A HISTORY OF THE MONROE DOCTRINE

A History
of the
MONROE DOCTRINE

*A New Revision of the book
originally published under the title*
HANDS OFF: A History of the Monroe Doctrine

by
DEXTER PERKINS

Little, Brown and Company · *Boston* · *Toronto*

LIBRARY OF CONGRESS CATALOG CARD NO. 55-10752

D

*Published simultaneously in Canada
by Little, Brown & Company (Canada) Limited*

PRINTED IN THE UNITED STATES OF AMERICA

To
W. L. P.

Acknowledgments

THIS book is, in part, a summary of my detailed studies of the Monroe Doctrine, and in part a continuation of those studies on a less intensive scale. In penning these words of acknowledgment, I think back inevitably to the many persons who, by their assistance in my early work, have helped to make it possible. To all of them I have already expressed my gratitude, and I take this occasion merely to reiterate it. The list of my obligations has, however, grown with the preparation of this volume. From Dr. E. Wilder Spalding and Mr. George V. Blue I received the friendliest welcome and the heartiest assistance in my labors in the State Department. To Mr. Robert H. Haynes of the Widener Library, who has made the labors of many a summer so pleasant for me, I also wish to express appreciation. To Professor Clarence Haring, who read the last two chapters, giving me the advantage of his wide knowledge of Latin-American affairs and of his critical acumen, I am extremely grateful. To Dr. Albert K. Weinberg, especially familiar with the development of the theory of isolation, and from whose friendly criticism I benefited in the preparation of the first chapter, I wish to offer my thanks. To Arthur M. Schlesinger, my friend and counselor of many years, I once again pay warm and affectionate tribute.

I have been aided in my writing, also, by assistants to whose intelligent and patient labors I owe much. Mr. Irving S. Bernstein spent most of the last summer with me at the Widener Library, and played a large part in the assembling of materials used in the writing of Chapter VIII, besides being of great service in many other ways. Miss Marjorie Gilles, my secretary, has been indispensable. In the preparation of the manuscript, in the checking of references, in the securing of the illustrations, and in countless other ways she has given always the most cheerful and the most efficient aid. Scholarship inevitably involves drudgery. To these two persons, who have shared the drudgery with me, I express my hearty thanks; both are my former students, and I have valued not only their help but the friendly spirit in which it has been rendered.

Of the merits and defects of my book I shall naturally leave the reader to judge. It attempts a general view of an important subject; its scale, I have already said, is broader than that of my previous studies. Like every such study, it is, after all, the product of many minds. The synthesis, however, is my own.

DEXTER PERKINS

Foreword

~~~~~~

I BELIEVE strictly in the Monroe Doctrine, in our Constitution, and in the laws of God." This interesting sentence stood at the head of a full-page advertisement in the *New York Times* on December 2, 1923, the hundredth anniversary of Monroe's message. It was written by Mary Baker Eddy. However it strikes the reader as to its form, there is no doubt that it expresses something widely felt and widely believed. In the field of politics, there are few more unqualified faiths than the faith of the American people in the Monroe Doctrine. Few persons can define it; but that does not matter. One does not have to analyze in order to believe. Without distinction of party, or section, or position in society, most Americans in our own time would be willing to declare their loyalty to the principles laid down in the message of 1823. In the summer of 1940 they were approved by the virtually unanimous vote of both houses of Congress. They are at the heart of our creed with regard to foreign policy.

There are few subjects, therefore, in American diplomatic history that have so great an importance as the story of the Monroe Doctrine, an importance attested by the immense bibliography of the subject which today exists. There are few which have so great a contemporary significance. The course of events in Europe, the appearance of a new philosophy, perhaps a conquering philosophy, alien to the thought and the interests of the New World, have large implications in terms of the message of 1823. The declaration of President Roosevelt with regard to Canada, the acquisition of new bases in the Caribbean, the conference of Havana to consider the problem of the French and Dutch colonies in this hemisphere, the statement of Herr von Ribbentrop that the United States under the Monroe Doctrine must keep out of Europe if it wishes Europe to

keep out of America, all suggest the living interest and the necessity of understanding the full import of the principles laid down by
Monroe.

There are few subjects, too, with regard to which it has been
necessary to clear away so many misapprehensions. Many Americans believe that the Monroe declaration prevented the reconquest
of South America by a wicked combination of European powers.
Many Americans believe that Theodore Roosevelt, a new Saint
George pitted against a German dragon, staved off an occupation
of Venezuela by the navy of the first Reich. Many Americans believe that the Monroe Doctrine prescribes complete abstinence
from participation in European affairs. Many Americans believe
that Latin Americans have been, are, and ought to be grateful for
the doctrine. Not one of these things happens to be true.

Where so many misapprehensions exist, then, despite the flood
of literature on the subject that has already poured from our print-
ing presses, there is a distinct need for a fresh consideration of this
vital subject. The foreign policy of a democracy must be based
upon informed opinion. The pages that follow are intended to
contribute to the understanding of a set of principles that have
played, now play, and in all human probability will play, a role of
the first importance in the evolution of our diplomatic action.

Preface to the New Edition

$\sim\!\sim\!\sim\!\sim\!\sim\!\sim\!\sim\!\sim\!\sim\!\sim$

SINCE I wrote *Hands Off: A History of the Monroe Doctrine* in 1941, momentous events have taken place in the international sphere. These have influenced the development, and conditioned the character, of the Monroe Doctrine. The changes that have taken place I have described in this new edition, bringing them into focus and estimating their significance. In the performance of this task I wish to make acknowledgments to my two assistants at Cornell University, David H. Tiffany and Lin Webster. As always, my secretary, Miss Marjorie Gilles, has given not only her aid but her devoted interest to the work.

DEXTER PERKINS

Ithaca, New York
April, 1955

Contents

~~~~~~

A HISTORY OF THE MONROE DOCTRINE

I

The Separation of the New World and the Old—Republican America and Monarchical Europe

We are their [that is, the Latin Americans'] great example. Of us they constantly speak as of brothers having a similar origin. They adopt our principles, copy our institutions, and, in many instances, employ the very language and sentiments of our revolutionary papers.

But it is sometimes said that they are too ignorant and too superstitious to admit of the existence of free government. This charge of ignorance is often urged by persons themselves actually ignorant of the real condition of that people. I deny the alleged fact of ignorance; I deny the inference from that fact, if it were true, that they want capacity for free government; and I refuse assent to the further conclusion, if the fact were true, and the inference just, that we are to be indifferent to their fate. . . . It is the doctrine of thrones, that man is too ignorant to govern himself. I contend that it is to arraign the dispositions of Providence himself, to suppose that he has created beings incapable of governing themselves, and to be trampled on by kings.

In the establishment of the independence of Spanish America, the United States have the deepest interest. I have no hesitation in asserting my firm belief, that there is no question in the foreign policy of this country, which has ever arisen, or which I can conceive as ever occurring, in the decision of which we have had or can have so much at stake. This interest concerns our politics, our commerce, our navigation. There cannot be a doubt that Spanish America, once independent, whatever may be the form of the governments established in its several parts, these governments will be animated by an American feeling, and guided by an American policy. They will obey the laws of the system of the New World, of which they will compose a part, in contradistinction to that of Europe. . . . The independence . . . of Spanish America is an interest of primary consideration. Next to that, and highly important in itself, is the consideration of the nature of their governments. That is a question, however, for themselves. They will, no doubt, adopt those kinds of governments which are best suited to their condition, best calculated for their happiness. Anxious as I am that they should be free governments, we have no right to prescribe for them. They are and ought to be the sole judges for themselves. I am strongly inclined to believe that they will in most, if not all parts of their country, establish free governments.

— HENRY CLAY *in the House of Representatives, March 24, 1818*

THE MONROE DOCTRINE, in its broad lines, is a prohibition on the part of the United States against the extension of European influence and power to the New World. It does not necessarily imply (and the point will be later discussed in detail) that the United States must abstain from all diplomatic activity or all interference in the affairs of other continents. But there can be no denial of the fact that it is, in many minds, connected with a more general principle, the principle of the separation of the New World from the Old, and that it is regarded as a complement, if you will, as a foil, to the principle of no entangling alliances and no binding political connection with any European power. Monroe himself, in issuing his caveat against the plans of transatlantic states, drew a sharp distinction between America and Europe, and justified himself by calling attention to the abstention of the United States from any intervention in European affairs. It seems reasonable, therefore, at the outset of this study, to trace briefly the evolution of the principle of separation and nonentanglement in the years which preceded the enunciation of the message of 1823.

It is obvious that with the founding of the American colonies not merely a new country, but a new social order, began to develop in the New World in the seventeenth and eighteenth centuries. It is, of course, easy to exaggerate the difference between the two continents. The seeds of change were germinating on both sides of the Atlantic. Yet it might be contended with much plausibility that American society, despite an aristocratic veneer, was unlike any other. Nowhere else, to the same degree, was the career open to talents. Nowhere else was the gulf between rich and poor so narrow. Nowhere else were class distinctions so unimportant. The consciousness of these facts was, of course, sharpened by the outbreak of the war with the mother country. From the very outset of its career as a nation there was in America the ferment of new conceptions, the consciousness of new destinies. From this sense of differentness there was bound to flow the notion that the rupture of the political connection with time-worn Europe ought to be as complete as possible, that nonentanglement was the true basis of American foreign policy.

Nowhere is this conception more clearly expressed than in the works of the great pamphleteer of the Revolution, Thomas Paine. In *Common Sense*, the clarion call to independence, written in the late fall of 1775, Paine writes as follows: —

Our plan is commerce, and that, well attended to, will secure us the peace and friendship of all Europe. . . . I challenge the warmest advocate for reconciliation to show a single advantage which this Continent can reap by being connected with Great Britain. . . . But the injuries and disadvantages which we sustain by that connection are without number; and our duty to mankind at large, as well as to ourselves, instructs us to renounce the alliance; because any submission to, or dependence on, Great Britain, tends directly to involve this continent in European wars and quarrels, and sets us at variance with nations who would otherwise seek our friendship, and against whom we have neither anger nor complaint. As Europe is our market for trade, we ought to form no partial connexion with any part of it. It is the true interest of America to steer clear of European contentions, which she never can do, while, by her dependence on Britain, she is made the make-weight in the scale of British politics.[1]

Tom Paine, in speaking thus, was advocating no exotic doctrine of his own. The same viewpoint was expressed by other eminent figures of the time, never more cogently than by John Adams. "The principle of foreign affairs which I then advocated," wrote Adams years later, ". . . was, that we should make no treaties of alliance with any European power; that we should consent to none but treaties of commerce; that we should separate ourselves, as far as possible and as long as possible, from all European politics and wars." [2]

It is true that in practice the policy of nonentanglement broke down before the new republic had had two years of life. It is true that the French treaty, the alliance of February 6, 1778, seemed to be the flat denial of the maxims of the corset maker of Bristol and the lawyer of Boston. It is true that the aid which was accorded the Americans by a foreign power was a vital, and conceivably a decisive factor in the winning of their national independence, and in launching the new republic on its career. But the French alliance was the product of bitter necessity. It was only very reluctantly indeed that the leaders in the Continental Congress moved toward the forging of this foreign bond, and it is clear from the correspondence of the time that the opposition to any foreign connection was extremely tenacious. The first draft of a treaty, drawn by John Adams, was submitted to Congress in July of 1776. It proposed commercial intercourse with France on a most liberal basis, but it looked to no united action of the two nations against Great Britain.[3] It went no further than to pledge the United States not to assist its former mother country in any war which might arise between the British and the French. Even after Washington had been beaten at the Battle of Long Island on August 27, and the military situation was altering for the worse, the same position was maintained. Only the very unfortunate events of the late fall of 1776 produced a change in tone. It needed the Battle of White Plains (October 28), the surrender of Fort Washington with its garrison of about three thousand men, the dreary retreat across New Jersey, and the threatened dissolution of the Revolutionary Army to bring the Congress to the point where it was ready to seek military and naval action on the part of France in support of American independence. And in the voluminous dispatches of the year 1777, the Committee on Secret Correspondence, while constantly urging the American commissioners in Paris to press for French entry into the war, makes no use of the word "alliance," suggests no binding commitment such as would thereby be implied. It was Franklin and his associates, not the Congressional leaders, who perceived that some form of association and compact would probably be indispensable to the winning of French aid, and who, as early as February 1777, resolved to support one another in the drafting of such a compact.[4] The treaty of February 6, 1778, which bound the two nations to make war and peace together, while welcomed when it was finally consummated, was not drafted in direct accordance with instructions from Philadelphia, but, on the contrary, transcended these instructions.

There are indications, moreover, that distrust of entanglement was not absent from the minds of the negotiators. Some reward for the exertions which France was about to make they had, of course, to offer. Accordingly, such islands of the West Indies as were then in the possession of Great Britain were generously promised to the Most Christian King — if he could take them. But in accordance with precedents to be found in the Congressional instructions of September 1776, a prohibition was erected against the French conquest of "the islands of Bermudas, as well as any part of the Continent of North America, which before the treaty of Paris 1763, or in virtue of that treaty, were acknowledged to belong to the Crown of Great Britain, or to the United States, heretofore called British Colonies, or which are at this time, or

have lately been under the power of the King and Crown of
Great Britain." [5] Thus carefully were the French excluded from
the conquest of Canada, or Nova Scotia, or Newfoundland; thus
obvious was it that the Americans were on their guard against
the substitution of one European nation for another on their
very borders. The compact with Louis XVI was a necessity; but
the signs are many that just so was it regarded.

Nor can it be said that the treaty of 1778 operated in such a fashion as to encourage the Americans to similar engagements. Even
during the war itself there was plenty of friction. There was much
resentment at the somewhat futile operations of the Comte d'Es-
taing in 1778; there was disillusionment once more when the same
naval commander withdrew in 1779 from the operations before
Savannah; there was a curious indifference on the part of France
to the American struggle in 1780; it needed the brilliant operations of 1781, culminating in the surrender of Cornwallis at York-
town, to give to the alliance a genuine and indeed a fundamental
military triumph.

And when it came to the peace negotiations of 1782, uneasiness at the association with France soon made itself manifest. It
was not keenly felt, it is true, by the venerable Franklin. But by
John Adams, congenitally suspicious, it was not only felt, but
frankly avowed, not only to Congress, but even to the British nego-
tiator, Oswald. His famous conversation of November 18, 1781,
has often been quoted: —

"You are afraid," says Mr. Oswald today, "of being made the tools
of the powers of Europe." "Indeed I am," says I. "It is obvious that
all the powers of Europe will be continually manoeuvring with us, to
work us into their real or imaginary balances of power. They will all
wish to make of us a makeweight candle, while they are weighing out
their pounds. . . . But I think it ought to be our rule not to meddle;
and that of all the powers of Europe, not to desire us, or perhaps, even
to permit us, to interfere, if they can help it." [6]

The consequence of this suspicious attitude was reflected in the
negotiations themselves. Disregarding the instructions of Congress,

which had adjured the fullest and most confidential relations with the French court, and overruling the objections of Franklin, the other negotiators, Adams and Jay, conducted their conversations with the British plenipotentiaries with little reference to Vergennes, the French Foreign Minister, and confronted him with the draft of a treaty only when that draft had been virtually completed. There was not, in all this, any breach of, or derogation from, the compact of alliance itself; but there was, very obviously, a distrustful attitude, an aloofness, that had its roots in dislike of any dependence on any European court. Nor were the commissioners alone in this attitude. It is clear that in Congress itself, as the necessity for French aid disappeared, a certain restlessness soon manifested itself with regard to the connection with the court of Louis XVI. Especially significant of the drift in sentiment is the resolution of the spring of 1783, in which Congress, in rejecting the idea of a League of Neutral Nations put forward during the war, declared it to be "the fundamental policy" of the United States to remain "as little as possible entangled in the politics and controversies of European nations."[7] Thus early in our history the isolationist point of view with regard to foreign policy was hardening into dogma.

The period of the Confederation and of the drafting of the Constitution sees the consolidation of this sentiment. In practice, there were still exceptions to the rule which was being forged. Thus, for example, in the negotiations with Spain carried on by John Jay in 1785 and 1786, negotiations looking to the conclusion of a commercial treaty and to the opening of the Mississippi to American trade, Jay, as a *quid pro quo* for commercial concessions, proposed a mutual guarantee of Spanish and American possessions, a virtual alliance.[8] A young deputy in Congress, who enjoyed the confidence of Madison and Jefferson, the most notable figures in Virginia, and whose name was James Monroe, would, it appears, have been willing to acquiesce in such a guarantee if the price had been not trade privileges, but the freedom of navigation of the great river.[9] And at about the same time that these discussions were going on, Thomas Jefferson, then our minister to France, drafted a plan for united action on the part of European powers and the United States against the pestiferous pirates of Barbary. But Jay's proposal was never even submitted to Congress; it would not have had the slightest chance there. And the indifference of the great European states to ending the plague of piracy doomed to impotence the ambitious proposal of Jefferson, and perhaps did something to convince that great American of the futility of attempting co-operative action with the courts of the Old World.

Far more important, indeed, than these abortive attempts at closer association with transatlantic states was John Jay's tentative effort to free the United States from the obligations of the French alliance. That alliance contained within its text no limit of time whatsoever; and though Franklin had on several occasions assured the British negotiators that it would terminate with the end of the war, such emphatically had not been the view of Vergennes, the French Foreign Minister,[10] nor, so far as one can discover, of Adams and Jay, at the time of the peace negotiations. None the less, when the French Minister, the Marquis de Moustier, presented his credentials in the early winter of 1788, the American Secretary of State took occasion to comment upon the allusion in them to "France's ally," and to express the opinion that the treaty of ten years before had been drawn with a view to the securing of American independence, and that it had lapsed with the attainment of that end. Confused and obviously annoyed, de Moustier transmitted his conversation with Jay to the Comte de Montmorin, French Foreign Minister. The reply was prompt and emphatic. "You will correct the ideas of Mr. Jay," wrote Montmorin; "you will assure him that the King regards his alliance with the United States as unalterable; that his Majesty has always taken and will not cease to take a true interest in their prosperity, and will continue to contribute thereto so far as he can without prejudice to his own interests. This is the doctrine which you ought to develop, and which the King's Council is surprised to see so ill understood." [11] Thus the French alliance stood, and was to stand unchallenged for some years to come. But Jay's maneuver reveals America's waning interest in the connection, and the drift of American policy towards detachment.

Indeed, since the very moment independence was won, the writings of American public men have abounded in expressions of the desire to remain aloof from European affairs. Franklin, it is true, still appeared to cling to the connection with France. But Hamilton, writing to Washington on March 24, 1783, declared, "It now only remains to make solid establishments within, to perpetuate our Union, to prevent our being a ball in the hands of European powers, bandied against each other at their pleasure." [12] Richard Henry Lee, whose "soul had panted for" the alliance, expressed the hope that the United States would now become "independent indeed, not of one only, but of all the nations on earth." [13] Sam Adams urged that "we shall never intermeddle with the quarrels of other nations." [14] George Mason, author of the Virginia Bill of Rights, seems to have endorsed the opinion of his son that the new nation "ought to have as little to do with the politics of Europe as possible." [15] And John Adams, consistently with views long and sturdily held, went so far on one occasion as to declare that he "sometimes thought" it would "be the best thing we can do to recall every minister from Europe and send embassies only on special occasions." [16] Perhaps the most extraordinary statement of all is that of Thomas Jefferson, in a letter of October 13, 1785. "Were I to indulge my own theory," writes the future President, "I should wish them [the United States] to practise neither commerce nor navigation, but to stand with Europe precisely on the footing of China. We should thus avoid wars, and all our citizens would be husbandmen." [17]

The dread of foreign influence is also clearly evidenced in the debates in the great Constitutional Convention of 1787. One of the strongest arguments for union lay in the danger that foreign countries might exploit the jealousies of the individual states; and the indignation of the delegates fell with peculiar force upon Gunning Bedford of Delaware, who was imprudent enough on one occasion to intimate that the small states, if not treated with sufficient deference, might seek "some foreign ally of more honor and good faith." [18] In the fixing of the treaty-making power, too, the isolationist temper displayed itself. The provision requiring a two-thirds vote for ratification was certainly due in part to a specific episode, to the resentment still felt against John Jay's willingness to waive American rights to the navigation of the Mississippi a few years before; but it was justified also on more general grounds by such important members of the Convention as Gouverneur Morris of Pennsylvania and Elbridge Gerry of Massachusetts.[19] Finally, the explicit prohibition in the Constitution against the acceptance by any American official of "any present, Emolument, Office, or Title, of any kind whatever, from any King, Prince, or foreign State" has an obvious relationship to the general doctrine of aloofness from European affairs. It is not too much to say that when the new government was set up in 1789 there had already developed a strong, though not as yet a completely consistent, tradition in favor of American abstention from European politics.

The events of the first decade of our history under the Constitution did much to consolidate that tradition. Almost contemporaneous with the setting up of our government were the meeting of the States-General at Versailles and the first steps in that vast unfolding drama which is known to history as the French Revolution. By the spring of the year 1792 the revolutionary movement had led to war with Austria and Prussia. By the winter of 1793, the invasion of the Netherlands and the execution of Louis XVI brought Great Britain into the struggle, and transformed a purely Continental conflict into one which was waged also upon the sea, and inevitably affected the interests of the United States. As to the merits of the struggle American opinion was deeply divided; men of the cast of mind of Alexander Hamilton inevitably viewed the onward surge of the revolutionary movement with a deep distrust; men like Jefferson and Madison, on the other hand, naturally sympathized warmly with the French republicans, and viewed with optimism the overthrow of the French monarchy and the birth pangs of the young French republic.

In circumstances such as these, it was the obvious dictate of prudence that the United States should pursue the course of neutrality. George Washington, "of all American public men the most invariably judicious," as William Edward Hartpole Lecky once put it, had clearly perceived, even before the actual outbreak of war, that neutrality in any European war should be the keystone of American policy. As early as 1790, when for a little the international situation appeared threatening, he had written in this strain to Lafayette.[20] In the fall of 1792, when the cabinet had under discussion the possibility of a rupture with Spain, and the ebullient Hamilton had brought forward, as he had two years earlier, the idea of an alliance with Great Britain, the President had declared that "the remedy would be worse than the disease." [21] And on March 23, 1793, in a private letter written after news of the British declaration of war on France, he indicated his hope that the United States would be able to hold aloof from the conflict.[22] In the position which he had thus come to assume consistently, he was to be backed by a united cabinet.

Thomas Jefferson, in 1793, was Washington's Secretary of State. There are those persons, even to this day, who persist in portraying Jefferson as a dreamy doctrinaire, moved more by emotional sympathy with democratic ideals and international brotherhood than by any hard conceptions of practical statesmanship and national self-interest. No conception could be further from the truth, especially with regard to foreign affairs. The author of the Declaration of Independence was, in fact, a singularly supple and flexible intelligence, with whom dogma was hardly likely to count against desirable concrete ends. He was the last man in the world to involve the United States in foreign war for nebulous or altruistic purposes, or for love of another nation. It is a calumny upon his memory to suggest such a thing.

In reality, speaking broadly, Jefferson's diplomatic notions had been based increasingly on isolationist conceptions. His correspondence shows that he had very early realized the maxim that Europe's anguish might be America's opportunity. As early as 1784, in the midst of a minor crisis between France and Austria, he had expressed to Monroe the belief that war might "renew that disposition in the powers of Europe to treat with us on liberal principles." [23] Three years later, in another tense moment, he wrote, "Should war take place, and should it be general as it threatens to be, our neutrality must be attended by great advantages." [24] And of war itself, when it came, he was ready to comment cynically, "Since it is so decreed by fate, we have only to pray that their soldiers may eat a great deal." [25] The man who could write such a line as that was no pallid sentimentalist, likely to sacrifice American interests to abstract ideas of democracy or world regeneration.

Nor were those other two Virginians in whom Jefferson often confided, and who were each to play a large role on the national stage, divergent from him in his conviction that the proper role for the United States in the European war was one of neutrality. Both James Madison and James Monroe were to become, perhaps we may say they had already become, ardently Francophile. But Madison, despite a censorious and suspicious attitude toward the administration, reluctantly declared, "Peace is no doubt to be preserved at any price that honor and good faith will permit." [26] And Monroe, arguing that neutrality would be more useful to the French republicans than war, admitted that the sentiment for neutrality appeared to be general.[27] On the part of the most ardent friends of France, then, it may fairly be stated that there was no disposition to plunge the United States into war on her behalf.

On the part of those whose prejudices led them to sympathize with Great Britain, the same thing might be said. Alexander Hamilton, the Secretary of the Treasury, had more than once suggested an alliance with Great Britain. But he was not so foolish as to bring forward any such proposal again, in the spring of 1793. On the contrary, he took what was in one sense a more strictly isolationist position than that of Jefferson: he sought to maintain the proposition that the alliance of 1778 with France was no longer applicable, and that the United States had been liberated from the obligations of the guarantee of the West Indies which was a part of that instrument. He argued that the alliance of 1778 had been made with "a *man* from whom essential benefits had been received"; that the execution of Louis XVI had been far from an act of national justice and that it might be argued that the grateful and honorable part for the United States would be to assist the coalition in restoring his heirs to the throne; that France was engaged in an aggressive war, whereas the agreement of 1778 spoke of a "defensive" alliance; that in such circumstances the treaty of alliance might at least be considered as suspended.[28] The argument was, perhaps, more ingenious than sound; but that it possessed some appeal is seen in part by the way in which Jefferson countered it. He did not deny that the compact was binding; but he suggested that the United States, if asked by France to fulfill its obligations and defend the West Indian islands, might wriggle out of the guarantee. In defiance of the peace treaty British troops still occupied border posts on the Great Lakes; no appeal had ever been made to the French to assist in ousting them therefrom; might it not be a proper question whether "a ten-year forbearance in us to call them into the guarantee of our posts entitles us to some indulgence?" [29] This ingenious suggestion, in answer to Hamilton's reasoning, is eloquent evidence of Jefferson's desire to avoid entanglement, and to keep out of the European struggle.

Acting on advice that was general, and that conformed with his own point of view, General Washington decided upon a policy of neutrality, and on April 22, 1793, issued that famous Neutrality Proclamation which has so often been cited as creating new precedents in international law. There were, it is true, those who criticized the manner and the matter of his action; and the student of American politics will not be astounded to learn that among other criticisms one which was strongly pressed was that of Presidential usurpation. But these criticisms appear, on the whole, of little moment; and when Congress met in the last months of 1793, and when Washington submitted to the two houses the draft of his proclamation, the House responded by a unanimous vote expressing approbation and pleasure, and the Senate by a similar resolution.[30] That the administration had pursued a course in accordance with public opinion was thus put virtually beyond question.

The contemptuous disregard of American rights and interests that was shown by both belligerents operated also to prevent, rather than to bring about, American involvement. Genêt, the first minister sent by revolutionary France to the United States, conducted himself with such arrogance, so clearly defied usage and treaty forms alike, so brazenly appealed to the American people over the head of their own government, that the partisans of France themselves stood confounded. On the other hand, so extreme were the misuses of British naval power, so supercilious British treatment of American complaints, that no foe of the French Revolution, however ardent, would have dared to advocate openly a connection with its great antagonist. Resistance, after such treatment, was thinkable; but union with one arrogant European nation against another equally arrogant was an idea that none but the most pronounced of Anglophobes or Francophobes would have deemed possible.

Neutrality, then, and nonentanglement were the watchwords of the Washington administration; and time only strengthened the conviction that such a policy was a wise one. It was not, of course, that the President or his advisers were detached in sentiment; few Americans have ever been that in the midst of a great European war; it was rather that the rise of factional feeling made the reasons for circumspection more compelling. To Washington it was, no doubt, the French faction that was particularly disturbing: he resented the heat with which they denounced the Jay Treaty, an honest, if not brilliantly successful effort to liquidate many of our disputes with Great Britain; he watched with dread the rise of "the democratic societies"; he was deeply disturbed by the all-too-obvious efforts of the French Minister, Adet, to interfere in American domestic politics with an eye to promotion of the interests of France. It was in part because of these things that he resolved to retire from office; in part because of them, too, that he determined to address to the American people parting words of counsel as to the perils which beset them. The result was the famous Farewell Address of September 17, 1796.

In its pervading temper, the Farewell Address expressed the general thesis of American separation from the affairs of the Old World.

Europe [wrote the first President] has a set of primary interests which to us have none or a very remote relation. Hence she must be engaged in frequent controversies, the causes of which are essentially foreign to our concerns. Hence, therefore, it must be unwise in us to implicate ourselves by artificial ties in the ordinary vicissitudes of her politics or the ordinary combinations and collisions of her friendships and her enmities.

Our detached and distant situation invites and enables us to pursue a different course. If we remain one people under an efficient government, the period is not far off when we may defy material injury from external annoyance; when we may take such an attitude as will cause the neutrality we may at any time resolve upon to be scrupulously respected; when belligerent nations, under the impossibility of making acquisitions upon us, will not lightly hazard the giving us provocation; when we may choose peace, or war, as our interest, guided by justice, may counsel.

Why forego the advantages of so peculiar a situation? Why quit our own to stand upon foreign ground? Why, by interweaving our destiny with that of any part of Europe, entangle our peace and prosperity in the toils of European ambition, rivalship, interest, humor or caprice? [31]

Words such as these express an influential philosophy and an important step in the development of the notion of the two spheres. But they do not mark (and the fact has been too little stressed) the complete triumph of this theory. There were qualifying phrases in the Farewell Address to which, in the interests of accuracy, attention needs to be called. They were almost certainly due to the influence of Hamilton; we get a hint of them in Hamilton's comments upon the President's preliminary draft of the Address; but they were accepted by Washington himself. It was, for example, only against *"permanent* alliances" that Washington warned his countrymen; he gave his endorsement to "temporary alliances for extraordinary emergencies." [32] With that keen pragmatic sense which distinguished him, which was indeed one of his most salient intellectual and moral qualities, he asserted no inflexible and irrevocable dogma, but a general principle of action, subject to possible qualification or modification.

It is undeniable, however, that the general principle which Washington laid down was rather to be strengthened than weakened by the events of the next few years. The arrogance of the government of republican France increased with time; the French had deeply resented the Jay Treaty with Great Britain; and they treated American commerce with an increasing disregard of international law. The emissaries whom Adams sent to negotiate with them were treated with nothing less than contumely; they were asked by outright bribes to buy good relations with France. The correspondence of these emissaries, when it came back to the United States, was published by the President; an explosion of popular feeling followed, and the country became engaged in an informal war with France. There were members of Adams' own party in these years who would have welcomed some kind of association with Great Britain; there were somewhat nebulous and ambitious projects for common action on the part of the United States and the former mother country with a view to despoiling Spain of her colonies. But the President himself, a sturdy if difficult personality, had no truck with any such ideas; and the net result of the war with France was the treaty of 1800, which, in re-establishing peace, also terminated the treaty of alliance of 1778. Thus the United States was liberated from its only close political connection with any other state, and liberated under circumstances that have more than a passing interest. For it was one of the earliest and one of the most determined advocates of the

doctrine of nonentanglement under whom the treaty was negotiated; and it so happened, owing to senatorial delays, that it was
proclaimed by Thomas Jefferson, the chief of a rival party and, as
it might appear, the pronounced friend of France. Indeed, in his
inaugural address, the new Chief Executive struck off a sentence
all too often attributed to Washington, which seemed to crystallize
the growing dogma of separation, "peace, commerce and honest
friendship with all nations, entangling alliances with none." [33]

As in the case of his great predecessor, however, Jefferson was
no doctrinaire observer of his own maxim. When in 1802 he received intimations that the far-flung province of Louisiana had
been ceded by Spain to France, and that a strong power was thus
about to be established upon the Mississippi, he at least played
with the idea of an alliance with Great Britain, and declared to
his friend Du Pont de Nemours that "the day that France takes
possession of New Orleans . . . we must marry ourselves to the
British fleet and nation." [34] At the same time, and rather inconsistently, the instructions to Monroe, sent out to France to purchase the "island" of New Orleans and the region of West Florida,
suggest a guarantee to France of the territories to the west of the
river in exchange for the proposed cession. Neither the one nor
the other of these propositions implies the exclusion of all European influence from the American hemisphere. But fate was kind
to the President. Monroe and Livingston, instructed to purchase
only the island of New Orleans and West Florida, seized the opportunity which was offered them for the acquisition of all Louisiana; and the upshot of their negotiations was the transfer to the
United States of a vast territory which had hitherto been under the
influence and the government of a European state. As a mere matter of geography, the treaty of cession represents an obvious re-
enforcement to the idea of separating the New World from the
Old.

We may, I think, go further than this, however. In the period
from 1783 to 1803, despite the general trend towards nonassocia-
tion with European powers, there had been occasional flirtation

with the idea of some closer understanding with one or another. In almost every instance, what had been involved was American interests in the valley of the Mississippi. John Jay had been willing to buy the friendship of Spain, the sovereign of that great river, with an alliance. It had been the lure of conquest in the Southwest that led Hamilton in 1798 to talk of understanding with Great Britain. It was the danger of the closing of the port of New Orleans that led Jefferson to write the famous letter to Du Pont de Nemours in 1802. Occasionally, as a detailed study of the period would show, other factors came into the reckoning when closer association with a European power was proposed. But in the main, deviations from the principle of nonentanglement turned on a single problem. And it is a fact that though only two years after the cession of Louisiana Europe was again to be involved in general war, this second war sees no such flirting with the idea of special compacts as had the first. Freed from any further danger of interference with the development of the West, more clearly than ever the great power of the North American continent, the United States no longer needed to seek in any kind of foreign commitment the preservation of its own essential economic interests. The acquisition of Louisiana freed American statesmen from a fear which had been constantly recurring, and satisfied an appetite which might otherwise conceivably have led to dangerous political commitments.

The consolidation of the nonentanglement idea may almost be said to date from 1803. It was alone, now, rather than in proposed concert with any European states, that Jefferson undertook the chastisement of the Barbary pirates, a legitimate operation of war which the exceedingly rationalistic President calculated to be less costly than treaties of tribute; and it was by a policy of isolation, in its strongest terms, that the Jefferson administration faced the storms of a general European war. Only a little while ago, before the outbreak of the present war in Europe, the thesis cropped up that by refusing to trade with European belligerents (except for cash), and particularly by refusing to sell them munitions of war and to travel in their vessels of commerce, the United States might avoid all danger of involvement in the struggles of Europe; but not even the most rabid supporter of curtailment of intercourse with the Old World at that time went so far as Jefferson went in 1807. His famous measure of the embargo was the complete suspension of foreign trade, the ultimate of the isolationist conception. That it was accepted, that even after its repeal the principle of nonintercourse as a substitute for war continued powerfully to influence American foreign policy for four and a half years, is a fact of great significance. In the hard, and as it proved the ineffectual, struggle of the Jefferson and Madison administrations to defend American neutral rights without recourse to war we hear nothing of any flirtations with European courts, and the historian who seeks to trace the development of the idea of nonentanglement finds the annals of these years short and simple indeed. And when English arrogance, and American ambition to make the conquest of the Canadas and Floridas, led to the declaration of war on Great Britain in June of 1812, no one proposed any association whatsoever with the France of Bonaparte. The war was unpopular enough in some parts of the country as matters stood; it produced the most violent political discontent in New England, and it was with difficulty that financial, military, or political support could be found there; nebulous projects that squinted at secession began to be entertained; and it was with almost universal relief that American opinion received the Peace of Ghent.

In the meantime, too, momentous events were happening in another quarter which operated to bring into still clearer relief the separation of the New World and the Old.

It was the Napoleonic invasion of Spain which provided the impetus for the outbreak of revolt in her American dominions. In the year 1810 juntas were set up at Buenos Aires, at Bogotá, at Caracas, at Santiago de Chile, ostensibly to hold the country for King Ferdinand, but undoubtedly with larger purposes in the background.[35] What began as a movement ostensibly loyal was soon transformed into a struggle for independence. By the end of

1811 this fact was already clear; President Madison alluded sympathetically to the new states in his message to Congress, and in the House of Representatives a resolution was passed expressing "a friendly solicitude in the welfare of these communities, and a readiness, when they should become nations by the exercise of their just rights, to unite with the Executive in establishing such relations with them as might be necessary." [36] Observing these events, the prescient Jefferson, always alive to the large philosophical implications of what was going on in the world, wrote to his friend Alexander von Humboldt words which state with crystal clearness the doctrine of the two spheres. [37]

But in whatever governments they will end, they will be American governments, no longer to be involved in the never ceasing broils of Europe. The European nations constitute a separate division of the globe; their localities make them a part of a distinct system; they have a set of interests of their own in which it is our business never to engage ourselves. America has a hemisphere to itself. It must have its separate system of interests; which must not be subordinated to those of Europe. The insulated state in which nature has placed the American continent, should so far avail that no spark of war kindled in the other quarters of the globe should be wafted across the wide oceans which separate us from them and it will be so. [38]

For a time, however, it seemed as if Jefferson's prophecy might be belied. With the ending of the war in Europe Spain made a tremendous effort to regain her American provinces. Mexico was reduced to order; in Venezuela and Colombia the army of the Spanish general, Morillo, won victory on victory, and drove Bolivar, the leader of the revolutionists, into exile; Chile fell before the royalist leader, Osorio. But in the year 1817 the tide began once more to turn; the republic of La Plata, which had successfully maintained its independence, dispatched its great general, San Martín, across the Andes, and with the victory of Chacabuco a great step was taken toward the liberation of Chile. Enthusiasm for the cause of Latin-American liberation began once more to express itself in the United States. President Monroe very early in his term sent a mission of inquiry to La Plata, on whose soil not a single Spanish soldier remained, and began to talk of the recognition of the independence of the new state. In Congress the nascent republics of the South found a sturdy and eloquent champion in Henry Clay, who saw the birth of an "American system" in the events that were taking place. The separation of the New World from the Old seemed to the more imaginative and poetic minds of the time to be in the way of becoming a reality, and on both sides of the Atlantic men began to talk as if it were a fact.

Nor was it merely the revolt of the colonies that in the first years of Monroe's administration sharpened the cleavage of the continents. There had been nothing very shocking to American opinion in the peace settlements that followed the Napoleonic Wars. The union of Great Britain, Austria, Prussia, and Russia to prevent a new outbreak of violence on the part of France was not illogical; the provisions of the treaty of November 20, 1815, calling for meetings at fixed intervals of the representatives of the great powers for "the examination of such measures as shall be judged most salutary for the peace and prosperity of Europe," were equally reasonable; nor could there be any objection in principle to the famous treaty of the Holy Alliance of September 26 of the same year, by which, under the leadership of the mystical Tsar Alexander, and in language as vague as it was pious, the sovereigns of Europe bound themselves to observe in their domestic and foreign policies "the duties which the Divine Saviour has taught to mankind." Amongst pacifists, untaught by the history of the race, there was even a disposition to hail this last-named document with positive enthusiasm. But events were soon to demonstrate that the association of the great powers contained ominous possibilities; as early as the Congress of Aix-la-Chapelle in 1818 projects were brought forward looking to the interposition of the members of the Alliance in the affairs of the Spanish colonies; and when in 1819 the Russian Minister at Washington, Mr. Poletica, sounded John Quincy Adams, the American Secretary of State, on the possibility of American adhesion to the compact of the Alliance he received very little encouragement indeed. In a remarkable dispatch to Middleton, our minister at St. Petersburg, the reasons for our attitude were clearly stated: —

For the repose of Europe as well as of America [wrote the son of the arch-isolationist of 1783], the European and American political systems should be kept as separate and distinct from each other as possible. If the United States as members of the Holy Alliance could acquire a right to ask the influence of its most powerful members in their controversies with other states (as suggested by Alexander), the other members must be entitled in return to ask the influence of the United States for themselves or against their opponents. In the deliberations of the League they would be entitled to a voice and in exercising their right must occasionally appeal to principles which might not harmonize with those of any European member of the bond. This consideration alone would be decisive for declining a participation in that league, which is the President's absolute and irrevocable determination, although he trusts that no occasion will present itself rendering it necessary to make that determination known by an explicit refusal.[39]

This was the language of Adams in 1820; the events of the fall and of the succeeding years made its cogency more and more apparent. For, in October, in the protocol of Troppau, the three Eastern courts, Russia, Prussia, and Austria, committed themselves to the doctrine that it was the sacred duty of the great states of Europe to put down internal movements of discontent by force of arms. In the course of the next year, movements looking to the establishment of constitutional government in Naples and Piedmont were summarily snuffed out, and there was already talk of similar action in Spain, where the worthless Ferdinand VII had been temporarily compelled to submit to a measure of constitutional control. Action such as this was a violation of the American faith in popular government; it underlined and emphasized in the most striking fashion the difference in point of view between the American republic and the principal states of the Old World.

The year 1822 was to carry still further this process of differentiation, with the recognition by the United States of the revolted colonies as independent nations. This step had been talked about as early as 1818, but for a variety of reasons it had been delayed. John Quincy Adams was no romantic; he did not share the popular enthusiasm for the cause of the Latin-American states; he doubted (and time has, to some extent, confirmed his doubts) whether all the governments to spring from the ruins of the Spanish Empire would be democracies in the American sense of the term. He was restrained, too, by the feeling that recognition ought to be accorded only when the result of the struggle was no longer doubtful; more important still, he was negotiating with Spain for the cession of the Floridas, and feared to wreck these negotiations by recognizing the revolutionists. Recognition, moreover, would be a sort of defiance to the Old World autocrats; and isolationist that Adams was by inheritance, conviction, and temperament, he yet appears to have hesitated to act in such flagrant disregard of the opinion of the chancelleries of Europe. In 1818 and 1819 he seems still to have hoped that recognition might be brought about by an accord with one or more European governments, though he would not be drawn into the deliberations of the Congress of Aix-la-Chapelle. But by February 1821, the Florida treaty had been duly ratified; in May, under the leadership of Clay, the House of Representatives voted resolutions indicating readiness to support recognition; in June, Bolivar inflicted a crushing defeat upon the army of Morillo at Carabobo; in July, his great associate and rival, San Martín, entered Lima, bringing the revolution to Peru, the last and most faithful of Spain's South American provinces; in August, the Spanish viceroy in Mexico was compelled to acknowledge the independence of that province. The facts of the situation pointed toward the complete success of the revolutionists. In March of 1822, President Monroe sent to Congress a message recommending recognition, and asking that provision be made for the sending of ministers. The administration, when it acted, acted with the most striking independence. It consulted with no European power; it gave no warning to any European chancellery of what was coming; and it paid no attention whatsoever to the situation which existed in Spain. It reckoned not at all with the fact that Ferdinand was in the power of his revolutionary subjects, and that recognition under such circumstances would be particularly distasteful to the legitimists of the Old World; it reckoned no more with the fact that the Spanish constitutionalists were making, or at least professing to make, new efforts at the reconciliation of the colonies with the mother country. Its action was taken on a purely American basis, and from a purely American point of view. The thesis of an American system appeared to be one step nearer realization in actual fact; the separation of the Old World from the New appeared to be still further advanced. But momentous events were still to come; and the fall of 1822 and the year 1823 were to march toward a crisis, or at any rate what seemed to be a crisis, which led to the public and vigorous expression of the doctrine of the two spheres, and to a new expression of its pervading spirit. This was the solemn warning to European states to keep their hands off America; this was the Monroe Doctrine.

II

The First Challenge
Monroe Hurls Defiance at Europe

These United States of America, which we have seen arise
and grow, and which during their too short youth already
meditated projects which they dared not then avow, have
suddenly left a sphere too narrow for their ambition, and have
astonished Europe by a new act of revolt, more unprovoked,
fully as audacious, and no less dangerous than the former.
They have distinctly and clearly announced their intention to
set not only power against power, but, to express it more exactly, altar against altar. In their indecent declarations they
have cast blame and scorn on the institutions of Europe most
worthy of respect, on the principles of its greatest sovereigns,
on the whole of those measures which a sacred duty no less
than an evident necessity has forced our governments to
adopt to frustrate plans most criminal. In permitting themselves these unprovoked attacks, in fostering revolutions
wherever they show themselves, in regretting those which
have failed, in extending a helping hand to those which seem
to prosper, they lend new strength to the apostles of sedition, and reanimate the courage of every conspirator. If this
flood of evil doctrines and pernicious examples should extend
over the whole of America, what would become of our religious and political institutions, of the moral force of our governments, and of that conservative system which has saved
Europe from complete dissolution?

— METTERNICH *to Nesselrode, January 19, 1824*

THE famous message of December 2, 1823, with the possible exception of the Farewell Address the most significant of all American state papers, contains two widely separated passages which have come to be known as the Monroe Doctrine. In discussing American relations with Russia, the President laid down the principle that "the American continents, by the free and independent condition which they have assumed and maintain, are henceforth not to be considered as subject for future colonization by any European power." This phrase occurs early in the document. In its closing paragraphs, on the other hand, Monroe turned to the subject of the Spanish colonies. In language no less significant than that just quoted, he declared that the political system of the allied powers, that is, of the Holy Alliance, was different from that of America. "We owe it, therefore, to candor, and to the amicable relations existing between the United States and those powers," he went on, "to declare that we should consider any attempt on their part to extend their political system to any portion of this hemisphere as dangerous to our peace and safety. With the existing colonies and dependencies of any European power we have not interfered and shall not interfere. But with the governments who have declared their independence and maintained it, and whose independence we have, on great consideration and just principles, acknowledged, we could not view any interposition for the purpose of oppressing them, or controlling in any other manner their destiny, by any European power in any other light than as the manifestation of an unfriendly disposition towards the United States."

These pregnant phrases express in unmistakable terms the ideological cleavage between the New World and the Old. We have already seen how this cleavage had become sharper and sharper in the years after 1815. To Americans European absolutism, in 1823, was a system as odious, as devoid of moral sanction, as that of Nazi Germany or Stalinist Russia seems to many citizens of the United States today. On the other hand, to many of the statesmen

of Continental Europe, the buoyant republicanism and the democratic faith of the people of the United States were a vast dissol-
vent which threatened destruction to the existing order, and unknown and incalculable perils for the future. The message of
Monroe had to do with specific situations which we must soon
examine, but it was based on general principles which played an
important part in the thinking of the President and his advisers.

That part of the message which was directed against Russia appears to have been the work of John Quincy Adams. There is,
perhaps, no figure more remarkable in the lengthening list of the
Secretaries of State. Acidulous, combative, suspicious, Adams was
none the less a great personality, great in his unswerving and intense patriotism, great in his powerful and logical intelligence, great
in his immense industry, great in his high integrity. No man who
ever directed American foreign policy came to his post with a
wider background of experience, with a better education, academic, linguistic, legal, with a broader conception of his task.
Adams was hard-headed and practical; but he also recognized the
importance of ideas and general principles. And this fact he was
to make clear in his working out of the so-called noncolonization
dogma. Long before 1823 the Secretary of State had begun to
formulate his ideas with regard to the exclusion of European influence from the American continents. When he negotiated the
Florida treaty in 1819, he took special satisfaction in the extension
of American territory to the Pacific by Spain's renunciation of all
rights north of 42 degrees. As early as November of 1819 he had
declared in the cabinet that the world "must be familiarized with
the idea of considering our proper dominion to be the *continent*
of North America." [1] In a heated dispute with Stratford Canning,
the British Minister, in January of 1821, over the title to the Columbia River region, Adams stated, "We certainly did suppose
that the British government had come to the conclusion that there
would be neither policy nor profit in cavilling with us about territory on this North American continent." "And in this," asked
Canning, "you include our northern provinces on this continent?"

"No," said Adams; "there the boundary is marked and we have no disposition to encroach upon it. Keep what is yours, but leave the rest of this continent to us." [2] These statements, compared with what followed, were remarkable only for their modesty. In July of 1822, in one of those Fourth of July addresses so dear to American national pride, the Secretary went on to attack the whole colonial principle, as applied to both North and South America. By November he was ready to confide to the British Minister that "the whole system of modern colonization was an abuse of government, and it was time that it should come to an end." [3]

In part, the position so boldly taken was a matter of political theory. The United States was not yet half a century from the Declaration of Independence, from its own shaking off of the chains of colonial tutelage. But, in part, Adams' doctrine had an economic basis. Adams disliked colonialism not alone because it was a reminder of political subordination, but because it was connected in his mind with commercial monopoly, and the exclusion of the United States from the markets of the New World. A New Englander of New Englanders, the representative of the great mercantile section of the Union, and that at a time when the American shipping interests were more important in relation to other interests than at any time in our history, the Secretary was to do battle for the trade of the American people no less than for more abstract notions of political righteousness. It was, indeed, a commercial controversy that sharpened his pen for the famous declaration with regard to colonization that we have quoted at the beginning of this page.

This controversy was one with Russia. In 1823 Russia still had colonial claims on the northwest coast of America. For more than a decade, indeed, there had been a Russian establishment, Fort Ross, at Bodega Bay on the coast of California, whose existence, though it had occasioned no diplomatic discussion, had been noted with some mild apprehension. But more important, in September of 1821 the Tsar Alexander, acting at the instigation of a corporation known as the Russian American Company, had issued an imperial decree which conferred upon this concern exclusive trading rights down to the line of 51 degrees and forbade all foreign vessels to come within one hundred Italian miles of the shore on pain of confiscation.[4]

This imperial decree was, from the outset, challenged by the American government. In connection with it John Quincy Adams, with a boldness that excelled that of his cabinet colleagues, wished to deny the right of Russia to any American territory. And though he was overruled in a measure, since the instructions to Middleton at St. Petersburg, sent in July of 1823, were based on possible recognition of Russian claims north of *fifty-five*, the Secretary nevertheless would not give up his viewpoint in principle. To Tuyll, the Russian Minister at Washington, he declared on July 17, 1823, that "we should contest the right of Russia to *any* territorial establishment on this continent, and that we should assume distinctly the principle that the American continents are no longer subjects for any new European colonial establishments." [5] Five days later he set forth the same theory in a dispatch to Richard Rush, our minister at London, and set it forth in some detail.[6] In December, when he came to draft for the President the customary sketch of foreign policy to be used in the preparation of the annual message, he used almost the identical words that had been used five months before in speaking to Tuyll, and Monroe took them over bodily and inserted them in his message of December 2.

This, in essentials, is the origin of the noncolonization clause, one of the two important elements in the enunciation of the Monroe Doctrine.

It cannot be said that this clause was particularly important or particularly influential in its immediate effects. It was not enthusiastically received by the general public. It was rarely commented upon in the newspapers. It occasioned no favorable word in Congress. The Tsar had already determined upon concession long before the message, as early as July 1822, and in the discussions at St. Petersburg Monroe's language was politely thrust aside by Alexander's Foreign Minister, who declared "it would be best for us to waive all discussions upon abstract principles of *right*." [7] The President's declaration was without effect upon the actual compromise which was worked out between the two governments, limiting Russian rights to the line of 54 degrees 40 minutes, and conceding American trading privileges north of this line for a period of ten years.[8] It was not favorably received by official opinion in any European country. In France Chateaubriand, the Foreign Minister, asserted on first reading it that Monroe's declaration "ought to be resisted by all the powers possessing either territory or commercial interests in that hemisphere." [9] In Great Britain Canning flatly challenged the new doctrine in an interview with Rush, our minister at London, early in January of 1824. Monroe's thesis, said the British Foreign Secretary, "is laid down broadly, and generally, without qualification or distinction. We cannot acknowledge the right of any power to proclaim such a principle; much less to bind other countries to the observance of it." Six months later, when Richard Rush attempted to introduce the Adams theory into the negotiations over Oregon, he was met with an "utter denial" of its validity, and with the categorical statement that "the unoccupied parts of America" were "just as much open as heretofore to colonization by Great Britain . . . and that the United States would have no right whatever to take umbrage at the establishment of new colonies from Europe in any such parts of the American continent." [10] In the immediate sense, the assertion of the noncolonization principle accomplished nothing positive, and aroused resentment rather than respect. There is room to doubt its wisdom as a diplomatic move, and a harsh critic might even go so far as to describe it as a barren gesture.

Nor is it easy to see on what logical basis Adams' declaration could rest. The Secretary of State attempted to found it upon the hypothesis that "the two continents" to which it referred "consisted of several sovereign and independent nations, whose territories covered their whole surface." But apart from the fact that in European eyes these "independent nations," as regarded Latin America, did not yet exist, it was certainly not true that all the continent of North America was in the possession of some civilized power. The very existence of the dispute between Russia and the United States was, indeed, eloquent testimony to the contrary. A vast hinterland in Alaska remained virtually unexplored, and this was equally true of much of what is now northwest Canada. Some kind of claim to exclude other powers from these territories Adams could succeed in making out, on the basis of the Florida treaty of 1819, and on the cession by Spain of her rights to the Northwest north of the line of 42 degrees. But these rights had always been rather shadowy and were very far from being clearly established, and to claim this whole Northwest on such a basis was hardly convincing. It is questionable, indeed, if Adams seriously believed his own argument. Certainly none of those to whom he presented it were in the slightest degree impressed. "The declaration of Monroe [declares one of the most acute students of the Monroe Doctrine] applied in part to territory discovered and claimed by Great Britain and Russia; in part, to territory presumed to be in the possession of insurgents whom the United States alone had recognized as independent; and in part, to any additional territory which the progress of exploration might reveal. In the view of public law, then, it was worthless. The United States could not by a declaration affect the international status of lands claimed, ruled, or discovered by other powers. They might proclaim in advance the policy which they would adopt when such questions should arise, but no unilateral act could change the Law of Nations. . . . The Law of Nations could be changed only by the renunciation, made tacitly or expressly, by every civilized power of its right to colonize any unoccupied part of the western hemisphere." [11] It is difficult to deny the justice of this reasoning. Often as the language of Adams has been cited since 1823, it rested upon an insecure foundation of logic and fact at the time.

More important, however, than the noncolonization clause are those resounding paragraphs of the message of 1823 which focused the attention of every European chancellery on the American attitude toward the new republics of the South. What was the origin and the occasion of these famous phrases? What was their reception? What was their effect? To answer the first of these questions we must go back to the events which were briefly described in the last chapter.

The march of reaction in the Old World was by no means checked at the Congress of Verona in the fall of 1822. On the contrary, the Continental powers decided upon a new intervention to put down revolt in Spain, with France as their agent. In January, after a struggle in the bosom of the cabinet, the French ministry of Villèle virtually determined upon war, and withdrew its ambassador from Madrid. In April, the French forces crossed the Pyrenees and marched upon the Spanish capital; in a few brief months they occupied almost the entire country, with the exception of Cádiz, whither the Spanish revolutionists had fled with King Ferdinand as their captive. Events such as these were bound to have their repercussion in the United States.

Despite the doctrine of isolation and American aversion to entanglement, there has, in fact, never been a time when Americans were indifferent to the general trend of events in Europe. A perfectly cynical foreign policy, a policy of stark and naked self-interest, may perhaps be possible for dictators who manufacture their own public opinion; but the diplomacy of a democratic nation will, in the very nature of the case, be shaped in some measure by general principles and by broad political ideals. The trend of the events in the Old World was not lost upon James Monroe or John Quincy Adams. In his annual message for 1822, indeed, the President already demonstrated a mild uneasiness — perhaps no more than a mild uneasiness — as to the future. Alluding to the European scene, he went on to say: "Faithful to first principles in regard to other powers, we might reasonably presume that we should not be molested by them. This, however, ought not to be calculated on as certain. Unprovoked injuries are often inflicted, and even the peculiar felicity of our situation might be with some a cause for excitement and aggression." [12] Six months later, when the French armies had occupied Madrid, he penned a too-little-noticed letter to Thomas Jefferson. "Our relation to Europe," he wrote, "is pretty much the same, as it was in the commencement of the French revolution. Can we, in any form, take a bolder attitude in regard to it, in favor of liberty, than we then did? Can we afford greater aid to that cause, by assuming any such attitude, than we do now, by the form of our example?" [13] Language such as this suggests that a more positive attitude toward European reaction was ripening in the mind of the President.

Events, moreover, were strengthening his hand. For if the United States were to act in the cause of Spanish-American liberty, it was already at least likely, if not absolutely clear, that it would not take its stand alone. At the Congress of Verona Great Britain, through Lord Castlereagh as Foreign Secretary, had already made clear its increasing distaste for interventions in the interest of absolutism. It had made clear, too, a predilection even more vital. The Spanish-American revolutions had opened a whole continent to British trade. The commercial stake of Britain in the affairs of the New World no British government could afford to ignore. The recognition of the new republics by the United States in March had made it all the more necessary that London should seek their good will by a similar policy. Already, in May of the same year, the matter had been discussed with the government at Paris, in the hope of finding a common ground of action. At Verona the Duke of Wellington, the British plenipotentiary, was directed to bring the matter up in the most positive form. The question of Latin America was leading to the alienation of Great Britain from the powers of the Holy Alliance.

Moreover, the death of Castlereagh, shortly after the end of the Congress, brought to the Foreign Office George Canning, less attached than his predecessor to any highfalutin notions of European solidarity, and who, as member for Liverpool in the Commons, directly represented British trading interests. Under such a leader it could have been predicted that a bolder and more positive policy with regard to the new republics would be put into operation. Nor did the world have to wait very long to be made aware of this fact. For, on the occasion of the French intervention in Spain, Canning made his position entirely clear. "With respect to the Provinces in America," he wrote to Sir Charles Stuart, British Ambassador at Paris, "time and the course of events appear to have substantially decided their separation from the mother-country; although the formal recognition of these provinces as Independent States, by his Majesty, may be hastened or retarded by various external circumstances, as well as by the more or less satisfactory progress, in each State, towards a regular and settled form of government. Disclaiming in the most solemn manner any intention of appropriating to himself the smallest portion of the *late* Spanish possessions in America, his Majesty is satisfied that no attempt will be made by France to bring under her dominion any of those possessions, either by conquest, or by cession from Spain." [14] This declaration, while it did not entirely rule out the possible reconquest of Spain's former colonies in the interests of the worthless Ferdinand, at least made it wholly clear that there was to be no profit in the venture. The attitude of Canning was to have much to do with the message of 1823.

There were hints, indeed, in the spring and summer of 1823, that the two Anglo-Saxon powers were headed towards a political understanding. Canning's policy, his cousin Stratford Canning reported from Washington, had made the English "almost popular" in the United States, and even Adams "had caught a something of the soft infection." [15] The American Secretary of State, in his conversations with the British Minister, seemed to grow positively mellow with the progress of events. He commented with satisfaction to Stratford on the "coincidence of principle" which seemed to exist between the two governments. [16] In a tone far different from any that he had previously employed, he spoke of Great Britain and the United States as "comparing their ideas and purposes together, with a view to the accommodation of great interests upon which they had hitherto differed." [17] He seemed to suggest the possibility of a diplomatic rapprochement, and particularly of an agreement upon the question of Spanish America.

For a time, however, Canning hesitated. He had no romantic affection for the United States. No one had been more high-handed or arrogant than he in dealing with the American government at the time of the embargo. No Englishman could have been more superciliously confident of British superiority. And lurking always in his mind, as his correspondence shows, was the notion that the Americans might attempt a coup of their own in the New World, and possess themselves of Cuba. But with the month of August he decided to move forward. Might not diplomatic conversations with the United States result at one and the same time in American disclaimers of any acquisitive purposes, and American co-operation in a common opposition to the intervention of the Continental powers? So at least the British Foreign Secretary appears to have reasoned, and on the sixteenth of August, taking advantage of a "transient" observation of the American Minister, Canning began with Rush a series of important conferences that bulk large in the history of the Monroe Doctrine, and form an equally interesting chapter in the history of American political co-operation with European powers.

What Canning wished was a joint declaration on the part of the London and Washington governments. Its general outline was made clear in a note of August 20.

England [he wrote] had no disguise on the subject.

She conceived the recovery of the colonies by Spain to be hopeless.

That the question of their recognition as Independent States was one of time and of circumstances.

That England was not disposed, however, to throw any impediment in the way of an arrangement between the colonies and the mother country, by amicable negotiation.

That she aimed at the possession of no portion of the colonies for herself.

That she could not see the transfer of any portion of them to any other Power, with indifference.[18]

Holding these views, Great Britain would be very ready to declare them in concert with the United States. Could Rush sign a convention on the subject or, if this were not possible, could he consent to an exchange of ministerial notes? Rarely has an American Minister been asked more interesting questions. Rarely, in the history of the first fifty years of American diplomacy, had a more flattering offer of diplomatic co-operation been made.

But Richard Rush was both a shrewd and a cautious man. In a matter so important it would be perilous to act without instructions. After all, there was as yet no evidence that the Spanish colonies were in any particular peril, and though on the twenty-third of August Canning told him he had heard from Paris that at the end of the Spanish war a Congress would be called on the colonial question, such an intimation did not point to the necessity of immediate action on the part of the American Minister. Moreover, as Rush perceived, there was a difference in the American and British positions. The United States had already recognized the colonies. Great Britain had not. The one country was irrevocably committed; the other might be free to alter its policy and bring it into harmony with that of the Continental powers. Were there not risks in hasty action that far outweighed the benefits? Was not the proper course to refer the whole matter to Washington?

Thus, at any rate, reasoned the American Minister. He took no absolute stand against co-operation. He was willing to make it clear to Canning, indeed he did make it clear, that his country desired "to see the Independence of the late Spanish Provinces in America permanently maintained," and that "it would view as unjust and improper any attempt on the part of the Powers of Europe to intrench upon that Independence." [19] He even hinted that, should Canning assure him that the time had now arrived when Great Britain would recognize the colonies, he might be willing to consider more decisive action. But in default of such an assurance he could only refer the whole problem to his government. Nor, despite the importunities of the Foreign Secretary, would he budge from this point of view. Twice, after the note of August 20, Canning returned to the charge, once on the eighteenth of September, once again on the twenty-sixth. Twice Rush returned the same reply. Even Canning's suggestion that Great Britain might promise the *future* acknowledgment of the South American states failed to swerve him from his course. The possibility of a joint declaration months in advance of the famous message had thus to be discarded. The principal significance of the Canning-Rush interviews lies in the influence which they exerted upon the deliberations of President Monroe and his advisers.

Before we return to those deliberations, however, we should pause to underline once more the extraordinary nature of Canning's overtures. Today the United States is a great power, whose favor is a mighty matter. In 1823 conditions were far otherwise. In particular, our relations with Great Britain had for the most part been conducted on anything but a happy plane. Condescension commingled with arrogance had usually marked British policy, though there had been some improvement under Lord Castlereagh. Attentions as flattering as those that were paid to Rush might have turned the head of a less judicious representative of the United States. They must have been little less than thrilling to him.

Rush's first accounts of his interviews with Canning arrived in Washington early in October. Despite the French intervention in Spain the summer had, on this side of the water, been a tranquil one. In May Albert Gallatin, our minister at Paris, had talked with the Vicomte de Chateaubriand, the literary genius and diplomatic ineffectuality who conducted the foreign affairs of France. The American had stated frankly that the United States, in his judgment, "would not suffer others to interfere against the emancipation of America." [20] He received an answer "in the most explicit manner . . . that France would not make any attempt whatever of that kind, or in any manner interfere in the American question." [21] Speaking also to Pozzo di Borgo, the militant friend of repressive policies, and the Russian Ambassador at the court of Louis XVIII, Gallatin had made the American position clear, and had reported that the representative of the Tsar "seemed to coincide with me in opinion." [22] With these assurances, it is not strange that John Quincy Adams had fled the heat of Washington and spent the summer with his family at Quincy, his ancestral seat

But the Rush dispatches suggested that the tempo of the diplomatic drama might conceivably be quickening. Nor did they stand entirely alone. A letter of George W. Erving, a former Minister of the United States to Spain, written to Crawford, the Secretary of the Treasury, September 25, 1823, struck an alarmist note with regard to French and Russian intentions in Latin America.[23] And the language of the Tsar Alexander, on at least two occasions in this momentous fall, suggested that, whether or not there was to be a clash of arms, there was at least a sharpening of the issues between Old World doctrines of repression and New World doctrines of liberty. On the sixteenth of October, to make the point clear, Baron Tuyll called on Secretary Adams, and told him that his August Master would not receive any minister or agent from any one of the states just formed in the New World. He added, rather significantly as it appeared, that Alexander was highly pleased at the attitude of neutrality adopted by the United States in the war of the colonies with Spain, and still more pleased at its declared intention to continue to maintain that neutrality. The views thus expressed were embodied in an official note transmitted on the same day.[24] A month later came another communication written in much the same spirit. It did not utter any specific menace, unless such a menace could be read into the Tsar's general assertion that his "only object" was "to guarantee the tranquillity of all the states of which the civilized world is composed." [25] But in doctrine it could hardly fail to be offensive. To Adams, always suspicious and touchy, it appeared nothing less than "an 'Io Triumphe' over the fallen cause of revolution, with sturdy promises of determination to keep it down; disclaimers of all intention of making conquests; bitter complaints of being calumniated, and one paragraph of compunctions, acknowledging that an apology is yet due to mankind for the invasion of Spain, which it is in the power only of Ferdinand to furnish, by making his people happy." [26]

All in all, then, we can understand why it was that in November of 1823 Monroe and his advisers were ready to join issue on what

appeared to be, and in truth was, a fundamental divergence of
viewpoint between the New World and the Old. The discussions
that preceded the enunciation of the famous message of 1823
form one of the most interesting chapters in the history of the
Monroe Doctrine. They involved, as we shall see, not only the drafting of the President's message, but also the drafting of a suitable
reply to Canning's overtures, and an answer to the ideological pro-
nunciamento of the Tsar. Fortunately we have a most remarkable
record of them. For the Secretary of State of the United States
kept a diary, rising often in the wee small hours to fill in the narrative of events of high significance to posterity. And that diary,
despite its egocentric character, is a precious memorial of the discussions on the Latin-American question between the President
and his advisers.

The story of these discussions begins with the seventh of November. Very early it becomes clear that the President and John
C. Calhoun, the Secretary of War, were seriously concerned lest
the Holy Alliance should act in the New World to restore to Spain
her ancient dominions. The President, Adams reported on the thirteenth, was "alarmed far beyond anything that I could have conceived possible," and "the news that Cadiz has surrendered to the
French has so affected him that he appeared entirely to despair
of the cause of South America." [27] Calhoun, in the language so
characteristic of the Secretary of State, was "perfectly moonstruck"
at the danger.[28] In later cabinet meetings the panic of the President,
if panic it was, seems somewhat to have abated. But in these
later meetings he seems still to have believed in the peril, and in
this conviction he was, apparently, still supported not only by
Calhoun, but by Wirt, the Attorney General.

John Quincy Adams, on the other hand, took a very different
view. He was by no means averse to some ringing declaration of
policy; he positively yearned to try epistolary conclusions with
Baron Tuyll. But the peril he thought was much exaggerated.
Again and again, in the course of the cabinet discussions, he expressed skepticism as to the danger of intervention. Canning's

alarm, as indicated in his interviews with Rush, he believed to be affected; the real purpose of the British Minister, he suspected (and the suspicion, we have seen, was partly justified), was to obtain a self-denying pledge from the United States, and was only "ostensibly" directed against the forcible interference of the Holy Alliance against South America.[29] Judging, and, as the upshot was to prove, correctly judging, that self-interest and not romantic attachment to principle would be the real mainspring of the action of the Continental powers, he found it difficult to imagine that these powers would act at all. They would have no reason to restore the old commercial monopolies. Why should they seek to maintain the power of the decrepit Spanish monarchy across thousands of miles of ocean? "Was it in human absurdity to imagine that they should waste their blood and treasure to prohibit their own subjects upon pain of death to set foot upon those territories?" [30] No, if they took action at all, their object would be to partition the colonies among themselves. But how could they agree upon the spoils? And how could they induce Great Britain to acquiesce? "The only possible bait they could offer . . . was Cuba, which neither they nor Spain would consent to give her." [31] "I no more believe that the Holy Allies will restore the Spanish dominion upon the American continent," he stated in the cabinet meeting of November 15, "than that Chimborazo will sink beneath the ocean." [32] This view he reiterated on the eighteenth, and again on the twenty-first.[33]

But if Adams was inclined to minimize the actual danger, he was not, as we have said, inclined to let the situation pass without action. Like the President himself, like all the other members of the cabinet, he believed that the time was ripe for a state paper which would, if it did nothing else, thrill American pride and — even an Adams may have thought of this — tickle the ears of the groundlings. As early as November 7 he stated this view in the cabinet. The communications received from Baron Tuyll in October would, he believed, afford "a very suitable and convenient opportunity for us to take our stand against the Holy Alliance, and at the same time to decline the overture from Great Britain. It would be more candid as well as more dignified to avow our principles explicitly to Russia and France, than to come in as a cock-boat in the wake of the British man-of-war." [34]

In making this assertion, the Secretary of State was thinking in terms not of a Presidential message, but of diplomatic correspondence, correspondence which might, of course, be released for publication to the greater glory of the United States and of John Quincy Adams. It was the President and the President alone who decided that at least one of the methods of replying to the homilies of the Tsar and the overtures of Canning, and of making the American position clear, should be a straightforward declaration in the forthcoming message to Congress. In the message's sketch on foreign affairs, prepared by Adams for his chief, there is no mention of the Latin-American problem. In the famous diary there is no intimation of the Secretary's suggesting that the forthcoming communication to the national legislature deal with the matter of the former colonies. It was Monroe who, on his own initiative, brought into the cabinet meeting of November 21 the first draft of what was to become the very heart of the Monroe Doctrine. This draft was certainly not marked by timidity. It was, indeed, too strong for John Quincy Adams. It was, if our diarist is to be believed, a ringing pronouncement in favor of liberal principles in both the Old World and the New. It "alluded to the recent events in Spain and Portugal, speaking in terms of the most pointed reprobation of the late invasion of Spain by France, and of the principles upon which it was undertaken by the open avowal of the King of France. It also contained a broad acknowledgement of the Greeks as an independent nation, and a recommendation to Congress to make an appropriation for sending a minister to them." [35]

Never loath to express himself with vigor, Adams, both in the cabinet meeting and in private conversation with his chief, deprecated a line of thought and action which drew no distinction between republicanism in Europe and republicanism in America. The message, in the form in which the President had written it, "would," he declared, "be a summons to arms — to arms against all Europe, and for objects of policy exclusively European — Greece and Spain. It would be as new . . . in our policy as it would be surprising." [36] It was not for America to bid defiance in the heart of Europe. "The ground that I wish to take," he declared, "is that of earnest remonstrance against the European powers by force with South America, but to disclaim all interference on our part with Europe; to make an American cause, and to adhere inflexibly to that." [37] The President saw and accepted the point of view so cogently stated; on November 24 he showed Adams a new draft which was "entirely conformable to the system of policy" which he had recommended.[38]

On the twenty-fifth and twenty-sixth of November came further and final discussions on the famous message. William Wirt, the Attorney General, quite properly, as Adams admitted, remarked "upon the danger of assuming the attitude of menace without meaning to strike, and asked, if the Holy Allies should act in direct hostility against South America, whether this country would oppose them by war?" [39] Such a war he did not believe the American people would support. "There had never been much general excitement" in favor of the Spanish revolutionists.[40] To these objections the Secretary of State had a ready reply. He did not believe the danger of war to be great. But "if it were brought to our doors, we could not too soon take our stand to repel it." Were the Holy Allies to attack Latin America, "we must not let Great Britain get the sole credit for withstanding them." Such action "would throw them [the colonies] completely into her arms, and in the result make them her Colonies instead of those of Spain. My opinion was, therefore, that we must act promptly and decisively." [41] So, too, thought Calhoun, faithful to his persuasion that the reconquest of South America would be followed by action against the United States. So too, of course, thought the President. At the meeting on the twenty-sixth the die was cast in favor of the great pronouncement of 1823. It may be, however, that at the very last Monroe wavered. According to the journal of William Plumer, Jr., a few days before the actual sending of the message, the President expressed some "doubts about that part of it which related to the interference of the Holy Alliance with Spanish America," and "said he believed it had better be omitted, and asked him [that is, Adams] if he did not think so, too. Adams replied, 'You have my sentiments on the subject already, & I see no reason to alter them.' 'Well,' said the President, 'it is written, & I will not change it now.'" [42] Perhaps this story, which must have come through Adams, is somewhat embroidered. Whether embroidered or not, at any rate the decision of the cabinet meeting stood, and on December 2, 1823, the members of Congress had an opportunity to read the great declaration.

That declaration, as we have already seen, proclaimed the superiority of American institutions, and the peril to the United States of any attempt on the part of European powers to extend their political system to the New World. It was, of course, the expression of a faith rather than a closely reasoned justification of American opposition to the reconquest of the colonies. Monroe assumed these propositions rather than debated them; and perhaps the strength of the message lies in the unwavering firmness of its tone, and the complete confidence of the President in the postulates which he put forward. Yet there is, I think, much more than this to be said for it. Monroe rested his opposition to European intermeddling in Spanish America on the danger to "the peace and safety" of the United States. In so doing he took a strong position from both a legal and a moral point of view. He was basing American policy on the right of self-preservation, a right that is and always has been recognized as fundamental in international law. If in very truth the interposition of the Holy Alliance in the New World imperiled the peace and safety of the United States, then the right to protest against it was obvious. And of this who should be the judge if not the chief magistrate of the republic? How, at any rate, could any European challenge him? Did he not stand secure on his own ground?

The practical wisdom and the immediate effectiveness of the message are matters that will become clearer as this narrative proceeds. But before we examine in some detail the full significance of Monroe's pronouncement, we should turn aside for a moment to follow the evolution of two collateral state papers, the instructions to Rush concerning the overtures of Canning, and the answer to the "Io Triumphe" of the Tsar. In particular the first of these may well claim our interest, for what was therein involved was the propriety of joint action with a European power to protect American interests. Was such action a violation of our tradition? Was it therefore to be avoided at all hazards? Or might it be both expedient and necessary?

The question, after all, was a very important one. So significant indeed did the President consider it that, shortly after the receipt of the first dispatches from Rush, he took the extraordinary step of sending them to two Virginians and ex-Presidents, to Jefferson and Madison. "If a case can exist, in which a sound maxim may, and ought to be departed from is not the present instance precisely that case?" he wrote to the sage of Monticello. "My own impression is that we ought to meet the proposal of the British government." [43] From both his famous confidants, Monroe received encouragement to go forward. "Great Britain," wrote Jefferson, in language which has a curious tincture on his pen, "is the nation which can do us the most harm of any one, or all on earth; and with her on our side we need not fear the whole world. . . . Not that I would purchase even her amity at the price of taking part in her wars. But the war in which the present proposition might engage us, should that be its consequence, is not her war, but ours. Its object is to introduce and establish the American system, of keeping out of our land all foreign powers, of never permitting those of Europe to interfere with the affairs of our nations. It is to maintain our principle, not to depart from it." [44] "There ought not to be any backwardness," wrote Madison, "in meeting her in the way she has proposed. Our co-operation is due to ourselves and to the world; and whilst it must ensure success in the event of an appeal to force, it doubles the chance of success without that appeal." [45]

Nor was this viewpoint without support when Monroe brought

the question before the members of the cabinet. Calhoun, from the beginning of the discussions, was in favor of giving Rush a discretionary power to act with Britain. So was Southard, the Secretary of the Navy. Not so, however, John Quincy Adams. Strongly distrusting the motives of Canning, always ruggedly independent both in the expression of his personal views and in his conceptions of American foreign policy, the Secretary of State wished not only to decline the overtures of Britain, but explicitly to state that without British recognition of Spanish-American independence "we can see no foundation upon which the concurrent action of the two Governments can be harmonized." [46] And Adams it was, in the main, who prevailed. The instructions which he drafted for Rush contained more than one sentence that reflected the isolationist temper. "As a member of the European community," he wrote, "Great Britain has relations with all the other powers of Europe, which the United States have not, and with which it is their unaltered determination not to interfere." Not having recognized the Spanish colonies, moreover, she might, "negotiating at once with the European Alliance and with us, concerning America, without being bound by any permanent community of principle," "still be free to accommodate her policy to any of those distributions of power, and partitions of Territory which have for the last century been the ultima ratio of all European political arrangements." In the circumstances it was difficult to perceive the "foundation upon which the concurrent action of the two governments could be harmonized." "For the effectual accomplishment of the object common to both governments, a perfect understanding with regard to it being established between them, it will be most advisable that they should act separately, each making such representations to the Continental European Allies, or either of them, as circumstances may render proper, and mutually communicating to each other the purport of such representation." [47] This was certainly the language of independence; and it undoubtedly represented the Adams cast of mind. The sentences thus penned, moreover, were to stand in the draft which was finally sent to London; the Secretary had his way with regard to them. Yet some concession to the contrary viewpoint had to be made, and, yielding perhaps to the solicitations of the President, Adams closed his dispatch by declaring that "should an emergency occur in which a joint manifestation of opinion by the two Governments may tend to influence the Councils of the European Allies, either in the aspect of persuasion or of admonition you will make it known to us without delay, and we shall according to the principles of our Government and in the forms prescribed by our Constitution, cheerfully join in any act, by which we may contribute to support the cause of human freedom and the Independence of the South American Nations." [48] Thus the door was left open to *eventual* common action as a possibility — eventual common action, however, to be decided upon not by Richard Rush, but by the administration in Washington. Adams had, in the main, won his point as to an independent course; but the stand which he took was not an absolute one, but one which might be modified by time and circumstance.

There is much food for reflection in this decision, in this year 1941. Does it justify the isolationists of our own day, or is it rather an argument for a policy of co-operation with Great Britain? The temptation, of course, for both schools of thought is to claim the unequivocal support of the men of 1823. But perhaps the fairest judgment takes a middle ground. Men like Adams clearly realized that American foreign policy must remain *American;* and so long as nations continue, as they doubtless will, to consult their own interests there must be a watchful regard and a prudent reserve as to the conditions of co-operation with any other power. Adams' reference to "those distributions of power, and partitions of Territory which have for the last century been the ultima ratio of all European political arrangements" is not to be forgotten. But, on the other hand, for those Americans to whom the doctrine of nonentanglement is a fixed and abiding principle, never to be violated, perhaps never to be debated, there is no great comfort in the position taken by Monroe and his advisers. Blind dogmatism was not the quality of mind most conspicuous in the men who made the great decisions of that far-off November one hundred and seventeen years ago. Neither Jefferson, nor Madison, nor Monroe, nor even Adams, closed the door to the possibility of co-operation with a European power where they were convinced that the interests of the United States would be advanced by such action. They took their stand not on formulas, but on facts. To the extent that they recognized a peril to exist, they were willing to join hands with Great Britain to avert it. In this, as in previous crises we have examined, the pure gospel of isolationism was accepted with some qualifications and exceptions.

But if Adams made a slight concession to the idea of co-operation with Great Britain in his dispatch to Rush, he preached the pure milk of the isolationist word in his answer to the communications of the Tsar. His purpose, as he described it, was, "in a moderate and conciliatory manner, but with a firm and determined spirit, to declare our dissent from the principles avowed in those communications; to assert those upon which our own Government is founded, and while disclaiming all intention of attempting to propagate them by force, and all interference with the political affairs of Europe, to declare our expectation and hope that the European powers will equally abstain from the attempt to spread their principles in the American hemisphere, or to subjugate by force any part of these continents to their will." [49] The "firm and determined spirit" of the Secretary of State could be taken for granted; his gifts of moderation and conciliation were less obvious. The dispatch which he penned began with a ringing declaration of the principle of government with the consent of the governed; its language was on occasion sarcastic, if not provocative; its tone something less than urbane. In the cabinet Calhoun was opposed to its being sent at all; and though no one supported the Secretary of War in this view, Wirt, the Attorney General, objected to the first paragraph as "a hornet of a paragraph," [50] and the President expressed the fear that the republicanism of the dispatch might "indispose the British Government to a cordial concert of operations with us." [51] The Secretary, as his diary shows, bore with no very good grace the criticisms directed toward him; the first paragraph was "the cream of his paper"; a "distinct avowal of principle" was "absolutely required." [52] But Monroe, with the tact which distinguished him (no one knew better how to handle the prickly New Englander), secured the deletion of the most offensive passages; and a modified and somewhat softened note was finally sent to Baron Tuyll. Yet the closing paragraphs of this note were unequivocal. "The United States of America," Adams wrote, "and their government could not see with indifference the forcible interposition of any European power, other than Spain, either to restore the dominion of Spain over her emancipated Colonies in America, or to establish Monarchical Government in those Countries, or to transfer any of the possessions heretofore or yet subject to Spain in the American Hemisphere, to any other European Power." [53] Such language left no doubt as to the point of view of the United States. At the close of 1823, the American government had in the dispatch to Rush, in the note to Tuyll, as in the famous message of December 2, taken a definite stand against the reconquest of the New World. Having analyzed these two collateral documents we may now once more fix our attention upon the declaration of Monroe itself, and seek to assess its wisdom, its influence, and its historical significance.

Perhaps the first question that we should ask ourselves is as to the extent of the danger against which the message was directed. There can be little question as to how the average American would respond. For at least half a century it has been persistently asserted that the President's action saved the New World from deadly peril, that it frustrated the wicked designs of the members of the Holy Alliance, and established the liberties of Latin America upon a basis secure and irrefragable. Unfortunately this notion is purely legend; and if we survey the facts candidly we must admit that the message of 1823 was directed against an imaginary menace. Not one of the Continental powers cherished any designs of reconquest in the New World in November or December of 1823.

As the Continental power with the most formidable navy and

the most important merchant marine, France might have seemed to be the probable agent of the Holy Alliance in restoring the colonies to Spain, all the more so as she had just intervened victoriously in the Peninsula. But in reality she had no stomach for any such venture. French policy was subject to contradictory influences which rendered it both hesitating and ineffective. On the one hand were France's increasingly important trading and mercantile interests, which desired, not the reconquest, but the recognition of the colonies. On the other were the Ultras, the proponents of the Spanish intervention, the apostles of reaction in general. Caught between these two groups, the French Prime Minister, Jean de Villèle, with Chateaubriand, his Foreign Minister, attempted a policy of compromise. This compromise was based upon an idea that had cropped up again and again in the preceding few years, and had, for a little, seemed to make substantial headway in the Argentine. It was the idea of independent Bourbon monarchies in the New World, under the governance of one or another of the Spanish Infantes. In June and July of 1823 it was seriously discussed in the bosom of the cabinet, and may be regarded, for a little while at any rate, as the aim of French policy. It implied the possibility of a measure of armed aid to Spain.

But it was very far from a project of reconquest. Jauntily disregarding the facts of the case, Villèle spoke of "a few troops and a little money" as sufficient for its realization.[54] In another of his letters, he alludes to "detachments," not great expeditions.[55] Sacrifices on a grand scale he obviously did not intend. He thought of the scheme as involving a minimum of effort, and furthermore he wished to make it contingent on Ferdinand's pursuing what France would regard as a reasonable policy in Spain.[56] To count on Ferdinand VII being reasonable as a condition of any course of action was almost to foredoom it.

But were we to take the Bourbon monarchy idea more seriously than it deserves to be taken, and to identify it with a broad policy of intervention, we should find any such judgment soon reduced to nullity by the events of the month of October, 1823. In the early days of that month there took place a series of conferences between George Canning and the French Ambassador at London, the Prince de Polignac. The results of these conversations were embodied in the famous Polignac memorandum of October 9. "The junction of any Foreign Power in an enterprise of Spain against the Colonies, would be viewed" by Britain, stated Canning, "as constituting an entirely new question; and one upon which they must take such decision as the interests of Great Britain might require." To this clear intimation of British opposition to intervention there came the following reply, dictated by René de Chateaubriand, the Foreign Minister of France. The French government "believed it to be utterly hopeless to reduce Spanish America to the state of its former relation to Spain. France disclaimed, on her part, any intention or desire to avail herself of the present state of the Colonies, or of the present situation of France towards Spain, to appropriate to herself any part of the Spanish possessions in America. . . . She abjured, in any case, any design of acting against the Colonies by force of arms." [57] Thus, two months before the Monroe message, France had given a pledge against an interventionist policy, in answer to a British warning. She did not, on that account, abandon all interest in the question of Latin America. Indeed, shortly after the events just described, she began urging the Spanish government to appeal to the powers for a Congress on the colonial question. But there is no evidence whatever that either Chateaubriand or Villèle thought of such a Congress as an introduction to any policy of coercion. Indeed, the events of the fall of 1823 point clearly in the opposite direction. The French squadron in the West Indies was weakened, not strengthened; [58] so, too, were the squadrons at home, several vessels of which were put out of commission. [59] "From whom," wrote Chateaubriand to Talaru, the French Minister in Spain, October 30, 1823, "can Spain expect aid to reconquer her colonies? Surely she cannot think that France would furnish her money, vessels, or troups for such an enterprise?" [60] Nor is the slackening of naval activity all that we have to go by as to French intentions. At the very time when Monroe was issuing his

warning against the nefarious designs of the Alliance the French
cabinet was preparing to send agents to the New World who
should reassure the new states as to the views of France. The instructions to these agents directed them to do their utmost to remove the impression that France had ever promised military or
naval aid to Spain.[61] France, it is declared, cannot wait indefinitely
on the good pleasure of Ferdinand before recognizing the new
states. She is willing to mediate between the new republics and the
former mother country on the basis of independence, with special
commercial privileges for Spain. Such language makes it crystal-
clear that the pledges given to Canning were given in good faith,
and that, if Villèle and Chateaubriand had flirted with the idea of
using force in June or July, they had ceased to flirt with it in November.

But what of the Tsar Alexander? What lay behind the note of
October 16, of which we have already spoken? What lay behind
the declamatory phrases of the "Io Triumphe over the fallen cause
of revolution" which so disturbed the tranquillity of John Quincy
Adams? The answer is, very little indeed of a concrete character.
Russian policy towards Latin America can hardly be said to have
crystallized at all in those last months of 1823. There is reason to
suspect — at least the French Minister suspected — that the brilliant Corsican, Pozzo di Borgo, who represented the Russian government at Paris, was coquetting with the idea of the resubjugation
of the colonies. In October he paid a visit to Madrid. There he
appears to have encouraged, rather than discouraged, the ridiculous ambitions of Ferdinand, and even to have urged the King to
appeal to his allies for aid.[62] But if he took such action, he took it
on his own authority. No instructions which dealt with the colonial
question came from St. Petersburg, to him or to any other Russian
representative, until November 26, 1823, only six days before the
American President sent his message to Congress. And when indeed they did come, they were phrased in mellifluous generalities,
declaring only that the colonial question concerned "the interest
of all the Allies, and that it is between them and with the King of

Spain that this important question ought to be treated and decided by common accord." [63] Still opposed to the recognition of the hydra of revolution, Alexander yet realized, and clearly indicated, that the fate of Latin America could only be decided after an understanding with Great Britain. Very specifically he declared that preliminary conferences with the Court of St. James's were the indispensable prelude to that Congress to which he, in common with the French Court, looked forward as a forum for the consideration of the affairs of Latin America.[64]

If Alexander thus pursued a policy of caution, what was to be said of Metternich, the Austrian Chancellor, and Count von Bernstorff, who directed Prussian policy? With regard to the first of these two men, the answer is given in a series of long and able dispatches designed to make their impression upon the Tsar. Metternich was, it is true, a reactionary, in some respects the arch-priest of reaction; but he was no romantic, and no crusader in causes that had nothing to do with the interests of Austria. He recognized that the Spanish-American revolutions had already largely succeeded. "It appears to us," he wrote, "that all that wisdom should dictate at this time is to keep open the question of legal right. It is certainly not over this immense part of the American continent which Spain formerly possessed as colonies that the efforts of the mother-country can now be directed with any chance of success whatsoever. In deeming it possible to regain all, she would be practically sure to lose all." [65] His views were echoed by his Prussian colleague. As for the allied powers, wrote Bernstorff, they "lack arms to reach America, or even a voice to make themselves heard there." [66]

It is possible, then, to state with definiteness and with assurance that the powers of the Holy Alliance had no designs against the liberties of the New World at the moment when Monroe launched his famous declaration. The story that the President prevented a terrible danger is legend and nothing more; as legend it deserves to be recorded. It assumes a material strength on the part of the United States which closer examination reveals not to have existed; it assumes that the United States was a great power, in the modern sense of the word, in 1823. It assumes that this country was listened to then with the same respect which it commands today.

One of the striking facts, indeed, about the events we have been examining is the attitude of the Continental powers toward the American government. With one exception, that of Russia, they proposed entirely to ignore it in their projected Congress on the colonial question. When, for example, Canning suggested in the course of the Polignac conversations that the administration at Washington ought to be represented at any Congress on Latin-American affairs, Chateaubriand and Villèle were nothing less than shocked. To the former the British proposal seemed "malevolent" and "short-sighted"; [67] to the latter it seemed better to have no Congress at all than to admit a country "whose political principles are directly at variance with those of every other Power." [68] In a later pronouncement Chateaubriand went even further; the exclusion of the United States from European gatherings "might serve in case of need as a supplementary article of the public law of Europe." [69] Views such as these were welcomed in Vienna and Berlin. When Adams, in one of his dispatches to Rush, indicated that his government would refuse to participate in a Congress if invited to do so, his resolution was superfluous; it was a certainty from the beginning that no invitation would be extended.

It would be pleasant if with these last sentences we could terminate the deflation of the message of 1823, from the standpoint of its contemporary effect; but candor compels us to press on still further before turning to the more agreeable task of indicating the many strong points of Monroe's declaration. We shall have to examine its reception in the Old World and the New; we shall have to ask what were its effects upon the policy of Old World monarchies or New World republics.

First of all, then, how was it received by Europeans? How were its resounding periods judged by European statesmen?

On the continent of Europe, there were here and there individuals, the friends of liberty, who hailed it with delight. The venerable Lafayette thought it "the best little bit of paper that God had ever permitted any man to give to the World," [70] and Barbé-Marbois, always well-disposed to the United States, thought it "not only the best but the best-timed state paper which he had ever read." [71] But to most Continentals, the message came as a most unpleasant surprise. They knew, of course, nothing whatever of its background; innocent of nefarious designs, they could hardly be otherwise than resentful of the imputations of the President. Without any preliminary warning or exchange of views, without any effort to establish the facts, in a document intended only for the American national legislature, Monroe and Adams had laid down the principles on which they expected the policy of the Old World to be governed in relation to the New. These doctrines were nothing more nor less than a challenge to the monarchies of Europe; they were as odious to a Metternich or a Chateaubriand as the diatribes of Hitler or Mussolini are to a convinced friend of liberty today. "Blustering," "monstrous," "arrogant," "haughty," "peremptory" — these were some of the terms applied to the message. And veritably vitriolic criticism came from the pen of the great Metternich.

These United States of America [wrote the Austrian Chancellor], which we have seen arise and grow, and which during their short youth already meditated projects which they dared not then avow, have suddenly left a sphere too narrow for their ambition, and have astonished Europe by a new act of revolt, more unprovoked, fully as audacious, and no less dangerous than the former. They have distinctly and clearly announced their intention to set not only power against power, but, to express it more exactly, altar against altar. In their indecent declarations they have cast blame and scorn on the institutions of Europe most worthy of respect, on the principles of its greatest sovereigns, on the whole of those measures which a sacred duty no less than an evident necessity has forced our governments to adopt to frustrate plans most criminal. In permitting themselves these unprovoked [sic] attacks, in fostering revolutions wherever they show themselves, in regretting those which have failed, in extending a helping hand to those which seem to prosper, they lend new strength to the apostles of sedition, and reanimate the courage of every conspirator. If this flood of evil doctrines and pernicious examples should extend over the whole of America, what would become of our religious and political institutions, of the moral force of our governments, and of that conservative system which has saved Europe from complete dissolution? [72]

Yet though there was widespread irritation at the message of 1823, there was not, on the part of any Continental power, any protest against it. It may be that Chateaubriand considered such action; he had, as we have seen, told Stuart that the noncolonization clause "ought to be resisted by all the powers possessing either territory or commercial interests in that hemisphere." [73] But the idea, if held, was soon abandoned. It would not have been strange if the Tsar, with his passion for dialectic and high-sounding principles, had wished to answer the philippic of Monroe; but when Tuyll proposed such action to his August Master, he was answered that "the document in question enunciates views and pretensions so exaggerated, it establishes principles so contrary to the rights of the European powers, that it merits only the most profound contempt. His Majesty therefore invites you to preserve the passive attitude which you have deemed proper to adopt, and to continue to maintain the silence which you have imposed upon yourself." [74] Alexander evidently believed that further discussion would serve only to dignify the American manifesto. And the cabinets of Madrid, of Vienna and Berlin, despite their irritation, emulated his silence.

This silence is not to be regarded as flattering to the United States. It proceeded from a sense of American weakness, rather than American strength. Following a habit which European ministers seem early to have developed in evaluating American foreign policies, there was a distinct disposition to set the message down to the exigencies of domestic politics. Menou, the French chargé at Washington, believed it was part of John Quincy Adams' campaign for the Presidential succession in 1824. [75] Stoughton, his Spanish colleague, took a similar view, and thought the pronouncement a mere *brutum fulmen.*[76] And on every hand, in the diplomatic correspondence of the time, one becomes painfully aware of the low estimate in which the physical power of the United States was held. The charge of materialism, a hoary weapon in the European arsenal of criticism of the United States, was reiterated again and again. The Americans would not fight, because they were too much interested in making money. They could not be brought to any real sacrifices. Such was the judgment of Menou, of Stoughton, of Tuyll. And if, perchance, they did take up the sword, their power would be anything but formidable. Financially, Tuyll reported, the Union "would . . . find itself a prey to considerable embarrassment." Its army was small, nor was it possible to raise forces to cope with a powerful expedition. "The sluggishness inherent in the forms of a federal republic [mark well these words, reader of today], the scanty powers and means of which this government disposes, the lack of inclination of the inhabitants of this country to make pecuniary sacrifices which offer them no bait of considerable and direct gain, the irritation which would be aroused among the merchants by the cessation of their commercial relations with France, Spain and the North . . . will tend to make such a war . . . rather a demonstration which circumstances have rendered indispensable and which is entered upon reluctantly with the secret desire of seeing it ended as soon as possible, than one of those truly national enterprises sustained by every means, and with every bit of energy, which might make it a very embarrassing obstacle. The attitude which the government of the United States has assumed," the minister concluded, "is undoubtedly of such a nature as to demand in an American expedition undertaken by Spain and her Allies a considerable development of means and of military force. But once the decision is taken to attempt it, I should not think that the course taken by the United States, unsupported by Great Britain, would be of a nature to change such a decision." [77]

One might set down remarks such as these, remarks which have their parallel in the language of Chateaubriand and many others, as nothing more nor less than wishful thinking. Yet one can but admit that an analysis of the naval strength of the United States in 1823 does something to sustain the view frequently expressed. In 1823 this country had a naval establishment which, numerically, was about a quarter that of France in ships and men, and less than an eighth that of Russia. These are crude figures, it is true; and even were we to accept them at face value, we should have to remember that, even with Havana and the French Antilles as bases, the Continental powers would have been at a severe disadvantage in waging war on this side of the Atlantic. We have to take account, too, of the numerous American privateers which might have been unleashed had war come. But even making such allowances it still remains true that in all human probability a combined French and Russian intervention in American affairs would have constituted a considerable menace, and that the forces of the Allied powers would have outnumbered those of the United States. We shall be making a gross error if we attribute to the United States of 1823 the material strength of a later age.

We shall be making an error, also, if we imagine that the *policies* of the European powers were much influenced by the solemn warnings of Monroe. The plans for a Congress on the colonial question went forward none the less rapidly because of the message of the President; indeed, Chateaubriand and Metternich and many others were led to hope that the flaming republicanism of the American pronouncement would operate to bring Great Britain into line with the Continental powers. The idea of Bourbon monarchies in the New World, dissociated from the use of force, was fully as vital in 1824 as it had been in 1823; and in St. Petersburg the Tsar Alexander seems to have played with the idea of intervention for the first time after, and not before, December of 1823.[78] If his thoughts on this subject never got beyond the point of nebulous conversation, the reason lay not in the attitude of the United States, but in the frigid indifference of the other Continental courts, and in the obvious and vigorous opposition of Great Britain. That opposition was underlined by Canning's refusal, at the end of January, to attend a Congress on the colonial question. Never really seriously entertained, the whole idea of intervention in the New World became little less than an absurdity by the spring of 1824.

Yet it will not do, because the peril to the independence of the new states was in large degree illusory, to depreciate unduly the significance of Monroe's message. To say nothing of its long-time importance, of its epoch-making character in the perspective of more than a century, there is still much to be said for it from the viewpoint of 1823. We should not assess the President's action in the light of the knowledge of today. We must obviously assess it in the light of its own time. Viewed from this angle, it must first of all be said that the Presidential declaration took a considerable amount of courage. The cabinet discussions make it clear that whether or not a serious danger existed, Monroe *thought* it existed. So, too, with the exception of Adams, did his advisers. It needed, therefore, a certain audacity for the young republic of the West to throw down the gauntlet to the great states of Europe. True, there seemed some reason to believe that if emergency arose the United States would be supported by the power of the British navy. But there could be no real confidence that this would be the case. There was always the possibility, as Adams and Wirt had both pointed out, that Great Britain was playing a double game.[79] There was, indeed, something suspicious in the way in which Canning had handled the whole matter. The President himself and Richard Rush, as well as Adams, were quick to question his motives. They could not but remark that in September the overtures of the British Minister had suddenly ceased. The silence that followed might be easily interpreted as the sign of a shift in British policy. In such circumstances, to speak out boldly was no mere cheap and easy gesture, no mere *brutum fulmen,* launched in the secure knowledge that the step taken would be made good by the armed might of Britain. It was an act, if not of unmitigated audacity, at least of calculated courage.

Moreover, from one angle, at any rate, it was an exceedingly skillful piece of diplomacy. Great Britain and the United States were inevitably rivals for the favor of the young republics of Latin America, rivals for their favor and their commerce. By the declaration of December 2, 1823, Monroe anticipated Canning in giving open expression to opposition to the reconquest of the new states, and in the public assurance of the will of another power to protect them. And the records of the time clearly indicate the chagrin of the British Minister at having been thus outplayed in the diplomatic game. True, it strengthened his hand in refusing the invitation to the projected Congress on the Latin-American question. "The Congress," he wrote joyfully to A'Court, British Minister to Spain, "was broken in all its limbs before, but the President's speech gives it the *coup de grâce*." [80] But this pleasurable reaction to Monroe's pronouncement was short-lived. From exultation Canning soon changed to suspicion and jealousy. Hard on the reception of the message, he communicated the Polignac correspondence to the agents of Great Britain in the New World, and labored to show (with some accuracy, it must be confessed) that his own country had been first in assuming the protection of the new states. [81] There are clear signs, too, that he dreaded the extension of the American political system in the New World, and labored to circumvent it. "The great danger of the time," he wrote to one of his friends in 1825, "a danger which the policy of the European System would have fostered, was a division of the World into European and American, Republican and Monarchical; a league of worn-out Govts. on the one hand, and of youthful and strong Nations, with the U. States at their head, on the other." [82] With this thesis in mind, Canning himself seems to have flirted with the idea of Bourbon monarchy in the winter of 1824. [83] He bent his every effort to settle the dispute between Portugal and its revolted colony, Brazil, with a view to preserving the monarchical system in the latter country. And at the same time, never the doctrinaire, always the ardent servant of British commercial interests, he pressed harder than ever before in the cabinet and at Madrid for the recognition of the colonies. Indeed, he even went so far as to offer King Ferdinand the guarantee of the island of Cuba if that obdurate prince would come to some kind of understanding with his former subjects on the mainland.[84] He sought to persuade his colleagues that "the ambition and ascendancy" of the United States made forthright action imperative. And at more than one American capital he sought to undermine the prestige and throw doubt upon the motives of the American government. The message of Monroe had struck home; and the activity of British diplomacy in seeking to counteract it demonstrates clearly enough with what shrewdness Monroe had acted in proclaiming independently, and in anticipation of the Court of St. James's, the opposition of the New World to invasion or penetration from the Old. From this angle alone, despite its false assumptions, the message was a brilliant diplomatic document.

Nor is this by any means all that ought to be said. The *method* of the warning to Europe is no less interesting than the matter. Monroe and his advisers might have confined themselves in 1823 to the ordinary courses of diplomatic correspondence. They might have contented themselves with an answer to Tuyll, perhaps with a similar communication to France. They chose instead the course of open diplomacy. And how, indeed, could they have chosen better? Granted the premises upon which they acted, what could have been more skillful? How much more effective the declaration to Congress than an unostentatious diplomatic protest; how much more gratifying to the national pride, how much more productive of prestige in South America, how much more disconcerting to Europe! No wonder that the British chargé, Addington, could write as follows of its reception in the United States.

The message seems to have been received with acclamation throughout the United States. . . . The explicit and manly tone, especially, with which the President has treated the subject of European interference in the affairs of this Hemisphere with a view to the subjugation of those territories which have emancipated themselves from European domination, has evidently found in every bosom a chord which vibrates in strict unison with the sentiments so conveyed. They have been echoed from one end of the union to the other. It would indeed be difficult, in a country composed of elements so various, and liable on all subjects to opinions so conflicting, to find more perfect una- nimity than has been displayed on every side on this particular point.[85]

Whatever else the President had or had not done, he had certainly interpreted the sentiments of his countrymen, and aroused their enthusiasm and their loyalty.

And, indeed, he had done more. He had stated with remarkable force and clarity the divergence in the political ideals of the Europe and the United States of 1823. Absolutism and democracy, these were the opposing principles which the President made clear. To Alexander, to Pozzo, to Metternich, whatever practical obstacles might stand in the way of the reconquest of the colonies, the fun- damental postulates of the situation were perfectly clear. Sover- eigns held their power by the will of God. No revolution could divest them of these rights. In theory, then, they could naturally assist one another in the putting down of their rebellious subjects. In theory, the republics of Latin America were outside the pale, and their success the symptoms of the dissolution of world order itself. "The Christian World," wrote Pozzo di Borgo, "tends to divide into two parts, distinct from, and I fear, hostile to, one another; we must work to prevent or defer this terrible revolution, and above all to save and fortify the portion which may escape the contagion and the invasion of vicious principles." [86] Against this Old World order, based on the doctrines of absolutism, Monroe opposed a new one, based on the right of the peoples of the world to determine their own destiny, and to govern themselves. The principles which he expressed were more than the principles of his own government; they were the principles of the nineteenth and early twentieth cen- turies. They were the principles that, in the main, were to triumph, in the years that lay ahead, to triumph not only in the New World, but in a large part of the Old. Framed only for the continents of the West, they were to have an ecumenical significance for several gen- erations of men. The liberty which Monroe desired and defended for the republics of Latin America was, in the course of the century, to be diffused throughout no small part of Europe as well. The President of the United States spoke not only for his people, but for his age. He spoke, indeed, for more than his age. It is a measure of the significance of the declaration of 1823 that it has today, in this year of grace 1941, a relevancy no less great than when it was framed nearly a century and a quarter ago.

III

*The Challenge Recalled
Polk Revives Monroe*

. . . Near a quarter of a century ago the principle was distinctly announced to the world, in the annual message of one of my predecessors, that —

"The American continents, by the free and independent condition which they have assumed and maintain, are henceforth not to be considered as subjects for future colonization by any European powers."

This principle will apply with greatly increased force should any European power attempt to establish any new colony in North America. In the existing circumstances of the world the present is deemed a proper occasion to reiterate and reaffirm the principle avowed by Mr. Monroe and to state my cordial concurrence in its wisdom and sound policy. The reassertion of this principle, especially in reference to North America, is at this day but the promulgation of a policy which no European power should cherish the disposition to resist. Existing rights of every European nation should be respected, but it is due alike to our safety and our interests that the efficient protection of our laws should be extended over our whole territorial limits, and that it should be distinctly announced to the world as our settled policy that no future European colony or dominion shall with our consent be planted or established on any part of the North American continent.

— JAMES K. POLK'S *First Annual Message, December 2, 1845*

IN THE diplomatic history of the United States there is an irregular but very obvious rhythm. There are periods when the problems are few, and the public mood calm and pacific; there are others when the great issues are at stake, and when a militant spirit makes itself felt among the body of the people. The years just preceding the War of 1812, for example, were years of rising nationalism; and this temper lasted beyond the war and helped to shape the momentous declaration of December 2, 1823. But then an era of comparative quietude seemed to set in, and from the inauguration of John Quincy Adams to the administration of John Tyler the diplomatic waters were, for the most part, untroubled or stirred only on their surface. Curiously enough, the administration of Andrew Jackson, who could hardly be described as a mild or forbearing person by natural temper, was amongst the least eventful in our diplomatic annals. In the middle forties however, the American mood seemed once again to change: a new wave of militant feeling swept over the country; once again it came to war, this time with Mexico, our neighbor to the south. The aggressive spirit took possession of the nation for almost a decade and a half; and never was the American democracy more bumptious and irritating in its bearing toward other nations than in the decade of the fifties. The unblushing manifestations of sympathy for revolution in Europe, and the equally unblushing manifestations of the acquisitive instinct at home, were extraordinary; and it was only the growing division over slavery which acted as a check upon American nationalism in action. With secession, however, the situation again drastically changed; the Civil War engaged the full energies of the government of the Union, and when that war was over another period, calmer and more drab, was opened in American diplomacy.

What produced these oscillations of opinion? The most probable explanation is to be found in the American movement of expansion. In the first two decades of the century, the region between the Appalachians and the Mississippi was filling up; the men of the frontier viewed with natural suspicion and hostility the British intrigues with the Indians of the Ohio Valley, and the lawlessness on their southern border; the War of 1812 was an expression of their spirit; in its course it broke the Indian power to the east of the great river, and in 1819 the purchase of Florida rounded out the American domain in the Southeast. Thus the way was paved for a relatively quiet period, as settlers in large numbers flowed into the older West, and new stars appeared upon the emblem of the republic. But the frontier spirit was insatiable; gradually new horizons beckoned, and Texas and Oregon became the objectives of new generations of pioneers. With this new land hunger the nationalist spirit flared up once more; American statesmanship assumed a new tone; and the fact that a great issue was coming to divide the American people at home may have operated to intensify the temper in which they faced the more important questions of diplomacy. In all countries it has been traditional to seek to forget internal problems and the weaknesses of internal economy by a vigorous policy with regard to foreign nations. At any rate, the spirit mounted; and it ceased to mount only with the rupture of the Union itself.

In these years from 1823 to 1861, the evolution of the Monroe Doctrine follows the course of our foreign policy in general. Caution and something very like indifference characterize the years from 1823 to 1841; and then comes a period in which popular attention is once more drawn to the principles of 1823. Those principles express, indeed, something of the American faith in democratic government; the exclusion of European powers from the New World fits well with American expansionist ambition; it is not strange that the two go hand in hand. By degrees, then, between 1841 and 1860 the people of the United States come more and more to accept the words spoken in 1823 as having a broad and a general application, as fixing not a specific, but a universal rule of policy, as governing their conduct with foreign nations. This earlier period of quiescence, this later period of widening acceptance of the Monroe Doctrine, we must now examine.

We should begin, however, by a word or two more than has yet been said with regard to the message. For one thing, we should emphasize the fact that there is no evidence that Monroe was in any degree aware that he was enunciating maxims which should govern *in perpetuo,* or at least for a long time to come, the foreign policy of the United States. The language of the message related to a specific situation, it was directed against the "allied powers" — that is, the Holy Alliance; it was fashioned to meet a concrete, though as it turned out an imaginary, danger. We cannot be too clear with regard to the proposition that the fifth President of the United States had little conception of the far-reaching influence of the words which he enunciated.

We should be wholly clear, also, on a second point already mentioned. In the field of international politics, at that epoch it was Great Britain which occupied the center of the stage. So far as the fear of intervention by the Holy Alliance existed, and there was much less such fear in Latin America than in Washington, Latin Americans looked for succor to the mistress of the seas rather than to the young republic of the North. This was true of Bolivar, the Liberator, who wrote in January of 1824 that only England could change the policy of the allies. It was true of Santander, the Vice-President of Colombia. It was true of Alamán, the Mexican Foreign Minister. It was true of Rivadavia, the Foreign Minister of Argentina. And when the danger had definitely passed, all of these men recognized that the British attitude had been the really decisive one even though they did not ignore the role of the United States. It is, after all, anachronistic in the highest degree to give greater weight to the immature American democracy in 1823 than to the power whose prestige was never greater, whose force was never more impressive, than eight years after the defeat of Napoleon at Waterloo.

Bold, indeed, as had been the language of Monroe, it was hardly to be translated from brilliant generalities into binding political commitments. Though Henry Clay, the steady friend of the new republics, introduced into the House of Representatives a resolution endorsing the principles which the President had laid down, the voice of criticism occasionally made itself heard. John Randolph of Roanoke, for example, always bilious in opposition, characterized the Presidential declaration as quixotic, and declared that, if the governments of South America, having achieved their independence, had not valor to maintain it, he would not commit "the safety and independence" of the United States in such a cause.[1] Floyd of Virginia denounced the message, so he tells us at a later date, as "assuming an unwarrantable power; violating the spirit of the Constitution; assuming grounds and an attitude toward European Powers, calculated to involve us in the strife which there existed, and in which we had no interest; and indirectly leading to war, which Congress alone had the right to declare." [2] These statements, no doubt, are to be regarded as exceptional, but what is more remarkable is the cautious language of the State Department itself in the diplomatic correspondence of 1824 and 1825, when the new republics of the South began to seek to realize on the draft of friendship proffered by Monroe. The first of these republics was Colombia, which, as early as July 2, 1824, alarmed at the rumors of a French mission which might have the re-establishment of monarchy in view, solicited a treaty of alliance with the United States, and based its appeal upon the famous declaration of December.[3] Cool, indeed, was the tone of John Quincy Adams' reply. Minimizing the danger which the President had exaggerated seven months before, the Secretary of State reminded Salazar, the Colombian Minister, that the ultimate decision in such matters must rest with the legislative body. Should the crisis recur, the President would recommend to Congress "the adoption of measures exclusively of their resort, and by which the principles asserted by him would with the concurrence if given, be on the part of the United States, efficaciously maintained." But this was not all. The words which followed were "weasel words" indeed, for they confessed American dependence on Great Britain. "It is obvious," wrote the American Secretary of State, in terms which he would have blushed to have published, "that the United States could not undertake resistance by force of arms, without a previous understanding with those European Powers, whose interests and whose principles would secure from them an active and efficient co-operation in the cause. This there is no reason to doubt, could be obtained, but it could only be effected by a negotiation preliminary to any alliance between the United States and the Colombian republic, or in any event coeval with it." [4]

We must not, of course, exaggerate the extent of this retreat from the bold language of the message. The Monroe Doctrine was not, and was not intended to be, anything else than a unilateral declaration of policy. From that day to this American statesmen have insisted upon its purely American character, upon the right of the United States to interpret it in its own fashion, and on the basis of its own interests. Despite the answer of Adams to Salazar, Monroe reiterated the principles of 1823 in his message of 1824. But the reference to British assistance is none the less revealing. Very evidently the American government was readier to be bold in speech than it was to be decisive in action.

The alliance that was denied to Colombia was to be denied a few months later to new claimants to American favor. In January of 1825 the monarchy of Brazil sought an offensive and defensive alliance with the United States against the former mother country, Portugal, and against any European powers which should seek to assist Portugal in the subjugation of her former dominion.[5] Once again the request was denied.[6] In August of 1825 came a third incident of similar character. A French fleet was dispatched to Haiti to put diplomatic pressure on the government of this former colony of France, and to extort a large indemnity as the price of recognition of Haitian independence. The American government remained disinterested, and indeed it was not strange that it did, in view of the influence of the slave states in American politics, and the fact that the Haitians made no representations in Washington. But the presence of the French squadron aroused considerable apprehensions in other quarters; and the government of Mexico, fearing invasion, addressed to Joel Poinsett, our minister at Mexico City, an appeal for aid.[7] But Poinsett, before he would accept the note addressed to him, insisted that there be stricken from it any phrase which assumed the existence of a commitment on the part of the United States. And Henry Clay, now Secretary of State, gave no assurances whatsoever when the matter came to his attention; indeed, as had Adams a year before, he minimized the danger.

But still more striking evidence of the strong American distaste for translating the broad generalities of the message into more concrete terms is to be found in the debates in Congress on the mission to Panama. In the year 1826, on the initiative of the Liberator himself, a conclave of the American states was called to meet upon the Isthmus to deliberate matters of common concern. To this conclave the United States was invited, invited formally by Colombia, by Mexico, and by Central America, invited, as at least the Colombian invitation shows, with the hope of securing a definite commitment from the American government. President Adams and Secretary Clay were not averse to accepting this invitation. But they had no illusions, so far as one can discover, as to what would be possible at Panama. In nominating two commissioners, the President explicitly stated that the object was "neither to contract alliances, nor to engage in any undertaking or project importing hostility to any other nation." [8] The most that he proposed (and this in connection with his own cherished principle of noncolonization) was "an agreement between all the parties represented at the meeting, that each will guard, by its own means, against the establishment of any future European colony within its borders," [9] together with a possible denunciation of interference from abroad. But even this was subject for suspicion. The partisan opponents of Adams, eager to discredit him, and to promote the candidacy of Andrew Jackson for the Presidency, launched a ferocious attack upon the mission itself. Misrepresentation of motives, of facts, and of intentions was as rife as in the Senate debate on the League of Nations in 1920. But what emerged and emerged with clarity, was a very real determination not to be entangled in the affairs of the states to the south. To the report of the Committee on Foreign Affairs endorsing the mission was appended an amendment explicitly declaring that there must be no "departure from the settled policy of this government, that, in extending our commercial relations with foreign nations, we should have with them as little political connexion as possible." [10] The amendment also frowned heavily upon any joint declaration with regard to either European colonization or European interference with the new states. The language not only of its supporters, but of its opponents, demonstrates beyond the shadow of a doubt that it represented the conviction of the great majority of the members of Congress, as it did also, no doubt, of the people of the United States. By the year 1826 it was established as firmly as could be that Monroe's declaration implied no entangling alliance, indeed no intimate political connection, with the republics of the Southern continent.

Indeed, one may go further than this. The debates of 1826 often allude to the "Monroe Message." But they give no hint that it has become doctrine; they did something to preserve the memory of it, but little to enshrine it in the public mind; and for the decade and a half which follows on the debates over the Panama Congress allusions to the President's declaration are few and far between. Fugitive references one finds; on one occasion, and on one occasion only, the declaration of 1823 is cited in the deliberations of the Congress; but never is it cited, or even alluded to, by those responsible for the foreign policy of the United States. Very distinctly, it falls into the background.

The nations of Europe, during these fifteen years, paid no respectful homage to the prejudices or the policies of the American republic. They did not abstain from interference, or even from territorial aggrandizement in the New World. But the steps which they took were none of them very dramatic, nor did they seem to touch the vital interests of the United States.

On the part of France, for example, there are two episodes to be recorded, which at some other period might conceivably have aroused the susceptibilities of the American people. The bourgeois monarchy of Louis Philippe attempted in the year 1838 two separate naval enterprises in the New World, the blockade of Mexico

and the blockade of Argentina. The blockade against Mexico resulted in no land operations whatsoever, except for a brief and temporary debarkation at Vera Cruz. In Argentina the French went
further, occupying the important island of Martín García in the
Río de la Plata, and intermeddling scandalously in the domestic
politics not only of La Plata, but of the neighboring republic of
Uruguay. But in both cases the objectives which the cautious regime of Louis Philippe had in mind were the redress of commercial grievances, and not the permanent occupation of American
soil. And in both instances American opinion remained for the most
part inert. In the House of Representatives Caleb Cushing of
Massachusetts, a brilliant figure in the period just ahead, did indeed introduce a resolution based on the message of 1823, and calling for American mediation; but the administration took no heed.
Argentina was far away; our own relations with Mexico were badly
strained in 1838; no public clamor dictated action. Conservative
and cautious in matters of diplomacy, President Van Buren and his
able but circumspect Secretary of State, John Forsyth, were quite
content to let Great Britain interpose its good offices between the
disputants, and bring both the Mexican and Argentinian disputes
to a close.[11]

Equally striking was the indifference of American official opinion, in the decade of the thirties, to the encroachments of Great
Britain. It is not that the government in London had any grandiose
schemes of expansion in the New World. For the most part, it was
content to consolidate its strong, its unrivaled, commercial position in Latin America. But now and again, in the casual British
way, it strengthened its territorial position as well, and did so without a word of protest from the United States. It is not perhaps
strange that the American government took no action when Great
Britain occupied the Falkland Islands in January of 1833. Hardly
any New World territory could have been more remote; our relations with Argentina, the American government which possessed
a rightful claim to the territory in question, were suspended at the
time; it would have been difficult to say what American interest

was involved.[12] But it is hardly the same, one would think, with regard to Central America. There British encroachments might well seem more important. In that region already might have been foreshadowed the clash which actually occurred in the decade of the fifties.

In three different parts of Central America Britain might have been accused of violating Adams' famous principle of noncolonization in the period between 1830 and 1841. In the first place, the colony of British Honduras, which had existed before 1823, extended its boundaries into territory which was claimed, certainly with some color of right, by the Republic of Central America. In the second place, without any justification whatsoever, the British superintendent of Belize in the year 1838 seized one of the Bay Islands, the island of Ruatan, lying off the coast of Honduras. In the third place, taking advantage of a hazy sort of protectorate over the Mosquito Indians, the British consolidated their position on the west coast of what is now Nicaragua, and in August 1841 occupied the port of San Juan, at the mouth of the river of that name, thus gaining control of one of the most important communication routes across Central America. In every one of these instances, it is fair to say, the initiative seems to have come from ambitious British agents in the New World rather than from the Foreign Office; but in every one of them, also, the activities of these agents was watched with complacency and with approval by the government in London.

It seems extraordinary indeed that no one of these acts of aggrandizement, unostentatious though they were, should have provoked a protest from the administration at Washington. With regard to one of them, extension of the southern frontier of Belize, a specific appeal was made to the United States by the Central American government at the end of 1834.[13] But the Central American agent, Galindo, received from Forsyth, the Secretary of State, the chilling answer that it was not deemed expedient to interfere in the matter. The case of Ruatan passed completely unnoticed; the occupation of San Juan no less so. Preoccupied with internal affairs, the American people and their governors paid precious little attention to foreign politics in the decade of the thirties.

In truth, in this period of quiescence the relations of the United States with the governments of Latin America were never close, and were, in many instances, hardly more than sporadic. With Mexico relations were frequently strained; with Central America there was only fitful contact; with New Granada and Venezuela there was little friction, though hardly cordiality, and an appeal on the part of the former state to the principles of 1823 against a British blockade went unanswered; [14] with Argentina there was a long period of diplomatic nonintercourse; with Ecuador and Peru there was a very minimum of communication; with Chile nothing that could be described as a significant friendship. American influence was unimportant and even minute as compared with that of Britain; the nations of the Southern continent, taught by the rebuffs of the twenties, only rarely appealed to their Northern neighbor; the role of the United States in world affairs was still a much restricted one.

But events were unfolding, none the less, that were to lead to the vigorous reiteration of the principles of 1823. If these principles were not applied in the instances which we have been examining, it was fundamentally because American interests had not been sufficiently touched; given a situation which clearly involved those interests, it might have been foreseen that Monroe would come into his own again. With the rise of the Texan question, with the whetting of the American appetite for Oregon and California, what would be more natural than that a solemn warning should be issued against the intrigues and the appetites of the wicked powers of the Old World? What would be more natural than a new appeal to the emphatic precedents of an earlier age?

Thus it was that on the second of December, 1845, James K. Polk, president of the United States, explicitly revived the Monroe Doctrine. The events which led him to do so deserve to be examined in some detail.

In the year 1836 the Texans had cast off the yoke of Mexico, and had declared themselves to be an independent state. The next year began those long and tortuous negotiations which were at long last, after eight years, to result in the annexation of Texas to the United States. From the outset, France and Great Britain labored to prevent such a consummation. Far from recognizing American hegemony on the North American continent, these two powers set to work to counteract the influence of the young republic, and to invoke the European doctrine of the balance of power as a principle that might regulate the affairs of the New World as it already did those of the Old. They urged the Texans to remain independent; they even played with the idea of a guarantee of that independence, a guarantee which might imply the obligation to use force to preserve it.[15] Their maneuvers were well known in Washington from the beginning; as early as 1842, with Texas in mind, President Tyler inserted a sentence of warning in his annual message. "Carefully abstaining from all interference in questions exclusively referring themselves to the political interests of Europe," he wrote, "we may be permitted to hope an equal exemption from the interference of European Governments in what relates to the States of the American Continent."[16] Tyler's observation was premonitory of others to come. In the debates on the abortive treaty of annexation of 1844 Senators more than once cited the declaration of Monroe. But the statesmen of France and Great Britain took no note of these utterances, and though the annexation of Texas was in the way of consummation by June of 1845, the French Prime Minister, Guizot, in the same month went out of his way to proclaim with unconscious imprudence the validity of the principle of the balance of power in the New World. "France has a lasting interest," he declared sententiously, with Texas in mind, "in the maintenance of independent states in America, and in the balance of forces which exists in that part of the world."[17] Such observations, needless to say, were picked up by the Democratic press. They were read by the hard and narrow, but able man who occupied the White House in 1845. They had something to do with his re-enunciation of the Monroe Doctrine.

But Texas had been annexed before Polk transmitted to Congress his annual message. It might not have been worth while to revive the principles of 1823 if only an issue already settled had been involved. Besides Texas there was, however, Oregon, an unliquidated problem in 1845. This region had been under the joint occupation of the United States and Great Britain since 1818. For some time after the agreement of that year it had attracted little interest. But with the early forties American settlers began to occupy the Willamette Valley, and in Congress an agitation began for the organization of a territory in the disputed region. This agitation crystallized in the so-called Linn bill, first brought out and debated in 1843. In the course of these debates the Monroe message was invoked as justification of American title. It was mentioned by Sevier of Tennessee as "a sentiment to which he most cordially responded," [18] and by Woodbury of New Hampshire was described as "a noble declaration" in which he thoroughly concurred.[19] Still more significant, it was cited by the House committee which reported on the Oregon question as having "deservedly come to be regarded as an essential component part of the international law of the New World." [20] More strikingly than in the case of Texas, American public opinion, in its zeal for expansion, began to invoke the Continentalism of the declaration of December 2, 1823.

In addition to Oregon, there was California. To this fair province Americans had no title in 1845. But no one is forbidden to hope, and James K. Polk and many another American with him hoped for California. And since hope and fear go hand in hand, Polk looked with dark suspicion upon the machinations of Great Britain in the Far West. Sinister rumors came from the American Consul at Monterey of British agents whose presence boded no good to American interests; [21] and while nothing definite could be proved, and while historical research has later demonstrated that little was intended, there was smoke enough to rouse the President's suspicion of fire.[22] Polk definitely told Senator Benton of Missouri that he meant to reassert "Mr. Monroe's doctrine against permitting foreign colonization, and that in doing this he had California and the fine bay of San Francisco as much in view as Oregon." [23]

Texas, Oregon, California — all these together might have been reason enough for serving new notice on the Old World as to the inviolability of the New. But events in the Southern Hemisphere as well as in the Northern suggested the possibility of action. For in the fall of 1845 the French and British squadrons combined were engaged in naval interference in La Plata; the press was full of denunciations of their action; *Niles's Register,* one of the most influential of newspapers, was mournfully declaring that Monroe's words had become a dead letter; [24] the American chargé at Buenos Aires was almost tearfully pleading for the re-enunciation of the principles of 1823.[25] A much milder man than James K. Polk — and mild is certainly not the adjective to apply to the gentleman from Tennessee — might well have thought the moment propitious for a reaffirmation of the dogma which had been enunciated twenty-two years before.

Of the immediate circumstances attending the message of 1845 we have no such masterly account as that to be found in the diary of Adams for the earlier declaration. Polk, too, kept a diary, it is true; but it is narrow and pinched and often uncommunicative, like the man himself. We do not read of any long deliberations; we do not even hear of a cabinet debate. Buchanan, the Secretary of State, as more than one of his diplomatic dispatches attest, obviously approved of the course which was in mind. The President's advisers certainly expressed no word of dissent when the message was read to them late in November. It probably would not have mattered if they had. As early as April, 1844, before he was yet even a candidate for the Presidency, Polk had written in a public letter, "Let the fixed principle of our Government be, not to permit Great Britain, or any other foreign power, to plant a colony or hold dominion over any portion of the people or territory of either [continent]." [26] Tenacious, unafraid, definite-minded, the President had probably crystallized his own views long before December 1845, and would with difficulty have been shaken from them.

The statement which he sent to Congress on December 2 is probably one of the most thoughtful, as it is one of the most complete, expressions of the spirit of Monroeism. It is no mere parroting and iteration of the message of 1823. It bears the imprint of a strong personality, and of a mind that was both clear and vigorous. In one respect, it out-Monroes Monroe. For Polk sounds a challenge, not only against intervention by force of arms, not only against the invasion of European forms, but also, with Guizot and with the balance of power in mind, against European diplomatic intrigue, against any intermeddling with American states in their relations with one another.

Jealousy among the different sovereigns of Europe [he wrote] . . . has caused them anxiously to desire the establishment of what they term the "balance of power." It cannot be permitted to have any application on the North American continent, and especially to the United States. We must ever maintain that people of this continent alone have a right to decide their own destiny. Should any portion of them, constituting an independent state, propose to unite themselves with our Confederacy, this will be a question for them and us to determine without any foreign interposition. We can never consent that European powers shall interfere to prevent such a union because it might disturb the "balance of power" which they may desire to maintain upon this continent.[27]

The language was clear and unequivocal; the challenge of these words was a sweeping one; it carried the American veto on European action in the New World far indeed; perhaps it went further than could easily be justified. Certainly, France and Great Britain in offering friendly counsel to Texas, or even in proposing to guarantee its independence, were well within their rights as independent states. Moreover, Polk's principle was, certainly in the circumstances of 1845, impossible to enforce in practice. And yet one is rather glad that it was made. For the application of the principle of the balance of power to America would have been an odious and a dangerous thing, would be so today or tomorrow. It was worth while to denounce it, to call it emphatically to the attention of

American and European opinion, to issue a warning against it. Polk's message was an extension, but a useful extension, of the general principles which underlay the declaration of Monroe.

But if, in one respect, Polk went beyond his predecessor, in another he took ground rather less advanced. He did not, as some authors have said, confine the Monroe Doctrine to the North American continent. He was far too intelligent for that. But he did suggest that geographical propinquity might have something to do with the practical enforcement of the general principle. He did explicitly declare that it applied "with greatly increased force" to the establishment of any new colony in North America. He was not abdicating the exercise of American influence in Latin America; but he was suggesting that there were certain areas where the United States, perforce, must take a perfectly clear and unequivocal stand. It might take one attitude toward a blockade of the Río de la Plata, another toward the British occupation of Oregon. In making this distinction the President was opening the door to much debate in the future; but even in these days of rapid communication it still seems possible that there is a difference in American interest between the Panama Canal and Tierra del Fuego.

In one other matter, too, Polk extended the gist of the maxims of 1823. The message of that year, while warning against reconquest and the imposition of European political forms on the new states, had said nothing about the transfer of territory in the New World. John Quincy Adams, in his note to Tuyll, had warned against the cession of "any of the possessions heretofore or yet subject to Spain in the American hemisphere, to any European Power." [28] Henry Clay, in 1825, closely connected Monroe's declaration with a warning to France that the United States could not permit Cuba to come into the hands of any other state; [29] and warnings of a similar character with regard to that island follow from time to time in the decade of the thirties. But Polk was the first public man explicitly to bind together the prohibition on colonization and reconquest, and on the cession of territory to a European power. No doubt with the fear of the transfer of California to

Great Britain in mind he declared in plain terms that "it should be distinctly announced to the world as our settled policy that no future European colony or dominion [the two words are important] shall with our consent be planted or established upon any part of the North American continent." [30] Such language certainly barred the cession of territory from an American to a European state, no less than it did the colonization of any part of the New World.

It would be pleasant to record of the message of 1845, as it would of the message of 1823, that it had an epoch-making influence in its own time. But the truth of history compels a different view. However, the Polk declaration was nowhere received with great enthusiasm. In the United States itself the age was one of intense partisanship; Americans then as now no doubt believed in theory that this partisanship should stop at the water's edge; but then as now (most unhappily, it well may be) it did not stop there. Accordingly, while the Democratic papers applauded the statesmanship of a Democratic President, the Whig sheets were either chary of comment or positively critical. "All the gas of the Message about 'the balance of power' on the Continent, and our resistance to further European conquest and colonization," wrote the irrepressible Horace Greeley, editor of the *New York Tribune,* "is the paltriest fishing for thoughtless huzzas, worthy of a candidate for constable rather than of a President of the United States," and with regard to Oregon he added, "We shall betray a conscious weakness in our pretensions if we resort to foolish gasconade about 'the balance of power' and 'this continent' as without the proper sphere of European interest or observation." [31]

In Congress, too, there appears to have been no intense enthusiasm for the revival of the Monroe Doctrine. On January 14, 1846, Senator Allen of Ohio, chairman of the Committee on Foreign Relations, asked leave to bring in a resolution endorsing the stand of the President. The resolution, it is true, was a rather formidable and bellicose one. Undoubtedly it went far, declaring that European intermeddling would "incur, as by the right of self-preservation it would justify, the prompt resistance of the United

States." [32] But the action of the Senate is none the less significant. The very moment that the resolution was brought forward, the attack on it began, led by John C. Calhoun of South Carolina, whose disappointment at not having received the office of Secretary of State in Polk's administration may have sharpened the vigor of his assault. Allen's proposal, Calhoun declared, involved commitments that the country could not possibly discharge, and which it had not yet arrived at a sufficient state of maturity to assume. The original declaration of President Monroe, declared the South Carolinian, had been without practical effect, and had indeed even produced certain embarrassment. There was no necessity of reiterating it now, especially in language that might involve the choice of the "path of error and danger." [33] In the face of this attack the supporters of Polk, interestingly enough, were silent. And when the vote came, Senator Allen was refused leave to bring in his resolution, every one of the Whigs aligning himself in opposition. To the Congress of 1846 the message was a domestic gesture, rather than a diplomatic maneuver, and as such was the object of partisan rivalry, and not of united approval. Nor, as one reads the debates therein, does one discover any widespread endorsement of the views of the President.

If the message did not arouse unanimous support at home, it was hardly likely to evoke any particular burst of enthusiasm abroad. In England, the statesmen in power passed it by in dignified silence. But the British press, on the other hand, was not in all instances so restrained. The *Morning Chronicle* regarded its language as "rather gratuitous," and as the assertion of a policy that might prove "dangerous to peace." [34] *The Times*, almost professionally anti-American, adopted a severe tone of moral indignation at the idea that the New World could be or should be separated from the Old. "We are not accustomed," it declared, "to hear statesmen and rulers announce new principles of public morality, to demand an insulation from the universal laws and sympathies of their kind, and in their place to erect a convenient system of original and axiomatic claims. . . . The Old and the New World are separated by much less distances than those which divide the constituent nations of each. If America is a world of its own, then also is each of the four conventional quarters of the globe. In fact there is no more reason why America should segregate itself from the universal system and universal code than any other quarter." [35] Language such as this no doubt found an echo in the minds of many other Englishmen, and for that matter many other Continentals as well.

Certainly, it found an echo in France. There Polk's message was naturally not well received by those in power. The American Minister noted that at the New Year's reception of 1846, both Louis Philippe and his Prime Minister seemed "unusually reserved and stately" in addressing him.[36] And not long after this Guizot took up the gauntlet which had been thrown down by Polk, and on January 12, 1846, reiterated in the Chambers his favorite doctrine of the balance of power. The speech is the first public challenge that was ever made to the Monroe Doctrine and as such it deserves quotation. "Gentlemen," said the French Premier, in answer to Polk's contention that European states should abstain from intermeddling in the New World, "the maxim is a strange one. The United States is not the only nation of North America. There are, on the North American continent, other independent nations, other legally constituted states; I will name only Mexico. These states have the same right to seek or to reject alliances, to form such political combinations as appear to them to accord with their interests. The proximity, the existence of the United States cannot in any degree limit their independence or their rights." With these states, the Prime Minister went on, France had relations, relations which she would maintain. "These bonds that we have with the other nations of the American continent, these relations that we have contracted with them, that they had a right and we had a right to make, these commercial, political, even territorial interests will be maintained; we will maintain them without any feeling of hostility toward the United States, indeed, with the same sentiments of good will and friendship which we have long professed and practised toward them; we will maintain them without giving the United States any just subject of complaint, but also without yielding to any unfounded pretension." [37]

This formal repudiation of the doctrine of the two spheres, it is only fair to say, was not supported by all French politicians, or by the unanimous voice of the French press. Adolphe Thiers, bitterly partisan opponent of Guizot, defended the American position and declared that the declaration of principle with regard to European colonization was fundamentally sound.[38] The opposition papers took the same view.[39] But there can be little doubt, none the less, that in the longer perspective Guizot expressed the view of most Frenchmen, and that the time had not yet come when the principles of 1823 would be generally and tolerantly accepted by any considerable part of European public opinion.

Polk's message, then, we must reiterate, was not received with respect or with enthusiasm in every quarter, domestic or foreign; nor did it, candor compels us to declare, influence decisively any pending negotiation of the United States. The Texan question, indeed, had been liquidated long before the President penned his message; on July 4, 1845, the Texan legislature had formally consummated the uniting of the Lone Star republic with the Union. As for California, the declaration was, in all probability, superfluous; British agents might dream of the acquisition of that fair and verdant province; but the dispatches of Lord Aberdeen, the British Foreign Secretary, show that he vetoed any thought of positive action there, and was ready, albeit with some jealousy and some reluctance, to let events take their course. The failure of the British Admiralty to strengthen its forces in the Pacific points to the same conclusion. Finally, with regard to Oregon, the language of Polk was, if not repudiated, one might almost say contradicted in practice. The President had been elected in a hectic campaign in which the words "Fifty-four forty or fight" appeared to express the sentiments of his constituents; he had expressed an earnest desire "to look John Bull in the eye"; he had denounced the convention of joint occupation of 1818; he seemed to be taking, in his message, a high, an unyielding, an uncompromising tone. Yet despite all this, the year 1846 saw a solution that fell short of American extreme demands, and the line of 49 degrees was drawn as the boundary between the United States and the possessions of Great Britain. It was drawn, certainly not because of Polk's declaration, but almost in contradiction with it; it was no diplomatic triumph for the principles of 1823.

In many respects, moreover, the Polk administration, in its subsequent action, was to demonstrate the difference between the declaration of a principle and its positive execution. In more than one instance it was far from bold in carrying out the language of the declaration of December 2. Take, for example, the case of the Argentine Republic, where, as we have already said, the joint navies of France and Great Britain were engaged in operations against the dictator Rosas. So far as dogma was concerned, American intervention in this controversy would have been wholly justifiable. The war against Argentina involved the seizure of the important strategic island of Martín García; it involved domestic intrigues with the enemies of Rosas, and the provoking of civil war; it swept Uruguay into the struggle, and there it implied the maintenance in power of a faction which was not averse to a closer connection with Europe, perhaps even a British or a French protectorate; it developed in such fashion as to threaten the sending of a French expeditionary force across the seas. True, the perils which might have eventuated were never realized; and the jealousy of Britain no doubt acted as a check on the policy of France, none too resolute or fixed in any case. But Polk and Buchanan could not have foreseen the collapse of the intervention; and, to reiterate, in theory they might well have made the position of the United States clear. They had, however, other fish to fry nearer home; they had in early 1846 to think of the Oregon dispute; they had, after the month of May, to think of the war with Mexico which American policy had done something to provoke. And so they did nothing. Buchanan's instructions to Mr. Harris, sent out to Buenos Aires, make it clear that the Secretary of State believed that France and

Great Britain had "flagrantly violated" the Monroe declaration,[40] but "existing circumstances," he confessed, "render it impossible for the United States to take a part in the present war." [41] The most that the administration could do was to urge neutrality upon Paraguay, which threatened to take a hand in the crushing of the hated Rosas. And even this gesture was ineffectual.

It was the same in the region of Central America. There, as we shall see, new British encroachments led to specific appeals to the principles of 1823. But the administration remained inert, and contented itself with mere lip service to the dogma of Monroe. "To suffer any interference on the part of European Governments with the domestic concerns of the American Republics and to permit them to establish new colonies upon this continent," wrote Buchanan, "would be to jeopard their independence and to ruin their interests. These truths ought everywhere throughout this continent to be impressed upon the public mind. But what," added the Secretary of State in his forcible-feeble way, "can the United States do to resist such European interference whilst the Spanish American Republics continue to weaken themselves by division and civil war and deprive themselves of the ability of doing anything for their own protection?" [42] Language so little militant as this stands in striking contrast with the declaration of December 2, 1845.

Yet in 1845, as in 1823, the American declaration of diplomatic principle ought not to be regarded as insignificant, or trivial, or unwise, merely because it was not immediately translated into effective action. The efficacy of the Monroe Doctrine (and the truth never needed greater emphasis than in these days in which we live) depends, in large measure at least, upon the material power of the United States. The practical effectiveness of any diplomatic tenet may finally have to be determined by the caliber of a nation's guns, the number of its ships, the effective organization of its armed force. This country had to grow up to the Monroe Doctrine, looking at the matter from this point of view. But it does not follow that it is always futile to enunciate a dogma which one has not yet the power to make respected in every set of circumstances and among all conditions of men. James K. Polk, in 1845, was performing a work of education, if nothing more. He was recalling to the American mind a great principle. It may well be contended that Monroe's words needed recalling, that the American people needed to be so educated. In this sense his action was justifiable, and useful. It was he, in a sense, who reinvigorated the message of 1823, and inaugurated the fashion of citing it in diplomatic controversy, and set it in the way of becoming a generally accepted dogma.

There are signs, many of them in fact, that Polk's words took hold both in the United States and, to a lesser, but significant, extent, in Latin America. After 1845 allusion to Monroe's dogma becomes so frequent as to be almost usual in American politics; the process of consolidating it in American opinion, if by no means finished, had been well begun. And after 1845 it is extraordinary to discover the number of references to it in the correspondence of the Latin-American states.

Take, for example, the curious episode of General Flores and of the Congress of Lima of 1847.[43] General Juan José Flores was a perennial figure in the politics of Ecuador. In 1845 he had been driven from the country, and had taken refuge in Spain, where he was attempting to raise an armed force for the reconquest of his country, and for the establishment of a Spanish Prince there. At a little later date he extended his activities to Great Britain, where he bought some ships and raised some troops for his projected expedition. Great, indeed, was the excitement in Spanish America at this ambitious enterprise. And, with the Polk declaration in mind, we find the Ecuadorian Minister at Washington writing to Buchanan on November 26, 1846, reminding him of "the solemn protests which have at all times, and particularly at the present, been made by the cabinet of Washington, against all European intervention in the political affairs of America," and expressing the hope for "the effective co-operation and aid of the illustrious Republic of the United States." [44] Only a little later a similar request came from Peru. With a view to aiding Ecuador in the defeat of Flores, President Castilla asked Prevost, the American Consul at Lima, for the sale of two large steamers, and Prevost transmitted the request with the comment that to grant it would be "a service to Republicanism and Humanity, as the United States have proclaimed long since to Europe that all attempts to interfere in the domestic affairs of these and subvert their institutions would be viewed as an act of hostility toward the American people." [45] Fortunately for the Polk administration, by the time these appeals had been received, the danger from Flores' plans had largely vanished. The British government had forbidden the sale of the vessels he had chartered, and the enthusiasm of the Spanish government for the project was rapidly fading away. It was not necessary to take any action, and with the certainty that he would not be challenged Buchanan could reiterate the principles of 1823 in his instructions to an outgoing minister to Quito. [46]

But the flurry of fear over General Flores had an interesting sequel. It led to the calling of an American Congress to meet at Lima in the winter of 1847. To this Congress the American government was invited to send a representative, with a view to convincing "the Governments of Europe that all America, north and south, will unite to oppose and put down any attempt at conquest or subversion of American institutions." [47] Though Polk and Buchanan appear to have treated the whole matter very casually, though they sent no special envoy to the assembly, the Congress, when it met, passed, at the instance of the American Minister, J. Randolph Clay, resolutions reaffirming the noncolonization principle, and denying the right of European powers to intervene in the affairs of the New World. [48] One might even say that the Monroe Doctrine was taken fully as seriously at Lima as it was in Washington.

Still more striking is the interest awakened by Polk's declaration in the states which had a stake in the building of an interoceanic canal, from New Granada (the modern Colombia) on the south to Nicaragua and Honduras in the north. All of these states viewed with a justifiably jaundiced eye the pretensions and the ambition of Great Britain. The claims of this greatest of contemporary powers on the east coast of Central America seemed ever to be enlarging. The kingdom of the innocent Mosquitoes, under British tutelage, appeared by 1844 to extend far to the south of their primeval limits, beyond the states of Central America into the dominions of New Granada itself. Agitated at the course of events, the New Granadan government undertook those negotiations with the Polk administration which resulted in the famous treaty of 1846, for the guarantee of the neutrality of the isthmus at Panama. In initiating these negotiations, the Colombian Minister of Foreign Affairs made confident appeal to the spirit of the Monroe Doctrine.[49] In urging the ratification of the compact in Washington, Señor Herran, the Colombian plenipotentiary, did likewise. In specific terms his instructions called attention to the repeated declarations of American statesmen with regard to European intervention and colonization in the New World, and urged the United States to assume the leadership of an American confederation, opposing to the avaricious proposals of Europe the humane and disinterested principles of the young democracies of the New World.

Unfortunately, as we have already said, the Polk administration showed no ardor to advance its principles in practice. It left unanswered the appeals of Nicaragua; it signed the treaty of guarantee with New Granada, but (strikingly enough) did so with an expression of the hope that France and Great Britain might participate in similar guarantees, and thus divorced itself from any strict idea of Continentalism; it showed no interest in what had taken place at Lima. Concerned, no doubt, chiefly with the war with Mexico, it spent little of its diplomatic energies in advancing the diplomatic principles of 1823.

One exception to this rule there is, and that an important one. It is the case of Yucatán, in which for the first time the Monroe Doctrine was made to serve the purposes of what may fairly be described as imperialism, if by imperialism is meant the extension of American political control over a people of wholly different stock and origin. The idea of the annexation of Yucatán did not, it is true, originate in Washington. In the winter of 1848 a commissioner from that province appeared in the capital urging that the Americans take control in order to forestall occupation by some other power, and citing explicitly the language of the famous message.[50] In March, a more concrete suggestion made its appearance. Desperate at the danger from the Indian civil war which had unfolded itself in the peninsula, the authorities of Yucatán offered "dominion and sovereignty" simultaneously to three different states, to the United States, Great Britain, and Spain.[51] President Polk was evidently much disturbed at the catholicity of Yucateco political principles, and fearful that one of the other powers appealed to might close with the offer that had been made. On April 19, 1848, he laid the question before the Congress, and, while not explicitly recommending annexation, cited with fixed purpose the message of Monroe and his own declaration of 1845, and expressed the opinion that Yucatán would be "dangerous to our security" in the hands of a European power. With questionable accuracy, so far as the records of the State Department show, he also asserted that he had authentic information that if the United States did not grant some measure of aid, "some European power" would probably do so.[52]

But Congress was considerably less excited than was President Polk. A bill for the temporary occupation of the province was, it is true, reported out to the floor of the Senate. But there it was subjected to a powerful assault, in which the rising dogma of Monroe itself was sharply challenged.

The most important speech of this important debate was that of John C. Calhoun, and it must have derived especial weight from the fact that Calhoun had been a member of the cabinet of 1823. The declaration against the Holy Alliance, declared the South Carolinian, was not to enunciate any general principle whatever; it was directed at a specific peril. Only by a forced construction could it be applied to the situation of 1845. It was "an absurdity" to assert that the attempt of any European state to extend its system of government to this continent, the smallest as well as the greatest, would endanger the peace and safety of this country. As for the idea of noncolonization, this had not even been discussed in the cabinet of 1823, and was in any case completely inapplicable to the situation in Yucatán. Taken all together, Calhoun went on, Monroe's declarations were "declarations — nothing more. Not one word in any of them in reference to resistance. There is nothing said of it; and with great propriety it was omitted. Resistance belonged to us — to Congress; it is for us to say whether we shall resist or not, and to what extent." The President "tells you that these declarations have become the settled policy of this country. What, the declarations? Declarations are not policy, and cannot become settled policy. He must mean that it has become the settled policy of this country to resist what these declarations refer to; and to resist, if need be, by an appeal to arms. Is this the fact? Has there been one instance in which these declarations have been carried into effect by resistance? If there be, let it be pointed out. Have there not been innumerable instances in which they have not been applied? Certainly." "The principle which lies at the bottom of his recommendation . . . puts it in the power of other countries on this continent to make us a party to all their wars; and hence I say, if this broad interpretation be given to these declarations, we shall forever be involved in wars." [53] What then, according to the Senator from South Carolina, was the proper course of action? It was not to repudiate what lay behind the Monroe message, any more than it was to extend it. It was to deal with each case as it arose, never being seduced by a broad general principle, and never being quite unmindful of it. We shall do Calhoun injustice if in his attack on Polk we think of him as merely tearing down what others had set up; he was the advocate of a judicious opportunism in the application of the famous dogma, rather than its foresworn and uncompromising foe. In speaking as he did, he raised a question which was bound to recur, indeed is still bound to recur. Is the maxim of the Doctrine to be applied unbendingly, unequivocally, in a spirit of pure literalism? Or is it rather to be applied when, where, and if it represents the clearly defined national interest of the United States? Many times since 1848 the problem had been raised; and, as we shall see before this story ends, it is still present in the vast events of 1940 and 1941.

Calhoun, in 1848, did not stand alone. As has clearly been seen, in the intense partisanship of the time, there was a tendency on the part of the Whigs to question the Monroe principles just because a Democrat had revived them. And so, on the Whig side of the Senate, the South Carolinian's arguments were embroidered and refurbished; Polk's policy "would have led to perpetual war with the world, or at least with England, the mightiest power in it," declared Niles of Connecticut; [54] it becomes "an authority justifying any and all schemes of aggression or ambition," lamented Davis of Massachusetts and continued by saying, "We who traffic in nations, and when we cannot buy, conquer them to make acquisitions, have a monopoly, a patent right to this particular trade, and hold the right to restrain others from engaging in it." [55]

To these assaults the Democrats, on the whole, responded rather tamely. Houston of Texas and Bagby of Alabama thought the principles of 1823 inapplicable to the case of Yucatán; [56] Dix of New York declared the carrying out of the President's theory to be "a question of prudence"; [57] even such a stout partisan as Lewis Cass doubted whether it had been involved in the case of La Plata, or meant anything more as regarded the matter before the Senate than that if we did not act, we could not legitimately complain if Spain or Britain did.[58] But there were other bolder Senators who defended their party leader without reserve, and Hannegan of Indiana, in charge of the occupation measure, declared that the principles of 1823 had become among the "cardinal doctrines of the American political creed." [59] In theory at any rate the issue was joined; in practice it was avoided. A change of government in Yucatán resulted in the withdrawal of the proposal that the province be taken under American — or other — protection, and the bill that had been introduced in the Senate was dropped after an intermittent discussion of about a fortnight. The danger of Spanish or British action had never been real; it had disappeared entirely by the late spring. And with its disappearance disappears too, for a season, all mention of the Monroe Doctrine.

By the year 1848, indeed, as the above events make clear, the status of that Doctrine in the public mind was still somewhat doubtful. It had been revived, discussed, defended, extended; it had attained a new importance, and been assimilated by a wider public; but it was hardly yet a national tenet. The Democrats, the party of a vigorous and perhaps a self-assertive foreign policy, were on the whole its partisans and friends; but their Whig opponents still dared assail and mock it; they were, when they came to power, almost to make a virtue of ignoring it; and nothing as yet indicated that the risks of such a course were excessive. Nor could it be said that the Doctrine had been effectively used in the promotion of American interests, or even brought forward directly in diplomatic conversations with another government. It had not altered a whit the solution of any one of the problems to which it had been applied; and while it had been cited more than once in the instructions of Buchanan to American representatives abroad, the Secretary of State had never committed the imprudence of using its authority to buttress the American position in his intercourse with foreign chancelleries. Still insufficiently assimilated at home, still inadequately supported by superior military and naval power, it was only slowly making its way to that dominating position in the American mind and in American policy which it was later to occupy. The Monroe Doctrine, it cannot be too often emphasized, grew and was bound to grow *pari passu,* and only *pari passu,* with the growth of the United States as one of the great nations of the globe.

Yet it must again be emphatically declared that Polk's re-enunciation of the principles of 1823 was a matter of high importance. In the years from 1826 to 1845 these principles had been to a large extent neglected; to revive them was a public service, and one from which much of American foreign policy was to flow. And if the silent Tennessean had not died only a few months after laying down the Presidency, he might have witnessed in the decade of the fifties the further consolidation of the dogma he had revivified, and its continuing influence upon American opinion. In the Central American controversy with Great Britain, the Doctrine figured to no small degree, and, if it did not play the central role in the diplomatic conversations or in the settlement arrived at, it was at least a major factor in the problem.

The role of the British government in the region of Central America we have already noticed. Cynical or brutal, frankly imperialistic or sinister, the policy of the London Foreign Office certainly was not. Still less was it directed at a clash with the United States. In the decade of the forties, the large investments which British capital had made in the rising republic of the West, the vast importance of the cotton trade, yes, even a certain sentimental partiality for the unruly offspring of British power, all combined to make the statesmen of the Court of St. James's draw back from too sharp a collision with the government at Washington. We shall completely misunderstand the character of the period, we shall completely misunderstand the position of the British government, if the salient and vital facts are not comprehended. Great Britain was no menace to the states of the New World, to their independence or to their institutions, such, perhaps, as contemporary Germany may be in the decade which lies ahead. The British, it may reasonably be contended, throughout the nineteenth and early twentieth centuries in the main used their vast power, their dominating place in world politics, with remarkable moderation. And never was the spirit of conscious imperialism and territorial expansion weaker in the British Foreign Office and among the British people than in the decades of the forties and fifties. The burly and often tempestuous Palmerston, a stormy petrel in the politics of Europe, was in 1848 ready to go so far as to propose a general treaty of arbitration with the United States.[60] The play of both political and economic forces tended to preserve good relations, if not to foster good manners, between the two great Anglo-Saxon peoples.

But this is not to say, of course, that the interests of the two did not conflict in the region of Central America. Chatfield, the British Minister to the five republics of this region, was an ambitious and trouble-making individual, who sought by every kind of activity and intrigue to consolidate the position of Great Britain and even to extend its territorial power. Had he been able to have his way, Great Britain might have taken one or more of the turbulent states of the Isthmus under its protection. And while his activities were not encouraged in London, on one point the Foreign Office did consistently sustain him. Whether from sentiment or interest (and the analysis of motive cannot be entirely clear), Lord Palmerston was determined to maintain the integrity of the Mosquito kingdom. It was with his support, as we have already said, that the town of Greytown had been occupied in January of 1848, to the great agitation of the government of Nicaragua, and the rending of the air with appeals to the United States.

Now the question of Greytown might not have been important to the administration of James K. Polk, with only a year of office ahead of it, and a Presidential election in view. But it was to become important in 1849. The cession of California, and its organization as a state, had immensely increased interest in interoceanic communication. It had led, indeed, to the formation by American capitalists of a company for the construction of a canal across Nicaragua, with one terminus at Greytown. And shortly after this company had signed a contract with the Nicaraguan government, Chatfield had served notice upon the latter that the whole of the San Juan River from its mouth to the Machuca rapids belonged to the Mosquito kingdom, and could not be disposed of without reference to the tinsel sovereign of that region and his protector the government of Great Britain.[61] A little later the Foreign Office directed Barclay, the British Consul at New York, to serve notice to the grantees not to begin work on the canal, as the territory of Mosquitia would be bisected by it.[62]

This action naturally precipitated a diplomatic controversy. At Washington and London the controversy was conducted with urbanity; but in Central America the case was otherwise. The Taylor administration sent out to that interesting region a young and ardent commissioner with a taste for archeology, and still more with a taste for a quarrel with the opponents of his country. This worthy, George Ephraim Squier by name, engaged in a bitter diplomatic duel with the ubiquitous, and overzealous, Chatfield. And in the course of this duel, be it noted with interest, he secured from the Nicaraguan, Honduran and Salvadorean legislatures a ringing appeal to the United States based upon the principles of 1823.[63]

But the Whig administration had no exaggerated deference for the dogma of Monroe. It was not averse to a tripartite diplomatic intervention with Great Britain and France, in an effort to put an end to the war then raging (if raging be the proper word) between Haiti and the Dominican Republic. It watched with complacency the actual coercion of the black potentate of Haiti by European diplomats. With regard to Central America, it cared not a straw for general principles. The Secretary of State, John Middleton Clayton, had not hesitated to poke fun at the Polk appeal to Monroe in 1848. At an early state of the diplomatic controversy we are discussing, he had explicitly told Crampton, the British Minister, that he and the President "in no way adopted" the favorite dogma of his predecessor.[64] He knew that he could not merely let the matter lie. But what he sought was not the invocation of a general principle, but the making of a specific and binding compact which should open the way to the building of a canal, and operate to check the expansion of British interests in Central America. The result was the famous Clayton-Bulwer Treaty of April 19, 1850. This treaty provided for the joint protection of the projected canal by Great Britain and the United States. And by its first article the two governments concerned declared that they would not "erect or maintain any fortifications commanding the same, or in the vicinity thereof, or occupy, fortify or colonize, or assume or exercise any domination over Nicaragua, Costa Rica, the Mosquito Coast, or any part of Central America."

At a later date there was to be infinite debate as to whether or not the compact thus signed was a violation of the Monroe Doctrine. Buchanan, faithful to the expansionist interpretation of the Doctrine that had appeared so early in Polk's message on Yucatán, declared that Clayton had "reversed" the principles of 1823, by binding the United States not to colonize Central America.[65] As events unrolled, moreover, it became clear that the British, taking advantage of ambiguities in the wording of the agreement, were far from intending to withdraw from the regions which they had occupied, some of them, as we have seen, in violation of the great American dogma. Finally, the very idea of joint protection of an interoceanic canal was, in the course of time, certainly by 1880, to be regarded as a possible infringement on Monroe's dictum. But this is to regard only one side of the case. If the Clayton-Bulwer Treaty did not drive the British out of Central America, it certainly opposed a barrier to the further extension of their influence; its language with regard to colonization might almost be regarded as the first recognition by another power of the tenet which John Quincy Adams had laid down twenty-seven years before. And with regard to the question of joint protection of the canal itself, it might be contended that if an administration so attached to the Monroe Doctrine as that of James K. Polk could contemplate with complacency, as we have seen that it did, the notion of a joint guarantee of the transit route across the Isthmus, then Clayton might reasonably be absolved from treason to the Doctrine in framing an instrument of similar character only four years later. It would have marked a prodigious growth indeed in the principles of 1823 if they had undergone so great a change as this in the space of less than half a decade.

Having regard, indeed, to the material power and the existing interests of the United States, there was much to be said for the Clayton-Bulwer Treaty. Its vice lay, not in the essentials of its terms, but in the ambiguities of its language, which took some time to clarify, and which appear to have encouraged the British government to courses not always well received on this side of the Atlantic. In particular, its vice lay in the fact that it did not define the region of Central America, and that it therefore left British establishments in Belize and the Bay Islands in a position which was bound to be the subject of later debate. Within two years, indeed, such a debate actually took place. For acting with complacent disregard of American objections, acting, perhaps, as it thought, within the limits of its rights, the British government on March 20, 1852, declared that Ruatan, Bonacca, and four neighboring islands were erected into the British "Colony of the Bay Islands." The repercussions of this step were, it is true, not immediate; the American people were in the midst of an election year; but once they had elected Franklin Pierce, the representative of militant Democracy, to the Presidency, it was perhaps inevitable that there should be a revival of discussion of the Monroe Doctrine. Inquiries as to the nefarious purposes of Britain were set afoot; the Senate Committee on Foreign Relations examined British policy in detail, and came to the conclusion that any permanent establishments by Great Britain in the neighborhood of the Isthmus must necessarily excite concern and, if persisted in, "lead to consequences of the most unpleasant character." [66] And when the new President of the United States took the oath of office on March 4, 1853, he went so far as to declare that the American people regarded "the idea of interference or colonization on this side of the ocean by any foreign power beyond present jurisdiction as utterly inadmissible." [67] It was clear that the annexation of the Bay Islands had precipitated the whole Central American question into the area of controversy, and that a heated diplomatic debate lay ahead.

In the winter session of the Congress which expired on March 4, 1853, Lewis Cass, Democratic wheel horse and candidate for the Presidency in 1848, sought to strengthen the hands of the incoming administration by pressing for the adoption of a resolution endorsing the Monroe Doctrine. The debate which took place revealed the fact that the partisan flavor still adhered, at least in some measure, to the principles of 1823. In general the Whigs deprecated any invocation of those principles. In particular, a relative newcomer in the Senate, destined within a brief eight years to become Secretary of State of the United States, took his stand against any appeal to the developing American dogma. William H. Seward (such was this newcomer's name) declared the Cass resolutions to be in opposition to the "deliberate judgment" of the Committee on Foreign Relations, and further stated that they could not possibly secure a majority "either in the Senate, or in the Congress, or in the country." "The principles involved," he went on, in language which, in its frank opportunism, suggests Calhoun in 1848, "have become a tradition among the American people, and on acknowledged occasions they would act upon them vigorously and with unanimity. On the other hand, the Americans are a practical people, engrossed with actual business affairs; and they will not act upon abstract principles, however approved, unless there be a necessity, or at least an occasion." [68] No such occasion, he maintained, existed at the time. The case of the Bay Islands came under the Clayton-Bulwer Treaty, and ought to be argued on the basis of that treaty. It ought *not* to be argued on the grounds which Great Britain might not accept, and which she might indeed sharply challenge.

The language of Seward is of considerable interest. In one sense it is highly critical of the Cass resolution. Yet the New Yorker admitted, it will be observed, that the "principles involved" had "become a tradition," and in this admission he was not alone. For the first time, indeed, in the debates of 1853, the declaration of 1823 becomes the Monroe *Doctrine*. In earlier discussions the references are almost invariably to "principles" of Mr. Monroe, or to the "Monroe declaration." But now, in Congress and in the press, appears this new phrase, so judiciously chosen, so full of flavor, so clearly connoting secular, if not divine authority for the propositions with which it deals. If words were centrally significant, indeed, we should have to date the birth of the Monroe *Doctrine* from 1853.

We see, therefore, in the debate on the Cass resolution some indication of the development of the great dogma. At home its authority was growing; but it was still, as events were to prove, of very little value in a diplomatic negotiation. In the prolonged discussions on the Central American question in which the Pierce administration was to engage, it was to be brought forward, brought forward specifically, by James Buchanan, now the American Minister in London. In an able memorandum of January 6, 1854, Buchanan wrote: "Mr. Monroe, one of our wisest and most discreet Presidents, announced in a public message to Congress, in December, 1823, that 'the American continents, by the free and independent condition which they have assumed and maintain, are henceforth not to be considered subjects for future colonization by any European powers.' This declaration has since been known throughout the world as the 'Monroe Doctrine,' and has received the public and official sanction of subsequent Presidents as well as of a very large majority of the American people. Whilst this doctrine will be maintained," he continued, "whenever in the opinion of Congress the peace and safety of the United States shall require it, yet, to have acted upon it in Central America might have brought us in collision with Great Britain, an event always to be deprecated, and, if possible, avoided." [69] This language was discreet and guarded, it is true. But it provoked an answer nonetheless from Lord Clarendon, the British Foreign Secretary, an answer which declared that the famous Doctrine "could be viewed only as the dictum of the distinguished personage who announced it, and not as an international axiom which ought to regulate the conduct of European states." [70] This flat denial of the Monroe dogma as of binding force in international relations Buchanan could neither refute nor ignore. He chose the course of skillful evasion. "If the occasion required," he wrote in a new note, "Mr. Buchanan would cheerfully undertake the task of justifying the wisdom and sound policy of the Monroe doctrine, in reference to the nations of Europe, as well as to those of the American Continent." [71] And having thus turned the edge of Clarendon's challenge, he proceeded to argue the American case in Central America by reference, not to the message of 1823, but to the Clayton-Bulwer Treaty.

Lord Clarendon's criticism of the Doctrine was echoed by at

least one other distinguished Englishman. Speaking in the house of Commons two years later, a future Prime Minister of Great Britain, and one of its greatest, Benjamin Disraeli, took occasion to express himself in the most definite of language. "Now, sir," he exclaimed, "the Monroe Doctrine is one which, with great respect to the Government of the United States, is not, in my opinion, suited to the age in which we live. The increase in the means of communication between Europe and America have made one great family of the countries of the world; and that system of government, which, instead of enlarging, would restrict the relations between those two quarters of the globe, is a system which is not adapted to this age." The United States, he went on, "instead of vaunting that they build their greatness on the Monroe Doctrine, which is the doctrine of isolation, should seek to attain it by deferring to the public law of Europe, and by allowing their destiny to be regulated by the same high principles of policy which all the European communities that have a political system have invariably recognized." [72] Thus does it become clear that in the middle fifties British political leaders were very far from recognizing the binding force or the political propriety of the principles of 1823.

But nonetheless, in practice, and naturally with some reluctance, the British government beat a retreat in Central America. It was hardly to be expected that it would abandon its position in Belize, which went back, in part at least, to treaties almost coeval with the existence of the United States, but by the agreement finally reached in 1860 it returned the Bay Islands to Honduras; the guileless Mosquitoes were recognized as under the sovereignty of Nicaragua and Honduras, and Greytown was made a free port. The American prejudice against the extension of European power in the New World was in considerable measure deferred to; and if the citation of the great American dogma in the negotiations themselves accomplished little, the public opinion which it stimulated and which lay behind it must be esteemed an element in the final settlement. Perhaps, indeed (but the point must not be overemphasized), we may say that the treaties of 1860 represent the first diplomatic victory, and that a modest one, in which Monroe's dogma really figured.

We must not, however, delude ourselves with regard to the position that the dogma had attained in the decade of the fifties. Though it was undeniably growing in popularity at home, not even there had it yet become a truly national principle; and one even discovers in the debates in Congress in 1855 on the Central American question a tendency to soft-pedal the Monroe principles and take stand on the Clayton-Bulwer Treaty. "The less our statesmen at home and diplomats abroad say about it, the better," thought Wilson of Massachusetts.[73] Other Senators echoed his viewpoint, as did the *North American Review* for April 1856, in the first article in any periodical bearing the title "The Monroe Doctrine," in which the author concluded by declaring that the principles advocated in the name of Monroe, "are wholly unhistorical, and without foundation in any legitimate interpretation of his guarded language." [74] Language such as this makes it clear that there was still plenty of dissent to the formula which Polk had revived in 1845.

Still less must we assume that formula commanded the respect of Europe. There is, it is true, no positive menace to New World states in the late forties and in the fifties, but there is plenty of intrigue which is either ignorant or contemptuous of American opinion. Perhaps, in this regard, the French were the worst offenders. In the island of Santo Domingo, in particular, their influence was always active. As early as 1841 Levasseur, the French Consul-General at Port-au-Prince, had recommended the seizure of Samaná Bay; [75] and when the eastern half of the island, now the Dominican Republic, revolted against the rule of the sable government of Haiti, this same gentleman was in the thick of things, urging the acceptance of a protectorate, encouraging the revolt, securing the active co-operation of French naval vessels with the revolutionists. In 1846 a French counselor of state, in a ponderous volume, advocated the acquisition of Samaná Bay.[76] In 1849, the protectorate idea was again revived. In 1851 appeared a series of articles in the *Revue des Deux Mondes,* probably written by Rey-baud, Levasseur's successor, which are nothing less than propaganda for an active policy in the Caribbean.[77] And in 1854, when the American government, its interest finally stimulated, sought to secure a leasehold of Samaná for itself, French influence was strenuously and successfully exerted to prevent the ratification of the agreement which the American agent succeeded in negotiating, and which he defended in the name of the Monroe Doctrine.[78]

Nor is the French attitude illustrated only by this example. In Mexico French influence was steadily exerted against the United States, in a fashion which we shall have to analyze later; in Central America a French newspaperman, Félix Belly, appears in 1858, intriguing against the American government, and actually securing a contract for the construction of a canal; as far to the south as Ecuador the idea of a French protectorate appears in the dispatches of the Quai d'Orsay.[79] To be sure, as happens again and again, responsible directors of policy were less aggressive than their agents; but in such matters as these one discovers no exaggerated respect for the influence of the United States.

The Spaniards, too, were incubating plans by no means friendly in the decade of the fifties. Their influence rivaled and then succeeded that of France in the Dominican Republic. In 1846 a Spanish fleet cruised off the island and tried to make political contacts looking toward Spanish control; the next year Dominican commissioners appeared at Madrid with a project of protectorate; [80] in 1852 a Spanish agent published a book frankly arguing for the extension of control, and blandly ignoring the Monroe Doctrine; [81] in 1854 came new negotiations. And as the decade comes to an end, the way is clearly being prepared for that reoccupation of the island which was actually to be consummated in the days of the Civil War. In the dispatches of this period there is no reference, not even a contemptuous one, to the principles of 1823.

All this, no doubt, was natural, for the United States was not yet a great power. On what other basis than force, in the last analysis, can European diplomacy be said to rest? It need not be surprising that the American dogma had not yet commanded the respect of Old World statesmen; it is perhaps more disconcerting to find that it had not won the gratitude of Latin America. In Central America, in particular, one might have expected that the United States would have enhanced its prestige. But such was not, in fact, the case. Guatemala and Costa Rica had always been somewhat pro-British; an anti-American faction gained control in Salvador in 1853; in Nicaragua disillusionment as to the generosity of American motives led to a similar reorientation of policy in the same year; only Honduras, hopeful of American influence in the question of the Bay Islands, remained on friendly terms with the government at Washington to the end of the period. In 1855, moreover, came an event which scandalized and terrified the inhabitants of the Isthmus. The filibustering expedition of William Walker, his seizure of the government of Nicaragua, the tolerance and finally the recognition accorded him by President Pierce and his advisers, all seemed to show that unscrupulousness and covetousness had more to do with American policy than anything else. There had been the Mexican War less than a decade before; there had been a bullying policy toward Mexico almost ever since, except for a few brief years of Whig rule (and these not impeccable); and now there was the toleration of this ruthless, if unofficial, imperialism. Was it any wonder that Latin Americans were not extravagantly grateful to the Colossus of the North, as it was coming to be called? Many of them, it is true, were far away, and therefore safe; but few of them were disposed to cordiality. The policy of New Granada becomes anti-American after 1856 with the aggressive stand of the United States in the Panama riots. In Ecuador, as we have seen, there was an effort to establish a connection with France; in Argentina the most influential of its publicists was pronouncing the exclusion of the United States from the counsels of Latin America; in Chile and Peru the writings of important political figures bear witness to the fear of aggression. "Look at the empires which pretend to resuscitate the old idea of the domination of the globe," wrote the Chilean Bilbao, "Russia and the United States. The first is very far away; the second is very near; Russia is limiting her warlike operations; the United States are extending theirs every day . . . we already see fragments of America fall into the clutches of the Anglo-Saxon boa constrictor, and involved in its coils; yesterday Texas, after that northern Mexico and the Pacific salute a new lover; today the advance guard of guerillas scour the isthmus, and we see Panama, that future Constantinople of America, hang in suspense, view its destiny in the abyss, and ask, 'Will there be a south, will there be a north?' . . . We commence to follow the steps of the Colossus, which steadily advances without fearing anyone. . . . We understand this colossus always more impetuous and audacious, which believes in its right to rule as did imperial Rome, and which, already infatuated with the long roll of its felicities, advances like a tide to discharge its waters like a cataract over the south; we see that this nation, which had always been our star, menaces the autonomy of America; the Saxon of the North gathers his forces, unites his efforts, harmonizes the heterogeneous elements of his nation to attain the possession of Olympus, which is the absolute dominion of America." [82]

To an American such words as these seem overstrained indeed; overstrained, in fact, they were. But they are important none the less; and in the fifties, unfortunately enough, they were only the exaggerated reflection of American militancy and nationalism. They illustrate how scrupulous in action the United States must be to win the confidence of the Southern republics. The Monroe Doctrine, enunciated and re-enunciated, is certainly not enough. We cannot even be sure that the great dogma itself will always attract, and not repel.

By 1860, at any rate, the Doctrine had not won Latin-American friendship, or European recognition. But it was taking root in American consciousness, and whether Europeans or Latin Americans liked it or not, it was, undeniably, serving American interest. It had been of some assistance in the solution of the Central American question; it expressed a natural, a justifiable, opposition to the extension of European dominion and European political influence in this hemisphere. The country had not yet grown up to it in material power; but it was growing up to it; it was to be able, with the years, to make it good. And, indeed, the demonstration was not long in coming. Out of the weakness of the United States, out of the bitter tragedy of civil war, were to arise two challenges, both arrogant, one highly dangerous to the principles of 1823; out of the victory of the North was to come a new respect for American might, and a new vindication of those principles. We turn to the Spanish invasion of Santo Domingo, and the French occupation of Mexico — the quixotic adventure of Prince Maximilian.

IV

The Hour of Peril
France and Spain Defy the Monroe Doctrine

Resolved, That the Congress of the United States are unwilling by silence to have the nations of the world under the impression that they are indifferent spectators of the deplorable events now transpiring in the Republic of Mexico, and that they think fit to declare that it does not accord with the policy of the United States to acknowledge any monarchical government erected on the ruins of any republican government in America under the auspices of any European power.
— *Resolution of the House of Representatives, April 6, 1864*

The Monroe Doctrine summed up amounts to this, that all the European nations should abandon the great and legitimate interests which they have acquired in America during more than three centuries at the cost of blood and immense sacrifices, leaving to the inhabitants of those countries liberty to constitute themselves anew, as if a lacerated and debilitated body could thus attain health.

On the same principle it should be permitted still to the barbarians, to attack the merchant vessels of all peoples, whose tribulations were the victims of their cruelty, and whose wealth was the prize of their avarice. On the same principle the Mexican should have been permitted to adore his idols, the Chinese to continue to sacrifice their children, and to remain like the Japanese cut off from the commerce of the world; the cannibals should be permitted to devour their prisoners, and lastly, all the savages should be abandoned to the grossest errors, to the most repugnant moral practices, to the most ferocious instincts.

— MARTIN Y OÑATE, *España y Santo Domingo*

IN THE struggle of the nineteenth century between democracy and older governmental forms, between the spirit of the Old World and the New, the decisive point, in a sense, is the beginning of the decade of the sixties. In the period of sixty years since the beginning of the century the democratic spirit had won as yet only partial and indecisive victories in Europe. In England the middle classes had been admitted to power by the great Reform Bill of 1832; but in France the rising democratic tide, which engulfed the Orleans monarchy in 1848 and swept to power the republicans of that same year, soon ebbed again, and, using the mechanics of democracy to aid his rise to authority, Louis Napoleon, half genius, half scheming politician, established a semi-authoritarian regime which for some years at least expressed largely his own will and purpose. In Central Europe the revolutions of 1848 had, for the most part, failed; in the East there still remained unshaken the august power of the autocrat of all the Russias; and as the guns began to thunder at Manassas, and free-necked men responded to the call of Lincoln, it was still possible to wonder whether the great democratic experiment might not prove to be unworkable, and the chief of democratic nations be riven asunder by sectional jealousy and internecine strife. The issue of the Civil War was to fortify immensely the democratic principle, but the war itself gave opportunity for a European sovereign to offer a most serious challenge to the position of the United States in the Western Hemisphere. The intervention of the French in Mexico is an episode of the first significance in the clash between the system of the Old World and the system of the New.

The monarchical principle in Latin America, it must be understood, did not expire with the message of 1823. For one thing, in part due, as we have seen, to the exertions of Canning and Metternich, it was preserved intact in Brazil. Nor was all hope of its continued existence abandoned in other parts of America. As late as the year 1829, there was a movement in Colombia for the restoration of monarchical forms, with Bolivar as the first sovereign. In Central America one finds hints of a similar tendency. In Ecuador there was the rather grotesque episode of General Flores. It will not do, of course, to make too much of incidents of this kind. In no one of the cases mentioned was the establishment of monarchy ever at all near to realization. But all indicate the survival of the old ideas, and if it be said that these are, after all, rather insignificant movements, the same can hardly be asserted with regard to the royalist activity in the republic nearest to the United States, the republic of Mexico.

There, indeed, the monarchical idea demonstrated a real vitality. The first movement of independence had resulted in the establishment of an Empire, under the upstart monarch, Itúrbide. Though the constitution of 1824 was modeled after that of the United States, Alamán, Minister of Foreign Affairs in the new administration, was a convinced believer in the royalist idea. In 1829, indeed, he sounded Pakenham, the British representative in Mexico City, on the feasibility of setting up a government under a European prince,[1] and a similar overture appears to have been made again in 1834.[2] The next year, Santa Anna being president, there appears at the Foreign Office the dominant figure, one might almost call him, in the history of Mexican monarchy, Gutiérrez de Estrada. This man, who pursued for a quarter of a century with inexorable tenacity the realization of the monarchical idea, does not seem to have made any direct overtures to European governments at that time. But in 1840 he published a pamphlet which produced a great sensation, calling for a Convention which should give to Mexico a royal form of government under a European prince. "I can discover," wrote he at that time, "no other means of saving our nationality, in deadly peril from the Anglo-Saxon race, which, translated to this continent, prepares to invade it all, supporting itself, on the democratic principle, element of life and strength for it, but the germ of weakness and death for us." [3]

This appeal earned Gutiérrez nothing but execration at the time, and he was obliged to flee the country. The mass of Mexicans identified republicanism with nationality itself; undoubtedly then, as later, they had no stomach for the European connection. But the monarchical idea, nonetheless, continued to be cherished, cherished not only in Mexico, but also in Spain, some of whose statesmen still dreamed of re-establishing the bond which united Spain's oldest continental province to the mother country. In 1846, encouraged by the advent of Paredes, an avowed monarchist, to the presidency, the Spanish government embarked upon an intrigue which, despite its futility, is still an interesting illustration of the attitude of Europeans toward the problems of the New World. The plan was the old one — the establishment of a Bourbon monarchy in Mexico, this time under the rule of Don Henrique, son of the Infante Francisco de Paula.[4] In pursuance of this idea Bermudez de Castro was sent to Mexico City as the Spanish Minister, well supplied with funds for the persuasion of the Mexicans. More than half a million dollars were expended by this individual in the course of his activities,[5] and in the spring of 1846, with an exuberant optimism that no doubt went beyond the facts, he reported that the President and Council were with him, that ten or twelve thousand troops were at the disposal of the monarchists, and that a meeting of distinguished Mexicans had been held at his house to sign a declaration in favor of calling a Spanish prince to the throne. More than this, the Spanish government made overtures to France and England, to enlist their support in the enterprise, declaring in a memorandum to these courts that action was necessary to prevent "gigantic plans" on the part of the United States to "sweep away the Spanish race and swallow it up in the gulf of the Union." The question, this memorandum goes on, is European, not Spanish. All nations were declared to have an interest in "not allowing the American territory to be subject to the influence of a single Power, especially if this Power be animated by a spirit of rivalry towards the ancient Continent, proclaiming as the basis of its policy to exclude all European nations from any participation in the rule of, or influence upon, the New World." [6]

The Spanish project of 1846, despite the activities of de Castro, collapsed with the coming of the Mexican War; and it is but fair to say that it never received encouragement from Paris or from London. Standing alone, it might seem hardly worthy of comment; but just as it had its roots in the past, so too it adumbrated events of similar character in the future. For a few years after the war with the United States Mexican monarchical sentiment appears to have languished; but by 1853 its exceedingly active proponents were once again busy with their schemes, schemes which derived much of their significance from the fear and hatred with which many Mexicans regarded the United States. The clash between the republican and the monarchical systems was never better illustrated and underlined than in the events of this decade.

It is hard for any people to see itself as others see it. Naturally, we Americans put a favorable interpretation not only upon our present motives, but upon our past actions. It is desirable, perhaps, for that matter, that we should not always see ourselves too clearly, or at least that we should not fall into any mood of self-depreciation or weakness. For self-depreciation and weakness are deadly perils to a nation. But with whatever complacency we may contemplate our own historical role, we shall have to admit, if we study the documents at all, that in the period of the fifties Americans were generally regarded in Europe as a bumptious and absurdly self-confident folk, aggressively preaching their national faith of democracy without much regard for good manners, and expanding where they chose to expand at the expense of others with little regard for moral scruple. And since it is easy to moralize one's own actions, as it is to impugn the morality of the actions of others, it became with certain European statesmen a matter of right conduct, one might almost say, to oppose some obstacle to the onward march of the militant North Americans. Mexico furnished the central area of conflict; in the years between 1853 and

1860 a battle of systems was fought out there, in which each side doubted the scrupulosity and good faith of the other, in which each believed that it was contending for some universal good.

The Mexican government of Santa Anna, which came into power in 1853, had no love for the United States. There was plenty of reason to distrust American motives and American manners, and as early as April of the year just mentioned, Alamán, once again Foreign Minister, sounded the French Minister in Mexico City with regard to a tripartite guarantee of Mexico against its northern neighbor.[7] The idea is repeated in a memorandum of October 24. If the "new Vandals and Goths" are to invade the territory of their helpless neighbor, why should France stand helplessly aside? Why should it not guarantee Mexico against spoliation? Why should it not (and this is hinted rather than expressed) ally itself with the struggling republic which bars the way to Anglo-Saxon imperialism?[8]

In different circumstances this appeal might perhaps have been answered. But the Crimean War had broken out in Europe, and so long as it lasted nothing could be done for Mexico. The French Minister in Mexico City, ably assisted by his British colleague, had to content himself with intriguing against the United States, and with writing home eloquent dispatches in which the Americans were most unflatteringly compared with the Russians, and Mexico and the Isthmus of Tehuantepec with Constantinople. "Ambition, the abuse of strength, and aspirations toward universal domination are the distinctive traits" of both the Russian and the American peoples, he wrote. "Russia aspires to dominate in Europe in the name of despotism, and the United States to dominate in America in the name of liberty. The principle of monarchy, imposed with all its exaggerations and abuses by the sabre of the Tsar and the lance of the Cossacks, and the democratic principle, imposed by the rifle of Yankee adventurers, end in the same results, absolutism and tyranny."[9] But the language of jealous rivalry was not used only by the Frenchman. "The Europeanizing of all Mexico, of all South America," wrote Gadsden, American Minister to

Mexico in 1853, ". . . has to be fought here." "Believe me, Sir," wrote his successor, John Forsyth, "we cannot afford to play the 'dog in the manger' with our Monroe Doctrine. Mexico . . . must lean upon some power. Shall it be Europe or the United States? I answer unhesitatingly the United States, by every consideration of humanity, good neighborhood, and sound policy. For if it be Europe, I can see a multitude of contingencies that will make Mexico the battleground for the maintenance of American supremacy in America; the theater for the practical illustration of the value and virtue of the Monroe Doctrine." [10]

The clash of French and American interests in Mexico becomes sharper with increasing anarchy in Mexico itself. In 1855 the liberal elements had once more come into power, and in 1857 they promulgated a Constitution which dealt hardly with the Church and with the other great landowning interests, and which was modeled after that of the United States. But their power by no means remained unchallenged. A bitter civil struggle ensued; by 1858 a reactionary government had established itself in Mexico City, while, on the other hand, at Vera Cruz was installed the regime of one of the greatest of Mexican liberal leaders, the Zapotec Indian Benito Juárez. Torn between two contending factions without scruple and without pity, Mexico lapsed into conditions so disorganized as to offer an easy excuse for outside intervention.

Americans who condemn the intrigue and the ambition of Louis Napoleon and Maximilian will do well to remember that in the last years of the fifties the annexationist spirit made itself strongly felt in the United States. As early as January, 1858, Senator Houston of Texas, the hero of San Jacinto and the Texan revolution, introduced a resolution looking to the establishment of a protectorate over Central America and Mexico, and followed it up with a discourse filled with references to the Monroe Doctrine. The resolution was defeated in June by a decisive vote; but as the situation grew steadily worse, Buchanan in his message of 1858 actually recommended the partial occupation of Mexican territory, and especially of Sonora and Chihuahua. As the same time he warned the nations of Europe. "It is a duty which we owe to ourselves," he wrote, "to protect the integrity of Mexico's territory against the hostile interference of any other power. Our geographical position, our direct interest in all that concerns Mexico, and our well-settled policy in regard to the North American continent render this an indispensable duty." [11] The message of 1859 went even further, and looked toward intervention and assistance to the forces of Juárez. It, too, contained the by now inevitable reference to our "established policy." And it was followed by a treaty, the so-called McLane-Ocampo Treaty, by which the liberal faction in Vera Cruz virtually put itself under an American protectorate, conceding to the United States hardly less than a general right of intervention and a general power of police in the distracted country to the south. Had it not been for the slavery issue, which effectively neutralized the expansionist spirit so far as the North was concerned, the closing years of the fifties might well have seen the extension of American dominion over its southern neighbor.

It is against some such background as this that we must measure the policy of Louis Napoleon. It seemed as if Mexico might be swallowed up by the United States; against such a peril De Gabriac, the French Minister in Mexico, constantly sent his warnings to Paris. Buchanan's message of 1858 caused him the most acute anguish; it was received, he wrote, with "general stupor." [12] The recognition of Juárez was "the application of the Monroe Doctrine in the form of a defiance of Europe"; [13] the McLane-Ocampo Treaty foreboded nothing less than a general catastrophe. [14] The time had come for Europe to step in, for the foundation of a monarchy in the Constantinople of the West, for the preservation of the "equilibrium" (the phrase recalls that of Guizot) so necessary to the well-being of the New World.

Such counsels were not uncongenial to the imperial dreamer in the Tuileries. They were not uncongenial to the shallow and beautiful Empress whom he had called to share his throne. And they were supplemented by the urging of the Mexican monarchists: by Gutiérrez de Estrada, who, by the middle of 1857, had established relations with the French court; by José Hidalgo, who in 1858 at the imperial castle of Compiègne held long conversations with the imperial pair on the grand design of the restoration of the monarchy in Mexico. But again war, the war of Italian liberation, supervened in Europe; and when the French Foreign Office sounded Great Britain on the project of monarchy, it received the blunt reply that the best way out of the Mexican imbroglio was annexation by the United States.[15]

The Emperor Louis Napoleon, however, possessed a serene tenacity that had carried him far; the dream which he cherished was postponed, not surrendered, and soon events favored his plans. Obviously, American influence in Mexico was seriously shaken by discord at home; in December 1860 came secession; in April 1861, war. And the government of Juárez played into the hands of the interventionists. It was incapable of preserving order, or of meeting the legitimate demands of other powers; by the summer of 1861 it had suspended its international obligations; it seemed bent on quarreling with everyone. In circumstances such as these it was not difficult to shape a plan for joint action against Mexico, with redress of grievances as its ostensible object; and in this plan Great Britain and Spain were induced to join. The result was the London Convention of October 30, 1861, and the tripartite agreement which followed on its heels.

Of the governments associated with France in the original expedition of 1861, that of Great Britain may well be acquitted of any ulterior purposes. It was ready, indeed, to see the United States associated with the enterprise — a sure sign of good faith; and it sent only a small force of seven hundred marines to Mexico. It disbelieved (at least Lord John Russell, its Foreign Secretary, disbelieved) in the practicability of the monarchical idea. It was, in the course of time, to use its influence, unsuccessfully as the event proved, to dissuade Maximilian from venturing across the seas. But the second of Napoleon's original partners, Spain, had somewhat different views; it desired intervention, not a mere operation for the redress of grievances; and there was certainly a party at the Spanish court which, with a nostalgia that is somewhat pathetic, still hoped for the establishment of a Bourbon prince upon the throne of Mexico. The Queen, a dull and doltish sovereign, the Foreign Minister, Calderón Collantes, a subtle and shifty politician, the Spanish Minister at Paris, Señor Mon, a confirmed reactionary, all cherished hopes for the future. These hopes were echoed in the press, and in at least two pamphlets of the time, in one of which, it is interesting to observe in passing, the Monroe Doctrine was moderately described as "most unimportant and common-place on its face, but subversive and anarchical in its results." [16] But there was also in Spain another faction, more realistic and more statesmanlike. To it belonged O'Donnell, the Prime Minister; and to it also belonged the liberal politician-soldier Prim y Prats, who was put in command of the Spanish troops which went out to Mexico. With such divided counsels there was small hope of positive accomplishment; and as is well known, the troops of the three intervening powers had not been long in action before a bitter quarrel broke out between the Spaniards and the Frenchmen. The details of this quarrel we do not need to examine; the upshot of it was the withdrawal of the forces of General Prim, and the transformation of the tripartite intervention into an enterprise of the French government alone. Happily rid of its associates, that government could now march forward to the realization of the monarchical dream.

That dream, of course, was from the beginning in the mind of Louis Napoleon. He probably did not think of it as involving the brutal imposition upon the Mexicans of a regime which they disliked; on the contrary, misled and misinformed as to the actual situation, he began by believing that there existed in Mexico a strong and powerful monarchical faction which it would be easy to install in power, and which could without difficulty maintain itself once it was placed there.[17] He probably did not believe that such a government could be antipathetic to the Mexicans; he intended that it should be based upon a plebiscite, and perhaps he did not regard this plebiscite as a mere solemn farce. Unctuously, but perhaps not wholly insincerely, he wrote to Flahault, his ambassador at London, "I seek nothing but good; convinced that to try to make a people prosperous is to work effectively for the prosperity of all." [18]

But it would, of course, be incredibly naïve not to understand that Napoleon's dream of monarchy was conceived as a check upon the power of the United States. The famous letter to Forey of July 3, 1862, accurately explains his views in this regard. "There will not be lacking," he wrote to his commander across the seas, "people who will ask why we are going to spend men and money" in this enterprise.

In the actual state of the civilization of the world, the prosperity of America is not indifferent to Europe, for it nourishes our industry and gives life to our commerce. We are interested in seeing the United States powerful and prosperous, but we have no interest in seeing that republic acquire the whole of the Gulf of Mexico, dominate from this vantage-point the Antilles and South America, and become the sole dispenser of the products of the New World. Mistress of Mexico, and consequently, of Central America and of the passage between the two seas, there would be henceforth no other power in America than the United States. If, on the contrary, Mexico conquers its independence and maintains the integrity of its territory, if a stable government is constituted there by the arms of France, we shall have opposed an insuperable barrier to the encroachments of the United States, we shall have maintained the independence of our colonies in the Antilles, and of those of ungrateful Spain, and this influence will radiate northward as well as southward, will create immense markets for our commerce, and will procure the materials indispensable to our industry.[19]

A franker expression of hostility than this could hardly be looked for. The irritation at American jingoism, the suspicion of American purposes based upon Buchanan's messages and the McLane-Ocampo Treaty, these may help to explain such a view as that expressed above, but they cannot alter its fundamental character, or shake in any manner the clearly established thesis that one of the principal objects of the Mexican intervention was to checkmate the United States. No more sinister project, in terms of American interest, American influence, and American ideas, has ever been conceived in the history of the Monroe Doctrine.

Obviously, however, so long as the United States was involved in Civil War, the cards in the Mexican game were in the hands of Louis Napoleon. Freed from his allies, he sought to press forward, and though there were unhappy delays, and even a stout resistance, particularly at the city of Puebla, though in French counsel itself doubts were felt as to the wisdom of the Emperor's course, by the summer of 1863 French troops had entered Mexico City, a Council of Notables had been summoned, and the throne of the new Mexican monarchy had been offered to the Archduke Maximilian. The month of Gettysburg and Vicksburg, ominous for French plans for the future, was also the month in which the monarchical idea took concrete and irrevocable form. In April of 1864, just as Grant was about to initiate his great campaign on the Potomac, the Austrian archduke formally accepted the throne and set sail for the New World.

The tragic fate of Maximilian has cast the aura of romance around him, and around his consort, Carlotta, amongst the most beautiful, as she was surely amongst the most unfortunate, women of her time. Yet never did mortal man, perhaps, fare forth more quixotically and with less clarity of vision than did the scion of the Hapsburgs. Warnings there were for him, warnings aplenty. Sir Charles Wyke, the British Minister in Mexico at the outset of the intervention, talked to an emissary of the Archduke in September of 1863, and specifically declared against the enterprise. The French had so thoroughly identified themselves with the clericals and the reactionaries, he asserted, as to make their role in Mexico odious from the beginning.[20] Rechberg, the Austrian Foreign Minister, had talked with Motley, the American Minister at Vienna, as early as February of 1862, and had been told that opposition to the establishment of a monarchy in Mexico would be "universal and intense."[21] From that time forward he had observed the greatest caution with regard to the venture, and had warned against its being attempted unless the support of England as well as France could be secured. Francis Joseph gave no enthusiastic support to his brother's daydreams. And even if none of these men had taken the position that they did, Maximilian, if he had been even halfway well-advised in 1864, might have seen that the victory of the North was presaged in the Civil War, and that a Union flushed with victory and ablaze with martial spirit would not stand idly by while the flag of monarchy was planted on the castle of Chapultepec. In a way he *did* barely glimpse the difficulty. He wrote to Louis Napoleon in August of 1863 that "the most serious obstacle . . . would come from North America, the recent news of which appears to foreshadow the reconstitution of the Union, which is as greedy of aggrandizement as it is hostile to the monarchical principle in the other hemisphere." [22] Yet he persisted in moving forward, and at a time when he ought to have been analyzing with the greatest care the perils immediately in the way, he was dreaming romantic dreams of the marriage of his brother, Ludwig Viktor, to one of the daughters of the Emperor of Brazil, and even of the gradual absorption of Central America by the government which he was to found in Mexico.[23] In international politics, the guerdon of victory goes not to the just or yet to the unjust, but to the well-informed and the well-prepared. A clear-eyed appraisal of the facts, a resolute will, effective military power — these are usually the essentials of successful action in great enterprises. Maximilian was egregiously misinformed, one might even say self-deceived; he was not so much resolute as obstinate; and he was dependent, and ought to have known he was dependent, upon the loyalty and military support of the Emperor of the French. This was an insecure basis upon which to rest his great adventure. No doubt he was personally brave; no doubt he yearned to do good; no doubt when the time came he could meet death with dignity. But in a practical world it is not these things that count in statesmanship; and however much we may pity the Archduke we cannot possibly admire him as a director of policy and a man of large affairs.

It has just been said that Maximilian ought to have seen that he was dependent upon the support of Louis Napoleon; the observation brings us back to French policy, which we must analyze for a little before we turn to the attitude of the United States. For the Mexican adventure never had the cordial and widespread support of French public opinion, and it was entered into with misgivings even by Louis Napoleon and his ministers. As early as 1862, within the limits permitted by the censorship, the French liberal papers were attacking the expedition with an energy of which there had been no example since the establishment of the Empire. In 1863 the press attacks grew stronger, and the critics did not hesitate to predict American hostility to the whole enterprise. Should the North win the Civil War, wrote one author, it "will emerge a military democracy, led by a more centralized and compact government. Imagine peace concluded, will these arms and hearts disarm as if by enchantment? What is to be done with them? What employment shall be offered to their ambition? What diversion to these hatreds? What food for these passions? . . . The field of battle . . . is already indicated; it will be Mexico. On the other hand, the South has always been expansionist in character; an independent Confederacy will soon absorb the regions which lie nearest at hand to satisfy its rapacity and its ambition." [24]

Language such as this might or might not be significant; but it was surely food for reflection when the French Chambers let their misgivings with regard to Mexico be heard and expressed. In the legislative session at the opening of 1863, the Corps Législatif expressed the hope that it would see "the happy and early end" of the whole expedition.[25] A year later it stated that the Mexican adventure had "beyond question disquieted many minds," [26] while the Senate expressed a hope that "the enterprise gloriously commenced should receive as soon as possible a solution worthy of the Emperor and of French interests"; [27] and in the discussions of 1864 orator after orator conjured up the specter of American opposition to the designs of Napoleon, and at least one of them, Jules Berryer, specifically declared that the Monroe Doctrine had been challenged — and would be vindicated.[28]

Even in the circles of the Emperor himself there was no enthusiasm for the Mexican enterprise. Marshal Randon, the Minister of War, had never been its partisan and was opposed to the
sending of further troops in 1863; [29] in June of that same year,
Drouyn de Lhuys, the Minister of Foreign Affairs, drew up instructions which seem to abandon the whole idea, and look to the
withdrawal of the French from Mexico.[30] Had not these instructions been nullified by the action of Marshal Forey in calling the
Mexican Council of Notables, and in facing the French government with a *fait accompli,* the matter would have ended then and
there; Louis Napoleon himself frankly admitted to Sir Charles
Wyke in November 1863 that he had got the bear by the tail and
did not dare let go.[31] Wyke urged that the Council of the Regency
be dissolved, and that in order to ascertain the will of the people a
Congress be summoned in accordance with the fundamental laws
of Mexico. "That," replied the Emperor, "would amount to admit-
ting a mistake, and in France it is no longer permissible to make
mistakes." [32] If in 1864 the imperial politician who guided — or
misguided — the destinies of France was determined to see the
matter through, it was in part because he was not strong enough
or brave enough to admit that his hand had been forced, and to
shape his policy on a new basis. That unquenchable enthusiasm,
that indomitable resolution, that clear view of the facts of the case,
which are the preconditions of successful policy, were lacking in
Napoleon's enterprise in Mexico. The obvious threat which it offered to American interests and American ideas was in some measure diminished by the halfhearted manner in which, almost from
the beginning, it had to be carried on.

But what, in the meantime, of the great democracy of the
North? What of American opinion when the squadrons sailed for
Vera Cruz in 1861; while French armies pressed forward toward
the capital; when the Archduke Maximilian set sail from Trieste
to redress the balance of the New World by the founding of a
monarchy in the city of the Montezumas? And what of the policy
of the government of the United States? What of Congress? And of

its leaders? These are the cardinal questions to which we must now turn. At the risk of anticipating the story itself, it is worth while to say at the outset that the Monroe Doctrine played an enormous role in public discussion and diplomatic action in connection with the Mexican question. It has been more than once pointed out that Seward never mentioned the Doctrine explicitly and by name in his copious diplomatic correspondence on Mexico; and this statement is correct. But it would be more to the point to indicate that the upholding of the principles of 1823 is implicit in all the more important of his dispatches; that those principles were again and again invoked by the Mexican Minister in Washington; that they were on the lips of most American public men, and in the columns of many of the newspapers; and that they exercised a powerful influence upon the course of events at home and abroad. The years from 1861 to 1867, in truth, demonstrate that whereas at the beginning of the Lincoln administration the Monroe Doctrine had not yet attained the importance of a truly national principle, while some atmosphere of partisanship then still clung to it, it emerged from the events which we are about to examine immensely strengthened, and firmly anchored in the thought of the American people and in the policy of their government.

William H. Seward, who was to speak for the American people in the great question of Mexico, was one of the really great Secretaries of State of the United States. He began badly, it is true; and the fantastic suggestion which he made to the President, appropriately enough on the first day of April, 1861, that the North and South should be united by a policy of quarreling with the principal governments in Europe, has done something permanently to diminish his fame. His first few months, indeed, were by no means brilliant; and, as we shall see, when he attempted to use the Monroe Doctrine to condemn the Spanish government's reoccupation of the Dominican Republic he was roundly and smartly snubbed. But Seward (and what more can be asked of any man?) learned from experience; after the disillusion of Bull Run, it was clear that the time for braggadocio was over; and the alternative policy which the Secretary of State adopted was to serve extremely well the interests of his country.

The first efforts which Seward made to deal with the Mexican problem had as their object the forestalling of the threatened intervention of the European powers. To Corwin, the American Minister in Mexico City, he proposed that the United States assume the interest charges on the Mexican debt for a period of three years, taking in exchange a lien on the public lands in the northern provinces of Lower California, Chihuahua, Sonora, and Sinaloa. But such a proposal from the beginning had very little chance of success. It smacked distinctly too much of territorial ambition to be popular with anybody. Corwin himself declared that it would "probably end in the cession of the sovereignty" to the United States.[33] In London Adams reported that it had merely sharpened British suspicion of American purposes and seemed to be "but the preliminary to an entry for inevitable foreclosure." [34] In Paris Dayton was told by M. Thouvenel, the French Foreign Minister, that the American proposition would be wholly unsatisfactory to France, and was pointedly reminded that the danger of Mexican extinction had hitherto come from the United States.[35] In Spain the worst construction was put upon the American proposal.[36]

Nor was the idea really popular even in Washington. In advance of the actual negotiation of a treaty by Corwin, the administration decided to try to get a resolution of approval from the Senate of the United States, and Seward apparently worked energetically to this end. He was aided by the indefatigable Mexican Minister at Washington, Matías Romero. This remarkable man, of prodigious industry and energy, and a mere youth of twenty-nine in 1861, seems to have been a master of the art of personal politics. He formed contacts with all the most influential people in Washington: through Montgomery Blair, the Postmaster General, he gained a knowledge of what went on even in the secrecy of the cabinet; he enjoyed cordial relationships with Charles Sumner, the chairman of the Committee on Foreign Relations in the Senate; and with an understanding of democratic institutions remarkable in a

Mexican of the sixties, he resorted to an active propaganda in newspapers and periodicals. Romero had not really hit his stride at the end of 1861 and the beginning of 1862, but nonetheless he managed to win the members of the Committee on Foreign Relations to his point of view on the Mexican business. When the resolution endorsing the project of a loan was brought to the floor of the Senate, however, it was decisively rejected, and a resolution of wholly contrary tenor adopted declaring that it was not advisable to negotiate a treaty that would require the United States to assume any portion of the principal or interest of the debt of Mexico, or that would require the concurrence of foreign powers.[37] Though the loan project lingered on, though a treaty was actually negotiated by Corwin and submitted to the Senate, there was never any real prospect that this mode of solving the Mexican difficulty would be adopted. In his effort to forestall European intervention Seward was charting both a bold and an interestingly novel course; but the course was unsuccessful, and the squadrons sailed for Vera Cruz.

Once the intervention was begun, the American Secretary of State adopted an attitude of studied moderation, which was nonetheless clear as to the fundamental principle involved. Nothing in the Monroe Doctrine or in the history of our foreign policy in 1861 implied a denial on the part of the United States of the right of European nations to wage war against an American state for the redress of grievances. The French blockade of Mexico and Argentina in 1838 had passed unchallenged. The Anglo-French operations in the Río de la Plata in 1845 had been the subject of no protest from Washington. The Buchanan administration itself, most sensitive on the subject of the principles of 1823, had explicitly recognized the right of European powers to "wage honorable warfare" against Mexico in the famous La Reintrie circular of December 1860, communicated by the American agent to the members of the diplomatic corps at Mexico City.[38] Seward did not, therefore, question the right of the powers which had signed the convention of London to take action against the government of Juárez. When invited, as at British urging upon France he was invited, to participate in punitive measures, he refused, declaring that such association with other states was contrary to the traditional policy of the United States, and adding that Mexico, "being a neighbor . . . on this continent, and possessing a form of government similar to our own in many of its important features," was entitled to some measure of patience and indulgence.[39] He added a warning, the first of many, against the subversion of Mexican institutions. "The United States," he wrote in a circular memorandum of December 4, 1861, "have a deep interest which, however, they are happy to believe is an interest held by them in common with the high contracting parties and with all other civilized states, that neither the sovereigns by whom the convention has been concluded shall seek or obtain any acquisition of territory or any advantage peculiar to itself, and not left equally open to the United States and every other civilized state within the territories of Mexico, and especially that neither one nor all of the contracting parties shall, as a result or consequence of hostilities to be inaugurated under the convention, exercise in the subsequent affairs of Mexico any influence of a character to impair the right of the Mexican people to choose and freely to constitute the form of its government." [40] What was this but the re-enunciation of the Monroe Doctrine, stated delicately yet firmly, and without the irritating use of the phrase "Monroe Doctrine" itself?

The circular dispatch of December 4 was the first of many in which the American position was set forth. As yet, though Seward knew of the danger of a monarchical intrigue, he reckoned the danger trivial, as was natural for one of his optimistic temperament; he hoped and expected that the intervening powers would quarrel among themselves, as indeed they did; and he told Romero that their divergences of purposes would remove the sting from any far-reaching plans.[41] But as time went on the candidacy of the Archduke Maximilian began to be more and more freely discussed in the American newspapers, and even mentioned in the dispatches of Dayton, the American Minister at Paris, a gentleman not remarkable for his alertness or undeviating attention to the public business.[42] By March 1862, the Secretary of State deemed further insistence upon the American position desirable, and penned an interesting instruction to his representative at Paris, one of the suavest, cleverest, and most definite that ever came from Washington. Following an old but always valuable diplomatic technique, Seward began by expressing his full confidence in the sincerity of the professions of the intervening powers that they intended no interference in the internal affairs of Mexico. Still, he hinted, there were rumors of monarchical designs. "The President deems it his duty," taking these facts into consideration, "to express to the allies, in all candor and frankness, the opinion that no monarchical government which could be founded in Mexico, in the presence of foreign navies and armies in the waters and upon the soil of Mexico, would have any prospect of security or permanency. Secondly, that the instability of such a monarchy there would be enhanced if the throne should be assigned to any person not of Mexican nativity. That under such circumstances the new government must speedily fall unless it could draw into its support European alliances, which, relating back to the present invasion, would, in fact, make it the beginning of a permanent policy of armed European monarchical intervention injurious and practically hostile to the most general system of government on the continent of America. . . . In such a case," this great instruction goes on, in sentences all the stronger because they leave so much unsaid, and contain no word of menace, "it is not to be doubted that the permanent interests and sympathies of this country would be with the other American republics. It is not intended on this occasion to predict the course of events which might happen as a consequence of the proceeding contemplated, either on this continent or in Europe. It is sufficient to say that, in the President's opinion, the emancipation of this continent from European control has been the principal feature of its history during the last century." [43]

Thus Seward made the American position crystal-clear. He spoke the language of the Monroe Doctrine; he spoke also the language of the American people. For with the year 1862 there are multiplying signs of popular indignation at the course of events in Mexico; Francis Blair, General McClellan, John J. Crittenden, chairman of the House Committee on Foreign Relations, all were restive at the course of events. Romero, ever active, fanned the flames of indignation, and in a note no doubt intended for publicity and for American consumption made appeal to the message of 1823, whose lines, he declared, "seem to be written for the present occasion." [44]

But the tide of war in 1862 ran strongly against the North; McClellan was obliged to withdraw from before Richmond; then came the second Bull Run, the invasion of Maryland, the hard-won Northern victory of Antietam; and the year closed in gloom with the wintry holocaust of Fredericksburg. In circumstances such as these the Mexican question had to wait; and wait indeed it did except for occasional manifestations of public discontent, until Gettysburg and Vicksburg, and the turn of the fortunes of the North well toward the beginning of 1864. When interest revived that winter the fact was due, in part, beyond all question, to the indefatigable Romero. In touch with a host of newspapers and public men, Romero staged a dinner in New York, to publicize the woes of his country. The turnout was impressive: George Bancroft, Hamilton Fish, James J. Astor, Henry Clews, David Dudley Field, and Charles King, the President of Columbia, were among the guests. Still more important, the Mexican Minister was busy among the members of Congress. In particular, he pleaded and argued with Henry Winter Davis, now at the head of the Committee on Foreign Affairs. And largely owing to this insistence, Davis reported out from his committee on April 4, 1864, a famous resolution declaring that "the Congress of the United States are unwilling by silence to leave the nations of the world under the impression that they are indifferent spectators of the deplorable events now transpiring in the Republic of Mexico, and that they therefore think fit to declare that it does not accord with the policy of the United States to acknowledge any monarchical Government

erected on the ruins of any republican Government in America under the auspices of any European power." [45] The resolution passed
by a vote of 109 to 0.

But the victory of the North was not yet won; and Seward, wise
and self-restrained, still pursued a policy of caution. He did, of
course, refuse to acknowledge the regime set up under French
bayonets in Mexico City, declaring in a note of October 23, 1863,
that "the United States continues to regard Mexico as the theater
of a war which has not yet ended in the subversion of government
long existing there . . . for this reason the United States is not
now at liberty to consider the question of recognizing a government which, in the further chances of war, may come into its
place." [46] But he parried the attempts of the French chargé, Geoffroy, to draw him out further; when the Frenchman protested
against the Davis resolution, the Secretary, in a masterly reply,
pointed out that the House of Representatives could not and did
not fix the foreign policy of the United States. [47] The war between
the states moved on; slowly the lines tightened; Sherman marched
from Chattanooga to Atlanta, and from Atlanta to the sea; the
Lincoln administration was re-elected; the victory of the North became more and more certain, and with the spring of 1865 a nation
flushed with victory began to think seriously of Mexico.

There were numerous signs of the gathering tide of feeling in
the victory year which brought the Civil War to an end. Even before the surrender of Lee at Appomattox, there was talk, on the
part of such influential people as Francis Blair, of reuniting North
and South in a crusade for the restoration of republicanism. [48] With
Lincoln's permission, though not with his approval or encouragement, Blair went to Richmond at the end of '64, got in touch with
Jefferson Davis, and proposed that an armistice should be arranged, under cover of which the forces of the South should be
shifted to the banks of the Rio Grande, there to be united with
the liberal forces of Juárez. The idea died a-borning, but not before
it had received some favorable consideration from the President
of the Confederacy. A similar project, on the part of General Lew

Wallace, cropped up early in 1865, and, according to its author, was approved by the President himself.[49] General Grant, shortly after Lee's capitulation, became an ardent proponent of intervention in Mexico. He entered into close relationship with Romero, and gave no discouragement to the Mexican's schemes for enlisting a considerable force in the United States.[50] In June, he even pressed his views upon the President in a special meeting of the cabinet.[51] He joined in a remarkable, if unsuccessful, intrigue by which a high-ranking American army officer, General Schofield, was to lead an army against the Emperor Maximilian.[52] The victor of Appomattox was the very spearhead of the movement for a vigorous policy against the French.

But the advocates of such a policy were many indeed. By summer, the air was thick with appeals to the principles of 1823. Henry Winter Davis,[53] Montgomery Blair,[54] Secretary Harlan of the Interior,[55] former Secretary of War Cameron,[56] these are only some of the men who made clear their devotion to the cardinal tenet of the American diplomatic faith. To question it became an act of infidelity; it was, as the judicious Montholon reported, nothing less than the "idol of patriotism" with the masses.[57] As the months wore on, moreover, pressure for action increased; in the fall the conventions of the political parties in the various states produced a new crop of resolutions on Mexico; General Grant was as militant as ever; in the cabinet Dennison and Harlan were hot for vigorous measures; [58] the President himself felt much the same — indeed, he told Schofield that the question should have been settled the very moment the Civil War had ended. It was clear that the American people viewed with intense feeling the presence of the French in Mexico.

There were, of course, a few exceptions to the general rule. The most conspicuous friend of moderate courses was John Bigelow, American Minister in Paris, who saw the Mexican problem, very naturally, from a different perspective from that which prevailed in Washington. As early as 1863 Bigelow had written that nothing was more unpopular in Europe than the Monroe Doctrine, and "nothing was more absurd anywhere." [59] In 1865 he seems to have held the same view, and argued warmly in favor of a policy of restraint with regard to France. "I think you will find, when the question is raised in a practical shape, with all its attendant responsibilities before our people," he wrote, "that the opposition to the extension of European influence in the Western Hemisphere is a sentiment which they cherish, but not a policy of making ourselves the armed champion of all or of any of the Spanish American States, whose people belong to a different race from ours, who speak a different language, who possess a different religion, and who have been trained under social and political institutions having very little in common with those of the United States." As for European opinion, Bigelow was perfectly explicit. "I doubt if there is a power in Europe," he wrote, "that would formally sustain our pretensions under what is called 'the Monroe Doctrine,' while England, France, Spain, Denmark, Austria and Brazil would lend their moral support and some of them probably material support to any sovereign that would resist them. . . . In a war to redress the wrongs of Mexico or to propagate republicanism by the sword," he declared, "we should, in my opinion, be likely to fail." [60] The position thus taken by Bigelow was supported by McCullough, the Secretary of the Treasury, who declared that the country could not stand a new war,[61] and by Welles, the Secretary of the Navy. But these gentlemen expressed their views in private, not in public. Only in an occasional pamphlet or newspaper editorial was any such opinion publicly put forward. The vast weight of opinion was on the other side. Seward was not far from the truth, though he may have been speaking for effect, when he declared that the whole nation wished the Monroe Doctrine upheld. And President Johnson struck the popular note, beyond all question, when he declared in his annual message of 1865, "We should regard it as a great calamity to ourselves, to the cause of good government, and to the peace of the world should any European power challenge the American people, as it were, to the defense of republicanism against foreign interference. . . . The United States desire to act in the future as they have ever acted heretofore; they never will be driven from that course but by the aggression of European powers, and we rely on the wisdom and justice of those powers to respect the system of non-interference which has so long been sanctioned by time, and which by its good results has approved itself to both continents." [62]

That the French government watched nervously this gathering tide of opinion in the United States is absolutely clear. Even as early as April, 1864, at the time of the passage of the Davis resolution, Drouyn de Lhuys had revealed his agitation at the American attitude to Dayton, the American Minister. "Do you bring us peace or war?" he had asked, when Dayton came to see him. [63] Nor was there anything in the events which followed to allay his nervousness. During the summer Geoffroy, the French chargé, constantly warned of the mounting American sentiment against the intervention. In August he transmitted an intimation of Seward's that under no circumstances would Maximilian be recognized, [64] and at the turn of the year he sent word of the Blair mission to Richmond, which had as its object the uniting of the North and South against the French. [65] On February 13 he gave it as his sober opinion that when the Civil War was over the people of the United States would throw themselves upon Mexico, and that no one would dare oppose such action. On the twenty-seventh he declared that war with France was thought to be in the offing. In all probability under the influence of these events the Emperor Louis Napoleon on March 1 wrote a letter to Bazaine, the French commander in Mexico, in which he clearly revealed apprehension of the United States, and directed the Marshal to concentrate rather than diffuse his forces. [66] A few weeks later a nervous dispatch went forth from the Foreign Office to Geoffroy. "We cannot believe," wrote Drouyn de Lhuys in words that show only too clearly that he *could* believe, "that they [the United States] are thinking of using them [their forces] in an expensive and unjust war against a country that has never given them cause of complaint — in a war, in fact (and we say it because we do not wish to repeat it), in which circumstances will force the United States to meet and oppose a power that was once their ancient ally." [67] For a few months after this extraordinary dispatch the apprehension in Paris appears to have lessened. For Seward, the architect of American policy, remained calm and composed. It was not until summer that he began the great diplomatic campaign which ended in the assurance of French withdrawal from Mexico.

That campaign was one of the most brilliant in the annals of our foreign policy. It was impregnated with the Monroe Doctrine. It is true that the American Secretary of State never once mentioned the Doctrine by name in his correspondence with the French; he probably thought and thought correctly that such citation would serve no useful or constructive purpose. But the spirit of the Doctrine was constantly present in his dispatches, and the vindication of the Doctrine was essentially his aim. He saw his problem clearly, and with eyes undimmed by passion; he took into careful accounting the unpopularity of the Mexican expedition with French public opinion, and the difficulties of Maximilian; in the cabinet meeting in June he stoutly opposed hasty action or provocative measures, declaring that the whole miserable business would be over in six months, perhaps in sixty days; he indulged, therefore, in no ultimatum, but step by step pushed the French government into a retreat that finally became complete.

Seward already knew, in the early spring of 1865, that there was some nervousness in the French Foreign Office with regard to the attitude of the United States. But it was not till July that a certain measure of acerbity began to creep into his tone, and not until August that he went so far as to declare, in his instructions to Dayton, that "the sympathies of the American people for the Republicans of Mexico are very lively, and that they are disposed to regard with impatience the continued intervention of France in that country." [68] This delicate language brought a reply at once proud and conciliatory. France, it was declared, would not be swayed by "haughty injunctions or threatening insinuations." It was unwilling to leave anarchy behind in Mexico, "but it would gradually withdraw its troops, and it was ready to engage in a frank exchange of views with the American government." [69] Taking advantage of these admissions, in September the Secretary spoke more frankly. His instructions of September 6 contained no threat, but once again alluded to the tension which the Mexican situation created, and to the strong prejudice of the American people in favor of republican government.[70] Once again the answer came that France desired to withdraw, with the suggestion of a bargain, the recognition of Maximilian by the United States in exchange for the evacuation of the French troops.[71] Further encouraging news followed, an indication from the French Foreign Minister, Drouyn de Lhuys, that the reduction of French forces would go on as fast as possible, and hinting at the possibility of a commercial treaty if the United States would acknowledge the puppet Emperor.[72] It is obvious from what has just been said that Seward's tactics were producing an effect. Nor can it be chance that only a few days after the Secretary's first representations, Drouyn de Lhuys wrote a querulous dispatch to M. Dano, the French Minister at Mexico City, in which for the first time he hints at the abandonment of the unhappy Emperor.[73] At almost the same time the Emperor wrote to Bazaine, declaring that relations with the United States were assuming a grave character, and that it would be necessary to take into account the possibility of an invasion, and concentrate the French forces.[74] This advice was echoed by Marshal Randon, the Minister of War, who, in a letter of August 21, spoke of not permitting the intervention to last a moment longer than necessary.[75] On the other hand it is clear, also, that the French government had not yet determined upon a specific course of action; it was playing for time; it gave no assurances to the United States, except an assurance of willingness to bargain.

In the meantime, the date for the reassembling of Congress drew nearer; in order to avoid a storm Seward knew that he must press on with the Mexican matter. Accordingly, in November he went a long step further. His famous dispatch No. 300, of early November, declared the French intervention in Mexico to be "disallowable and impracticable," stated flatly that there was not the slightest chance that the United States would recognize the monarchical regime, and expressed regret that "no communication, formal or informal, which has been received from the government of that country [that is, France] seems to justify us in expecting that France is likely soon to be ready to remove, as far as may depend upon her, the cause of our deep concern for the harmony of the two nations." [76] At the same time the administration nominated General Logan, a partisan of war with France, as its minister to the government of Benito Juárez.

On the thirtieth of November Bigelow transmitted to Drouyn the instructions contained in No. 300. A heated discussion followed; there were the expected assertions that France could not be bullied, a querulous question as to why Seward did not say war if he meant war, the not novel defense of Maximilian's empire as based upon the will of the people. But from the conversation as a whole Bigelow drew the distinct impression that if the United States insisted upon it, there would be an end of the Mexican experiment. [77] And Bigelow was right; though he could not know it, on the very day after his discussion with Drouyn de Lhuys, the Emperor gave orders to Bazaine to prepare for the evacuation. [78]

By this time Seward was supremely confident. He now knew that the cards were in his hands. To the members of the Foreign Affairs Committee of the House he declared, "You can pass whatever resolutions you want now. I am ready for anything." And to Drouyn de Lhuys in a note of December 6 he declared that friendship with France would be "brought into imminent jeopardy, unless France could deem it consistent with her interest and honor to desist from the prosecution of armed intervention in Mexico"; he intimated that Congress might have something to say about the subject; and he declared with pointed candor that there had yet been no step on the part of France which authorized "an expectation on our part that a satisfactory adjustment of the case can be effected on any basis that thus far has been discussed." [79] He stated the issue in terms which made avoidance impossible.

By December, then, the victory was virtually won. On the twenty-first Bigelow tactfully intimated to the French Foreign Minister that the fixing of a date for French withdrawal would have "a tranquillizing and salutary effect upon both sides of the Atlantic." [80] He received the reply that the Emperor would speak upon the subject of Mexico at the opening of the Chamber, and that "I might be sure that what he would say would be satisfactory." [81] On Christmas Eve Bigelow had a talk with Louis Napoleon, who told him that he expected all French troops to be back by the following autumn.[82] Though there was further exchange of notes, though the general assurance of withdrawal had to be translated into more specific terms, the essence of the matter was settled by January 29, 1866, and the danger of monarchy in Mexico was ended with the denial of French support to Maximilian. Gradual withdrawal began in the fall of 1866 and Maximilian maintained himself a year more, atoning in some measure for the ill-judgment that had brought him to Mexico by the courage with which he faced the firing squad at Querétaro.

Such is the story of the foreign policy of William H. Seward in regard to the gravest international problem which he faced during his eight years of office. The Mexican question had in it many elements of danger; it was handled with masterly restraint, with a minimum of international friction, with complete diplomatic success. And beyond all question, and most emphatically, the French withdrawal from Mexico was in part due to the attitude of the United States. The course of events just described, the interesting synchronism between French decisions as to Mexico in August and in November, and the representations of Bigelow, establish this fact beyond the shadow of a doubt.

Nonetheless, in estimating the influence of the principles of 1823 upon the final decision of Louis Napoleon to withdraw from Mexico, we must preserve a due sense of proportion and of historical moderation. The American attitude was a major factor in the French withdrawal; it was distinctly not the only factor, and it may even be that other causes would have been sufficient to contribute to the result. Louis Napoleon, as we have seen, had tried to extricate himself from the Mexican adventure in 1863 and from the very outset of it he had faced a decided measure of domestic opposition. He had to consider this opposition; he had, too, to consider the state of French finances. And finally, he had to take into account the situation in Mexico itself.

Of the unpopularity of the Mexican expedition with the French people there cannot be the slightest doubt. From an early period it was the target of opposition speeches; and by 1865 the hostility to the enterprise was intense. As early as March a speaker in the Chambers predicted that the termination of the contest between the North and the South would see the French army in Mexico taken prisoner.[83] A month later, Jules Favre, in a speech signalized by brilliant eloquence and cutting invective, flayed the policy of the government, while the ministerial benches remained silent.[84] By June, Bigelow was writing that he did not believe there was a single man in France who thought that the Archduke could remain long in Mexico except "at an unprofitable waste of money and blood"; and early in December he wrote to Seward of "the universal unpopularity of the Mexican expedition" as making it impossible for the Emperor to pursue any other course than withdrawal.[85] In the press, attacks upon the French policy were frequent. The *Revue des Deux Mondes*, of the highest standing, and by no means anti-imperialist in its general views, expressed itself more and more frankly as the year wore on;[86] and early in 1866 M. Saint-Marc Girardin in a series of brilliant articles in the *Journal des Débats* assailed the course of Louis Napoleon.[87] In the Chambers the spokesmen of the government itself admitted that the whole trend of public opinion ran against the prolongation of the Mexican experiment. Tenacious though the Emperor was, cling as he might to his grandiose dream of monarchy in the New World, he could hardly fly in the face of his people for an indefinite period, or diminish his prestige by obstinate adherence to a course of action so widely condemned.

And, after all, the Mexican expedition was costing money — and a lot of money. By the end of 1865 the bill had run to 274,698,000 francs.[88] The drain was, of course, continuous; it was counterbalanced by very meager payments from Mexico to the French treasury. In addition, throughout 1865, the Mexican Finance Minister, Ramirez, was opposing an obstinate resistance to the payment of the French claims for the satisfaction of which the original intervention had been undertaken in 1861.[89] In the French Chamber, the budget discussions revealed a wide measure of dissatisfaction; and Frenchmen, gallant though they have often been in the field, have never been particularly heroic when it came to the bearing of a great weight of taxation. To continue a costly enterprise at the price of rising popular discontent would have been, in any case, a risky business.

And there is another factor that remains to be considered — the gallant resistance of the Mexicans made stouter by the weakness of Maximilian's government. They could not have fought so well if they had not received a measure of assistance from the United States; but the French in Mexico discovered that they had to beat down the resistance, not only of armies in the field, but of guerillas who sprang up wherever the French forces were not present in considerable numbers. Maximilian himself, complained Bazaine, was without energy or high capacity; the Mexican authorities of the Imperial regime were constantly at loggerheads with the French; the new government lost steadily in popular support the longer it was in operation. The monarch of the Tuileries had hoped, had even expected, that his protégé would rally round him the best and the most numerous elements of the nation; he found, instead, that the intervention in Mexico was assuming the proportions of a major military enterprise, and of an enterprise of conquest, at that. His disgust with the course of events was, no doubt, real, and he may well have meant what he said when, as early as February 1865, he declared to Bigelow, "What I really want is to get out of Mexico altogether." [90]

It is possible, then, that without American diplomatic action the Mexican adventure would have ended exactly as it did. But the

French have a saying that fits the case exactly: "One does not re-make history by hypothesis." While to claim for the role of the United States a total influence would be an error, to claim for that role a major influence would certainly be correct. The intervention in Mexico marks not only the consolidation of the Monroe Doctrine in American public opinion; it marks also its vindication and its triumph. The withdrawal of French troops from Mexico is the symbol of the end of an era, and of the beginning of another. It marks a great and vital step in the affirmation of the principles of 1823.

Less dramatic, but also not without significance in the years of the Civil War, is the episode of the Spanish reoccupation of Santo Domingo. As we have already seen, the ruling politicians of that republic had, all through the fifties, been flirting with the representatives of any foreign government which might help to maintain them in power. In the last years of the decade they had been evincing a special preference for Spain, or so, at least, had General Santana, who was then President. Clandestine aid was secured from General Serrano, the Governor General of Cuba, and negotiations for a close understanding, political and economic, were opened at Madrid. For a time the Spanish government under Marshal O'Donnell hesitated. It feared that premature action would, amongst other things, make "the contending parties in America forget their internal discords, might lead them to group themselves under the Monroe Doctrine, a principle accepted without reserve by the slave states no less than those where free labor prevails." [91] Its hand was forced by the course of events in the Antilles. On the twenty-first of February, 1861, Serrano, frankly avowing his own desire for annexation, wrote to Santana asking him what preparations should be made for the occupation of the island when the time for decisive action had arrived. Thus pointedly encouraged, the Dominican President on March 18 proclaimed the annexation on his own account; Spanish troops appeared from Cuba; the ministry at Madrid found itself in a position from which it was difficult to retreat; on May 19, a little more than a month after the firing on

Fort Sumter, by royal decree it declared Santo Domingo to be once more Spanish territory.[92] The course of events in America, as O'Donnell frankly stated to the British chargé Edwards, was not without influence upon the final decision.[93]

The events just recounted occurred when Seward was in the first, and effervescent, phase, of his incumbency at the State Department. Where, in the Mexican matter, he was full of suavity and self-restraint, in the Dominican affair his tone was one of bluster. As early as April 2, 1861, perhaps still under the influence of his fantastic idea that fanfaronade would unite the South and the North, he addressed an arrogant and imprudent note to the Spanish Minister. "An attempt to introduce Spanish authority within the territory of Dominica," he declared, ". . . cannot fail to be taken as the first step in a policy of armed intervention by the Spanish Government in the American countries which once constituted Spanish America, but have since achieved their independence; and as it cannot be known where the next demonstration of the ambition it would imply would take place, it must be regarded as threatening Haiti, Mexico, the seven States on the Spanish Main, and even those once Spanish-American states, which having been peacefully acquired and admitted into the American Union, now constitute a part of this republic." This was strong and sweeping language, but, intoxicated by his own rhetoric, Seward went on to make insinuations and threats with utter recklessness. The islands of Cuba and Puerto Rico were, he declared, "on many accounts very attractive to the American people." The forbearance exercised with regard to these tempting territories was based upon the assumption that Spain would not be "an inquiet or aggressive neighbor." "The President will not willingly believe that these proceedings [that is, in Santo Domingo] have been authorized by the Government of Her Catholic Majesty, or that they can receive its approval. But I am directed to inform you, and also the Government of Her Catholic Majesty, that if they shall be found to have received at any time the sanction of that Government, the President will be obliged to regard them as manifesting an unfriendly disposition toward the United States [the very words of the message of 1823], and to meet the further prosecution of enterprises of that kind in respect to either the Dominican Republic or any part of the American Continent or islands with a prompt, persistent, and if possible, effective resistance." [94] This was strong language, much stronger than the political situation warranted. But it was followed by another document of similar, and almost equally bellicose, tenor. On June 19, acting on the instructions of the Secretary of State, Horatio J. Perry, the chargé d'affaires at Madrid, presented a diplomatic note making specific and concrete appeal to the Monroe Doctrine, and protesting in formal terms against the Spanish decree of annexation.

The Government of Her Catholic Majesty [the note declared], was not ignorant of the settled policy of the United States well known to all nations having any interest in the Western Hemisphere. It was precisely in reference to the possible future of the Republics formed from the ancient colonies of Spain in America that this policy was first announced by President Monroe in 1823 and has since been strictly adhered to by the United States and respected by Europe [sic!]. . . .

We were the first and the most considerable of the American Republics. It became us therefore to take resolute ground against the projects then attributed to the Allied Powers, and to say to the nations of Europe with all respect but with firmness and dignity that we would not see with indifference the condition of things thus established, changed or put in peril by the intervention of any monarchical or aristocratic government. We could not permit any new colony to be planted by Europe in America though with such as already existed and had not obtained their independence we had no intention to interfere. . . .

The U. S. declared at the same time their purpose not to take any part in the international politics of Europe, nor to meddle with the interior concerns of European states. The political systems of the two Continents had come to be radically distinct, and whilst we would ourselves refrain from all interference with the governments of Europe, reciprocally we claimed the right to say, we would not suffer patiently the intervention of any European power in the internal affairs of the nations of America. . . .

The material interest of the U. S. in the change which has been attempted in the island of S. Domingo is as small as it could well be. Perhaps in no other part of America would the overthrow of a republican government and substitution of the power of a European state in its stead really affect the interests of the U. S. so little as the introduction of the Spanish jurisdiction in the Island of San Domingo.

It is the moral and political significance of the act of Spain which gives it importance, and because this is the first instance since the foreign policy of the U. S. was announced to the Allied Powers of Europe in 1823, that any nation has failed to see its own clear interests in the maintenance of that policy on the one side and the other.

Spain alone and for the first time has chosen not to respect it. . . . By the act of Spain the U. S. are no longer bound to that policy which up to this time has been faithfully observed on their part, as well as in their relations with the people of the different nations of Europe as with their colonies.

Whether the U. S. will decide still to adhere to their time honoured policy or to depart from it in the case of this nation must depend hereafter upon their own appreciation of their duty and interest without reference to the wishes or interests of Spain.

Filled with profound regret at this unhappy state of affairs, the undersigned has now to fulfill the duty imposed upon him by the President, and in the name of the government of the U. S. of America solemnly protests against the assumption or exercise of Spanish authority in the island of San Domingo; and this protest the U. S. in every case will expect to maintain.[95]

This remarkable note is, with the exception of the Olney dispatch of July 20, 1895, the fullest exposition of the Monroe Doctrine that was ever addressed directly to a foreign government. A captious historical critic might quarrel with some of its assertions. There had been violations of the Doctrine, as we have seen, before 1861. The government of Spain might perhaps have complained that respect for the American colonial *status quo* had not always been marked in the attitude of the American government and some of its representatives toward the island of Cuba. Perry himself, indeed, recognized this fact, and apologized for the notorious document known as the Ostend Manifesto,° on the grounds that this was the product of a party which "has since gone into open war and rebellion against the government of the United States itself." [96] But in its statement of general principles the note of June 19, 1861, expresses the very essence of the Monroe Doctrine. For this reason, if for no other, it is one of the most important diplomatic documents in the history of our foreign policy.

But it was wholly without immediate effect. The Spanish government could and did make out a plausible case for the point of view that it had occupied the island of Santo Domingo at the request of the Dominicans themselves, that it had merely responded to the solicitations of the leader of the Dominican people, President Santana. How could a democratic people such as the American deny the validity of action so soundly based? As for the Monroe declaration, what authority could it possess in an international sense? "I ought to say, in regard to the government of Her Majesty," wrote the Spanish Foreign Minister, Calderón Collantes, somewhat tartly to Perry, "that this is the first time that the existence of such a policy has been officially and directly communicated to it. The Government of the Queen neither accepts nor declines this policy, it limits itself to saying that it does not think this an opportune time to discuss it, because it does not see the usefulness or the convenience of entering at present into such an examination. . . . It is not easy to comprehend," he added, "how the United States, which recognize as the fundamental principle of their political existence that of universal suffrage — that of popular sovereignty in all its extent & followed out to the last consequences, can deny to other peoples constituted in a manner analogous to their own the right to exercise their sovereignty in accepting the

---

° The Ostend Manifesto was a joint statement of James Buchanan, John Y. Mason, and Pierre Soulé declaring that if Spain would not sell Cuba, the United States might be justified in taking the situation into its own hands. It was not intended to be made public, and was brought to public view as a factor in the partisan maneuvers of the fifties.

form of Government which they think most convenient, or in re-constituting themselves in the way which they may judge most advantageous to their interests and their future well-being." [97]

The language of Calderón Collantes has a contemporary, no less than a historical, interest. If democracy is slain in the New World, as it has been so widely slain in the Old, it is likely that the murder will be accompanied by the proclamation of democratic principles, and defended on democratic grounds. The self-determination of Santo Domingo in 1861 was a farce, and nothing more; the speedy development of armed opposition was to testify to this fact; but the regime of Santana had gone through all the forms of respecting the popular will; and whatever the real facts may have been, it was highly embarrassing to Seward, as it may easily prove to be embarrassing to some future Secretary of State, to question the procedure. It is by just such a plausible argument as this, and by such means as were employed by Spain in Santo Domingo, that the subversion of American liberties is likely to come about, if it comes about at all.

In this particular instance which we are examining there was really nothing to be done; the armies were gathering on the Potomac for the initial battle of a four years' struggle for national unity; Seward's challenge to Spain had been imprudent and ill-timed. He was, indeed, compelled to beat a diplomatic retreat. On the eighth of July Tassara asked him bluntly what was meant by the language which the United States was employing toward Spain and whether a threat was implied. Seward responded weakly and evasively, even saying that the United States desired to preserve its friendly relations with Spain.[98] On July 29, in a later interview, he was more adroit. He could hardly retreat with dignity from the position that he had assumed, and so he began by declaring that Perry's protest had been made under instructions, and that the United States was obliged to consider the conduct of Spain as "un-friendly and injurious to the interests of this country." But there was not much reason, he added, for the Spanish government to ask if a menace was intended. The United States was not accustomed to utter threats, and Congress alone had power to take action. It seemed certain, he went on, that the Congress just called in extraordinary session would not concern itself with regard to Santo Domingo. At the regular session in December, matters might be different, but the Executive could not anticipate the action which might then be taken. With this not wholly dignified evasion of the question propounded by the Spanish government, the interview with Tassara came to an end.[99]

It is, I am afraid, one of the particular weaknesses of democratic governments in foreign policy to bluster where they are not ready to act, to be "willing to wound, and yet afraid to strike." Such action is dangerous in the extreme; and the statesman who seeks popular applause at the expense of the dignity and interest of the nation must be severely condemned. The action of the American Secretary of State in the Dominican episode is highly reprehensible, but there are at least two things to be said in extenuation of it. In the first place, as has been seen, Seward himself learned from the episode, and learned fundamentally; and the self-restraint, the moderation, and the wisdom with which he conducted American relations with France in the far more dangerous challenge of the intervention in Mexico do much to atone for, as they are certainly in large measure the result of, his unnecessary braggadocio with Spain. In the second place, it cannot be said that, in this particular instance, any unhappy consequences flowed from his action; the course of events, if it was not changed for the better, was also not changed for the worse; Spain went on its way in Santo Domingo, without manifesting any particular resentment toward the United States or altering its policy toward the American government. The reannexation of Santo Domingo appears to have been generally popular in Madrid; and the general attitude of the Spanish public was apparently one of indifference toward the United States and the Monroe Doctrine.

But the years which followed 1861 were soon to alter the complexion of the matter. Spanish rule in Santo Domingo, so lightheartedly assumed, was from the first a failure, almost incredibly tactless and shortsighted. Santana himself, the genius of reannexation, was alienated within a twelvemonth; it was not long before revolt flared up, and it became serious by the fall of 1863. By the end of that year there were 13,000 Spanish troops in the island, busily persuading the Dominicans to be loyal to the flag which they had spontaneously (?) welcomed in 1861.[100] Throughout the year 1864 there were reinforcements, and by the beginning of 1865 more than 25,000 soldiers had been sent to the island.[101] General Gándara, who assumed the supreme command in the spring of 1864, was an able and energetic officer. But it was impossible for him to prevail in the field against the guerilla warfare of the revolutionists which had, as he himself confessed, assumed the proportions of a general rebellion. The suffering from disease was frightful. Yellow fever took its heavy toll, and in December 1864 had reduced by 50 per cent the number of the Spanish effectives.[102] The costs of the whole enterprise were becoming staggering. Even the Spanish commander himself was ready to admit by the end of the year that there was no advantage in trying to hold the island, though with the pride of his caste and race he wished to evacuate only after the insurrection had been put down.[103]

In the meantime, through the imprudence of an overzealous naval officer, and an equally overzealous diplomat, Spain had become embroiled elsewhere in the New World. A wholly unnecessary quarrel with Peru, fomented on the spot by the Spanish Minister, had resulted in the seizure of the Chincha Islands. In the circumstances, such an act of violence was bound to rouse suspicions, both in Latin America and in Washington; and the long tolerance which Seward had displayed toward the court of Madrid was now about to be broken. On May 19, 1864, he instructed Koerner, the American Minister, to "make it known to Her Catholic Majesty that the United States cannot yield their assent to the positions thus assumed in the name of Spain; or regard with indifference an attempt to reduce Peru by conquest and reannex its territory to the kingdom of Spain." [104] He then went on to a franker and more inclusive expression of policy. The states of Latin America allege "that several of the European states, which once had colonies here, are now seeking to reduce them again to the condition of dependencies. These apprehensions are not unlikely to be entertained by the whole people of the United States. The proceedings of Spain in Peru give them a color which is deeply to be regretted. Indeed, a general discontent with the forbearance of this government is already manifest. Should the sentiment of this country demand a reconsideration of the policy of neutrality which this government has hitherto maintained, it is much to be feared that new complications might arise, which would not merely disturb the existing systems of commerce, but might endanger the general peace of nations. . . ." [105]

In taking this high tone, even in the dark days of the Wilderness campaign, Seward was perfectly safe. Spain had no sinister intentions in the Pacific. As soon as the news of the seizure of the Chinchas reached Madrid, the Prime Minister, Señor Mon, told Koerner that there was no intention to retain the islands,[106] and on June 21 the Foreign Secretary, Llorente, addressed a circular to the diplomatic corps in which he expressly disavowed all thought on the part of Spain of recovering any part of her ancient colonial dominion in Latin America.[107] Two months later, Llorente declared to Perry that he could assure him, "without any hesitation, that the Monroe Doctrine of the United States would not be called in question by any proceeding of Spain in or against Peru. If President Monroe were alive and on the spot, he should see nothing running counter to his famous declaration." [108] Such language must have been sweet consolation for the very different tone of Tassara and Calderón Collantes in 1861.

By September 1864, moreover, the Spanish government had made up its mind to abandon the unhappy adventure in Santo Domingo. It may have been influenced by the course of events in Virginia; but it had reason enough to withdraw from an enterprise so thoroughly unhappy and unsuccessful. The ministry of General Narváez was compelled to proceed slowly; it was not till May 1865 that the last debates in the Cortes took place, with only occasional references to the position of the United States; but while the Union armies were returning to their civilian pursuits after four years of bloody war the Spanish squadrons were retiring their forces from Santo Domingo. The two occurrences were symbolic of that victory of the democratic principle and of the Monroe Doctrine which was to be crowned by the withdrawal of the French from Mexico and the death of Maximilian at Querétaro.

The episodes which we have been examining mark an important, one might almost say a decisive stage in the evolution of the Monroe Doctrine. They represent the sharpest challenge, historically, which has ever been made to the principles of 1823. And they had been defeated. The national sentiment of the people of the United States, and their growing attachment to the great dogma, had been a potent if not a decisive influence in frustrating the designs of Louis Napoleon. No informed publicist, no responsible statesman, could henceforward ignore the existence of a powerful prejudice among the American people against the intervention of Old World states in the affairs of the New. The dispatches from every important European court, from Great Britain, from France, from Spain, demonstrate that the significance of Monroe's principles was now thoroughly understood. And in 1865 there stood behind it, and the world was aware that there stood behind it, immense material power. The sprawling democracy of the West, the object of the jealousy and envy of Europe, had emerged triumphant from its fiery trial. Its way of life had been vindicated. Its capacity for effective action had been proved. The passage of the second Reform Bill in Great Britain in 1867, with its widening of the suffrage, the establishment of universal suffrage in the North German Confederation which Bismarck set up after his defeat of Austria, the emergence of the Third Republic in France after the disaster of Sedan — all these are in some measure the tribute which Europe paid to the men who answered to the call of Lincoln and the orders of Grant and Sherman. In 1865 the world appeared to belong to democracy; and the two American continents appeared to have been preserved from invasion by the ancient principles of monarchy or despotism. In this new climate of opinion the voice of the United States might well be heard with a new respect; and the self-confident nation which rose to greatness might ask a still wider recognition of the tenets of its faith, political and diplomatic. Not, of course, that the battle was completely won; Europe recognized in a measure, but certainly not unreservedly, the force of the Monroe Doctrine in 1865. But the change that had come about was a great one; and if, to the superficial mind, it appears relatively unimportant today, it is only because the years ahead were to bring greater changes still.

V

~~~~~~~~~~

New Pretensions and Interpretations
Self-Confident America Extends the Doctrine

~~~~~~

Is it true, then, that the safety and welfare of the United
States are so concerned with the maintenance of the independence of every American state as against any European
power as to justify and require the interposition of the United
States whenever that independence is endangered? The question can be candidly answered in but one way. The States of
America, South as well as North, by geographical proximity,
by natural sympathy, by similarity of governmental constitutions, are friends and allies, commercially and politically of
the United States. To allow the subjugation of any of them by
an European power is, of course, to completely reverse that
situation and signifies the loss of all the advantages incident
to their natural relations to us. But that is not all. The people
of the United States have a vital interest in the cause of popular self-government. They have secured the right for themselves and their posterity at the cost of infinite blood and
treasure. They have realized and exemplified its beneficent
operation by a career unexampled in point of natural greatness
or individual felicity. They believe it to be for the healing of
all nations, and that civilization must either advance or retro-
grade accordingly as its supremacy is extended or curtailed.
Imbued with these sentiments, the people of the United States
might not impossibly be so wrought up to an active propaganda in favor of a cause so highly valued both for themselves and for mankind. But the age of the Crusades has

passed, and they are content with such assertion and defense of the right of popular self-government as their own security and welfare demand. It is in that view more than in any other that they believe it not to be tolerated that the political control of an American state shall be forcibly assumed by an European power.

— OLNEY *to* BAYARD, *July 20, 1895*

THE STATEMENT has been often made and is, with many, an article of faith that the Monroe Doctrine protected the nations of Latin America in the second half of the nineteenth century from the victorious imperialisms of Europe, and from the fate of much of Asia and Africa. Like many another broad historical generalization, this particular assertion cannot be absolutely denied, or dogmatically contested; for it is, of course, possible that had it not been for the position of the United States new ambitious enterprises might have been attempted on this side of the Atlantic. Yet there is much reason to believe that such an assumption is a false one; and that the developments of the period from 1865 to 1895 would not have been materially different if Monroe and his successors had not interposed a veto upon the colonization of the New World, or the subversion of its republican governments.

For this period of thirty years we must, in the first place, rule Germany entirely out of the picture; German unity was not attained till 1871; and for a time thereafter the policy of Prince Bismarck was distinctly hostile to any projects of colonial expansion. "It is far from our purpose," wrote the German Chancellor in 1871 to the American Minister in Washington, "to get a footing anywhere in America, and we recognize in relation to the whole continent the predominant influence of the United States as founded in the nature of things, and compatible with our interests." [1] By the eighties, it is true, the appetite for colonies, which had been generally aroused in Europe, had communicated itself also to the leaders of German policy, but it was in Africa and the islands of the Pacific, not in Latin America, that the effort was made to satiate this appetite. When the young William the Second "dropped the pilot," Bismarck, in 1890 shortly after his accession to the throne, the policy of the Reich toward the states of the New World remained, for a time at any rate, unchanged. Caprivi, the successor of Bismarck, was no apostle of aggressive courses; [2] and the language of Holstein, the genius, albeit the evil genius, of the Wilhelmstrasse, shows clearly that the sensitiveness of the American government to European intermeddling in the New World was clearly recognized. "To intervene in Brazil," wrote this important permanent official in 1893, "without the co-operation of the cabinet of Washington, is to give to the latter an opportunity, as exponent of the Monroe Doctrine and protector of Pan-Americanism, to magnify its position at our expense." [3] Nor need we put our faith in words alone, so far as the Germany of the nineteenth century is concerned. The all-important fact to be remembered is that during this period the naval power of the empire was still inconsiderable; the agitation of the German Navy League with its momentous consequences attains significance just at the turn of the century. The physical power to accomplish anything really significant in the New World was simply not there; and this fact, added to the silence of the German archives, conscientiously explored by Count Stolberg-Wernigerode,[4] enables us to state categorically that there was no danger to Latin America from the Berlin government in the years which stretch from the evacuation of Santo Domingo by the Spaniards to the Venezuela message of 1895.

The policy of France during this same period is almost equally exempt from suspicion, though here we speak from less exact knowledge, since the French archives after 1871 are not open to the historical investigator. But on the positive side there is an interesting episode of the eighties which sheds some light upon French policy. Of all the regions of the New World, that which might most reasonably have attracted French interest and ambition was the Republic of Haiti. After all, Haiti had once been French; the trade of the island was largely with France; the language of upper-class Haitians, of the governing class, was the language of the Quai d'Orsay. And in the year 1884 the temptation came to meddle in the affairs of this perpetually turbulent little state. President Salomon, who then occupied the shaky seat of power, appears to have resorted to an expedient of Caribbean politicians not then entirely outmoded, and to maintain himself in office instructed the Haitian Minister in France to suggest to the French government the cession of the Môle Saint-Nicholas, valuable for a naval station, in exchange for a commercial treaty.[5] It was furthermore coyly suggested that if this offer were refused, Haiti would be compelled to turn to the United States. But the French government maintained a perfectly correct position. "We are very far from seeking in the New World advantages of any sort which might expose us to confront the redoubtable Monroe Doctrine," said the permanent official Billot to Vignaud, the American chargé. "I do not believe personally in the liberality, wisdom and force of this doctrine," he added. "A doctrine which tends to maintain the nations of the world apart instead of bringing them closer to each other is contrary to the aspirations of our time; but be this as it may, you shall not have, this time at least, an occasion to apply it to us."[6] There seems no good reason to doubt the sincerity of this utterance. Nor is there aught else in French policy, so far as can be discovered, to suggest that it was the object of the Third Republic to poach upon the preserves of the New World.

After all, so far as its acquisitive instincts were concerned, the Quai d'Orsay was able, in the eighties and nineties, to do fairly well elsewhere. In 1881 came the French protectorate over Tunis; in 1883 a protectorate over Annam; in 1885 the annexation of Tonkin; in the same year a measure of control over Madagascar, transformed into annexation in 1895. Nor are these very considerable gobbets of empire the whole story; in the great partitioning of Africa which took place in the eighties and nineties France secured vast areas on the Congo and the Niger, and consolidated her hold upon the Senegal. In 1898 came the dramatic clash at Fashoda, in which French and British interests met in the Sudan, and in which the former were compelled to give way. In the scope and extent of French-African ambitions was ample opportunity for the energies of the renascent France of the Third Republic. One of the greatest colonial empires in history had been created; it seems almost fantastic to assume that to all this, in the circumstances of the time, there could have been added policies of aggression in Latin America. After all, the Mexican experiment was not only a failure, but a vivid memory; and the states of the New World had attained in the period we are reviewing a consistency and a sense of national individuality that made them far less attractive objects of imperial policy than the Negroes of the Sudan or the yellow men along the Mekong.

There remains, then, as the third power which needs to be discussed as a possible foe of Latin-American independence, or a possible enlarger of its territories in the New World, the Empire of Great Britain. And here one major controversy emerges, of which the reader in due time shall be the judge, the highly important dispute between the British and the Venezuelan — and, in the upshot, the American — governments with regard to British Guiana. But when we have said this, we have said virtually all; no other project of colonial expansion in the New World reveals itself in the archives of the British Foreign Office; and the inherent probability that no such project existed is strengthened by the fact that Britain, like France, was engaged elsewhere in these thirty years from 1865 to 1895. Egypt and Burma, a large share of colonial Africa, the development of a great empire in India, these might well be regarded as worthy of engaging a fair share of the energies of the greatest — and perhaps the wisest and most moderate — of all imperial peoples. The assumption that, without the veto of the United States, Latin America would have been added to this far-flung dominion appears somewhat gratuitous. Nor can it ever be regarded as flattering to the pride of those whom Monroe described as "our southern brethren." The citizens of Argentina, or of Chile, or of Brazil, it is high time for us to realize, resent the complacency of the Anglo-Saxon which compares them in the latter half of the nineteenth century with the dusky denizens of Central Africa, or with the fellaheen of Egypt, or the betel-chewing inhabitants of Burma. They are ready to assume, as many Americans, alas! are not, that their claim to independence, and their ability to make it good, are not precisely those of Sudanese or Kaffirs. They believe that they could have defended themselves; perhaps they are right. At any rate, the plain fact of the matter is that nothing in the records of diplomacy indicates, in any positive sense, that the states of Latin America were in any peculiar peril from European ambition in the period which we intend to traverse in this chapter.

The real significance of the period is far otherwise. It consists, in the first place, in the expansion of the Monroe Doctrine at the hands of American statesmen; it consists in the second place in the promulgation of the Doctrine in terms that bore the character of an ultimatum, in the Venezuelan dispute with Great Britain. The new interpretations of the principles of 1823 are the signs of the growing self-confidence of the United States; the unqualified manner in which the Cleveland administration applied it to an insignificant boundary controversy was a landmark in the increasing importance of the principles at home and their increasing importance abroad.

We should begin our study of the new interpretations of the Monroe Doctrine by a retrospective glance at the period already traversed. Down to 1867, Monroe's great dogma had, in the main, been interpreted in very conservative fashion. There were, it is true, some exceptions to this generalization; Polk would have used it, had he been able, to acquire possession of the province of Yucatán — that is, for an adventure, as it must have been, in colonialism; Buchanan would have used it, or might at any rate have used it, for the assumption of imperial responsibilities in distracted and unhappy Mexico. But the American people had rejected any such ideas; and with Seward the Doctrine assumed its original character, and was stamped with every quality of moderation. Perhaps the best illustration of this fact is the attitude which was assumed toward the Spanish-Chilean war which broke out in 1865. This unhappy and unnecessary conflict was, from the first, a struggle over questions of prestige, not questions of territory; [7] and although the Chileans sent a propaganda mission to the United States under the distinguished publicist, Benjamin Vicuña Mackenna, and worked up a certain amount of public sentiment, Seward refused to interfere. In a famous dispatch to Kilpatrick, our minister at Santiago, he laid down conservative and orthodox principles with regard to the Monroe Doctrine. "We concede to every nation," he wrote, "the right to make peace or war, for such causes other than political or ambitious as it thinks right and wise. In such wars as are waged between nations which are in friendship with ourselves, if they are not pushed, like the French war in Mexico, to the political point before mentioned, we do not intervene, but remain neutral, conceding nothing to one belligerent that we do not concede to the other. . . ." [8] Though the disgusted Mackenna came to the conclusion that the Monroe Doctrine was "mostly humbug," [9] the Secretary of State was entirely right. Nothing in the principles of 1823, as construed in the nineteenth century, made necessary or inevitable the interposition of the United States in a war between an American and a European power, if this war were prosecuted for ends other than territorial aggrandizement or the subversion of republican government. Indeed, it was not till the Venezuela blockade of 1902 that a contrary view began to be brought forward, and to receive the approval of at least part of the American people.

The years after 1866, however, saw some interesting additions to the great American dogma. The first of these, a highly important one, which has received impressive affirmation within the last twelvemonth, is the proposition that territories in the New World are not to be transferred from one European power to another, or from an American to a European power. This conception, it is true, was not entirely novel. Considered in relation to a specific territory, East Florida, it was enunciated as early as 1811 in a resolution of Congress which declared that the United States

could not "without serious inquietude see any part of the said territory pass into the hands of any foreign power." In the note to
Baron Tuyll of the fall of 1823, John Quincy Adams had declared
that the American government "could not see with indifference the
forcible interposition of an European Power to transfer any of the
possessions heretofore or yet subject to Spain to any other European Power." [10] But these declarations could hardly be said to
mark the development of any general principle. In the two messages of President Polk, the same idea appears, this time undeniably in a form that gives it something of a doctrinal character.
But in the case of the message of 1845, the President's statement
awakened very little comment, and in the case of the message of
1848 it was sharply challenged. Furthermore, neither of these communications deals with the type of situation which is likely to be
most menacing in connection with the no-transfer ideal. Neither
has to do with the transfer of sovereignty from one European
power to another.

How little hold the general principle of no-transfer had taken on
the American mind in the period before the Civil War is illustrated by the language of the State Department and of Congress
with regard to Cuba. Statement after statement can be found in instructions to American ministers abroad declaring that the United
States would never permit the cession of this precious island to any
other power. In not one of these instructions is there any reference
to the Monroe Doctrine. In the debate on the Cass resolution for
the reaffirmation of Monroe's declaration occasional allusions to
Cuba occur.[11] But they are insignificant in number, and in the
prolonged debate of 1857–1858 on the purchase of the island,
though speaker after speaker declared his hostility to the alienation of the island by Spain, there is not a single reference to the
principles of 1823. We are warranted, then, in connecting the consolidation of the no-transfer idea with the administration of General Grant, and with the Secretariat of State of Hamilton Fish.

Cynical Europeans, always unwilling to believe that the Monroe
Doctrine is a mere prohibition against the aggression of others,

always ready to assume that it is merely a cover for American expansion, might in the temper of the period after the Civil War have found some support for the idea that, in reasserting the no-transfer principle, the United States was merely marking out for itself a right of reversion to the possessions of others in the New World. The idea that the American continents belonged to the Americans, that their connection with Europe would become more and more tenuous and would finally dissolve altogether, was a not unnatural consequence of the self-confident republicanism that followed the victory of the North. "Comprehensive national policy," wrote Johnson in his message of 1868, "would seem to sanction the acquisition and incorporation into our Federal Union of the several adjacent continental and insular communities as soon as it can be done peacefully, lawfully, and without any violation of national justice, faith, or honor." [12] "Our city can be nothing less than the North American continent, with its gates on all the surrounding seas," declared Sumner.[13] The formation of the Dominion of Canada, thought General Banks, was contrary to the interests and the future expansion of the United States; was, indeed, a violation of the Monroe Doctrine.[14] Taking into account this interesting temper, it was more than natural that the more imaginative American statesmen should look askance at the transfer of American territory to any European nation, and should regard the colonies of the New World as marked out, sooner or later, for a happy union with their own political system.

In the days of the Johnson administration, however, no public pronouncement was made on the matter. Secretary Seward desired to acquire by purchase the Danish West Indies, and twice in the course of his negotiations he stressed American objections to the transfer of the islands to any European power, even declaring that "*no* transfer of colonies in the West Indies between European powers can be indifferent to the United States." [15] But these declarations remained in the files of the State Department, and had, in all probability, no contemporary influence. It was left to the next administration to take a definite and categorical stand on this important corollary to the principles of 1823. The first expression of this stand had to do with Cuba, involved in 1868 in a desperate struggle for liberty against the archaic government of Spain. Alluding to the Cuban war in his message of 1869, President Grant declared: —

The United States have no disposition to interfere with the existing relations of Spain to her colonial possessions on this continent. They believe that in due time Spain and other European powers will find their interest in terminating those relations and establishing their present dependencies as independent powers — members of the family of nations. These dependencies are no longer regarded as subject to transfer from one European power to another. When the present relation of colonies ceases, they are to become independent powers, exercising the right of choice and self-control in the determination of their future conditions and relations with other powers.[16]

This declaration did not connect the no-transfer idea specifically with the message of 1823. But soon the connection was to be made, in reference to the President's famous passion for the acquisition of Santo Domingo. The details of this extraordinary and rather shoddy episode in Grant's administration we do not need to examine here. As happened on other occasions, the Dominican leader in power, in this case Buenaventura Baez, sought to buttress his position by selling his country to a convenient purchaser. The disagreeable aroma of land deals and private ambitions clung to the whole transaction. But the President had the most fantastic ideas as to the desirability of acquiring the territory in question. On very tenuous evidence, evidence refuted by the documents in the German Foreign Office, he persuaded himself that the North German Confederation had its eye on Samaná Bay.[17] In a message of May 31, 1870, he declared the annexation of Santo Domingo to be "an adherence to the Monroe Doctrine." In the same message, he declared, "the doctrine promulgated by President Monroe has been adhered to by all political parties, and I now deem it proper to assert the equally important principle that hereafter no territory on this continent shall be regarded as subject to transfer to a European power." [18]

Grant was destined to suffer a severe defeat on the Dominican question. The treaty of annexation was rejected in the Senate. But the no-transfer principle was not, on this account, abandoned by the administration. On the contrary, in a long and able memorandum of July 14, 1870, addressed to the Senate of the United States, Secretary Fish again asserted its validity, linked it closely with the Monroe message and explicitly declared it to be the fixed and unalterable policy of the United States. From that date forward, opposition to cessions of territory to European powers may be considered as an accepted corollary of the message of 1823.

Such a corollary receives today, it is fair to say, the adhesion of the large proportion of the people of the United States. Its reason and logic appeal to most of us. The author of this volume is prepared to endorse it. But we must not blind ourselves to unpleasant facts with regard to it. Obviously, the Grant doctrine, if we are to call it that, is a prohibition upon acts of peaceable transfer which may be perfectly legal in themselves. It is in derogation of the sovereignty of European nations; it can rest only upon an inherent right of self-defense, upon the existence of a vital national interest. On this ground we must sustain it, and on this ground alone. Yet is this ground valid? Yes, most persons would agree, for the area of the Caribbean. But is it valid for regions more remote, for the Falkland Islands, shall we say, for Crusoe's island in the Pacific? Not all Americans would answer this question in the same fashion. Grant seems himself to have limited his doctrine (whether consciously or not we cannot say) by speaking in the two declarations cited above of "this continent" not "these continents." Perhaps he was wise in so doing. As to that only the future can tell.

In actual fact, at least for many years after Grant's declaration, the no-transfer principle can hardly be said to have been seriously tested. There are a number of occasions when the government at Washington appears to have feared that it might be violated. Secretary Fish himself was nervous, for example, lest the Danish West Indies be acquired by Germany, and thrice between 1869 and 1877 instructed the American ministers at Copenhagen and Berlin to warn of the opposition of the United States; [19] similar warnings were twice addressed to the government of the Reich with regard to Santo Domingo; [20] and once notice was given of American opposition to the cession of Puerto Rico.[21] In 1884, the French government was advised that "the acquisition of Haitian territory by France would conflict with the principles of our public policy known as the Monroe Doctrine"; [22] in 1887 rumors of the cession of the island of Tortuga to Great Britain brought forth prudent inquiries at the Court of Saint James's.[23] In 1888 rumors of a French protectorate over the black republic led Secretary Bayard to instruct the American Minister at Paris to "leave no doubt with regard to the attitude of the United States upon these important topics." [24] But in every one of these cases the administration at Washington appears to have acted on rumors which had no basis in substance. It was well, no doubt, that it did act; it was worth while to iterate and reiterate the no-transfer idea; but it cannot be seriously stated that in any one of the instances just cited anything in the nature of a cession of territory was really intended.

In a very minor case, however, the new formula for the protection of American interests was ignored. In August of 1877, the government of Norway and Sweden ceded the island of St. Bartholomew to France. Since, seven years before, Fish had expressed his opposition to any transfer of this little territory to Italy,[25] it is probable that the transfer was undertaken, not in ignorance of, but in disregard of, the position of the United States. At any rate, the American government was not consulted; it was not even informed until after the treaty was signed; and Secretary Evarts, then in control of the State Department, acquiesced in the *fait accompli*, doubtless on the reasonable ground that so unimportant a change of ownership was hardly likely to provide a good occasion for the assertion of a novel principle in intercourse with a foreign government.[26] Not until the rise of German naval power, and the re-emergence of the question of the Danish West Indies at the close of the century, was the opportunity to be given to assert in unqualified terms the essence of the declaration that was made by Grant and Fish in 1869 and 1870.

Yet the emergence of this new corollary to the Monroe Doctrine was a symbol of the growing self-confidence of the United States; it signified, as has been pointed out, that the right of reversion to European colonies in the New World might conceivably be claimed by this country; it demonstrated the growing American sensitiveness to any violation of the concept of the two spheres. And before long this corollary was followed by another, unknown to the generation that preceded the Civil War. The Americans discovered for the first time that European participation in any project for an interoceanic canal was a violation of the Monroe Doctrine.

In the decades of the forties and fifties, militant and mild administrations alike had been perfectly content to accept the principle of an interoceanic canal under international supervision. When James K. Polk negotiated the treaty of 1846 with New Granada, it will be remembered, he was wholly ready to see the guarantee of the isthmus which he then extended to that state participated in by France and Great Britain.[27] Four years later John M. Clayton negotiated a compact with Great Britain which distinctly provided for joint protection of interoceanic communication across Central America; and this compact was ratified by the Senate by the decisive vote of 42 to 12. But the new nationalism of the postwar epoch took a very different view. As early as 1868 William H. Seward negotiated a treaty with Colombia which gave to the United States the sole right of constructing a canal, justifying his action on the ground that the Clayton-Bulwer Treaty did not apply to regions so far south. This treaty, however, was never ratified; and it was not till some years later that the canal question was thrown into the forum of international discussion, with the dramatic enterprise of Ferdinand de Lesseps.[28] That great engineer became identified with the project for the building of an inter-oceanic waterway in 1879. In that year an International Engineering Congress met at Paris; declared in favor of the Panama route, to the disgust of some of the American representatives there present; and paved the way for the activities of the French concessionaires who had made an agreement with the Colombian government the year before. A canal built by European capital and guaranteed by European powers was thus projected. After years of discussion it seemed as if at last the dream of transisthmian communication were about to be solved through the genius of the great Frenchman.

But in the United States these events were watched with a sour and a jaundiced eye. A rival company was organized for the construction of a Nicaraguan canal; General Grant was invited to accept the Presidency, and in August, being then in the course of his famous tour around the world, telegraphed his willingness to do so; in Congress voices began to be heard invoking the Monroe Doctrine, especially the voice of Senator Burnside of Rhode Island, the unhappy Union commander at Fredericksburg seventeen years before. The construction of a canal by European capital under the protection of a European government or by the authority of a European charter was, in Burnside's opinion, "dangerous to our peace and safety." Five million men would rally against such "foreign intervention." "Having perfected and strengthened our own existence, having attained a high standard of moral and intellectual excellence, we must not permit any infringement on our rights on this continent, or suffer any steps to be taken on any part of it which will interfere with progressive independence, civil or religious." [29]

The language of Senator Burnside may appear to some persons a bit perfervid. But there is no doubt that thoughtful students of public affairs were considerably aroused by the de Lesseps project. Edwin Lawrence Godkin was certainly no jingo. Yet he wrote in the *Nation* of February 5, 1880, with regard to an interoceanic canal, "We must be prepared to protect it against the evil of local revolution, and foreign aggression, and seize it when necessary, and successfully defend it against the two greatest naval powers of the world." [30] Senator Bayard of Delaware, later to be Cleveland's Secretary of State, was no jingo. Yet he took the same view. "Our power may be questioned, but it will be maintained. Every counsel of wisdom, therefore, exhorts us to 'seize the day,' and in time of peace prepare for war, for it is the surest way to avert it." [31] The *North American Review* was no fire-eating periodical. Yet it took a similar stand to that of Bayard and Godkin.[32] The *New York Times* was no yellow journal. Yet it, too, opposed the project of de Lesseps. In Congress a flood of resolutions attested the state of popular feeling. Cautious and conservative, President Hayes himself, and his equally cautious and conservative Secretary of State, Evarts, took a positive stand for a canal under American control. "The United States," wrote the President in his message of March 8, 1880, "cannot consent to the surrender of this control to any European power or to any combination of European powers. . . . The capital invested by corporations or citizens of other countries in such an enterprise must in a great degree look for protection to one or more of the great powers of the world. No European power can intervene for such protection without adopting measures on this continent which the United States would deem wholly inadmissible." This language was definite enough. But Hayes, frigid though he generally was, went further. "An interoceanic canal across the American Isthmus," he declared, "will essentially change the geographical relations between the Atlantic and Pacific coasts of the United States and between the United States and the rest of the world. It would be the great ocean thoroughfare between our Atlantic and Pacific shores, and virtually a part of the coast-line of the United States. Our merely commercial interest in it is greater than that of all other countries, while its relations to our power and prosperity as a nation, to our means of defense, our unity, peace, and safety, are matters of paramount concern to the people of the United States." [33]

In this important declaration, strong as it was in its terms, there was no mention, it will be observed, of the Monroe Doctrine. Hayes never connected the Doctrine with the canal. But there were plenty of persons who did. Indeed, it is not too much to say that the canal question was responsible for the most voluminous literature on the principles of 1823 which had yet appeared. Three periodical discussions appeared in the fall of 1879 and the spring of 1880, and a year later John A. Kasson, an important member of Congress, a leading Republican, contributed two articles to the *North American Review* in which he sought to prove the applicability of the great American formula to the question of the Isthmus. The language of this sober and sensible man with regard to the Doctrine is well worth quoting. "In every conflict of European with American interest on the two Western continents," he declared, "our countrymen make their appeal to the Monroe Doctrine. It is quoted as the supreme, indisputable and irreversible judgment of our national union. Among the very few maxims which serve to guide public opinion in our country, this ranks as the chief. . . . It has also taken fast hold on the popular mind. A President of the United States, justly appealing to it in an emergency, could not fail of unanimous following of patriotic citizens, even in the presence of a consequently impending war." [34]

Views such as these were echoed in the Congress of the United States; they were expressed in Congressional resolutions; they were affirmed in Congressional hearings. They indicated a tremendous popular interest; and they were sooner or later to lead to diplomatic action. By the time the Hayes administration went out of power, indeed, the plot had decidedly thickened. Secretary Evarts had tried to come to an agreement with Colombia for an American canal; the Colombian Minister at Washington had declared that his government adhered to the Monroe Doctrine; [35] but when he signed a protocol which recognized in rather sweeping language the special position of the United States, he went further than those in Bogotá dared go; and the instrument that he had negotiated was subjected to numerous mutilations by the Colombian Senate. Fears of American hegemony animated the breasts of the statesmen in Colombia; and the more the United States complained of a European guarantee of a canal, the more desirable such a guarantee seemed. Dichman, our minister, reported that negotiations were to be undertaken with the principal courts of the Old World looking towards the neutralization of the projected waterway, and, confronted with this situation, Secretary Blaine, Evarts' successor, hastened to make the position of the United States clear. In a circular of June 24, 1881, he reiterated the statement that the canal would be virtually a part of the coastline of the United States. A treaty of international guarantee, he somewhat extravagantly declared, would be regarded as "of the nature of an alliance against the United States," and "as an indication of unfriendly feeling." And then, in language which distinctly suggests the Monroe Doctrine, the Secretary pointed out that "while . . . observing the strictest neutrality with respect to complications abroad, it is the long-settled conviction of this government that any extension to our shores of the political system by which the great powers have controlled and determined events in Europe would be attended with danger to the peace and welfare of this nation." Directing the American representatives to give "discreet expression" to these views, the dispatch went on to say that the policy indicated "is nothing more than the pronounced adherence of the United States to principles long since enunciated by the highest authority of the government, and now, in the judgment of the President, firmly confirmed as an integral part of our national policy." [36]

This effort to connect the Monroe Doctrine with the canal question, and to emphasize this connection to foreign powers, was not particularly effectual. The Continental powers made no reply to these representations; Lord Granville, the British Foreign Secretary, after one of those long and tantalizing delays which all too often characterized British diplomatic manners toward the United States, responded that "the matter in question had already been settled by the engagements of the Clayton-Bulwer Treaty." [37] There for a time the matter rested, and in his instruction of November 10 to Lowell, Blaine turned aside from the principles of 1823 to plead for the modification of the treaty engagements of 1850.

But Frelinghuysen, who came into office at the end of 1881, imprudently attempted the tactics that had proved none too effectual when employed by his predecessor. In a long instruction of May 8, 1882, he brought the Monroe dogma once more into the center of the picture, and precipitated a new and, as it happened, none too fortunate discussion.

The views which were entertained by President Monroe [replied Lord Granville in language which was not without its logic] have not always been accepted by his successors; nor have the same views always been entertained either by the American Congress or by the Secretaries of State of the United States; but the mere fact that a treaty was concluded between this country and the United States in 1850 (twenty-seven years after the so-called "Monroe Doctrine" was enunciated), for the express purpose of establishing communication by ship-canal across the isthmus of Central America, and of jointly protecting any such communication which might be made, is a clear proof that neither the American administration of that day nor the United States Congress which sanctioned that treaty considered that they were precluded by the utterances of President Monroe in 1823 from entering into such a treaty with one or more of the European powers. How, then, can it be said, at the present day, that the Clayton-Bulwer treaty is opposed to the "Monroe Doctrine"? [38]

The effort to use the authority of Monroe's name in defense of an American-controlled canal must be pronounced to have been unsuccessful; as Buchanan had failed in 1854, as Seward failed in 1861, so Frelinghuysen failed in 1882, when he sought to inject the principles of 1823 into an international discussion. And it ought frankly to be stated that the position which he had assumed did not have the unanimous backing of his own countrymen, and aroused anything but friendly comment abroad. In America there were, from the first, skeptics about the applicability of the Doctrine to the canal question. E. L. Youmans, the able editor of

Popular Science Monthly, pooh-poohed the idea; [39] so, too, did Allen Thorndike Rice, editor of the *North American Review;* [40] so, too, did the venerable Gustave Koerner, whose comment derived authority from the fact that he had been minister to Spain in the years of the Civil War.[41] With men like these aligned on the other side of the argument, it is not surprising to find European periodical comment anything but acquiescent. The *Edinburgh Review* pronounced the appeal to the Doctrine to be "singularly inappropriate"; [42] a scholarly article in the *Preussische Jahrbücher,* written with more detachment, came to the same conclusion; [43] and a writer in another German review indulged in a slashing attack on the principles of 1823, which he pronounced to be nothing more than a propaganda for democratic and Protestant ideas, and for American hegemony, and declared to be incompatible with peace in the New World.[44]

Yet, despite refutations of the thesis at home and abroad, the idea that the Monroe dogma was connected with the Isthmian question took hold, and it was to be reiterated, by such a distinguished American as Theodore Roosevelt, in the debates at the close of the nineteenth century which finally led to the abrogation of the Clayton-Bulwer Treaty and to the conclusion of another compact which gave the United States what it wanted — uninterrupted and unchallenged control of any interoceanic canal. While we may not agree, then, with the logic of those who injected the Doctrine into the discussion of 1880 and 1881, we must recognize that the invoking of it was a factor in the crystallization of American public opinion. We must, indeed, recognize something more. We must concede that the interests of the United States were well served by its invocation. It was desirable, highly desirable, that a transisthmian waterway in the New World should be controlled by this country; those who devoted themselves to this end were animated by a clear sense of reality; and there would be few Americans indeed today, in this age of triumphant force and possible foreign menace, who would not willingly concede that the statesmanship of Hayes, of Blaine and of Garfield, of Frelinghuysen, of McKinley and Hay in later days, of Roosevelt himself, was directly toward a desirable goal. In the strictest of logic, a case could be made out against tying up the canal question with the principles of 1823; but just the same we shall not regret that the thing was done. Logic, after all, is not life.

We need not follow the course of the canal question in its detail after 1882. The Arthur administration followed up its diplomatic note writing by negotiating in 1884 the famous Frelinghuysen–Zavala Treaty with Nicaragua, which looked to an American-owned and American-controlled canal, and was a flat violation of the Clayton-Bulwer Treaty; but it was unable to secure the assent of the Senate to an agreement thus brashly put forward in violation of a previous compact, and the Cleveland administration reverted to a more cautious policy. The project of de Lesseps met with serious obstacles, and finally collapsed in the midst of a great scandal; the peril of a French-owned and French-operated canal evaporated. Never, in point of fact, had the French government taken any hand in the project; only two weeks after Hayes's message, the French Minister at Washington, Outrey, had given assurance that his government "in no wise proposes to interfere therein [that is, in the canal project] or to give it any support, either direct or indirect." [45] This attitude, so far as we can say, was consistently maintained.

The theory of no-transfer, the theory of an American-controlled canal — these are two of the new expressions of the principles of 1823 in the years between 1865 and 1895; to these two must be added a third, only adumbrated and not yet sketched in. This is the theory of preventive action, as it may be called; the theory that, in order to avoid embarrassing situations, the United States should act to forestall the use of armed force by European powers in the New World. It was not the theory of William H. Seward, as we have already seen; it did not take shape in any complete form until the administration of Theodore Roosevelt; but it was beginning to appear in the period we are now reviewing. There are a number of episodes that help to make this clear.

The first of these is the attitude assumed by Secretary Fish toward a possible common diplomatic front of European powers against Venezuela in 1871. That republic, at the time we speak of, was a prey to one of the most ferocious of its civil wars, in which, as was to be expected, the property and persons of foreigners had not escaped unscathed. On the first of June, Baron Gerolt, the German envoy in Washington, spoke to Secretary Fish concerning a circular sent by his government to its representatives at London, Florence, Madrid, and Copenhagen, "proposing a joint and concerted movement to urge on Venezuela a more orderly government" [46] and better observance of her engagements. Whether coercion was intended he did not make entirely clear, but at least once in the course of his conversation he alluded to a "combined fleet" and "guns." [47] He also asked whether the United States would be disposed to receive such a proposal.

In reply to this overture Secretary Fish did not deny the right of Germany to make diplomatic representations to Venezuela, or even to wage war against her; but he did declare that "the United States could not look with indifference upon any combination of European powers against an American state"; [48] if Germany's proposal looked to "a forcible demonstration of coercion by a combination of European states, the United States could not regard it with indifference." [49] In this language he clearly displayed American distaste for common action by European states for the redress of grievances in the New World. Four years later, when the ebullient Venezuelans got into a row with Holland, and when military action threatened, Fish offered his good offices to prevent the use of force by the Dutch.

Fish's action was emulated by Evarts, his immediate successor, and in still more striking fashion by James G. Blaine. Evarts proffered good offices in 1877 in a dispute between the German and Nicaraguan governments which looked as if it might have led to coercive action; Blaine acted vigorously when a new critical situation drew attention once again to the affairs of Venezuela. In the year 1880 that republic revised its schedule of payments to its various creditors, and at the same time brought forward the proposal that the United States should receive and disburse the sums due the respective governments. In answer to this application the State Department went beyond the original suggestion, and in June, influenced no doubt by the dire prophecies which came from Caracas of coercive action which would be "naught else but an occupation of American territory by a European state," [50] offered to assume direct administration of the Venezuelan customs. The idea, so important in the twentieth century, died a-borning at this time; Secretary Frelinghuysen, who soon succeeded Blaine, was not favorable to it; the Venezuelans appeared unenthusiastic; other expedients for the satisfaction of the creditor states were found feasible. But the view which the "man from Maine" had taken was, in essence, a new interpretation of the Monroe Doctrine.

We must not imagine, however, that, speaking broadly, the United States, in the period with which we are dealing, pursued a consistent policy looking to the discouragement of a show of force against American republics by the states of the Old World. The recurrent chastisement of the Haitians, for example, never seems to have been regarded with much emotion in Washington. France in 1869,[51] Spain in 1871,[52] Germany in 1872,[53] Great Britain in 1877,[54] France, Spain, and Great Britain in concert in 1883,[55] Russia in 1885,[56] Great Britain again in 1887,[57] resorted to force or the threat of force against the black politicians of Port-au-Prince without a word of protest from the State Department. The British in 1874, the Germans in 1878, the French in 1882, made minatory gestures against the Nicaraguans without arousing any concern in the United States. The Italians had a short-lived brawl with Colombia in 1886 which awakened no mention of the Monroe Doctrine. The French used coercive measures against the Dominican Republic in 1893 without the lifting of a hand at Washington. In principle, the United States opposed no veto during the nineteenth century to the punishment of the unruly states of the New World for their misdeeds or their turbulence. A new point of view was suggested, but it had not crystallized in doctrine.

And now we come to the last of the significant reinterpretations of the principles of 1823 which fall within the period we are considering, the famous controversy with Great Britain over the Venezuela-Guiana boundary. The story is one that needs to be told in some detail, and its background must be sketched in. The first discussions with regard to the matter took place in the eighteen-forties. At that time a boundary line had been drawn by the British geographer, Sir Robert Schomburgk, a line perhaps not illiberal to Great Britain. But Venezuela had protested, and the British government, not violently excited about the whole matter, proposed a compromise. The compromise was rejected; in 1850 both parties agreed not to encroach upon the disputed territory, and a long period of silence followed. But in 1875 the colonial government of British Guiana sent a small force into the disputed zone to recapture a criminal, and immediate protests issued from Caracas, accompanied by claims that the British boundary was on the Maroco, far to the east of the Schomburgk line. Sometime later gold was discovered in the disputed region; and while the presence of this mineral could not alter the legal or moral aspects of the question, it is a historical fact that Foreign Offices sometimes respond to impulses outside the legal and moral sphere. New discussions between the Venezuelan and the British governments took place; it cannot be said that all was reason on the one side and unreason on the other; Great Britain was, at one time at any rate, ready to yield the mouth of the Orinoco, and to fix the boundary very substantially to the east of the line of 1841. But the Venezuelans were intransigent and persistent; disgusted with efforts at negotiation, the British responded by proclaiming the Schomburgk line as the boundary in 1886, and a rupture of relations followed.

During all this period of discussion the authorities at Caracas did not forget the interest of the United States in the Monroe Doctrine. In 1876,[58] in 1880,[59] in 1881,[60] in 1884,[61] on three different occasions in 1887,[62] Venezuelan Ministers in Washington made appeal, sometimes explicitly, sometimes in terms not quite so definite, to the principles of 1823. For the most part, especially at the outset, these appeals were far from efficacious. At the expiration of his term of office, Secretary Evarts did indeed allude, in a note to the Venezuelan Minister, to "the deep interest which the Government of the United States takes in all transactions tending to attempted encroachments of foreign powers upon the territory of any of the republics of this continent," and declared that "this Government could not look with indifference to the forcible acquisition of such territory by England." [63] But no action followed. Under Secretary Frelinghuysen there were suggestions of arbitration, but great caution in going further. To the Venezuelan Minister, indeed, Frelinghuysen once stated that though "the moral position of the United States in these matters was well known through the enunciation of the Monroe Doctrine . . . formal action in the direction of applying that doctrine to a speculative case" would be distinctly "inopportune." [64] Secretary Bayard, who directed American policy in 1886 and 1887, was perhaps slightly more excited. Toward the end of the first-mentioned year he called the attention of the British government to "the doctrines we announced two generations ago, at the instance and with the cordial support and approval of the British government," and coupled this with the assurance that these doctrines had "lost none of their force or importance in the progress of time." [65] But these suggestive sentences were followed by expressions of confidence in British good faith, and a suggestion that American good offices might be accepted in the settlement of the controversy. The rupture of relations between Great Britain and Venezuela made the acceptance of any such suggestion improbable, and in February 1887, indeed, Lord Salisbury definitely refused it.

In the main, the controversy simmered during the six years between 1887 and 1893. Congress first took note of the matter in 1888, when the House of Representatives passed a resolution calling for information and reaffirming the Monroe Doctrine; [66] Secretary Bayard confessed to "grave disquietude" [67] in a dispatch to

Phelps, our minister in London, at about the same period; the Venezuelan Minister at Washington continued to indite laborious notes in which the principles of 1823 figured prominently.[68] For a moment in the fall of 1891, it appeared that Secretary Blaine, professionally a twister of the lion's tail, might interest himself in the matter; but he seems soon to have regained his tranquillity, and in January 1892 instructed Scruggs, our minister at Caracas, to express no opinion upon the boundary controversy.[69] Secretary Gresham, when approached, as he soon was, with new appeals for the defense of American righteousness against European wickedness, appeared for a time but mildly interested in the matter; and nothing more than a renewal of American good offices was suggested by the message of President Cleveland in 1894.

But with the autumn of this last-named year new forces began to be set in motion; and in particular the Venezuelan government engaged to assist its cause an individual whom the vulgar might describe as a propagandist, but who was to Venezuelans, of course, legitimately engaged in educating American public opinion. This gentleman was William L. Scruggs, erstwhile our minister at Caracas. Detached from his post with the incoming of the Democrats, he was in August of 1894 made the legal adviser and special agent of the Venezuelan government at Washington. By October he had prepared and was disseminating a pamphlet, *British Aggressions in Venezuela, or the Monroe Doctrine on Trial*. It went to the editors of newspapers and periodicals; it appeared in the mail of members of Congress; it found its way to the desks of governors of the various states; it received a place upon the shelves of clubs and libraries; it was sold upon the newsstands. It ran through four editions before December. Nor did Scruggs stop there. In January he sought out his Congressman, Livingston of Georgia, and on the tenth of January this statesman introduced a resolution "most earnestly" recommending arbitration to Great Britain and Venezuela; [70] on the sixth of February, this resolution was unanimously passed by the House of Representatives.[71] The surrender of the Monroe Doctrine, declared Livingston himself, would be "such a surrender of national prestige as would make us the jest of the civilized world. . . . Such an act of pusillanimity" he was sure "the people of the United States would never ratify." [72] Whatever the people of the United States might do, the Congressman was certainly right as to its politicians; on the thirteenth of February he had the satisfaction of seeing his resolution pass the Senate, here too by a unanimous vote; [73] on the twentieth it received the signature of President Cleveland.[74] The action of Congress produced its reaction in the press; by March the newspapers were beginning to take up the cudgels for the Monroe Doctrine; [75] on the twentieth of that month the question was discussed in the cabinet; and some time later, the rather lethargic but resolute temper of the Chief Magistrate of the Republic was stirred by an interview with Scruggs himself.[76] Secretary Gresham, so long indifferent, began to prepare a note to Great Britain upon the Venezuelan question; and it may be that his untimely death in May postponed a genuine crisis in our relations with the Court of Saint James's.

But Gresham, whatever his purposes, would have been suave in manner; his successor, Richard Olney, was more remarkable for forthrightness than for moderation; and his natural acerbity of temper may perhaps have been stimulated by the spirit of partisan rivalry. For as he set to work on instructions to Bayard in London, there appeared in the *North American Review* an article from the pen of the young Senator Henry Cabot Lodge.[77] This article was, perhaps, chiefly remarkable for the number and the grossness of its historical errors in tracing the evolution of the Monroe Doctrine; but it was distinguished, too, by a violent indictment of British imperialism, and the forthright charge that the object of British policy was the control of the mouth of the Orinoco. "The American people," concluded the Senator, "are not ready to abandon the Monroe Doctrine, or give up their rightful supremacy in the Western hemisphere. On the contrary, they are ready now to fight to maintain both." [78]

That Olney was definitely influenced by the language of Lodge

is something that cannot be proved. But the note which he prepared for Lord Salisbury was written in a similar spirit; though
shown to the President, who suggested "a little more softened
verbiage here and there," [79] it was not substantially altered by discussion; and it was forwarded to Bayard on July 20, 1895.

The Secretary of State incorporated in this remarkable instruction an historical description of the Monroe Doctrine. This description arrests the attention, but does not always command the
approval, of the historian; yet it was less remarkable than the conclusions which were drawn from it. It is still a moot question today
whether the boundary dispute between Great Britain and Venezuela was, as Olney asserted, "in any view far within the scope and
spirit of the rule [of the Doctrine] as uniformly accepted and
acted upon." [80] Though Colonel Lindbergh might approve the remark, the statement that "distance and three thousand miles of
intervening ocean make any permanent political union between a
European and an American state unnatural and inexpedient" was,
in view of the connection between Great Britain and Canada, very
far from a proposition that "would hardly be denied." [81] Nor were
Olney's generalizations on monarchical Europe and democratic
America as convincing in 1895 as they would have been in 1823.
The declaration that the republics of Latin America were "by
geographical proximity [*sic!*], by natural sympathy [*sic!*], by similarity of governmental constitutions" [*sic!*] the "friends and allies"
of the United States carried with it some exaggeration. Nor would
these republics, jealous of their own independence as they were,
accept without some demur the assertion that "the United States
is practically sovereign on this continent, and its fiat is law upon
the subjects to which it confines its interposition." [82]

But Olney was writing, not a historical tract, but a diplomatic
communication for the instruction of Great Britain, and also — one
cannot help believing — for the edification of the American people. Like the aggressive lawyer that he was, he put the case in
terms of the utmost vigor; he sought to arouse the languid interest
of Lord Salisbury and the pride of his countrymen. The picture

that he painted of the consequences of British success in the controversy with Venezuela was indeed a lurid one.

> The disastrous consequences of such a condition of things are obvious [he wrote]. The loss of prestige, of authority, and of weight in the councils of the family of nations, would be the least of them. Our only rivals in peace as well as our enemies in war would be found located at our very doors. Thus far in history we have been spared the burdens and evils of immense standing armies and all the other accessories of huge warlike establishments. . . . But with the powers of Europe permanently encamped on American soil, the ideal conditions which we have thus far enjoyed cannot be expected to continue. We too must be armed to the teeth, we too must convert the flower of our male population into soldiers and sailors, and by withdrawing them from the various pursuits of peaceful industry we too must practically annihilate a large share of the production energy of the nation.[83]

There are few Americans, I believe, who, reading this famous instruction today, will not find the language somewhat overstrained as related to a boundary dispute between Venezuela and Great Britain, with regard to territory largely jungle, and remote from civilization; but Olney's conclusion was less extreme than his premises, for what he asked of the British was, after all, nothing more nor less than the arbitration of the matter in issue. He asked this, as was his nature, in a tone that was anything but persuasive; the threat of force lay in the closing lines of the note which described the British assertion of title as "injurious to the interests of the people of the United States as well as oppressive in itself"; [84] it was hardly veiled in the sentence which declared that "while the measures necessary or proper to the vindication of that policy [that is, the Monroe Doctrine] are to be determined by another branch of the Government, it is clearly for the Executive to leave nothing undone which may tend to render such determination unnecessary"; [85] but the demand put forward by the United States was not, after all, a demand to which the British government could not in dignity accede.

Lord Salisbury, however, who directed the foreign policy of

Great Britain in 1895, was a British Tory of the most supercilious type. An old hand at the diplomatic game, he was as unmoved by bluster as he was untouched by any misleading idealism. To move him to action was difficult; and although the communication of the Olney note was followed in course of time by an unmistakable press polemic against Great Britain, the British Foreign Secretary allowed months to pass before he deigned to answer the communication of the American Secretary of State. To do him justice, he apparently meant to have his answer ready for the administration with the opening of Congress in December, but, through casualness or ignorance, the date of the reassembling of that body was misunderstood; and though the answer was drawn up on November 26, it was sent through the mails instead of by cable and had not arrived in Washington at the beginning of the session. That Olney and Cleveland were somewhat chagrined at this cavalier treatment, as it seemed to them, was natural; and their feelings of resentment could hardly have been allayed by the language of the British Foreign Secretary. For Lord Salisbury, in a tone that was decidedly cocksure and perhaps patronizing, proceeded to traverse the arguments of Olney in no uncertain fashion. The Monroe Doctrine, he declared, had no more to do with the case than the flowers that bloom in the spring. The question was "simply the determination of the frontier of a British possession which belonged to the Throne of England long before the Republic of Venezuela came into existence." [86] To argue thus was bad enough; but worse, and more harrowing to the feelings of the President and his adviser, was to come. Not content with challenging the relevance of the Monroe Doctrine to the Guiana boundary controversy, Salisbury went on to challenge the Monroe Doctrine in general. "In the remarks which I have made," reads one of the most significant paragraphs in the note of November 26, "I have argued on the theory that the Monroe Doctrine itself is sound. I must not, however, be understood as expressing any acceptance of it on the part of Her Majesty's Government. It must always be mentioned with respect, on account of the distinguished statesman to whom it is due, and the great nation who have generally adopted it. But international law is founded on the general consent of nations; and no statesman, however eminent, and no nation, however powerful, are competent to insert into the code of international law a novel principle which was never recognized before, and which has not been since accepted by the Government of any other country. . . . The Government of the United States is not entitled to affirm as a universal proposition, with reference to a number of independent states for whose conduct it assumes no responsibility, that its interests are necessarily concerned in whatever may befall those States simply because they are situated in the Western Hemisphere." [87] Such language could hardly be otherwise than wounding; and though the British Foreign Secretary, in a sentence more gracious than most that he penned, admitted that changes in the territorial distribution of the New World would be "highly inexpedient," [88] there was no mistaking his challenge to the principles of 1823, or his refusal to arbitrate the dispute with Venezuela. He was right in his contention (to day most Americans would admit this) that the Monroe Doctrine was not international law; but he had been more anxious to score points in a diplomatic argument than to facilitate the settlement of a dangerous controversy; he had dealt rather with syllogisms than with substance; and his imperious tone, however gratifying to his own pride and intelligence, was to prove neither serviceable to Great Britain nor even capable of being maintained in practice with the unfolding of events. President Cleveland, indeed, was "mad clean through" as he read the reply of Lord Salisbury, and in Congress and in the press, though the terms of the British reply had not been made public, the clamor against Great Britain was increasing. It was clear that a genuine crisis in the relations of the United States with Great Britain was approaching.

Here and there, it is true, the voice of moderation occasionally made itself heard. Ambassador Bayard sought to temper the ardor of the administration in a letter to the President, written on De-

cember 5. "Our difficulty," he declared, "lies in the wholly un-
reliable character of the Venezuelan rulers and people, and results
in an almost undefinable, and therefore, dangerous responsibility for the conduct by them of their own affairs." [89] John Bas-
sett Moore, most distinguished of American international lawyers,
sought to persuade the administration of the error of its ways
through a letter to the Postmaster General. He pointed out the
extravagance of Venezuelan claims in the course of the controversy; the lack of precedent for the arbitration of a boundary controversy where no line had been previously determined; the fact
that so far as the mouth of the Orinoco was concerned (the point
of maximum geographical sensitiveness), Great Britain had frequently offered to yield the point. [90]

But the President and the Secretary were in no mood to listen
to such counsels; and on December 17 the President transmitted
to Congress a message in which he reasserted the American position, defended the Monroe Doctrine as finding "its recognition in
those principles of international law which are based upon the
theory that every nation shall have its rights protected, and its
just claims enforced," and made it clear beyond all question that
the United States was prepared, in case of British refusal to arbitrate its dispute with Venezuela, to examine the whole matter
independently, through the agency of an investigatory commission, which should report upon the matter with the least possible
delay.

When such report is made and accepted [the President declared] it
will, in my opinion, be the duty of the United States to resist by every
means in its power, as a willful aggression upon its rights and interests,
the appropriation by Great Britain of any lands or the exercise of governmental jurisdiction over any territory which after investigation we
have determined of right belongs to Venezuela. . . . In making these
recommendations I am fully alive to the responsibility incurred and
keenly realize all the consequences that may follow. . . . I am, nevertheless, firm in my conviction that while it is a grievous thing to contemplate the two great English-speaking peoples of the world as being

otherwise than friendly competitors in the onward march of civilization and strenuous and worthy rivals in all the arts of peace, there is no calamity which a great nation can invite which equals that which follows a supine submission to wrong and injustice and the consequent loss of national self-respect and honor, beneath which are shielded and defended a people's safety and greatness.[91]

The language of Grover Cleveland met with an instantaneous response from the greater part of the American people. It is the fearful responsibility of a President of the United States that he often may, if he will, call popular passion to his support; it is possible that a period of depression, such as that of 1895, is one in which the appeal to the instinct of bellicosity is particularly easy, and it is certain that the press, with few exceptions, rang with approval of the stand which had been taken. In the Senate, upon the reading of the message, the usual decorum of that body was interrupted by what the London *Times* correspondent described as "the most spontaneous demonstration" in the memory of living Senators. [92] In the House there was similar enthusiasm, and on the very next day, Hitt, the Republican floor leader, introduced a bill for the creation of the investigating commission which the President had sought, and asked unanimous consent for its consideration. Amidst frequent outbursts of applause the bill was passed without a single dissenting vote.[93] In the Upper House much the same scene was enacted, with frequent appeals to the principles of 1823.[94] In the meantime no less than twenty-six state governors, in response to an inquiry from the *New York World,* declared their unqualified support of the administration.[95]

It would not have been surprising if the provocative tone of the President, the virtual ultimatum which he addressed to Great Britain, should have aroused strong resentment amongst the press and the statesmen of the British Isles. Such, indeed, in many quarters was the initial reaction. Papers like the *Times,* the *Telegraph,* and the *Standard* all declared the American position inadmissible,[96] and even "monstrous and insulting." [97] The venerable Gladstone spoke of the "astounding folly" of the President.[98] The

"THE COMPLIMENTS OF THE SEASON!!"

PRESIDENT CLEVELAND. "Waal, Salisbury, Sir, whether you like it or not, we propose to arbitrate on this matter ourselves, and, in that event, we shall abide by our own decision."

A BRITISH VIEW OF THE CLEVELAND MESSAGE

First Lord of the Admiralty, Lord Goschen, felt impelled to take precautions to put the fleet in readiness.[99] But Lord Salisbury, as little prone to nervous agitation as any man in British public life, expressed as early as December 19 the opinion that the excitement in America would "fizzle away"; [100] Mr. Arthur Balfour, his famous nephew, was from the first for conciliation; [101] and Sir Vernon Harcourt, the leader of the Liberal opposition, labored with whole-hearted zeal from the outset for a pacific settlement of the difficulty.[102] There were no such explosions of recalcitrant nationalism among British politicians as among Americans; and when the *New York World,* wisely and in fine public spirit, telegraphed for expressions of opinion from representative Englishmen in behalf of peace, it received replies from such leading churchmen as the Archbishop of Canterbury and the Bishop of London; [103] from such prominent politicians as Lord Rosebery and John Redmond; [104] and even a cablegram from the secretary to the Prince of Wales (later Edward VII) and the Duke of York (later George V), in which these two great figures, beyond the reach of politics, and despite the remonstrances of Lord Salisbury, expressed themselves in unequivocal terms. "They earnestly trust and can but believe," these two important personages were quoted as saying, "the present crisis will be arranged in a manner satisfactory to both countries, and will be succeeded by the same warm feeling of friendship which has existed between them for so many years." [105]

The moderation of British feeling will be set down by those who lean to the economic interpretation of history as the product of the vast British investments in the United States, of the significance of the American market as a source of raw materials, of the close relationship between the banking interests on the two sides of the Atlantic. That such ties existed is undeniable; that they played a part is equally so. But that they tell the whole story seems, at least, doubtful. Something, it appears to the writer, must be set down to sentiment; and the question may well be asked whether, by the close of the nineteenth century, it had not become extremely difficult for the British masses to envisage with complacency a war with the United States, with its similar instinct for democracy, its common language, and its ties of blood.

At any rate, whatever the reason, the Salisbury ministry bowed to the voice of the British people; like the solid, practical man that he was, Salisbury recognized that he had blundered; in the ministry the powerful influence of Joseph Chamberlain was exerted in favor of moderation; the leaders of the Opposition in Parliament were making clear their intention of attacking with vehemence any obstinate adherence to the formulas of the note of November 26; and just at the beginning of January came the famous Jameson raid, the incursion of British filibusters into the Transvaal, and the famous telegram of the Kaiser to President Kruger offering his congratulations on the repulse of the raiders. With pleasure the British press turned to belabor Germany; and perhaps its indignation and irritation made somewhat easier a diplomatic retreat in British relations with the United States. It seems an error to assert that the Kruger telegram was a decisive factor in the Venezuela matter; the tide was running toward conciliation before the telegram was sent; but it certainly did not make more difficult or less congenial the task of the British government.

The first maneuver was an extremely interesting one. Through a go-between, Lord Playfair, Lord Salisbury approached Mr. Bayard with a proposal for an international conference of all nations having colonies in America, on the subject of the Monroe Doctrine. Great Britain would accept the decisions of such a conference, would, indeed, accept the Doctrine itself. To such a conference might be submitted the question whether the Venezuela boundary controversy came within the terms of the message of 1823.[106] The American Minister appeared to be entranced by this proposal. Such action, he thought, "would make it [the Doctrine] binding, not only on them, but practically on all intermeddling alliances in the Western Hemisphere, by European powers under any pretext." [107]

But Olney and Cleveland had no intention of being thus beguiled. Following a line of action by no means original with them, or abandoned by their immediate successors, they fought shy of any action which would submit the principles of 1823 to international definition or international sanction. They were prudent in so doing. For, as we soon shall see, the great American dogma was not received with transports of rapture in Europe; and in any such conference as was proposed the United States might, and probably would, have found itself virtually isolated. "The United States," Olney cabled back, "is content with existing status of the Monroe Doctrine, which, as well as its application to said controversy, it regards as completely and satisfactorily accepted by the people of the Western Continents." [108]

But Mr. Olney, while rejecting the British overture, responded with one of his own. The first transports of enthusiasm over the Cleveland message had now died down. The evidences of dissent had grown stronger. The academic world was, in general, hostile to the principles promulgated by the President; [109] so, too, was the voice of the pulpit; [110] the precipitous decline of the stock market on December 19 and 20, the liquidation of American securities by British holders, had induced reflection; and as early as December 24 Lord Pauncefote had reported that "a strong undercurrent" had commenced to flow "in opposition to the war-like attitude of the President." [111] The Secretary of State of the United States was not insensible to all this; and on January 14, two days after the Playfair proposals, he suggested that in the arbitration which the United States was demanding, provision should be made "that long-continued occupation of territory by Venezuelans or British subjects shall, with all the attending circumstances, be considered by tribunal of arbitration, and be given all the weight belonging to it in reason and justice, or by the principles of international law." [112] This proposal was to serve as the basis of a certain amount of diplomatic haggling; but it offered a starting point for negotiation; and after some months of effort, in which the Venezuelan controversy gradually faded from the public mind and the public prints, agreement was arrived at which prescribed a period of fifty years' occupation as decisive of title. The British had, of course, argued for a much shorter term of years; on the whole, the final understanding was a victory for Mr. Olney.

The outcome of the arbitration itself, in its turn, might be thought to have vindicated, in some degree, the position of the American government. The boundary laid down did not in all respects follow the Schomburgk line; it excluded Great Britain from the mouth of the Orinoco and substantially altered the limits of Guiana in the extreme south; it restricted, in other words, the claims of the British government. Men will no doubt continue to debate whether this was an indispensable satisfaction of American interest or merely a convenient gratification to American pride; the policy of Cleveland will continue to be praised as the preservation of American principles and the protection of a weak American republic, and to be condemned as an unnecessarily risky and bellicose interference in a dispute which concerned neither the Monroe Doctrine nor the well-being of this country; but it cannot be denied that the action that the President had taken preserved to Venezuela territory which might otherwise today belong to Great Britain. Nor is it without significance that a similar boundary controversy between France and Brazil was settled a few years later by arbitration.

Whatever else one may say, moreover, the Venezuela crisis was full of momentous consequences. As a diplomatic episode it is of the first importance. In the first place, it stimulated and aroused the national pride of the United States, and marks the beginning of that more sensitive national consciousness and that more militant spirit which were, in less than three years' time, to express themselves in the war of 1898. One indication of this new spirit is to be found in the acceleration of the movement for a larger navy which followed on the enunciation of the principles of 1823. The disparity between the British and the American armed forces in 1895 had been shocking indeed. The Americans, one blushes to write, had just one modern battleship to pit against the mighty navy of Britain. But the Congress of 1895–1896 appropriated funds for three first-class battleships and ten torpedo boats; and while such appropriations could be only a beginning, they have none the less a significance of their own. The enforcement of the Monroe Doctrine rests fundamentally upon sea power. This fact was beginning to be recognized. These were the days of Alfred Thayer Mahan, and of his tremendously influential historical analysis of the role of naval force in human affairs. And those who adopted his viewpoint, and who accepted his famous thesis, were almost invariably the friends of the principles of 1823. Mahan himself was a disciple of Monroeism. In part owing to his influence, in part to the events just recorded, Americans began to take cognizance of the necessity of backing up their favorite dogma with physical force.

Abroad, the Venezuela message was a reminder, and a striking and emphatic one, of the significance in American foreign policy of the doctrine of Monroe. Before we conclude our account of the Venezuela crisis we must see how opinion reacted to it in Europe and Latin America.

On the continent of Europe the general reaction may fairly be described as hostile, fully as hostile, in fact, as it was in Great Britain. In France there was, no doubt, some pleasure at seeing the pride of Lord Salisbury humbled. But the French, like the British, had their boundary dispute in South America, between the colony of French Guiana and Brazil; they were, as has been said, to settle it by arbitration a few years later, perhaps in deference to American opinion; but they did not relish Cleveland's tone. Accordingly it was pointed out in the press and in learned periodicals that the Monroe Doctrine was a mere *"ex cathedra* pronouncement," [113] and it was even declared that Olney's construction of it "suppresses the law of nations." [114] The attitude of the President was described as "haughty and aggressive"; the Olney note was "a new manifestation of American chauvinism." [115] The semi-official *Temps* declared that there might well "be occasion for the Cabinets of the powers to examine, calmly and uninfluenced by any external pressure, up to what point they allow a precedent to pass by which might afterwards be brought up against them." [116] *La Politique Coloniale,* which represented the opinion of such eminent politicians as Gabriel Hanotaux and Raymond Poincaré, stated definitely: "Europe cannot admit that their intervention [that is, the intervention of the United States] should assume aggressive form, founded on a doctrine which tends to nothing less than the confiscation of territories lawfully belonging to nations who have occupied them, and who make them productive at the cost of heavy sacrifice." [117] The president of the republic himself had his critical word to say. "Who will put his trust," he asked the German Ambassador, "in a country, of which the highest executive in an ugly mood or for election purposes will plunge the country into a devastating war?" [118]

If French comment was caustic, so too was German. The newspapers almost without exception denounced the "over-weening pride" of the United States [119] and the "jingoism" [120] of the message; the jurist Ludwig von Bar declared the Monroe Doctrine to be "an arbitrarily invented principle, proven absolutely worthless hitherto" and "irrational" and an act of "usurpation." [121] The German nationalist and navalist, Ernst von Halle, wrote in the autumn of 1896 that "there ought to be an authentic interpretation of the views of the European cabinets, as to the fashion in which they are ready to accept the Monroe Doctrine as a recognized principle of the Law of Nations, as well as a clear assumption of the position that there is a limit beyond which the protagonists of Pan-Americanism will have to face a Pan-European intervention." [122] It was in the year 1896, too, that the great Bismarck, from his retirement, denounced for the first, but not the last, time the principles of 1823; and though the official policy of the German government was wholly circumspect, the signs multiply of the growth of that Pan-German spirit which began to cast its shadow over the republics of the New World.

In the case of France and Germany, self-interest might easily dictate the tone of criticism that we have just been noting; but foreign offices and foreign observers more detached from American events took the same view. In Vienna, the *Fremdenblatt,* often semiofficial in its utterances, declared that the Monroe Doctrine "had never before been carried, even in America, to such lengths as at present"; [123] Professor Lammasch, the leading Austrian authority on international law, declared the Doctrine to be only "a political program," and not international law; [124] Francis Joseph and Count Goluchowski, his Foreign Minister, condemned the position of the United States as "in defiance of the law of nations," [125] and from Rome the American Minister reported "a general solidarity of sentiment adverse to the position our Government has assumed." [126] In Spain, in Holland, even in Russia, newspaper comment reflected a highly critical attitude.[127] From the angle of European opinion it is fair to say that the Cleveland message contributed to the intense dislike, based largely on jealousy, with which the United States was already regarded in Europe.

One might imagine that this dislike was compensated for by the favor with which the states of Latin America received the message of 1895. Certainly Cleveland's message had its enthusiasts in the countries to the south. The Venezuelans, naturally, were enchanted; a crowd of no less than 20,000 persons gathered in front of the American legation, and expressed themselves so enthusiastically that the building was nearly wrecked.[128] The Venezuela Academy of History held a special meeting to voice its "profound gratitude"; [129] a great demonstration in favor of the United States took place on Christmas Day.[130] In Colombia the same spirit prevailed; there were laudatory editorials in the papers, and Colombian publicists and poets united in paying homage to the "spirit of elevated justice" and "magnanimity" of the American President.[131] In Brazil, in both houses of the national legislature, resolutions were passed endorsing the President's stand; [132] in Peru the American Minister reported "cordial endorsement" of the position of the United States; [133] in Central America similar sentiments prevailed.[134] But the chorus of praise was not unanimous, so far as the American republics were concerned. In Mexico, in Argentina, and in Chile the prevailing tone of criticism was suspicious and hostile, the language used premonitory of much that was to come later. In Mexico, there was a natural uneasiness at the renascent nationalism of the great nation of the North, which tempered the enthusiasm of press and politicians; in Chile, there were memories of the strained relations which had been precipitated by the Valparaiso riots of 1891; and in the Argentine, which even thus early was beginning to aspire to that leading role which is still the object of its ambitions, the approval of the American action was less profound than jealousy of the role of the United States. Ex-President Pellegrini, indeed, went so far as to declare the Monroe Doctrine to be "an anachronism"; it had, in his opinion, "no longer a *'raison d'être.'*" "There is not today a European Power," he asserted, "that could or would attempt to conquer territories belonging to nations whose independence all have recognized." [135]

Distrust, rather than confidence, is indicated also in the rather pathetic Congress which met in Mexico City in 1896. This gathering was attended only by the representatives of Ecuador, Santo Domingo, Mexico, and Central America (one delegate representing three of these states). It drew up a report upon the Doctrine which, along with much very bad history, suggested that the principles of 1823 were becoming dangerously broad and vague. "Such is the juridical novelty, so extraordinary is the political importance, of such immense significance for the future is the development of these affirmations, not included in the primitive text of the Monroe Doctrine, or even in its spirit," it declared, "that they imperatively demand the convocation of a conference from which there can come some definitive concert of views, and perhaps some treaty which would raise into the category of legal formulae proposals which look to guaranteeing the security and well-being of the contracting states." [136] At the same time it was suggested that study should be given to the right of intervention of the American peoples in the "destiny and political affairs of each." [137] Such language betrays only too clearly a nervous dread of the overweening power of the Colossus of the North.

The point is one that deserves to be underlined. Conscious of our own good intentions, as Olney, no doubt, was conscious of his, we

Americans in general expect Latin Americans to be grateful for the extension of our protecting arm; so, on occasion, perhaps, they are; but protection is not far removed from overlordship, and the note of national superiority which Cleveland's Secretary of State struck all too clearly in his note of the twentieth of July undoubtedly operated to counterbalance the element of disinterestedness which beyond all question existed in that communication. Never, perhaps, was the United States less actuated by economic gain or territorial ambition, or even by a sense of danger to its security, than in the Venezuela controversy; but in this cynical world of ours it is always easy to believe the worst of others; and even when our intentions are purest, the greatest circumspection is necessary in appealing to the principles of 1823 if we are not to offend the tender pride of the nations to the south. This is a truth that American statesmen have of late years gone far toward learning; but it cannot be said that it had been assimilated by Grover Cleveland or Richard Olney.

Yet in the case of Latin America, as in that of Europe, the Cleveland policy certainly marked one step further in the widening of the knowledge of the Doctrine. It is, of course, ridiculous to say, as the report of the Mexico conference said, that the Doctrine had appeared to be dead, or at least antiquated; it had, as we have had occasion to see, been very much alive throughout the whole period which we have traversed; but its significance, though known to European chancelleries, was as yet, perhaps, insignificantly appreciated by them. What it meant to the American people, how it could enter into their emotions, how it could become an article of faith, was no doubt not fully realized until 1895. Understood it had been, and only too clearly, to the plotter of the Tuileries in the years of the Civil War; not unknown to Granville or Ferry or other Europeans, not unknown to Juárez and Romero; but hardly measured in its full power. Lord Salisbury, after all, was a seasoned diplomat; but he had the bad judgment to challenge a great idea. His error was soon retrieved, and, as we shall see, the statesmen of Britain united to pay lip service to the principles of 1823. But it is after all significant that they did not realize, after the note of July 20, just what it was they were facing. It was the message of December 17 that roused them from their indifference, electrified not only Britain, but Europe and Latin America, and placed the Monroe Doctrine on a new pinnacle of regard in the United States. The historian, always more observer than judge, may think what he will of the wisdom of that policy; but he will be bound to admit that it marks an epoch in the history of the great American dogma.

VI

*The Shadow of Germany—and Other Matters
The Turn of the Century*

The Monroe Doctrine should be the cardinal feature of the foreign policy of all the nations of the two Americas, as it is of the United States. Just seventy-eight years have passed since President Monroe in his annual message announced that "the American continents are henceforth not to be considered as subjects for future colonization by any European Power." In other words, the Monroe Doctrine is a declaration that there must be no territorial aggrandizement by any non-American Power at the expense of any American Power on American soil. It is in nowise intended as hostile to any nation in the Old World. Still less is it intended to give cover to any aggression by one New World Power at the expense of any other. It is simply a step, and a long step, toward assuring the universal peace of the world by securing the possibility of permanent peace on this hemisphere.

During the last century other influences have established the permanence and independence of the smaller States of Europe. Through the Monroe Doctrine we hope to be able to safeguard like independence and secure like permanence for the lesser among the New World nations.

This doctrine has nothing to do with the commercial relations of any American Power, save that it in truth allows each of them to form such as it desires. In other words, it is really a guarantee of the commercial independence of the Americas. We do not ask under this doctrine for any exclusive commercial dealings with any other American State. We do not guarantee any State against punishment if it misconducts itself, provided that punishment does not take the form of the acquisition of territory by any non-American Power. . . .

Probably no other great nation in the world is so anxious for peace as we are. . . . Our people intend to abide by the Monroe Doctrine and to insist upon it as the one sure means of securing the peace of the Western Hemisphere.

— THEODORE ROOSEVELT, *Annual Message of 1901*

1. THE SPANISH-AMERICAN WAR AND THE DOCTRINE

THE YEARS at the end of the nineteenth and the beginning of the twentieth century are among the most interesting and important in the history of American diplomacy. They are years in which a period of caution and inaction, generally speaking, is followed by one of intense and fateful activity. From 1865 to 1895 there is hardly a major diplomatic crisis in the annals of our foreign policy. Between Cleveland's Venezuela message and the year 1903 or 1904, in the brief space of less than a decade, momentous decisions were made which reshaped the policies of the nation. In 1895, when Olney fired his twenty-inch gun, as he liked to call the note of July 20, the country had long been at peace. A new generation had grown to manhood since Lee gave over his sword to Grant at Appomattox; and a new wave of vigorous nationalism was preparing of which Lodge and the youthful Theodore Roosevelt were sufficiently typical. Out of this new nationalism came the war with Spain, a "splendid little war," as John Hay lightheartedly called it, insignificant, perhaps, in the military annals of the United States, but by no means insignificant in its diplomacy. As a result the American people for the first time assumed political responsibility for communities beyond the mainland of the American continent. They woke up in 1899 to discover that they were the actual possessors of a colony in the Caribbean, of the island of Puerto Rico; and though they kept their pledge that Cuba should be given its freedom, in withdrawing from the island they reserved the right to intervene in its affairs in case things went sufficiently wrong. Almost contemporaneously with these new commitments came the Hay-Pauncefote Treaty, which assured complete American control of any transisthmian canal; and shortly after that treaty was signed covert encouragement was given by the Roosevelt administration to revolution on the Isthmus, and the building of the canal itself was begun under circumstances which suggested that the Americans intended to brook no interference with their objectives on the part of Latin-American states. In these same years American interests widened in the region of the Orient. The battle of Manila Bay aroused the acquisitive instincts of the American people; in July Hawaii was annexed; and by acquiring the Philippines the United States gave hostages to fortune on the other side of the Pacific and found itself impelled to a higher degree of diplomatic activity there. In 1900 came the Boxer Rebellion; here again the American government did not remain indifferent, and the march of American troops to the relief of the legations in Peking was the symbol of a new policy; the Open Door notes of John Hay had a like significance. With Europe, also, there came about momentous changes. American delegates appeared at the First Hague Peace Conference of 1899, consorting with wicked Europeans on the very soil of the Old World; they participated in the discussion of the problem of armaments, a problem largely European; and, after more than three quarters of a century of uneasy, if by no means strained, relationships, the two Anglo-Saxon peoples began to talk of mutual association for mutual benefit; and an entente, if not an alliance, seemed to be forming between the United States and Great Britain. Not literally for the first time, but certainly for the first time in striking fashion, the rising power of Imperial Germany began to be questioned on this side of the Atlantic; a growing prejudice against this new, prosperous, and ambitious state affected the decisions of the State Department and the judgment of the American people. More than ever, Americans became suspicious of European purpose in the New World; more than ever they viewed with dislike the use of force by European powers, if only for limited ends, in their disputes with the states of Latin America; and more than ever, in this regard, the principles of 1823 began to figure in the public mind. In the course of a little more than half a decade the scope of American diplomacy was widened, and its spirit in some degree transformed.

We shall not seek, we have already said, to explain this phenomenon. Our friends, the economic determinists, so right in a measure, so wrong in assuming that the part contains the whole, would doubtless point in particular to the expanding vigor of American finance and industrial capitalism. They would emphasize the fact that the confident nationalism of the turn of the century was associated with the quest for widened markets; they would point to our investments in Cuba; they would underline the enthusiasm of American businessmen, at any rate by the fall of 1898, for a commercial entrepôt in the Orient; they would, of course, recall to our attention the notes of John Hay; they would, quite correctly, associate the building of the canal with the needs of an expanding commerce. They would, indeed, go even further; they would suggest that the entente between Great Britain and the United States was based, in part, upon their close financial and commercial relationships, and in part upon the hope of a partnership in commercial imperialism; they would call attention to an expanding trade interest in Latin America, of which an illustration was the Pan-American Exposition of 1901; they would see economic jealousies at the root of American-German suspicions and rivalry. And, in part, they would of course be right. But such an explanation of the American nationalism of the period must be regarded as incomplete. It explains much, beyond all question; but it is doubtful whether it can account completely for the enthusiasm with which the mass of the people embarked upon new courses of action in these fateful years. Accepting the importance of the economic factors, the movement of opinion seems so broadly based, so widely diffused, as to be insufficiently explained by these factors alone. Moods count for much in the formation of national policies.

After many years of tranquillity, the American people awakened from their quietude, and by some deep impulse began to play a larger part in world affairs.

In the movement of American imperialism, as cynical Europeans, at any rate, denominated the events of the Spanish-American War, the Monroe Doctrine figured far less than might have been expected. As we have already seen, it had more than once been made to serve the purposes of American expansion — by Polk in 1845, by Buchanan in the late fifties, by Grant in the question of Santo Domingo. It would not have been strange if, as the American people and the administration of President McKinley became more disposed to intervene in Cuba, they had rationalized their own desires by assuming some sinister purpose on the part of others, some ambitious design on the part of some European state. But in fact no such design existed; and, the principles of 1823 aside, the interposition of the United States in the Cuban question rested upon pretty solid grounds, upon the dangers and inconveniences of a revolt at our own doors, upon the shocking barbarities of the Cuban struggle, upon our large economic interests in Cuba, and our duty to protect our citizens. To mention these is not to accept them unqualifiedly; but in the eyes of American opinion they were apposite and convincing. The McKinley administration, then, steered clear of the dogma of Monroe; and in Congress there was a similar attitude. Save for a singularly forced reference in the report of the Senate committee recommending intervention in Cuba, the Doctrine was hardly mentioned. That body issued its veto against the "recolonization" of any part of the island by Spain,[1] an obvious reference to the principle laid down by Adams seventy-five years before; it also declared that, just as the balance of power justified intervention by European states in the affairs of one or another of their number, so the Doctrine was "a distinct announcement that the United States would intervene, under certain expressed circumstances, in the affairs of every Central American and South American State." [2] This dictum was a curious application of the Monroe principle; it found literally not an echo in the deliberations of the Senate itself. Indeed, when debate took place on the war resolution the Doctrine was not once mentioned in the House, and only rarely at the other end of the Capitol. Only Senator Lodge, always so acutely aware of peril to the great dogma, in some mysterious fashion managed to connect it with what was developing in the Caribbean.[3]

On the other side of the Atlantic, European publicists, by this time fully aware of the declaration of 1823, were able to prove to their own satisfaction that American intervention in Cuba not only was not justified by, but was forbidden by, the language of Monroe. Had not the President stated in his famous message, "With the existing colonies or dependencies of any European power, we have not interfered, and shall not interfere"? Was it not then an unwarrantable extension of the language of the celebrated Doctrine to meddle in Cuba? "We are witnessing," wrote one of these publicists, "the last evolution of the Monroe Doctrine; it was to have been foreseen. Up to now the government of the Union consented not to meddle in the relations of Europe with its American colonies, provided that it was permitted to decide freely as to the interests of American states. More confident in its strength, it becomes still more demanding, and soon America for the Americans or America for the United States of the North will become an absolute truth, without exception." [4] Language such as this might be set down to the general hostility with which Continental Europeans looked upon the American intervention in Cuba; but it is interesting to discover that in the remarkable work of Herbert Kraus, published fifteen years after the Spanish War, and one of the best studies of the Doctrine by a European, the thesis just set forth is supported, and the conduct of the United States in 1898 declared to be "an extraordinarily drastic and obvious repudiation" of the principles of 1823.[5]

Was there any validity in this viewpoint? I, for my part, do not believe there was. It is not reasonable to quote the words of Monroe with regard to the then existing colonies of Spain as if they constituted a self-denying ordinance for the future. The very men who promulgated the Doctrine, or were later to embroider it, would have been prompt to declare that the day might come when the United States would take possession of Cuba. They would have indignantly repudiated the idea that they had made a resolution of abnegation with regard to that fertile and important island. They were not making promises of any kind to Europe; they were stating a national policy, which, like any other policy, might be subject to the modifications of time and circumstance. It is a mere trick of semantics which makes of the war with Spain a violation of the great Presidential declaration. We need not maintain, we ought not to maintain, as did here and there an ardent patriot, that since the essence of the great dogma lies in the separation of the two spheres, in America for the Americans, that the expulsion of Spain from the New World was an inevitable consequence of Monroe's language; decidedly it was not, as the President's reference to existing colonies shows; but we can fairly say that it was prejudice, not reason, which led European critics to brand the intervention in Cuba as repudiation of the principles of 1823.

With regard to the situation in the Far East, in the debates of this period, the Doctrine was more frequently cited to check, rather than to encourage, American imperialism. The argument brought forward, both in this country and abroad, was a simple one. If the United States were to impose a veto on European intermeddling in the New World, was it not therefore implied that the American government should keep out of Europe and out of Asia? Was not the annexation of Hawaii a violation of our traditional policy? Was it not an abandonment of the theory that lay at the basis of our foreign policy? So argued Senator Allen of Nebraska, in the debates of July 1898.[6] So argued Senator Bate of Tennessee. Was it not "glaring inconsistency" to act in this fashion? Was it not "piracy in violation of" the famous dogma? Was it not the rifting of "our hitherto gnarled and unwedgeable oak," the declaration of President Monroe?[7] And if this were true with regard to Hawaii, was it not even truer, *a fortiori*, with regard to the Philippines? In the historic debate on the treaty of peace with Spain this view was frequently and eloquently expressed. "The Monroe Doctrine is gone," exclaimed that great champion of the anti-imperialist viewpoint, George Frisbie Hoar. "Every European nation, every European alliance, has the right to acquire dominion in this hemisphere when we acquire it in the other," [8] and Senator Berry of Arkansas echoed these words.[9] The *Springfield Republican,* brilliant and independent journal, spoke of "the smashing of the Monroe Doctrine." [10] The *Boston Herald* declared that to take the islands would be "such a departure from our traditional policy" as would "rend the Monroe Doctrine from top to bottom." [11] The *St. Louis Republic* declared that the American people would "think long before they exchange the right to guard the Western Hemisphere for the right of partnership in the colonizing schemes of European monarchies." [12]

If American statesmen and editorial writers could take this view, it is not surprising that such a thesis was eagerly adopted abroad. As early as August 2, 1898, a writer in the *New York Tribune* was complaining that it was the common assumption among English writers on international politics that Monroeism was dead. A cartoon in *Punch* depicted Dame Europa in conversation with Uncle Sam. "Who are you?" says the lady. "Uncle Sam," is the reply. "Ah! any relation to the late Colonel Monroe?" is the next inquiry. On the continent the same reasoning was brought forward. The *Kölnische Zeitung,* even before the war with Spain, had declared that there was a fatal inconsistency in devotion to Monroe's pronouncement and overseas expansion at the same time.[13] The *Kreuz Zeitung* thought the treaty of peace with Spain a "throwing out of the window" of the principles of 1823.[14] The Emperor himself thought that the Doctrine "had been ceremoniously buried." And on the other side of the Rhine, the author of the first important French work on the American dogma called attention to the fact that the Presidents had always set forth "in deference to the prescriptions which they impose, their perpetual disinterestedness in extra-American affairs." [15]

Were the Americans and Europeans who took this point of view

DOCTRINE AND PRACTICE

DAME EUROPA (*coldly*). "To whom do I owe the pleasure of this intrusion?"
UNCLE S. "Ma'am – My name is Uncle Sam!"
DAME EUROPA. "Any relation of the late Colonel Monroe?"

A BRITISH VIEW OF THE DOCTRINE IN 1898

sound? Was the acquisition of the Philippines in derogation of America's traditional policy? Again the answer, I believe, should be emphatically in the negative. There are many persons, distinguished students of American foreign policy like Professor Samuel F. Bemis, who regard the McKinley policy of colonialism as one of the major mistakes of our diplomacy, since it extended our commitments into a remote region in which it would be difficult to operate in time of war. On this point there is a great deal to be said. But it is not necessary to argue that this policy involved an abandonment of Monroeism. After all, Monroe could never have dreamed that his maxims had any application whatever to the regions of the Pacific; their only antithesis, if any, was between America and Europe. Moreover, the fact that the United States had special interests in the Americas which it sought to defend by appropriate measures did not mean that it had no interests whatever elsewhere; if we grant, what we do not need to grant, that there was a principle of mutuality in the Doctrine, this principle would apply to Europe but not to the Orient. Men might differ and differ reasonably as to the ethical aspects of the American policy of "imperialism"; but even the most severe critic of that policy could hardly claim that the retention of the Philippines was the violation of any pledge to the Old World. It might, perhaps, be maintained that the United States, having followed the European precedents and gone in for the acquisition of territory in the Far East, was in a less favorable position to protest those precedents should they be applied to America; but to any such line of reasoning the easy answer would be that in America American interests remained vital, no less vital than before. And so of course it was in practice. For the United States *did* acquire the Philippines, it *did* continue to demand of European powers respect for the Monroe Doctrine; the notion that the one policy annulled the other may have been a point for argument by jealous Europeans and by anti-imperialists, but it was to be refuted by events themselves.

2. The Monroe Doctrine and The Hague Conference

It is interesting that the McKinley administration not only had to consider the question of whether the Monroe principles stood in the way of a policy of colonial expansion; it also had to ask itself what was the relation of these principles to movements for the consolidation of world peace. In facing this problem, the President and his advisers proceeded at the outset on the wholly reasonable assumption that there was no fundamental incompatibility between the American dogma and the search for a better international order. Why should it be thought that President Monroe would have opposed a veto on American attendance at any European gathering whatever? What necessity was there for taking such a position? Where were the historic precedents for it?

The historic precedents, so far as they existed, may be said to have pointed in the opposite direction. Though Frederick H. Seward, the son of the great Secretary of State, had held up action on American adhesion to the great Red Cross conventions, apparently because he thought he remembered that his father considered such action contrary to the Doctrine,[16] these conventions had been ratified in 1882, and James G. Blaine, in speaking of the matter to Clara Barton, had declared sententiously that "the Monroe Doctrine was not made to ward off humanity." [17] The United States had attended the Berlin Conference of 1884 and 1885 on the opening up of Africa, though it had not adhered to the general act which resulted.[18] McKinley and John Hay, the Secretary of State, had support for their position when they accepted the invitation of the Tsar to the first Hague Peace Conference. The distinguished delegation which set out thither was in fact instructed to promote the creation of an international tribunal of arbitration, and in the draft of this proposal it was stated that "the contracting nations will mutually agree to submit to the international tribunal all questions of disagreement between them, excepting such as may relate to or involve their political independence or territorial integrity." [19]

Yet from the conference at The Hague was to come the first of those reservations by which the government of the United States has sought to bar any international agency from the consideration of the principles of 1823. The position that these principles are, in no circumstances, to be subjected to international review, or international adjudication, has had a great influence upon American participation in later projects of international organization; it has certainly impeded the free co-operation of the United States in such projects, as we shall clearly see; and the raising of this question at the conference of 1899 has, therefore, a very considerable historical importance.

The conventions which were drawn up at The Hague can hardly be regarded as revolutionary in character. The most important of them, perhaps, was a Convention for the Pacific Settlement of International Disputes. By Article 27 of this document, in the event of a serious dispute breaking out between two or more of the powers, the signatory states were to "consider it a duty" to call it to the attention of the disputants that the Permanent Court set up by the Convention was open to them, and this reminder was only to be regarded as a friendly act. No obligation existed to act on this reminder; the machinery of arbitration of which the Permanent Court was the nucleus was purely voluntary. The fact must be underlined, in order to understand what followed.

The dominating member of the American delegation at The Hague was Admiral Alfred Thayer Mahan, a friend of expansion and imperialism, an advocate of the "large policy" and militant nationalism that connects itself also with the names of Theodore Roosevelt and Henry Cabot Lodge. On July 22 Mahan called the attention of his colleagues to the portentous Article 27, and expressed the opinion that it was "likely to be considered as an infringement of the Monroe Doctrine." At this idea, the delegation was "greatly perplexed," said Andrew D. White, its chairman. "We fear," he wrote, "lest, when the convention comes up for ratification in the Senate of the United States, some over-sensitive patriot may seek to defeat it by insisting that it is really a violation of time-honored American policy at home and abroad — the policy of not entangling ourselves in the affairs of foreign nations, on this side, and of not allowing them to interfere in our affairs, on the other." [20] There was, of course, an answer to this apprehension. One might have expected of a distinguished college president and friend of international peace that he would have seen that answer. If "an over-sensitive patriot" brought forward any such contention as was feared, it might have been replied to him that to boggle over the mere interposition of good offices, especially when there existed not the slightest obligation to accept those good offices when offered, was to reduce almost to a nullity the hope of progress toward international peace. And it might also have been suggested that the Senate of the United States could be trusted to make any reservations that American national interest required, without bringing forward such reservations at The Hague itself. But these reflections either did not occur to President White and his associates or else they were overridden by their keen sense of the importance of the principles of 1823. On the morning of July 24, the head of the American delegation "scratched off with a pencil" a declaration to be made by him at the signing of the Convention; in its original form it did not really meet the necessities of the case, speaking merely of the American policy of nonintervention in European affairs, but Seth Low suggested an addition to the effect that "nothing should be considered to require any abandonment of the traditional attitude of the United States towards questions purely American," [21] and in this form, it was agreed, the reservation should be presented. After a sleepless night for Andrew D. White the day of signing came, and as soon as the final act had been read, the Russian secretary of the conference presented the American declaration. "The conference was asked whether any one had any objection, or anything to say regarding it. There was a pause of about a minute, which seemed to me about an hour. Not a word was said — in fact, there was a dead silence — and so our declaration embodying a reservation in favor of the Monroe Doctrine was duly recorded and became part of the proceedings." "Rarely in my life," wrote White some time later, "have I had such a feeling of deep relief; for, during some days past, it has looked as if the arbitration project, as far as the United States is concerned, would be wrecked on that wretched little article 27." [22]

In days when naked force seems once again to rule so much of the world, when across the Atlantic the spirit of international conciliation seems exhausted, and the peace of Europe through the free co-operation of the nations hardly more than an iridescent dream, the American reservation at The Hague in 1899 may well appear of slight importance. Yet it still may be said of it that never was a reservation to an international treaty more thoroughly inexcusable, and none set a worse fashion for the future, so far as the American role in the peace movement was concerned. The Monroe Doctrine contains at its heart sound and enduring principles of action; it has a deep significance today, as it has had in the past; but it is, in my judgment, thoroughly regrettable that it should have been invoked then, and was to be invoked in the years ahead, unduly to hamper and thwart the movement for the pacific settlement of international disputes. The reason of course is not difficult to discover; the Doctrine is the expression of national interests which to most Americans appear centrally significant; the years at the turn of the nineteenth century were years in which the current of national feeling ran strong; but the position assumed at The Hague can only be regarded as hypersensitive.

In the months following The Hague Conference, the extraordinary claim was put forward that, by their silence at the conference, the nations of Europe had recognized the validity of the principles of 1823. Frederick W. Holls, secretary to the American delegation, in an article published in the *Review of Reviews* for November 1899, declared that it had been "officially communicated to the representatives of practically all the great powers," and "received with all the consent implied by a cordial acquiescence and immediate and unanimous adoption of the treaty upon that condition." [23] "Our traditional foreign policy," he declared, was "announced, vindicated, and maintained more clearly and emphatically than ever before." [24] Two years later, Theodore Roosevelt advanced a similar contention in his first annual message to Congress. Occasionally, Latin-American publicists, such as the distinguished Alejandro Alvarez and the equally distinguished Luis Drago, endorsed this thesis; [25] and at least one eminent European international lawyer came to the same conclusion. [26]

But there are many dissenters from any such hypothesis; and both reason and history support them. In a matter so important as the international recognition of the Monroe Doctrine, a unilateral act cannot be thought of as sufficient; the language of the American declaration was vague; it is hardly to be believed that the powers of the Old World would accept, and accept by silence, principles whose precise extent and character were left undefined; it needed more than the minute of speechlessness which Andrew D. White described to bring about the general acceptance of the American dogma. The chancelleries of Europe in the years to follow certainly did not all of them either act or speak as if they had accepted the principles of 1823 at The Hague; nor was this ever claimed by American statesmen in any diplomatic document. Had such a claim been put forward, it would, in all human probability, have been rejected. Respect for the American position there certainly was; but acquiescence in it as a binding legal formula was an entirely different matter.

Nonetheless, it is significant that in the McKinley administration, for the first time, the principles of 1823 should be brought into the discussion of the great problems of international action for the preservation of world peace; and, whether one likes the fact or not, it must be admitted that the idea behind the reservation offered at The Hague took hold. It was, indeed, only one manifestation of the intense popular interest in, and approval of, the ideas which lay at the heart of Monroeism.

3. GERMANY AND THE DOCTRINE

At the turn of the century, as we have just seen, American opinion may be described as in the highest degree sensitive to any threatened invasion of the Doctrine. In the minds of many, a new menace to its tenets was appearing on the horizon. Abandoning the ancient jealousy of Great Britain, many Americans began to look with a deep and dark suspicion upon Imperial Germany. The story of our relations with the government at Berlin is, in many of its aspects, closely related to the evolution of the principles of 1823.

At the moment at which these words are written, the free peoples of the world are ready, and quite naturally ready, to believe the worst of those in the seats of power at Berlin. They have seen the public faith cynically and brutally flouted; they have seen the democratic principle not only menaced, but destroyed, in most of Europe; they know that the rulers of Germany, succeeding where they can by violence, are seeking also by intrigue to advance their view and purposes, and to eat away the foundations of the traditional order of things. In such an atmosphere it would be only too easy to intrude the passions of the present into the recollection of the past, and to interpret the policy of the Germany of forty years ago in terms of the same sinister and aggressive ambition that terrorizes so much of the world today. But history must be loyal to serenity and truth; and if it is thus loyal it will not describe the policy of Germany under William the Second in terms that are applicable to the genius of a Hitler. Forces there were in Germany which foreshadowed the dour events of our own day, the forces of Pan-Germanism and militarism; but these cannot be said to have directed, though of course they influenced, the foreign policy of the Reich.

But let us turn from generalities to specifics and ask ourselves precisely what was the point of view of Germans toward the Monroe Doctrine at the end of the nineteenth century. We shall have to begin with the observation that there were in the Reich powerful elements anti-American in spirit. The German *Junker* or landholding class, for example, could hardly be expected, from either an economic or a political point of view, to admire the United States; American institutions were repugnant, like American exports of foodstuffs; and American nationalistic formulae were also, of course, anathema. We have already seen how Bismarck, an excellent representative of this class, regarded the Doctrine in 1896; it may be interesting to quote some further observations on his part in 1897 and 1898. In the former year, in the *Leipziger Neueste Nachrichten*, he had already described the American dogma as "an extraordinary piece of insolence," [27] but in 1898, shortly before his death, he expatiated on this idea with much force in an interview with Wolf von Schierbrand. The former Chancellor began by denouncing the war with Spain as "indefensible." "And the Monroe Doctrine?" his interrogator inquired. "That is a species of arrogance peculiarly American and inexcusable," Bismarck said wrathfully, and his eyes gleamed. "You in the United States are like the English in that respect; you have profited for ages from dissensions and ambitions on the continent of Europe. That insolent dogma, which no single European power has ever sanctioned, has flourished on them. And how will you enforce it? And against whom? The powers most interested, now that Spain is out of the way, are England and France, the two leading naval powers. Will you drive them off American waters with your pigmy navy? The Monroe Doctrine is a spectre that would vanish in plain daylight. Besides, the American interpretation of this presumptuous idea has itself varied constantly, and has been buried out of sight for many years at a time." [28] Such was the language, no doubt, of an old man who easily vented his spleen; but it was representative of the class for which he stood.

But the *Junkers* were not the only group in Germany which was contemptuous of, or hostile to, the United States. The rising tide of German nationalism at the close of the century had been typified by the movement for a more powerful navy; the future of Germany, the Emperor proclaimed, was on the water; and the leaders of the big-navy movement naturally echoed this view. They had their eyes on a variety of interesting points which might serve as bases for the increasing forces of Imperial Germany. One of these points, for example, was the Danish West Indies, now the possession of the United States. As early as 1896 Ernst von Halle, a leader in the big-navy movement, called attention to their desirability; [29] to acquire them, it was maintained, could not be regarded as contrary to the Monroe Doctrine, because it did not enlarge the area under European control, and second, and rather inconsistently, because the Doctrine had never been recognized by Europeans as a principle of public law.[30] In ignorance or disregard of the no-transfer principle, more influential Germans soon took up the suggestion of von Halle. During the war with Spain, Admiral von Tirpitz, then in the seat of power, suggested to von Bülow, the Chancellor, that the moment had come to pick up a naval base in the Caribbean while the Americans were busy with the freeing of Cuba; the Chancellor remained indifferent, but the activities of the friends of an acquisitive policy continued. In the fall of 1898 was organized what was ostensibly a commercial company, for the exploitation of the trade with the island of St. John; but those behind the venture, especially the fabulous Captain Christmas, a storybook figure of intrigue, made no bones about declaring that the real purpose was the eventual transfer of the territory to Germany. That this little venture had the encouragement of the German Naval Office is beyond question.

Through the treachery of Christmas himself, moreover, it soon became known in the United States. The Danish intriguer in the fall of 1899 came to this country, and talked with John Hay, Admiral Dewey, and Senator Lodge. The result was an outburst of feeling truly remarkable. On April 27, 1900, Secretary Root, at a dinner in New York in memory of General Grant, pronounced the following veiled but hardly equivocal warning. "No man who carefully watches the signs of the times can fail to see that the American people will within a few years have either to abandon the Monroe Doctrine, or fight for it, and we are not going to abandon it. [Cries of hear! hear!]" [31] A few days later Senator Lodge was even more specific. "I think," he said on May 11 in the Senate, "the safety of the United States rests upon its naval strength. . . . The nation of Europe which dares to take possession of those [Danish] islands, and hold them, right there on the road to the canal, and

make of them great naval stations . . . would be by that very act
the enemy of the United States. . . . Such an act by any European
power would mean war. . . . I am by no means convinced that
some European power, perhaps one of those whose navy is just now
receiving a rapid increase, may [not] want to test that [Monroe]
doctrine. . . . I am not conjuring up imaginary dangers. I think
that they exist and are very real." [32] Such utterances von Holleben,
the German Ambassador at Washington, set down as evidences of
a "truly hysterical irritation"; [33] the irritation would have been
greater if all the designs of the German Naval Office had been
known.

For we must not imagine that the Virgin Islands were the only
bit of territory which interested the sea lords at Berlin. In 1899
these gentlemen had their eyes on the Galápagos, important because of the opportunity which they afforded to control the passage
of the projected transisthmian canal; [34] Curaçao also attracted the
roving eye of von Tirpitz. [35] In 1900 the Admiral definitely suggested to the budget commission of the Reichstag the possibility
of a naval station on the coast of southern Brazil. [36] In 1902 he
thought it might be useful to acquire all the possessions of Holland
in the West Indies, Saint Eustatius and Dutch Guiana as well as
Curaçao. [37] And, in a different order of activity, during these same
years, he and his friends played with the notion of encouraging
European capital to undertake the building of the interoceanic
waterway across Panama. [38]

To the *Junkers* and the naval men, fixed in their antagonism to
the United States, must be added a third group, the Pan-Germans,
those apostles of race and German domination whose doctrines and
ambitions were to find their expression forty years later in the
triumph of National Socialism. These men talked and wrote in a
temper and spirit which recked little of the prejudices of American
opinion. Using, as well they could, the steady expansion of German
trade and finance in the countries of Latin America as the justification of their demands, they boasted of the "authoritative position"

which Germany occupied in the republics of the New World.[39] In particular, they called attention to the large number of Germans, over 300,000 by the end of the century, who had taken up their habitations in southern Brazil. They sought to organize German emigration to this promising region; they made it clear that German schools and churches must be maintained; Germany, wrote one author, must regard these settlements as outposts which she "cannot afford to lose, and which she must strengthen by instilling into the minds of the colonists the consciousness that they belong to her, and that with her they stand or fall." [40] Language such as this could hardly be otherwise interpreted abroad than as veiling political hopes and ambitions for the future. Nor was it rare that Pan-Germans, in dwelling on the Brazilian future, made very clear indeed the inevitable competition of German influence with that of the United States, and clearer still the possibility that the maintenance of Germany's interest might conceivably lead to an armed clash with the Americans. The Pan-German agitation was thus closely bound up with the movement for a greater navy which we have already discussed. "Unless our connection with Brazil is always secured by ships of war," wrote Professor Schmoller, "and unless Germany is able to exert pressure there, our development is threatened." [41] "The defense of South America," wrote another German academician, von Schulze-Gävernitz, "is a vital interest for Germany." [42] "We cannot and will not allow ourselves to be shut out from the only portion of the globe still left to us," wrote a third representative of Pan-Germanism, and went on to argue for a great fleet as the only way to prevent such a consummation.[43] That such utterances should have been not without effect, that they should have found their way into American and British periodicals, and even into books, that they should have operated to diminish the cordiality of, if not actually to embitter, American-German relations, is distinctly understandable.

Finally, the Emperor himself from time to time talked as if he belonged to the militants. The Monroe Doctrine, as we have seen, he proclaimed to have been buried at Santiago. "What is necessary for our navy must be done," he declared on another occasion, "even if it displeases the Yankees." [44]

Yet there is, emphatically, another side to the matter. The jingo elements in Germany were noisy and also numerous, but they did not control policy; the Chancellor and the Foreign Office pursued a course which, to the furious nationalists, seemed positively craven in its deference to the United States. Von Bülow and Holstein, the presiding genius of the Wilhelmstrasse, fully realized the sensitiveness of American public opinion. They turned a deaf ear to the solicitations of von Tirpitz and the Pan-Germans; they kept the Kaiser well in hand; and they pursued a wholly reasonable and considerate policy in dealing with the questions of German influence in the New World. The point is one that deserves to be embroidered and filled in.

Take, for example, the question of naval bases. The striking contrast between the attitude of the Naval Office and that of the Wilhelmstrasse is well illustrated by the curious case of the Dominican Republic. Ulises Heureaux, the president of this little state, after nearly two decades of personal rule found his power shaken and menaced. Rebuffed in his proposal of a closer commercial understanding with the United States, he turned in his extremity to Germany, and in the summer of 1898, apparently without any suggestion from any German source, proposed to the government at Berlin that it enter into closer relations with his regime, and be given a coaling station or other concession in return. Confronted with this interesting proposal von Bülow turned at once to von Holleben, and asked him what impression would be created in the United States by the acceptance of the American offer. The answer was unequivocal. The reception of any such step would be "most unfavorable"; in fact, wrote the minister, "I dare not estimate to what extent of hostility public opinion and even the administration would be carried against us." [45] And that was the end of the proposal. It was in much the same fashion that the Foreign Office dealt with the various proposals of von Tirpitz and his fellows. In the matter of the Galápagos, for example, the recommendations of the Naval Office were left six months unnoticed, and then, as in the Dominican case, the matter was referred to the German Minister at Washington. Von Holleben once more advised against action; he had wished the Galápagos to become German, he sighed, twenty years before; but it was now too late. "For the rest, it could not damage our interests, if England broke the Monroe Doctrine through the acquisition of South American islands." [46] In the case of the Danish West Indies, the same attitude was displayed. The acquisition of the island of St. John was discouraged. In this instance, indeed, when a propaganda article appeared in the semi-official journal of the Naval Office, von Bülow demanded of the Emperor that its author be rebuked; [47] and by order of the Kaiser himself he signified to Admiral von Tirpitz that in view "of the existing political and economic tension" such an agitation for the acquisition of territory in the West Indies was "especially inopportune." [48] And Holstein, than whom no one had more influence in the formation of Germany's real policy, was clear as to the necessity of maintaining good relations with the United States. [49] Germany kept her hands entirely free despite the numerous legends to the contrary, when in 1902 the American government negotiated a treaty of cession for the Virgin Islands. [50] If the treaty failed, as fail it did, this was on no account due to the machinations of the Wilhelmstrasse.

In the case of the island of Margarita the Foreign Office went still further. In March of 1901, a German warship taking soundings in these waters aroused the deep and not wholly unjustifiable suspicions of an American naval commander in the same region. "The Germans," as this gentleman observed, "are not much given to unselfish work for the benefit of mariners. . . . They are pressing the Venezuelan government for some claims of a German railway company . . . and being well aware of the feelings toward us on the part of the Castro government, they may offer to compromise by the cession to them of Margarita in perpetuum or 99 years lease." [51] This communication led Secretary Hay to direct the

American chargé in Berlin to make inquiries with regard to the matter, and to state "discreetly and informally, but decisively," that any attempt to carry out such a plan would constitute a source of apprehension to the American government, and might even lead to disturbing the friendly and cordial relationships with the empire.[52] The result was as satisfactory as diplomatic assurances can possibly be. The Wilhelmstrasse made not only a specific but a general denial of all acquisitive ambitions in the New World; in the fall of 1901 von Holleben, acting on instructions, explicitly stated that "all the reports that are circulated concerning German plans of conquest in South and Central America are lies and slanders of our enemies," [53] and on November 18 of the same year the minister, in a public interview, declared that the rumor that Germany was engaged in seeking possession of coaling stations or of any *point d'appui* whatever in South America or in the West Indies was circulated by "ill-disposed persons, who looked with envy upon the highly friendly relations between Germany and the United States." [54] Nothing in the correspondence of the Foreign Office, so the meticulous researches of Professor Alfred Vagts have proved, authorizes us to view with cynicism this positive assurance of the German Ambassador.

Nor is it at all clear that the Wilhelmstrasse was pursuing any ambitious policy in Brazil. In June of 1899, for example, it caused to be published in the *Kölnische Zeitung* an article vigorously attacking the uncalled-for ambitions of the German press in this regard.[55] In January 1900 von Holleben gave to the *New York Herald* a clear denial of German designs,[56] and these assurances were repeated in November 1901.[57] The German Minister at Rio himself wrote that Germany's efforts must be exerted in the economic and ethical sphere,[58] and his American colleague repeatedly assured the State Department that there was really little to fear from the temper of the German settlers, who had become identified with the country in which they made their homes, and who understood the Monroe Doctrine.[59]

But what, says the skeptical reader, influenced perhaps by the opinion of today, of the famous Venezuela episode? Is it not true that Germany was plotting nefarious designs on the independence of that state in 1902 and 1903? Did she not aim at the establishment of a naval base in the Caribbean? Did not a gallant and forthright President of the United States, President Theodore Roosevelt, virtually deliver an ultimatum to the German government, and at the point of the sword, so to speak, induce it to desist from its nefarious designs? And does not this episode make all these other minor questions seem insignificant? Does it not definitely indicate the hostility of Wilhelminian Germany to the United States and to the Monroe Doctrine?

Such is the legend, and nothing more than the legend, which has taken root in the American mind, and which is widely believed today. It rests upon the utterances of Theodore Roosevelt himself; and especially upon a letter of his to the historian, William Roscoe Thayer. And perhaps the best way of dealing with the problem is to cite that letter, or a large portion thereof, as it was written some fifteen and a half years after the event, and at a time, be it noted, when this most ardent and bellicose of Americans was sighing for war against the Reich.

There is now no reason [Mr. Roosevelt began] why I should not speak of the facts connected with the disagreement between the United States and Germany over the Venezuela matter, in the early part of my administration as President, and of the final amicable settlement of the disagreement.

At that time the Venezuelan Dictator-President Castro had committed various offenses against European nations, including Germany and England. The English Government was then endeavoring to keep on good terms with Germany, and on this occasion acted jointly with her. Germany sent a squadron of war vessels to the Venezuelan coast, and they were accompanied by some English war vessels. There was no objection whatever to Castro's being punished, as long as the punishment did not take the form of seizure of territory and its more or less permanent occupation by some Old-World power. At this particular point, such seizure of territory would have been a direct menace to the United States, because it would have threatened or partially controlled the approach to the projected Isthmian Canal.

I speedily became convinced that Germany was the leader, and the really formidable party in the transaction; and that England was merely following Germany's lead in rather half-hearted fashion. I became convinced that England would not back Germany in the event of a clash over the matter between Germany and the United States, but would remain neutral; I did not desire that she should do more than remain neutral. I also became convinced that Germany intended to seize some Venezuelan harbor and turn it into a strongly fortified place of arms, on the model of Kiauchau, with a view to exercising some degree of control over the future Isthmian Canal, and over South American affairs generally.

Influenced by these considerations, Mr. Roosevelt, so he says, tried "for some time" the usual methods of diplomatic intercourse. Germany "declined to arbitrate"; she "declined to say that she would not take possession of Venezuelan territory, merely saying that such possession would be temporary — which might mean anything." Accordingly the President "assembled our battle fleet," so his story runs, "ready to sail at an hour's notice," and told John Hay that he would see von Holleben, the German Ambassador.

I saw the Ambassador [continues his letter], and explained that in view of the presence of the German Squadron on the Venezuelan coast I could not permit longer delay in answering my request for an arbitration, and that I could not acquiesce in any seizure of Venezuelan territory. The Ambassador responded that his government could not agree to arbitrate, and that there was no intention to take "permanent" possession of Venezuelan territory. I answered that Kiauchau was not a "permanent" possession of Germany — that I understood that it was merely held by a 99 years' lease; and that I did not intend to have another Kiauchau, held by similar tenure, on the approach to the Isthmian Canal. The Ambassador repeated that his government would not agree to arbitrate. I then asked him to inform his government that if no notification for arbitration came within a certain specified number of days I should be obliged to order Dewey to take his fleet to the Venezuelan coast and see that the German forces did not take possession of any territory. He expressed very grave concern, and asked me if I realized the serious consequences that would follow such action; consequences so serious to both countries that he dreaded to give them a name. I answered that I had thoroughly counted the cost before I decided on the step, and asked him to look at the map, as a glance would show him that there was no spot in the world where Germany in the event of a conflict with the United States would be at a greater disadvantage than in the Caribbean Sea.

A few days later the Ambassador came to see me, talked pleasantly on several subjects, and rose to go. I asked him if he had any answer to make from his government to my request, and when he said no, I informed him that in such event it was useless to wait as long as I had intended, and that Dewey would be ordered to sail twenty-four hours in advance of the time I had set. He expressed deep apprehension, and said that his government would not arbitrate. However, less than twenty-four hours before the time I had appointed for cabling the order for Dewey, the Embassy notified me that his Imperial Majesty the German Emperor had directed him to request me to undertake the arbitration myself. I felt, and publicly expressed, great gratification at this outcome, and great appreciation of the course the German Government had finally agreed to take. Later I received the consent of the German Government to have the arbitration undertaken by The Hague Tribunal, and not by me.[60]

This extraordinary narrative has been widely disseminated; it has found its way into textbooks by distinguished historians; it ministers to American pride and to American prejudice alike. Yet it is filled with errors, errors which careful research among the documents inevitably reveals. Let us analyze it with the object of discovering the precise truth.

The Venezuelan question first comes above the diplomatic horizon in December of 1901. At that time the German government, in a memorandum to the State Department, outlined with candor, as we now know it to be, the position which it intended to take to bring the recalcitrant Castro to show some respect for the rights of foreigners. It expressly disavowed all territorial ambitions, but indicated that a blockade of the principal harbors of Venezuela might have to be considered, and added that if this measure failed of effect Germany "would have to consider the temporary occupation . . . of different Venezuelan harbor places and the levying of duties in those places." [61] This communication was received by Mr. Roosevelt and by John Hay, the Secretary of State, without a tremor; von Holleben, the German Minister, saw them both the very next day after the memorandum was transmitted; and from their tone he drew the conclusion that coercive action against the egregious Castro would cause no disturbance in official circles in Washington.[62] Not a word was said to discourage the government of the Reich from the enterprise it had in mind.

It was a year after the memorandum of December 1901 before actual measures of coercion were attempted against Venezuela — as we have seen — by Germany and Great Britain acting in consort. *A priori,* it would seem absurd for the Wilhelmstrasse to invite Great Britain to co-operate in measures of coercion if some sinister design for the acquisition of territory was in the wind. But we do not need to depend upon such reasoning. We know, from the British archives, that before the blockade was instituted, even the idea of control of the customs, mentioned in the memorandum of 1901, had been laid aside. Von Richthofen, the German Foreign Minister, explicitly repudiated it in the last days of November, 1902.[63] Such an idea, he declared, would require larger forces than were available, would probably lead to the establishment of a new line of customs posts by the Venezuelans further inland and — note well the observation — might involve trouble with the United States. The documents in the Wilhelmstrasse which bear upon the Venezuelan blockade have been searched with care by more than one historical scholar; not the slightest evidence of any acquisitive design has ever been discovered.

From the very first, moreover, the German government showed the greatest concern for American susceptibilities. The blockade was instituted on December 9. On December 11 the Venezuelan government requested Bowen, the American Minister at Caracas, to propose that the dispute be arbitrated.[64] On December 12 the

Secretary of State transmitted the Venezuelan proposal to London and Berlin, without commenting upon it or exercising any official pressure. On the fourteenth the German Foreign Office drew up instructions for Prince Metternich, its ambassador at London, declaring that Germany must accept American mediation, lest Great Britain get the credit for being more conciliatory than its associate.[65] On December 19, it accepted arbitration in principle. The blockade, it is true, was continued, and quite properly continued, while the terms of reference of the arbitration between Venezuela and intervening governments should be determined; but the acceptance of arbitration itself seems hardly the act of a government bent upon some sinister enterprise of force.

It would appear, then, from the foregoing, that Mr. Roosevelt was wrong in several of the key statements of his letter to Thayer; that he was wrong in assuming the intention of Germany to establish a "fortified place of arms"; that he was wrong in saying that "Germany declined to arbitrate"; that he was wrong in saying that in 1902 the government of the Reich even mentioned "temporary" possession — "which might mean anything."

But the rest of the Roosevelt story is no less inaccurate and untrustworthy. There are the strongest reasons for believing that the idea that an ultimatum was addressed to Germany was the product of the Rough Rider's exuberant imagination rather than of his memory. In the archives of the Wilhelmstrasse is not a word that confirms the story; there is not a word in the dispatches of Sir Michael Herbert, the British Ambassador at Washington; there is not a word in the State Department; there is not a word about any special orders to the American fleet in the Navy Department; there is not, in short, one single scrap of contemporary evidence that substantiates the Roosevelt narrative. Nor does one have to depend entirely upon negative evidence. In the papers of John Hay is the draft of a memorandum addressed to the blockading powers. This memorandum declares that the German government "spontaneously assured the Government of the United States that it did not contemplate the conquest or acquisition of any territory whatever"; it goes on to say that "the government of the United States . . . took pains to observe an attitude of friendly neutrality through all the painful incidents of the blockade that followed." [66] Could Hay have written these sentences if Roosevelt had talked to Holleben as, in 1916, he said that he had talked? Or take another bit of evidence — the speech of the President himself in April 1903, in which he declared that in the Venezuelan blockade "both powers assured us in explicit terms that there was not the slightest intention on their part to violate the principles of the Monroe Doctrine, and these assurances have been kept with an honorable good faith that merits the fullest acknowledgment on their part." [67] Had there been such a crisis as was described in the letter to Thayer, would Roosevelt have spoken thus a few months later? Or consider the language of the President in writing to Professor Münsterberg in the winter of 1903. "Germany, England and the United States," he wrote on January 23, "are the three great nations of the future. The Slavs need a hundred years, and the Latin races are played out. And the co-operation of these three peoples need have no limit — the Monroe Doctrine is no rigid article of faith." [68] Or consider one other striking, indeed overwhelmingly convincing, fact. Von Holleben, we learn from the German archives, was not even in Washington from the fourteenth to the twenty-sixth of December; and the President's visiting book shows that he saw the President on December 6, and reveals no other visit till the New Year's reception. When, then, could any ultimatum have been delivered? There is no reasonable answer to this question except the one word — never.

In coming to this conclusion, however, we have by no means done with the Venezuelan blockade from the standpoint of German-American relations, or that of the Monroe Doctrine. For the fact is undeniable that there existed in the latter part of 1902 and the first months of 1903 a very genuine resentment against Germany, and a very real tension in the relations of the two nations. "The outburst in this country against Germany," wrote Sir Michael Herbert in a dispatch of December 29, "has been truly remarkable,

and suspicion of the German Emperor's designs in the Caribbean
Sea is shared by the Administration, the press, and the public
alike." [69] On January 26 the British Minister again alluded to the
intense irritation against the Reich.[70] On February 7 he went so
far as to say that good relations with the United States would be
"seriously impaired" by further British co-operation with the government at Berlin.[71] On February 25 he expressed himself still
more emphatically. "Your Lordship would be amazed," he wrote,
"at the language held in regard to her [that is, Germany] by men
in the highest positions in Washington." [72] There seems every reason to believe that this analysis of American opinion was sound.
Roosevelt himself undoubtedly recognized the fact. "Are the people in Berlin crazy?" he was quoted as asking at the end of January. "Don't they know that they are inflaming public opinion more
and more here? Don't they know that they will be left alone without England?" [73]

Some explanation of this resentment may be found in the language of a large part of the German press. Naturally the Pan-
German papers were the most extreme. The *Alldeutsche Blätter*,
for example, on January 3 published a commentary on the Monroe
Doctrine which made up in violence what it lacked in accuracy.
The American dogma, it declared, was based upon a telegram (*sic!*)
and had long ago been properly condemned by Prince Bismarck.
The thesis it contained was a monstrous one, entirely "indefensible,
all the more so since the Americans were without the means to
enforce the principles which they so arrogantly laid down." [74] An
article in the *Gegenwart* was still more violent. Germany, declared
its infuriated author, had "humbly" asked for permission from the
"big-mouthed Americans" before entering upon the blockade. Only
the Yankees would be impudent enough to seize territory in the
Orient while they erected a fence around the American hemisphere. While it might not be wise to put the German pistol to the
American breast, the mailed fist was indispensable in dealing with
the arrogant and thoughtless Americans.[75]

Even papers less extreme took a view not so very different. The

Vossische Zeitung, for example, declared that no European nation had ever recognized the American dogma, and that no European country would ever do so.[76] The *Berliner Post,* a paper of similarly moderate views, declared that the Doctrine was a "non-binding monologue," and that there was no need for raising any questions with regard to it.[77] The *Hamburger Nachrichten* thought it merely "the personal opinion of the chief magistrate of the United States in 1823," and declared "utterly inadmissible . . . the inferences drawn from it" to the effect that "the United States may exercise a sort of supervision over the affairs of the various American states." [78]

College professors, moreover, some of them eminent, echoed the language of the press. Professor Eduard Hartmann warned against any "recognition" of American pretensions.[79] Professor Delbrück, a distinguished historian, commented on the "perfidious" policy of the United States.[80] Professor Wagner, an anthropologist of note, believed the Doctrine to be "a mere empty pretension, behind which is neither energetic will, nor actual power." Not even Napoleon had ever raised claims so extreme, he thought.[81]

In the face of what might almost be called a widespread manifestation of hostility to the United States, von Bülow and the Foreign Office sought to pursue a conciliatory policy, so far as possible; at the beginning of January, von Holleben, who had failed to gauge American feeling, was recalled, and a particularly acceptable ambassador sent out in the person of Speck von Sternburg, the friend of the President; and before leaving Berlin the new ambassador gave an interview to the press in which he spoke words that were smooth — and also vague. "The Monroe Doctrine," he declared, "is an unwritten law with Americans, and President Roosevelt interprets it, as he has on several occasions emphasized to the world, as a measure making for peace." [82] Arriving at New York at the end of the month, he was more specific. "The Emperor understands the Monroe Doctrine thoroughly. . . . He appreciates the American feeling for the Monroe Doctrine, and would not think of occupying a coaling station or territory. He would no more think of violating that doctrine, than he would of colonizing the moon." [83] On February 5 von Bülow stated in the Reichstag that Germany had no other object in Venezuela than to ensure the security of the lives, property, and commerce of German subjects,[84] and on March 19, a month after the lifting of the blockade, he spoke out strongly against "mare's-nests," and "most unfounded conscienceless rumors" [85] with regard to German territorial ambitions. Nor is it without relevance that at this same time the *Berliner Tageblatt* was refused official support in the dispatch of a special correspondent to Rio; [86] that the editor of the Pan-German *Grenzboten* was sharply censured for an article advocating the concentration of German colonizing energies in Brazil; [87] that in July von Bülow granted an interview to the Berlin *Lokal-Anzeiger* in which he publicly and authoritatively denied German ambitions in no uncertain terms.[88] Then, too, in the summer of 1903 the curb was placed on the often irritating and officious activities of German warships in the Caribbean; there can be no question that a really genuine effort was made to conciliate the United States.

One thing, however, the German government could not do, in the face of the more violent wing of its own public opinion: it could not state explicitly and unequivocally that it recognized the Monroe Doctrine. The possibility of such action was discussed; the question was raised by von Richthofen of the Foreign Office; but Admiral von Tirpitz was opposed to any such commitment, and none was made. Von Sternburg was reprimanded for his New York interview, and told to take more account of German sentiment; [89] von Bülow, in his speeches in the Reichstag, would make no specific allusion to the principles of 1823. And as perhaps was to be expected in this evil world, the omission of this act of obeisance counted for more with American opinion than all else; the Venezuelan episode apparently only reinforced the conviction of many Americans that Germany needed watching. From the blockade of 1902–1903 the Reich reaped nothing but mistrust.

It was far otherwise with Great Britain. In these years of growing anti-German prejudice the British played their cards superbly, to reap their reward a decade later in the days of the World War. They had done well in 1900 to abandon the Clayton-Bulwer Treaty, and, without any *quid pro quo*, to yield to the United States on the question of the canal; and they were now to show the same complacence once again. Downing Street, like the Wilhelmstrasse, had communicated its intentions in advance to Washington; [90] and on the thirteenth of November Sir Michael Herbert had informed his government that the way was clear. The Secretary of State, he declared, had announced that "although they regretted that European powers should use force against Central and South American countries, the United States Government could not object to their taking steps to obtain redress for injuries suffered by their subjects, provided that no acquisition of territory was contemplated." [91] The unfriendly reaction of American opinion to the blockade may, on this account, have been somewhat of a surprise; but the British ministers swiftly adjusted themselves to the facts. As early as December 15, for example, Lord Cranborne, who represented the Foreign Office in the Commons, declared that the United States had recognized that the British action was "in no way an infraction of the Monroe Doctrine . . . and that no nation in the world had been more anxious than England to assist them in maintaining that doctrine." [92] On February 14, 1903, the Prime Minister, Balfour, made a speech at Liverpool which even more categorically stated the position of the government. "We welcome," he declared, "any increase of the influence of the United States of America in the Western Hemisphere. We desire no colonization, we desire no alteration in the balance of power, we desire no acquisition of territory. We have not the slightest intention of interfering with the mode of government in any portion of that continent. The Monroe Doctrine, therefore, is not really in question at all." [93]

No two men could have spoken from the standpoint of the government with greater authority than those just cited; but what they said was matched by the language of Lord Lansdowne, the Foreign Secretary, and of other influential Conservatives in the

House of Lords. "I do not yield to the noble Lord [Lord Rosebery] or to any one in this House," said Lansdowne in late February, after the dispute had been liquidated, "in my desire that nothing should be done to give offense to the susceptibilities of the United States, or to indicate in any way that we have any desire to impugn the Monroe Doctrine." [94] And the Duke of Devonshire, that solid pillar of the British upper classes in the Balfour ministry, declared in the course of the same debate that Great Britain accepted unreservedly the principles of 1823.[95] In the debate on the King's Speech at the opening of Parliament, the spokesman for the government went even further. "The principle of the Monroe Doctrine," he declared, "has always received the unwavering support of successive Ministries in this country, and no temporary inconvenience will cause us to waver in our adhesion to the policy established by the American people." [96]

As to the opposition, they had from the first condemned the joint action with Germany as jeopardizing a much-valued friendship with the United States; and Sir Charles Dilke expressed their point of view when he asserted in Parliament that "in this country there is an overwhelming opinion in favor of the Monroe Doctrine." [97] And going on to let the cat out of the bag, as it were, he pointed out that Britain's enormous economic interests in Latin America could in no way be better served than by such a policy as the United States had laid down.

This chorus of praise for the great American dogma from British statesmen is a fact of fundamental significance. It comes very near to being an official recognition of the Monroe Doctrine; it comes very near to being the specific acceptance of the cardinal American policy. The spokesmen of no other nation have gone as far as the Britons went in 1902 and 1903; and the view then expressed was to remain controlling for years to come. Ulterior purposes lay behind this suavity, as we shall later see; but they cannot alter the fact that Great Britain is today, and for nigh forty years has been, the nation which has come nearest to wholehearted acceptance of the principles of 1823.

There is a final aspect of the Venezuela blockade that deserves attention here – that is, the sensitiveness of American opinion in 1902 to the coercion of an American state. Despite Mr. Roosevelt's romancing in 1916, it is clear from what we have already said that the administration hardly anticipated any such hostile reaction to the coercive measures of Germany and of Great Britain as actually occurred; in fact the President frankly stated as much to Speck von Sternburg. The go-ahead signal was given by the State Department to the intervening nations; it was in the course of the intervention itself that those in control of American policy discovered that they had to reckon with a public sentiment much more hostile to the use of force by European powers than on any previous occasion. It may be, as Sir Michael Herbert hinted, that part of this hostility came from the American naval men, and "the ship-building firms of Cramp in the East and Scott in the West, who want more orders for ships." [98] But in large part the feeling was genuine and sincere; it was merely one manifestation of the self-confident nationalism of the day.

The Venezuela blockade, then, marks still another stage in the evolution of the Monroe Doctrine; it marks a great change from the position assumed by Seward in 1866. That great Secretary of State had held that the use of force by European nations against American nations, provided no territorial ambitions or anti-republican aims were involved, was entirely licit; and European nations acted on this hypothesis in many instances during the succeeding thirty years. But in 1902–1903 American opinion, if not the American administration, tended to take a very different view; the State Department was obliged to set its machinery in motion and promote a peaceful settlement of the dispute almost as soon as it began. And, on the other hand, European nations acted differently from the way they would have acted at an earlier date: they sought in advance the approval of the United States; they were even ready, it might be added, to submit the question to American arbitration with the President of the United States as arbiter; they showed real concern for American susceptibilities, and one of them, Great Britain, virtually recognized the principles of 1823. No wonder that the *Westminster Gazette* could say, in comment on Venezuela, that "the Monroe Doctrine emerges with an immensely increased authority," [99] and that the *Saturday Review* proclaimed somewhat biliously that "Monroeism conquers in the voluntary departure of Europe from the American continents and adjacent islands." [100] No wonder that Henry White, then chargé at London, could declare that the events of the end of 1902 "served to further still more the acceptance of the Monroe Doctrine, and indeed to establish it on a very firm footing." [101] The America of Theodore Roosevelt, the America of the twentieth century, was a world power; its strength was more and more recognized at home and abroad; for better or for worse it was enlarging its view of its rights and responsibilities. Nor, in this regard, had the sands run out in 1903.

VII

The Policeman of the West
The Evolution of the Roosevelt Corollary

It must be understood that under no circumstances will the United States use the Monroe Doctrine as a cloak for territorial aggression. . . . There are, of course, limits to the wrongs which any self-respecting nation can endure. It is always possible that wrong actions toward this Nation, or toward citizens of this Nation, in some State unable to keep order among its own people, unable to secure justice from outsiders, and unwilling to do justice to those outsiders who treat it well, may result in our having to take action to protect our rights; but such action will not be taken with a view to territorial aggression, and it will be taken at all only with extreme reluctance and when it has become evident that every other resource has been exhausted.

Moreover, we must make it evident that we do not intend to permit the Monroe Doctrine to be used by any nation on this Continent as a shield to protect it from the consequences of its own misdeeds against foreign nations. If a republic to the south of us commits a tort against a foreign nation, such as an outrage against a citizen of that nation, then the Monroe Doctrine does not force us to interfere to prevent punishment of the tort, save to see that the punishment does not assume the form of territorial occupation in any shape. The case is more difficult when it refers to a contractual obligation. Our own Government has always refused to enforce such contractual obligations on behalf of its citizens by an appeal to arms.

It is much to be wished that all foreign governments would take the same view. But they do not; and in consequence we are liable at any time to be brought face to face with disagreeable alternatives. On the one hand, this country would certainly decline to go to war to prevent a foreign government from collecting a just debt; on the other hand, it is very inadvisable to permit any foreign power to take possession, even temporarily, of the custom houses of an American Republic in order to enforce the payment of its obligations; for such temporary occupation might turn into a permanent occupation. The only escape from these alternatives may at any time be that we must ourselves undertake to bring about some arrangement by which so much as possible of a just obligation shall be paid. It is far better that this country should put through such an arrangement, rather than allow any foreign country to undertake it. To do so insures the defaulting republic from having to pay debt of an improper character under duress, while it also insures honest creditors of the republic from being passed by in the interest of dishonest or grasping creditors. Moreover, for the United States to take such a position offers the only possible way of insuring us against a clash with some foreign power. The position is, therefore, in the interest of peace as well as in the interest of justice.

— THEODORE ROOSEVELT, *Annual Message of 1905*

A MAJOR theme of the history of mankind is the development of empire. Powerful nations invariably feel the urge to domination. Conscious of their material force, convinced of their moral superiority, they are often disposed to assert control over weaker and, as they are considered, inferior states. The degree to which this impulse exists, the extent to which it is gratified, the manner in which it is expressed, vary with time, circumstance, and national character. There is a vast difference between imperialisms. It is possible, for example, to make a great distinction between the manner in which Great Britain and France have exercised dominion over less highly organized peoples and the ruthless will to dominate of

Hitlerian Germany. There is such a thing as the moderate, and such a thing as the immoderate, use of national power. But the existence of the imperialist motive must be frankly admitted even with regard to the United States. Our democratic origins, the tolerant temper of our people, its aversion to foreign adventure, have been responsible for the fact that American imperialism has been imperialism with an uneasy conscience, imperialism which has usually justified itself as aiming at the preparation of less experienced political communities for the ordering of their own affairs; but this cannot and ought not to obscure the fact that the imperialistic temper has not been absent in our political life.

Never was that temper stronger than in the first years of the twentieth century. It found its economic roots in the growth of American industry, seeking new markets for its products; in the development of American finance, looking for new opportunities to lend under secure conditions and to invest with the assurance of protection for the investment. It received, very naturally, a powerful stimulus from the events of the Spanish-American War. It found spokesmen like Lodge in the political, and Mahan in the naval, and Strong in the religious field. And it brought the Monroe Doctrine to its aid.

In the development of the Doctrine, indeed, one of the most extraordinary and interesting objects of study must be the evolution of a theorem intended for the protection of the Latin-American states by the United States into one that justified and even sanctified American interference in and control of the affairs of the independent republics of this continent. This evolution attains peculiar importance in the period of the Roosevelt administration; but its roots lie, naturally enough, in the longer past. Had the Congress in 1848 accepted the position of President Polk, Americans would have extended their control over the population of Yucatán, albeit in this case at the invitation of Yucateco leaders; had the Congress yielded to the insistence of Buchanan, or followed the policy of the McLane-Ocampo Treaty, the United States might have extended its sway over Mexico in the years just preceding the

Civil War. The enunciation of the no-transfer principle by President Grant seemed to cynical observers to stake out claims for future American acquisition, at the same time it proclaimed that no European nation should disturb the *status quo;* and the eagerness of the hero of the Wilderness to acquire the territory of the Dominican Republic appeared to substantiate this view. Nonetheless, no extension of American control over any people outside the North American continent took place in the whole course of the nineteenth century, down to 1898; and the acquisitions of the Spanish-American War were never justified by the invocation of the principles of 1823. It was not until the first years of the twentieth century that there was to be deduced from the language of Monroe a right of positive interference in the affairs of independent nations. In these years grew up what came to be known as the Roosevelt corollary to the Monroe Doctrine.

The first occasion on which the government of the United States asked for, and received, recognition of its right to interfere in the affairs of an American state was the case of Cuba. By the Platt amendment to the army appropriation bill of 1901, it was stipulated that while the American forces were to withdraw from the island, the government of Cuba should consent to the exercise of an American right of intervention "for the preservation of Cuban independence, the maintenance of a government adequate for the protection of life, property, and individual liberty, and for discharging its obligations with respect to Cuba." The author of this amendment, however, in bringing it forward made no allusion to the principles of 1823; nor did the Senate debate itself reveal that there existed in the minds of most of the Senators any connection between the policy embodied in the amendment and the language of the Monroe Doctrine. Indeed when Senator Hoar, alone among the members of the Senate, declared that Senator Platt's proposal seemed to him "a proper and necessary stipulation for the application of the Monroe Doctrine to the nearest outlying country in America, except Mexico," [1] he was promptly brought to task. Senator Jones of Arkansas declared that he could not understand how the great American dogma "anywhere gives the United States the right to interfere in the internal affairs of any American state," [2] and Senator Morgan of Alabama stated the matter even more strongly: "This Monroe Doctrine never had anything to do with a proposition like this, the maintenance of a government adequate to the protection of life, property and individual liberty in any one of the American states. It has no connection with that." [3] No other Republican Senator, in answer to these strictures, rose to sustain the position of the Senator from Massachusetts. We cannot, therefore, regard the Platt amendment as based upon the principles of 1823.

In general, moreover, American newspapers and American public opinion did not draw from the Venezuelan blockade of 1902–1903 any conclusion that the United States must exercise a police power over the states of the New World. Irritation at German manners and methods, as we have seen, was widespread; but only an occasional editorial pronouncement suggested that the American government had any positive responsibility to maintain good order in the states of Latin America, in order to prevent such episodes as the blockade from ever arising. The thesis that if the United States would not permit others to intervene it ought to intervene itself first found general expression, not in the American, but in the British press, and in the language of British statesmen. Nor was this by any means a mere whim of circumstance; on the contrary, it may be stated with some assurance that British policy was consciously directed towards gently leading the administration at Washington in the pathway of imperialism. What could be wiser and more statesmanlike, indeed, from the standpoint of British interest than to win the good will of the United States by the recognition of the Monroe Doctrine, and at the same time to persuade the American government to assume the role of an international policeman in the New World, watching faithfully over vast economic interests which Englishmen had created there? What more reasonable assumption than that the principles of 1823 conferred responsibilities as well as rights, duties as well as privileges?

The signs of the development of this idea are to be found occasionally in years preceding 1902. Lord Salisbury in his reply to Olney had suggested it in a sort of reverse form, declaring that the United States, since it did not attempt to control the conduct of the Latin-American states, could not undertake to protect them from the consequences of their own misconduct. The *Living Age*, applauding Secretary Root's defiant utterance of April 1900, had declared that the right to shield the states of the New World from violence implied the duty to keep them in order.[4] It is not strange, therefore, that in the debates on the Venezuela blockade this same note should be struck again and yet again. In the House of Commons, for example, a government spokesman declared somewhat plaintively, "If the United States could see their way to the adoption of some effective course by which these almost periodical difficulties arising between the great Powers and some of the states of South America could be prevented, I think I may say it would meet with cordial concurrence in this country."[5] And there was the same suggestion behind the more guarded words of the Duke of Devonshire in the Lords. "Rightly or not, wisely or unwisely, probably wisely and rightly, the Government of the United States has not accepted any responsibility for the acts of the Republics established in South America; and if, in deference to supposed, and I believe erroneously supposed, susceptibilities on the part of the Government of the United States, we, or other powers of Europe, were to abstain from enforcing claims which we believe to be just and essential to the maintenance of our honor, such a course would make the Monroe Doctrine an object of dislike and opposition to every civilized Power in the world."[6] Thus cautiously did the Duke present to the Roosevelt administration, as he wished to view the matter, a choice between repeated interventions on the part of European powers and the assertion of a wider control upon the part of the American government itself.

The language of British statesmen was supported by the leading journals. The *Morning Post* raised the question in the clearest terms;[7] the pontifical *Times*,[8] the *London Standard*,[9] the *Daily Chronicle*,[10] and the *Daily Telegraph*[11] took the same view; such an important opposition paper as the *Westminster Gazette* adopted the same position.[12] And at Washington Sir Michael Herbert found occasion to bring the British attitude to the attention of the President himself. On the thirteenth of February Mr. Roosevelt took an opportunity to say to the British Ambassador that the American people were opposed to the collection of debts by force. "I observed," wrote Sir Michael to Lord Landsdowne, "that I supposed in that case he would be ready to police the whole American Continent and prevent the general repudiation which would most likely follow any declaration by the United States of such a policy." [13] This pointed observation certainly suggested in emphatic fashion that the principles of 1823 implied responsibilities as well as privileges.

Wholly apart, however, from observations such as these, it is entirely possible that the doctrine of the police power was taking root in the White House in the latter days of 1902 and the early days of 1903. Theodore Roosevelt was, of course, by instinct a policeman, this without reference to his specific employment in the years 1895–1897; his passion for righteousness was accompanied by an equally ardent desire to see his particular brand of this article imposed upon others; and a man who, as Henry Adams so well stated, was "pure act" must have found particularly irksome the role of passive observer to a large extent imposed upon him in the Venezuelan matter. The British and Germans had suggested that the President himself arbitrate their dispute with Venezuela; it was reluctantly, and at the insistence of John Hay, that this alluring prospect was put aside, and the controversy sent to The Hague Tribunal; from the White House came indirect assurances, emanations of Rooseveltian energy, that the United States would see that the award was carried out; [14] and in a most interesting conversation with Speck von Sternburg the Rough Rider gave still further evidence of his strong desire to play a more active role than hitherto.

The occasion of this conversation was the suggestion that came from Berlin of some international administration of Venezuelan customs. The great banking interest in Germany, especially the Disconto-Gesellschaft, had for some time nourished the hope of some such solution of the Venezuelan question; it had been discovered that Mr. Loomis, the Undersecretary of State, was not unfavorable; [15] the Wilhelmstrasse hailed with joy this sign of broadening outlook; and while it wished the initiative in any such scheme to come from America, it was not averse to Speck von Sternburg's discussing the question with his exalted friend of the tennis court and the riding path. The conversation took place near the middle of March, 1903. In the course of it the President boxed the compass of opinion; but at one point he gave utterance to these significant words: "A control of the finances of Venezuela through American and European financial institutions would be condemned by public opinion here. These wretched republics cause me a great deal of trouble. A second attempt of foreign powers to collect their debts by force would simply not be tolerated here. I often think that a sort of protectorate (*protektionistische Erklärung*) over South and Central America is the only way out." [16] The phrase was hardly uttered before it was virtually withdrawn; but it is full of meaning, nonetheless. The Roosevelt temperament was impatient; the instinct for the short cut and the dominating action was strong in the President; and before the year was out he was to give an excellent illustration of his natural temper. Impatient at the failure of the Colombian Senate to ratify the Hay-Herran Treaty, which paved the way for the construction of the canal, Roosevelt took speedy advantage of an uprising on the Isthmus to land armed forces there, hastily to recognize the government which was set up, and no less hastily to negotiate with it a compact which furthered his great ambition. This action vividly illustrated his distrust of Latin-American politicians (in this case so restrainedly described as "the homicidal corruptionists of Bogotá"), his conviction of the righteousness of the United States and of its mission for civilization, his willingness to use that "big stick" to which he so frequently alluded. His

policy, moreover, seemed to be successful; and this fact may have
its bearing upon his later treatment of the question of Santo Domingo.

In this little country, a prey to frequent revolutions at the turn
of the century, the control of the customs had been placed in 1893
in the hands of an American financial concern, which, with engaging optimism, described itself as the "Santo Domingo Improvement
Company." In 1901, the then existing government had annulled
the contract of this concern, and the concern itself had naturally in
its dudgeon appealed to the State Department. By the protocol of
January 31, 1903, it was agreed that the Improvement Company
should be compensated for the violation of its contract in the
amount of $4,500,000; and it was further stipulated that the man-
ner of payment should be left to three arbitrators, one appointed by
the President of the United States, one by the President of the
Dominican Republic, and one to be chosen by the Dominican government from the judges of the Circuit Courts of the Supreme Court
of the United States. This agreement was never submitted to the
Senate; it may not have been known to the President himself; but
its existence suggests that the State Department had begun to interest itself in the Dominican question from the standpoint of
American private interests before larger aspects of the problem
attracted the attention of the administration. Marxians will find in
this fact the sinister evidence of the influence of capitalism upon
American foreign policy; but the facts, so far as we have them,
demonstrate nothing oblique, or nothing particularly unusual.

And certainly it cannot be said that the Improvement Company
was the single or even the dominant factor in the events ahead;
other circumstances arose to arrest the attention of the administration, and to form its policy with regard to Santo Domingo. In the fall
of 1903, for example, Powell, the minister at Santo Domingo City,
an eager friend of intervention, reported that the Foreign Minister,
Señor Galván, was hostile to the United States, and busy promoting
some nebulous project for the neutralization of Dominican waters
and the establishment of free ports at Samaná and Manzanillo in

the interests of Germany.[17] In the name of the principles of 1823, in language more tortuous than eloquent, but beyond question charged with emotion, Powell protested to the Dominican Republic against the outrage; [18] what is more important, his suspicions, though in fact unjustified, seem to have been shared by the veteran of the State Department, Mr. Adee. As so often happens in matters of this kind, the administration was to be able to rationalize intervention in Dominican affairs on the ground that inaction might mean the aggrandizement of some other power. Nor was the German menace the only one raised. On October 17, 1903, the Belgian government, whose citizens had a substantial amount of Dominican securities, through its diplomatic representative at Santo Domingo City proposed joint action with the United States for the control of the customhouses, and the administration of the revenues by an international commission composed of representatives of the largest creditors — France, Belgium, and the United States.[19] In order to forestall such proposals, was it not necessary for the American government to take independent action of its own?

So at least it might reasonably have been argued; and such a position was made more cogent by the fact that the turn of the revolutionary wheel in Santo Domingo brought into power in the winter of 1904 a President who really desired the assistance of the United States. The Dominicans were by this time becoming universally unpopular abroad; their ardent pursuit of the sport of revolution was straining the patience of their European creditors; it was, and had been, a favorite expedient of the occupant of the uneasy seat of power in the republic to court the favor of some foreign state; and it is likely that President Morales was influenced by considerations such as these in the appeal which he made to the government at Washington. At any rate, whatever the reasons therefor, a Dominican agent appeared at the State Department late in January, and with references to the principles of 1823 besought the aid and assistance of the powerful republic of the North.[20] He had scarcely arrived there when another significant event occurred. The Hague Tribunal handed down an important decision with a bearing on the whole question of Caribbean politics. To the judges of this august body had been referred the question whether the powers which had used coercion against the recalcitrant Castro had a right to preferential treatment in the collection of their claims; and the answer to this question had been unanimously in the affirmative. Such a decision, as a prominent official of the State Department declared, "put a premium on violence"; [21] it seemed to make more necessary than ever the discovery of an alternative to the use of force by European states against American powers; it offered still another reason for listening to the Dominican appeal. Add to this that a few days later a dispatch arrived from Santo Domingo City indicating that the "outs" in the republic were making overtures to the German Consul for a secret understanding directed against the United States, [22] and we can understand why the Roosevelt administration began to consider seriously some form of positive action in the affairs of this troubled Caribbean state. Nor is it strange that in the winter and spring of 1904 American naval officers in Dominican waters seem to have given a covert, or even an overt, support to the government in power, with its predilection for an understanding with the United States. [23]

But the year 1904 was an election year, and the Presidential procedure was correspondingly cautious. A number of "educational articles" (when we do not approve their object, we describe them as propaganda) appeared in American periodicals; that they were stimulated by the State Department seems almost certain. By the month of May a *ballon d'essai* was launched by the President himself. At a banquet to commemorate the second anniversary of the independence of Cuba, Secretary Root read a letter from the chief magistrate of the republic. Declaring that the sole desire of the United States was "to see all neighboring countries stable, orderly and prosperous," Roosevelt went on to say that if a nation shows "that it knows how to act with decency in industrial and political matters, if it keeps order and pays its obligations, then it need fear no interference from the United States. Brutal wrongdoing, or an impotence which results in a general loosening of the ties of civilized society, may finally require intervention by some civilized nation, and in the Western Hemisphere the United States cannot ignore this duty." [24] Such language can only be interpreted as preparation for the specific intervention which lay only a little way ahead.

In July events still further strengthened the hands of administration; the arbitral commission chosen to determine the manner of payment to the United States, on account for the Santo Domingo Improvement Company, made its award; and, wonderful to relate, among its terms was a provision that in case of default the financial agent of the United States should take over the Dominican customhouses at Puerto Plata, and, if necessary, those at Sanchez, Samaná, and Monte Christi as well. [25] It certainly looks as if the eminent arbitrators had been reading the public pronouncements of the President of the United States. Two months later the event which the decision presaged actually occurred; the default took place, and an American financial agent, interestingly enough an official of the Improvement Company, installed himself at the customhouse in Puerto Plata. At this juncture foreign governments began to make themselves heard; the surrender of the revenues of this important port was a serious matter for the other creditors of Santo Domingo. It placed additional burdens upon the southern ports, the receipts of which were pledged to the French and Belgian bondholders, and upon Samaná, whose revenues had been hypothecated to the Italians. The situation was becoming exceedingly tense; the appeals of Morales for American aid became more and more insistent; the French government declared to the United States (not without reason) that its patience had become exhausted, and pressed for action. In these closing days of 1904 it was the invariably suspected Germans who were silent; but this is doubtless because they had no interest worth speaking of in the Dominican debt.

Freed from the embarrassments incident to a campaign for re-election, rendered confident indeed by a majestic victory at the polls, President Roosevelt in his message of 1904 reiterated the language of the letter of May 20; only this time he specifically declared that "in the Western Hemisphere the adherence of the United States to the Monroe Doctrine may force the United States, however reluctantly, in flagrant cases of such wrong-doing or impotence, to the exercise of an international police power." [26] The thesis which he thus expounded was amplified by Secretary Root at a dinner of the New England Society on December 22. Words were speedily followed by deeds. On December 30, Minister Dawson was formally instructed to ascertain "whether the Government of Santo Domingo would be disposed to request the United States to take charge of the collection of duties and effect an equitable distribution of the assigned quotas among the Dominican Government and the several claimants." [27] On January 5, the President named as special commissioner Commander Dillingham, a naval officer with wide knowledge of the island, to assist in the negotiations, and with the advent of the New Year two American war vessels cast anchor in the harbor of Santo Domingo to exercise, of course, a purely moral influence upon the discussions. By the seventh of February a protocol had been signed providing for American customs control; the preamble to this document declared that "the Government of the United States of America, viewing any attempt on the part of the governments outside of this hemisphere to oppress or control the destiny of the Dominican Republic as a manifestation of an unfriendly disposition towards the United States," was ready to lend its assistance in the straightening out of the finances of the distracted republic. Eight days later the President transmitted the protocol to the Senate, and once more, as in the message of December, he invoked the principles of 1823. "Either we must submit to the likelihood of infringement of the Monroe Doctrine or we must ourselves agree to some such arrangement as that herewith submitted. . . . We . . . are simply performing in peaceful manner, not only with the cordial acquiescence, but in accordance with the earnest request of the government concerned, part of that international duty which is necessarily involved in the assertion of the Monroe Doctrine. . . . This in reality entails no new obligation upon us, for the Monroe Doctrine means precisely such a guarantee on our part. . . . This protocol [the message concludes] affords a practical test of the efficiency of the United States government in maintaining the Monroe Doctrine." [28]

It was natural for Roosevelt, in proclaiming this new and interesting policy, not only to call the shade of Monroe to his aid, but to assert that the policy itself was no novelty. It is a habit of statesmen to justify innovations by stoutly maintaining that they are no innovations at all. But the fact remains that the administration of the customs of the Dominican Republic was, very decidedly, a breach with the past; and while in this instance there seems no reason to believe that the United States had exercised any coercion upon the Dominican government, it would not be a great step from the assumption of control at the request of the debtor state to the forcing of control upon a state which had not requested it at all, or to the extension of a control voluntarily acquiesced in to a domination by no means desired. Events were to demonstrate only too clearly the imperialistic connotations of the Roosevelt corollary to the principles of 1823.

In the Senate the protocol of February 7 failed of ratification before the rising of Congress. Determined not to be frustrated, the President directed the negotiation of a *modus vivendi* with the hard-pressed Dominican government; the timely arrival of an Italian cruiser on March 14 emphasized the necessity of urgent action; by the arrangement which was concluded, an American citizen named by the Dominican regime was to serve as collector of customs till the Senate should act upon the protocol. At the same time American warships were kept in Dominican waters, with what purpose Roosevelt revealed in September in an engaging note to the Secretary of the Navy. "As to the Santo Domingo matter, tell Admiral Bradford to stop any revolution. I intend to keep the island in the *status quo* until the Senate has had time to act on the treaty, and I shall treat any revolutionary movement as an effort to upset the *modus vivendi*. That this is essentially right, I am dead sure, even though there may be some technical or red tape difficulty." [29] This simplicity of judgment may be regarded as rather winning; but it illustrates the fine line which divides free consent from co-ercion in dealing with a turbulent Latin-American republic.

In what temper did the American people accept the Roosevelt corollary to the Monroe Doctrine? It is not altogether easy to say. Certainly there was no overwhelming popular approval of the action that had been taken. In the Senate the Democrats were al-most a body in condemning the course of the administration. Not only did they steadily oppose the protocol, but they actually de-termined in caucus upon a united opposition to it; and their atti-tude delayed ratification until the winter of 1907. Had public opin-ion decisively favored the agreement they would never have dared to take such action. Moreover, some very influential news-papers opposed the new policy. That the *Nation* or the *New York World* should do so could hardly cause surprise; but it was more significant to discover the *Springfield Republican* to be hostile; and it was still more impressive to find such stalwart Republican sheets as the *Boston Transcript*, the *New York Sun*, and the *Philadelphia Press* taking the same view. Of these various sheets, the *Transcript* put the case best — so well, indeed, that it deserves to be quoted.

There is a Latin-American side to Monroeism that ought not to be ignored [it wrote]. [It] may, should our policy become militant, place us in the unenviable attitude of coercing our southern neighbors at the behest of Europe. . . . Let "The High Finance" of the Old World lead itself up with these repudiated or semi-repudiated bonds at a few cents on the dollar, and receive a tip that the United States either can or may be made to intervene for a settlement or "readjustment" and there will be at once a "sharp advance," affording good profits and an embroglio on our hands. . . . The political Latin-American side of Monroeism is found in the possible unwillingness of nations of the rank and pride of Argentina, Brazil and Chile to accept an onerous degree of guardianship. They may insist that they prefer to do their own business in their own way, and that they can best make terms without intervention or intermediary. Supposing this should be their constitution, ought we to over-ride it, so long as the proposed settlement does not involve cession of territory? To prevent such cessions, to preserve the independence of South America . . . were the great ends sought by the simple Monroeism of Monroe. Since his day Monroeism has "expanded" by continued interpretations until there are signs to the southward that the public opinion in the countries affected views it with something very like distrust. It would be a strange, untoward outcome of eighty years of Monroeism if a secret combination of Latin-American countries should be formed in opposition to "the overlordship of the United States." [30]

The opposition expressed in such editorials as this affected in some degree not the fate of, but the form of, the Dominican treaty. The preamble of the original protocol was omitted. In contradistinction with the draft of February 7, 1905, the final text did not obligate the United States to assist in preserving order, or to interfere in domestic concerns except for the collection of customs. But the essentials of the Roosevelt program were retained; and on the final ballot not a single Republican voted in opposition to the administration. If there was no great wave of enthusiasm for the new policy, there was also no such determined opposition as might shake partisans loose from their moorings. Perhaps, after all, the prevailing popular attitude was inertia. Even in these days, when foreign affairs may be so vital, they remain a land of mystery to the average American; still more was this the case thirty years ago; why, in those dim days, should an insignificant Caribbean state arouse to any considerable pitch of emotion the great mass of the American people?

In Great Britain, which, as we have seen, had had something to do with the formation of the Roosevelt corollary, the position of the President was in general hailed with approval. The British bondholders who held Dominican bonds naturally profited from the customs control, and in a measure they were grateful. The report of the Council of Foreign Bondholders for 1906 comments with cordiality upon the action that had been taken, and then quite naturally goes on to ask for more of the same prescription. What about Costa Rica? What about Honduras? What about Guatemala? Why should not the United States still further widen its responsibilities? Why not indeed? [31]

If we turn from Britain to France, it is necessary to say that the best gauge of official opinion is to be found not in words, but in action. At the very time when the President was putting forward his new theory, France had on her hands a bitter dispute with the ever-troublesome Castro of Venezuela. In the fall of 1905 French ships began to gather in the Caribbean. The good offices of the government of the United States were offered. In December Ambassador Jusserand saw the President and the Secretary of State, and went so far as to say that if these good offices were not successful, and if a rupture occurred, France would "have to employ more telling measures than the mere sending of naval vessels into Venezuelan waters. She would probably be obliged to occupy temporarily one point or another, and seize perhaps some custom house; having recourse, in a word, to means which, while having chances of being felt, would avoid bloodshed." [32] Words such as these were nothing less than a challenge to the Roosevelt corollary; but surprisingly enough they awakened no opposition. M. Jusserand, on the contrary, was assured that "given especially the friendly and confident dispositions between the two countries it would surely be the easiest matter for France to follow a procedure which would not create such a precedent as would prove troublesome in the future. It might be agreed that, as soon as definite plans such as the above have been determined upon by the French Government, their Ambassador would write to the Secretary of State, giving the pledge that there would be no permanent occupation of Venezuelan territory, and that the landing of troops and the eventual seizing of a custom house would be of as limited a duration as possible." [33] Such language was indeed surprising; one is left to wonder why it was uttered; one asks oneself if the President's partiality for France and his detestation of Castro were responsible for his acquiescence within a year in the violation of the principles he had himself laid down; but one finds no answer to the question. The only thing that is clear is that the French government was, at the end of 1905, disposed to act in disregard of the Presidential pronouncement of 1904. In practice, it did not do so; the dispute was liquidated without coercion, after long delays; but the attitude assumed is interesting, nonetheless.[34]

In the French press, the general tone of comment was hostile to the new American formula. The *Temps*, often semiofficial, if not official, declared that the Monroe Doctrine had now "assumed an offensive character." [35] A critical author in the *Revue Générale de Droit International Public* spoke of the Roosevelt administration as having "resuscitated in the New World the old feudal theory of suzerainty," [36] and another went on to declare that the President's message represented "the rather hypocritical formula of the exclusive and selfish interest of the United States." [37] Two studies on the Doctrine published in 1905 under the eye of Louis Renault, eminent international lawyer, handled the Roosevelt corollary in anything but friendly terms. Only an occasional voice, indeed, was raised in its defense.

In Germany, comment was less widespread than in France. But the *Kreuz Zeitung*, that staunch champion of the *Junkers*, asked indignantly, "What right has the United States to such pretensions?" and answered its own question, "Absolutely none." [38] And the Kaiser, addicted to marginalia on the diplomatic dispatches which he read, commented on the Root speech of December 22 with the word, "This particular kind of Monroeism I cannot subscribe to." [39] But official policy was cautious. Neither von Bülow nor the Emperor had been willing to act against the chronically turbulent Haitians in 1904 though von Richthofen and Holstein were hot for administering chastisement; [40] in 1905, when an overzealous naval officer landed troops at the Brazilian port of Itajahy, after a sailor's brawl on shore, his action was disavowed and the officer himself recalled.[41] So circumspect, indeed, was German policy that Roosevelt himself admitted to his friend Cecil Spring-Rice that the Reich had no sinister purposes in Latin America.[42]

In Latin America the reactions to Roosevelt's policy were on the whole, and at the outset, surprisingly mild. In no one of the great states of Latin America was any official notice taken of the President's theory; in Brazil, in Chile, in Uruguay, and in Peru, the general tone of comment was favorable. In Argentina, where commercial jealousies and competition in the wheat and cattle markets tended to sharpen antagonism to the great nation of the North, there was more hostility. Such papers as *El Diario* and *La Prensa* did not hesitate to describe the President's thesis as "menacing" and as "the very negation of the independence of the Latin-American republics." [43] But other papers took a very different view; there was no official reaction; indeed, the Argentine Minister at Washington, in the spring of 1906, transmitted to the State Department favorable newspaper comment on the new policy with the obvious purpose of soothing the susceptibilities of the administration. [44] In 1905, in 1906, to the end, indeed, of the Roosevelt administration, one senses no widespread opposition to the new interpretation of the principles of 1823 in the reports of our ministers at the capitals of the Southern republics.

There are, perhaps, several reasons for this restraint. For one thing, there was certainly an element of consent in the whole Dominican transaction. The convention of 1907 was not forced down the throats of the Dominicans; it bore every evidence of a friendly understanding between the two nations concerned, and it seemed also to have averted a possible European intervention. In the second place, in August of 1905, in a speech that received much attention in Latin America and was, indeed, given publicity by the State Department there, President Roosevelt restated his position, in terms which made it clear that there would be no orgy of intermeddling. He declared that the United States would go to the "utmost limits of forbearance" before acting; that it would take no action save what was "absolutely demanded by our self-respect"; that it would seek "no territorial aggrandizement"; that it would make "every effort to avert" such a contingency; and that "no just and orderly government" had "anything to fear" from the

United States.[45] In his annual message of 1905 he reiterated these reassurances, and declared that some Latin-American states, having reached "stability, order and prosperity," were, "though as yet hardly consciously . . . among the guarantors of this doctrine," to be met "on a basis of entire equality" and "in a spirit of frank and respectful friendship." [46] In 1906, the administration went still further in its efforts to attract Latin-American good will. At the third Pan-American Conference in Rio de Janeiro appeared for the first time, if only for a season, a Secretary of State of the United States, in the person of Elihu Root; and with the tact that distinguished him Root avoided almost any reference to the principles of 1823, realizing clearly, it would appear, that the great American dogma was better adapted to domestic than foreign citation. In eloquent language he proclaimed the principle of equality of sovereignty, and assured his hearers that "we deem the independence and equal rights of the smallest and weakest member of the family of nations entitled to as much respect as those of the greatest empire; and we deem the observance of that respect the chief guarantee of the weak against the oppression of the strong." [47] Root visited Argentina, Uruguay, Chile, Peru, Colombia, and Panama, as well as Brazil; and everywhere he spoke the same language of friendship. Diplomatic addresses are not always accepted at their face value; but Mr. Root was sincere, and no doubt some of his hearers believed him.

In 1907, once again, the Roosevelt administration sought to do a service to the states of the South. In the midst of the Venezuela blockade of 1902–1903, the Argentine Foreign Minister, Dr. Luis Drago, had brought forward the principle that the use of force for the collection of debts was not to be tolerated, and was, indeed, at variance with the Monroe Doctrine, since financial interventions might easily lead to measures more sinister and far-reaching.[48] Secretary Hay had responded cautiously to this new theory; in magnificent circumlocutions he had avoided committing himself to its acceptance. But at the Hague Conference of 1907 the administration took a leaf from Drago; it proposed a convention which did not, it is true, go so far as the Argentine had proposed, but which forbade the use of force for the collection of contract debts until arbitration had taken place, or had been refused or thwarted by the debtor. This convention, it is true, was by no means received with enthusiasm by many of the Latin-American delegations; its ratification by them was often postponed, or denied, or accompanied by reservations; but the position assumed by the United States was, at least, a gesture of good will. It cannot fairly be said of the Roosevelt administration that it was unaware of the possible hostility that its foreign policy might arouse; or that it did nothing to soften the interventionist formula which it had so ingeniously invented.

The light touch of the Roosevelt administration, however, can hardly be said to have been emulated by President Taft or his Secretary of State, Philander C. Knox. At the distance of more than a quarter of a century, it can readily be seen that Mr. Taft, in discharging his high office, was by no means the ghastly failure which party spirit, and the venom of his predecessor, was to make him seem; his constructive achievements were many; but no man knew less than he how to endear himself to the multitude or effectively to publicize his policies. His choice of Mr. Knox, moreover, must be considered one of his major mistakes. A corporation lawyer of ability, but of choleric temper and limited view, supercilious in his attitude towards Latin Americans, and an easy victim of the prejudice which too often attaches to those connected with the interests of wealth, Knox managed in his four years of office to fail picturesquely and completely in attempting to follow and expand the policy of the previous years. In essence, the objectives pursued by the Secretary were in no sense sinister or irrational; what was desired and intended was to obviate the possibility of European intervention by setting in order the chaotic finances of such states as Nicaragua, Honduras, and Guatemala. This involved, as it had in Santo Domingo, loans by American bankers; it involved, as it had in Santo Domingo, some control over the customs; but whereas, when undertaken by the Rough Rider, it bore no sinister financial aspect, under Mr. Knox it early became stigmatized with the offensive title of "dollar diplomacy." The Secretary, most unfortunately, had been the representative of important mining interests in Nicaragua,[49] and this fact seriously hampered him in commanding respect for the policy which he inaugurated there. That policy we do not need to study in all its details; our interest naturally attaches particularly to the attempt to carry through the Roosevelt corollary; but the fact that the State Department, when revolution broke out in Nicaragua in the fall of 1909, before long took sides in the most emphatic fashion with the revolutionists against the President in office, and did so publicly, illustrates only too clearly the domineering and incautious spirit in which it approached the problems of Central America. Justice requires us to say that Mr. Knox, beyond question, was in his own estimation promoting the public interests of the United States; he obviously thought of himself as following out the line of action that had been traced by President Roosevelt; but he followed it with an ineptitude and a lack of success that are striking in the extreme.

Of the two loan conventions which Mr. Knox negotiated, the earlier is that with Honduras, the so-called Paredes-Knox Convention of January 10, 1911. The facts with regard to it will show that there was no sinister plot hatched in the State Department, indeed nothing sinister at all, except to those minds to whom bankers are by definition anathema. Honduras, at the period of which we write, was the possessor of a public debt, which, with arrears of interest, had reached the truly impressive total of $110,000,000. In 1908 the Council of Foreign Bondholders, representing British creditors (and the major creditors were British), drew up a contract for the funding of the debt, and this contract was diplomatically supported by the British government. But at this point the American Minister at Tegucigalpa intervened. On his own authority, as it appears, but with the subsequent approval of the State Department, he urged President Dávila to decline to accede to the agreement. There followed, after appropriate soundings, an appeal by the harassed chief executive to the United States for financial assistance. By April of 1909, only a month after Mr. Knox took office, it was already fairly clear that if American financiers could be persuaded to take a hand in the business, the loans of the past might be refunded on this side of the water, and the menace of European financial interests in Honduras permanently removed.[50] The British government offered no objection to the American plan — indeed, it behaved with great complacence toward the United States; and after rather complicated negotiations an agreement was reached. The terms of this agreement provided for the collection of the customs by a collector general appointed from a list of names presented by the fiscal agent of the loan (that is, the bankers) and approved by the President of the United States. "The Government of the United States," declared the closing sentence of Article IV, "will . . . afford such protection as it may find requisite." [51] This sentence was nothing more nor less than a paraphrase of that which appears in the Dominican convention of 1907. In the whole affair of the Honduran treaty, indeed, there is nothing that distinguishes it in principle from the compact with the Dominican Republic of four years before. In one respect, in fact, the Taft administration was more scrupulous than its predecessor. It will be remembered that President Roosevelt, in his own lighthearted way, had indicated that he would put down any revolution if one arose to thwart the evolution of his policy. In Honduras, on the other hand, when President Dávila, almost immediately after the signing of the treaty, found himself confronted with an uprising against him, and made appeal to the United States, he received no assistance whatever from Washington. President Taft and Mr. Knox were not ready, in this instance, to support the Roosevelt corollary by force of arms.

Unhappily, however, the administration acted differently, and much to its own disadvantage, in the case of Nicaragua. In that frequently distracted land there ruled in 1909 a dictator by the name of Zelaya. He was a man of undoubted capacity; and on both the material and the cultural side his sixteen-year rule had resulted in undoubted benefits to his country — in the construction of railroads, the stimulation of the coffee culture, and the beautification of the capital. But Zelaya was also corrupt, grasping, and unscrupulous, and in his foreign policy he was provocative as well, keeping Central America in turmoil. Since the Roosevelt administration had sought to bring about a good understanding in Central America by the exercise of its good offices, and by the Washington Conference of 1907, the activities of the dictator appeared particularly offensive. And it may well be that his moral turpitude was even more convincingly demonstrated when in the spring of 1909 he refunded the Nicaraguan debt, not where, of course, it ought to have been refunded, in the City of New York, but in the City of London with a concern known as the Ethelburga Syndicate. To an administration which was convinced of the peril of European loans to American states, such an act must have been distinctly irritating. Add to this the resentment felt at Zelaya's handling of claims questions and his cavalier treatment of American business interests, and it is not difficult to see that the temptation was strong to take advantage of any opportunity to rid Nicaragua and Central America of this truly baleful personality.

Revolution broke out in Nicaragua in October 1909. Undoubtedly some American firms had a hand in fomenting it. The American Consul at Bluefields was informed of it in advance. For a brief period the administration at Washington took no action of importance; but in November Zelaya executed two American soldiers of fortune who held commissions in the revolutionary army, and seizing upon this as a pretext the Secretary of State, in one of the sharpest notes that ever came out of Washington, excoriated the Nicaraguan president and terminated official relations with his representative in Washington.[52] This vigorous action had the effect of forcing the resignation of Zelaya; and it would not have been wholly unreasonable if thenceforward the United States had pursued a policy of absolute neutrality in the struggle of the Nicaraguan factions. Instead, the State Department acted to prevent the suppression of the revolt. When the forces of Madriz, Zelaya's successor, approached the port of Bluefields and took possession of the bluff commanding the town, at the same time posting a vessel of war off the harbor, the commander of an American naval vessel intervened, forbade fighting in the city itself, and insisted upon keeping the port open for the revolutionists.[53] Thwarted in their objective, the army of Madriz was finally compelled to withdraw from the coast, and the power of the President himself began to crumble. In August, the revolution triumphed, and General Estrada, the chief of the revolutionists, succeeded to the supreme power. Within two months of his installation in office a representative of the State Department appeared in Managua to negotiate a treaty for the control of the customs. In the course of the events just described a cynical mind might easily have detected a fixed purpose on the part of the United States to establish in Nicaragua a government that would do its bidding. In December, the selection of Adolfo Díaz, formerly secretary of an American mining company at Bluefields, as Vice-President of the republic had the air of confirming such a deduction. When in the spring of 1910 Estrada resigned (as it appears, on the insistence of the American Minister) and Díaz succeeded to the presidency, the chain of reasoning might well have seemed complete.

It was under circumstances such as these that there was signed at Washington on June 6, 1911, the so-called Knox-Castrillo Treaty, which, following the model of the agreement with the Dominican Republic and with Honduras, placed the customs of Nicaragua in the hands of an American official. On the very next day it was transmitted to the Senate, and in his message of transmission President Taft made his obeisance to the principles of 1823, as extended by the Roosevelt corollary. "A further responsibility is thrown upon us by the Monroe Doctrine," he wrote. "Much of the debt of Nicaragua is external and held in Europe, and while it may not be claimed that by the Monroe Doctrine we may be called upon to protect an American republic from the payment of its just foreign claims, still complications might result from the attempted enforced collection of such claims, from the involutions of which this Government might not escape." The policy advocated, the message went on to say, was especially desirable "with respect to countries in geographical proximity to the Canal Zone," and would "by contributing to the removal of conditions of turbulence and instability" enable them "to take their rightful places among the law-abiding and progressive countries of the world." [54] Seven months later, the Nicaraguan treaty and also the treaty with Honduras being unratified, Secretary Knox, in an able speech before the New York State Bar Association, expanded the argument of his chief. The Monroe Doctrine seemed to him to be connected with the "providential wisdom" of the founders of the Republic. "Mr. Roosevelt's corollary," he declared, would "diminish our responsibilities in proportion as we bring about improved conditions." In Santo Domingo, under American administration, the customs duties had been virtually cut in two, and the yield from them increased by nearly 80 per cent in seven years; "without any undue interference on the part of the United States" the new policy had "cured almost century-old evils." "It would not be sane," he concluded, "to uphold a great policy like the Monroe Doctrine and to repudiate its necessary corollaries and neglect the sensible measures which reason dictates as its safeguards." [55]

The Honduran and Nicaraguan treaties, however, were destined never to receive the adhesion of the Senate. It is not difficult to explain this fact. The Dominican treaty itself had barely gotten through, and had faced the almost united opposition of the foes of the administration. In the Senate of 1907 there were 31 Democrats. In the Senate of 1911–1912 there were 41. In the absence of strong popular pressure it was almost inevitable that most of these should align themselves against the administration. Nor should this all be set down to mere perverse partisanship. The traditional attitude of the Democrats had been that of opposition to entanglements with an imperialistic flavor. Cleveland had withdrawn the Hawaiian treaty of annexation from the Senate in 1893; Bryan had opposed the new commitments in the Orient; the platform of 1908 called for the grant of independence to the Philippines. Judging motives is always a precarious, and often an impossible, business; but it is fair to say that there may well have been sincere conviction behind the opposition to the extension of the Roosevelt corollary.

The Taft administration, moreover, was on no very strong ground in 1911 or 1912. It had been defeated in the elections to the House in 1910. Quite unfairly, it had been identified with Toryism and with undue complacence toward business interests. The background of the Nicaraguan matter was not alluring. Neither the President nor the Secretary had the gift of winning over the reluctant or the recalcitrant, or of dramatizing their case before public opinion. Most important of all, the administration had treated the Senate with a contemptuous indifference excelling that of President Roosevelt in the Dominican matter. As early as September 1911, while the Knox-Castrillo Convention was less than three months old, and not yet acted upon, it had encouraged the Nicaraguan government and the bankers to sign a loan contract for $15,000,000. A little later an advance of $1,500,000 was made, to be followed by smaller sums as the delay lengthened. In December an American official began to collect the customs. In March of 1912, the American bankers negotiated with the Ethelburga Syndicate, and secured a refunding of the former loan on very favorable terms, together with an understanding that the interest charges should be met through the customs revenues. In the same month the bankers secured an option on 51 per cent of the stock of the National Railway. When the Senate voted in May of 1912, Senators may well have felt some resentment at the course of the administration. They may well have found a malicious pleasure in doing what they could to thwart the Secretary of State. They may well have felt some justifiable prejudice against what might be regarded as an effort to coerce their judgment and anticipate their decision.

By this time, too, they may have felt some skepticism with regard to the Roosevelt corollary itself. The first effects of its application in the Dominican Republic had been really brilliant, as Mr. Knox had pointed out. But in November 1911, President Ramón Cáceres, the strong man of Santo Domingo, had been assassinated, and an era of turmoil was setting in that cast some doubt upon the infallibility of the Rooseveltian prescription for maintaining the peace of the Caribbean, and raised the question whether the mere control of customs was a conclusive remedy for domestic disorder. Moreover, in Nicaragua itself it seemed to become clearer and clearer that one thing led to another. President Díaz, the compliant friend of the United States, was by no means having things all his own way. He faced the constant hostility of his Minister of War, General Mena; he faced the hostility of the Nicaraguan Assembly, which the gentleman just mentioned controlled; as early as December 1911 he had proposed to the American Minister at Managua a treaty which would permit the United States to "intervene in our internal affairs in order to maintain peace and existence of a lawful government, thus giving the people a guaranty of proper administration." [56] In July 1912 he plucked up courage to dismiss the marplot Mena from office; but the result of his action was a new revolution, and a new appeal on his part for support from the United States. In August, American marines landed on the soil of Nicaragua; a few days later, under the command of the picturesque Smedley Butler, they entered the capital; on September 18, the American Minister made public a declaration that the United States intended to keep open the routes of communication and to protect American lives and property. On the twenty-fifth General Mena surrendered to an American admiral; a few days later American troops stormed a rebel position overlooking the railroad line; and a few days later still, they occupied León. The outcome of the Knox policy in Nicaragua was intervention — nothing less; and the occupation of Managua was the beginning of an episode that was not to be finally liquidated for some years to come.

In evaluating these events, however, we must not throw all the blame upon the Roosevelt corollary; we must remember that the Zelaya regime was offensive to the American government on grounds which had nothing to do with customs control; other factors than the financial undoubtedly entered into the problem. Yet surely the encouragement given to the bankers had a great deal to do with what followed; surely the events of 1911 and 1912 demonstrated that benevolent reorganization of the distracted finances of a Latin-American state was not as easy as it seemed. Surely the principle that American capital should supplant European capital, or supersede it, in the name of the Monroe Doctrine involved complications that were hardly foreseen in 1905 or 1907.

Mr. Knox, however, if he perceived this fact at all, was not deterred from the further prosecution of his policy in the case of a third Central American state, the state of Guatemala. There a long-lived despot by the name of Estrada Cabrera was in control. There, as in Honduras and Nicaragua, the public debt was largely in British hands. It had been refunded in 1895 and was supposed to be secured by the coffee revenues. The agreement to this effect had hardly been signed before it was violated. Interest payments were suspended, the coffee revenues diverted. Long patient or long indifferent, in 1912 the British government began again to press for a settlement of the debt question. And following the precedents he had created, Mr. Knox sought to secure a refunding of the Guatemalan debt, together with the administration of the customs by a nominee of the American banking group which should take up the loan. Such an arrangement, as he stated to the American Ambassador to Great Britain, seemed natural in dealing with "a general situation involving to a great extent the policy of this Government towards a portion of the world where the influence of the United States must naturally be pre-eminent." [57] But difficulties seem always to have attended this unfortunate Secretary of State. The British government was extremely suspicious, not without reason, of Estrada Cabrera; the bondholders were loath to give up the security of the coffee revenues, which had been pledged to them; they were loath to make new financial sacrifices; and although an agreement was signed with certain American banking groups in December, it proved wholly unacceptable to Great Britain. Demanding arbitration, which the Guatemalan government refused, the British finally determined upon a policy of menace. In May an ultimatum was presented by Sir Lionel Carden at Guatemala City; it stated that unless the coffee revenues were restored to the bondholders within five days diplomatic relations would be severed, and a British warship would be sent to collect the coffee tax. The Guatemalan government yielded, and the incident was closed.[58] Though naturally far from delighted at the British position, Mr. Knox, perhaps impatient with the authorities at Guatemala City, who wriggled and hedged even after the December agreement, used no strong or protesting language in his exchanges with Bryce; nor is there any evidence that the Guatemalan episode aroused even the faintest resentment in Congress or in the American press.

The discouragements which were met in putting into effect the Roosevelt corollary had certainly been many; the administration of President Taft had got nowhere in the case of Honduras, less than nowhere in the case of Guatemala, and had been dragged into an armed intervention in Nicaragua; but the policy it inaugurated was, interestingly enough, continued by the administration of Woodrow Wilson.

At first blush, it seems peculiar that a policy so intimately connected with banking interests, and so obviously implying a measure of control over the government and the lives of other peoples, should have been carried on, and indeed should have reached its climax, in the administration of a Democratic President who spoke much of self-determination, who wished to conciliate Latin-American opinion, who was much attached to general principles and peculiarly sensitive to any charge of pressure from financial sources. It is still more intriguing to find such a man as Secretary Bryan, a model of public piety and an anti-imperialist if ever there was such, marching along the path of his predecessor, the corporation lawyer Mr. Knox. Such a phenomenon deserves a word of preliminary explanation before we enter upon the details of the policy of the Wilson administration.

One reason for this, I rather suspect, lies in the fact that, to a degree which the American people do not always realize, American foreign policy, in its details though not often in its major directions, evolves from the permanent personnel of the State Department rather than from American public opinion. To a large number of international problems and policies the average American is entirely indifferent; his mind refuses to grapple with them; and within this range what is thought in the bureaus at Washington is infinitely more significant that what is thought by the man on the street. Secretaries of State, of course, when not influenced by public pressure, naturally tend to accept the view of their advisers, of those who have had experience and knowledge; and by the end of the Taft administration there had grown up a considerable body of official opinion in the Department which looked with favor upon the Roosevelt corollary and wished to see American control in the Caribbean area extended. This fact undoubtedly had something to do with the course pursued by the administration which came into power in 1913.

But there is another factor that needs to be taken into account. Woodrow Wilson and William Jennings Bryan were convinced believers in the universal efficacy of the democratic process, and in its triumph through the world. They believed they could assist the progress of democracy by their policy toward the states of Latin America. When the President declared, apropos of his Mexican policy, that he intended "to teach the Latin-American republics to elect good men," he spoke very much in character. His motive was disinterested to an extraordinary degree; but it was easy for him to be seduced by this same disinterestedness into measures of coercion. In the case of Mexico, the refusal to recognize Victoriano Huerta, because he had attained the presidency through violence, led to the occupation of Vera Cruz to prevent the dictator from getting supplies; and in the case of the smaller Caribbean republics it was but a step, and that not a very long one, from a benevolent supervision of their affairs to armed interposition. Influenced by very different motives than those of Knox, starting on different assumptions and guided, in part, by different objectives, the Democratic President and his Secretary of State came out in very much the same place. The fact is an extremely edifying one. It illustrates how the spirit of interference in the affairs of other nations may operate with men of widely divergent assumptions and points of view.

We need not, in this study of the Monroe Doctrine, consider except in passing the policy of the Wilson administration in Nicaragua. The marines remained at Managua; the customs continued to be collected by the designee of the bankers; the Secretary of State was ready to go even further than his predecessor and incorporate in a treaty an article conceding to the United States the right of intervention in Nicaraguan affairs; to Mr. Bryan, as to Mr. Knox, it seemed, "We cannot escape the responsibilities of our position." [59] But in all this we hear nothing of the principles of 1823 or of the Roosevelt corollary; and, in truth, it would have been strange had the fact been otherwise. For no European government took any action in the Nicaraguan problem, and there was not the faintest occasion for the administration, or even for the most sensitive and Monroe-minded of politicians, to make resounding appeal to the great American dogma.

Much the same thing can be said with regard to the Dominican Republic. The Taft administration, before it left office, had found itself compelled, by the responsibility assumed for customs collection, to interfere in the affairs of that interesting state; the customs service was temporarily suspended at some ports; the president of the day, if I may so put it, was obliged to resign. And here, as in Nicaragua, the Wilson administration out-Knoxed Mr. Knox: more and more the American Minister took a hand in Dominican affairs; the election of a constitutional convention in 1913 was partially supervised by American agents, despite the objections of the Dominicans; by 1914 American commissioners were sent to the island with instructions to compel the resignation of the chief executive, to demand an election under American supervision, and to insist that after such an election (were it honest) "revolutionary movements cease and . . . subsequent changes in the Government of the Republic be effected by the peaceful processes provided in the Dominican Constitution." [60] In the spring of the same year the United States had moved to extend its control over *internal* finances, sadly disorganized by revolution, and subject, perhaps, to supervision under a wholly possible — but disputed — interpretation of the convention of 1907. The story of what followed is not one that needs to be narrated here. By the summer of 1916, the Dominican government had been suppressed and American military rule existed in Santo Domingo. But all this had nothing to do with any threat from any foreign power; and the only relation of this interesting episode to the Roosevelt corollary is that it serves as an interesting and impressive illustration of how difficult it is to stand by complacently and watch revolutions revolve when one has already assumed a measure of positive responsibility in the affairs of another state.

The case of Haiti stands in a different category from that of Nicaragua and Santo Domingo. For here were not only the fine flower of the Roosevelt corollary and, in terms of the principles of 1823, the invocation of the Monroe Doctrine, but here also was the possibility of offensive interference on the part of European powers, of the Germans on the one hand and the French on the other. Historically speaking, the closest relations of this picturesque Negro republic were naturally with France. Haiti had, of course, been a French colony; and French interests subsisted when that relationship was terminated at the beginning of the nineteenth century. French diplomacy continued to play an active role at Port-au-Prince, and a French banking institution was the most important financial agency in the island. French warships not infrequently cast anchor in the harbor of the capital and at Cap Haïtien, and this continued to be true in the first decade of the twentieth century. Here was a situation that might bear watching. And in the Taft administration there appeared to be real reason for watching it. For with the spread of the idea of customs control in connection with foreign loans the Banque d'Haïti, a French institution, as we have said, began to put forward this idea and to urge the Haitian government to permit a French collector to be installed. The American Minister at Port-au-Prince got wind of this proposal and notified the State Department in February of 1909, suggesting that any such arrangement would be a violation of the Monroe Doctrine.[61] On February 23, Mr. Phillips, Assistant Secretary of State, responded that the United States would "view with much concern" any such arrangement as was proposed.[62] Almost contemporaneously with these occurrences came word of a proposal from the French Minister that France, Great Britain, and Germany join with the other powers in providing for the permanent station of a warship in the harbor of the Haitian capital.

At the time these events were taking place there were disquieting rumors with regard to Germany as well. The government of the Reich had shown a curious interest in the affairs of Haiti, which the prejudiced judgment of more than one American reporter connected especially with the furnishing of arms and ammunition to the Haitians to be used in their frequent revolutions. As far back as 1897 there had been a German naval demonstration at Port-au-Prince which, being undertaken for the redress of grievances, and especially for the indignity suffered, or alleged to be suffered, by a German subject, one Emil Lüders, had not provoked any action on the part of the cautious administration of President McKinley.[63] But such activity was supplemented by others; in the revolution of 1902 one of the candidates for the presidency was financed by German money in exchange for promises of concessions; in the same year the German gunboat *Panther* destroyed by gunfire the Haitian revolutionary craft *Crête-à-Pierrot*, which had captured a German vessel carrying arms to the regular government.[64] The president who came to power at this time was closely associated with German economic interests.[65] For a time after 1902 German foreign policy, intent upon sparing American susceptibilities, was cautious in its treatment of the Haitians. In 1904, when the French and German Ministers were stoned by a Haitian mob, the Kaiser and von Bülow refused to take any action, unless in concert with France, despite the urging of Holstein and von Richthofen.[66] No incident troubled the relations of the Negro republic with the Reich in the years of the second Roosevelt administration. But in 1909, when the question of customs control began to be mooted, the Germans, like the French, wished to have their finger in the pie; [67] and the news of their interest in the project combined with the previous advices from Port-au-Prince to urge the Taft administration into action.

It was, then, owing to the State Department, and on the initiative of the State Department, that in the fall of 1909 a proposal was put forward to reorganize the Banque d'Haïti and admit Americans to a voice in its administration.[68] Such a measure, of course, would serve as a check on the activities of the European governments and give the United States a voice in Haitian financial affairs. By the new arrangement the Americans held only a small fraction of the stock in the institution, and the fact that the proportion was no larger should be thoroughly digested by those cynics who trace everything in international politics to the sinister interests of high finance. It looks as if American bankers were by no means enthusiastic about investing their funds in the Negro republic, and as if they acted reluctantly on the solicitation of the State Department.

At Washington, indeed, the grounds for nervousness seemed more and more valid as time went on. In 1909, for example, a German commercial firm signed a contract with the Haitian government granting, among other things, the right to a coaling station. The provision in question was eliminated upon pressure from the State Department, but no doubt the incident rankled. German business interests continued to play an active part in Haitian affairs; German warships appeared in Haitian ports; German landing parties occasionally set foot on Haitian soil.[69] All this was troubling, to say the least, all the more so because of the turbulent conditions in the republic itself.

The Haitians had had a good many revolutions in their history, as a whole, but never did the political wheel revolve more rapidly than in the years from 1910 to 1915. In the five years just mentioned there were no less than six presidents, none of whom served so much as a year; the confusion was worse confounded; Haitian finances went not so much from bad to worse as from worse to infamous; and if ever anarchy invited the interference of a stronger power, this was the case in the affairs of the Negro republic. Early in 1914, moreover, came a move which helped to complicate the situation. In the conditions which existed the authorities of the Bank of Haiti naturally sighed for a strong hand; and there is no question whatsoever that by 1914 they willfully created a situation which they hoped would lead to intervention by withholding funds from the ephemeral government which was in power in the summer of that year. At the State Department Mr. Bryan, faced with the responsibilities of office, proved sympathetic to the bankers in this instance, as he had in the case of Nicaragua; when the Haitian government attempted to gain possession of the bank's funds, an American warship entered the harbor of Port-au-Prince, and transported these funds to New York to be held there in safekeeping until tranquillity returned to the distracted republic.

In the meantime, the question of customs control had come again to the fore. The French had cherished and still cherished the hope that they might be given a hand in the direction of Haitian finances. As early as March of 1914 M. Jusserand, the French Ambassador at Washington, had suggested that the customs administration be reorganized on an international basis, and that one of the three administrators thereof should be a Frenchman.[70] The suggestion was again discussed in July,[71] still again in February of 1915.[72] The Germans, too, began to get excited as Haitian matters went from bad to worse, and on July 25, 1914, only a few days before the outbreak of the World War, the German chargé addressed a note to Mr. Phillips, the Undersecretary of State, in which he declared that Germany had to consider its public opinion, which would not understand "if my government gave up their claim to participate in such a customs control."[73]

This German statement appears to have aroused considerable irritation; it was carried to the President, and in September it was answered by Woodrow Wilson himself in a dispatch which takes the strongest ground as to European financial control of American states. The dispatch deserves quotation.

Replying to the note of Your Government's Chargé, dated July 25, 1914 [it begins], regarding the matter of customs control in Haiti, I beg to say that the Government of the United States recognizes the large part which German merchants and German bankers have played in the development of the trade and enterprise of Haiti, and wishes to make this correspondence the occasion for expressing the pleasure with which it witnesses the employment of German capital and the activity of German men of affairs in this hemisphere; but represents to the Government of his Imperial Majesty that German interests are not the only interests which have played a conspicuous and highly influential part in the development of the Haitian Republic, and that the Government of the United States is well known to have taken for many years and without variation of policy the position that neither foreign mercantile influences and interests, nor any other foreign influence or interest proceeding from outside the American hemisphere could with the consent of the United States be so broadened or extended as to consitute a control, either in whole or in part, of the government or administration of any independent state.

The Government of the United States cannot depart from that policy, and feels confident that the Government of His Imperial Majesty will not expect it to do so.

Probably a participation of the Government of His Imperial Majesty in any method which might be agreed upon by which the Government of the Republic of Haiti should be assisted in the orderly, efficient and economical administration of its customs revenues did not present itself to His Imperial Majesty's Government as a departure from the traditional policy of the Government of the United States when its note was drafted. But this Government would regard such participation as a very serious departure from that policy alike in principle and in practice. The Government of the United States regards as one of the grave possibilities of certain sorts of concessions granted by governments in America to European financiers and contractors and of certain sorts of contracts entered into by those governments with European banking houses and financiers that the legitimate and natural course of enforcing claims might lead to measures which would imperil the political independence, or at least, the complete political autonomy of the American states involved, and might issue in results which the Government of the United States has always regarded as its duty to guard against as the nearest friend and champion of these states whenever they need a friend and champion.[74]

This was plain speaking to Germany; plain speaking to France was to follow, though at some distance. In February of 1915, when for the third time the French government brought up the question of control, Secretary Bryan asked the President for instructions. "The admission of any country to partnership in any political influence that we exerted there [in Haiti] would be inconsistent with the spirit of the Monroe Doctrine," he wrote.[75] "My own judgment follows and agrees with your reasoning in the letter altogether," responded Wilson.[76] And accordingly the Secretary wrote to Jusserand in this sense on the sixth of March. The Monroe Doctrine had been definitely applied to the question of European financial control over an American state.

The position that was thus assumed inevitably led to steps of interference similar to those which had proved necessary in Nicaragua and the Dominican Republic. At first persuasion was tried in an effort to bring about an understanding with the Haitian government which would give the American government control of the customs. But it was almost inevitably persuasion with coercion in the background. The first negotiations took place with President Zamor, as early as the first part of July, 1914, and before the German note. Apparently the Department of State wished to keep this dusky politician in office by force, if necessary. But Zamor fell suddenly in November, and was succeeded by President Théodore. This time the club of nonrecognition was held over the President's head to compel acquiescence in the American demands. It failed, as it failed with his successor of the winter of 1915, Guillaume Sam. Conditions in Haiti became frightful. French marines were temporarily landed at Cap Haïtien in June. At the end of July came the grisly uprising in Port-au-Prince, in which the president was murdered, dismembered, and his mutilated body paraded through the streets of the capital. The landing of American marines followed. Under the compulsion of American arms, the government of Haiti was brought to agree to a considerable measure of control, to American administration of its customs and internal finances, to the organization of a constabulary, to measures for the sanitation and public improvement of the republic; and at the same time it agreed not to surrender any of the territory of the Republic of Haiti "by sale, lease, or otherwise, or jurisdiction over such territory, to any foreign Government or Power except to the United States, nor to enter into any treaty or contract with any other foreign Power or Powers that will impair, or tend to impair, the independence of Haiti." [77] What was this but the reaffirmation of the Monroe Doctrine?

We do not need to carry the story of the Haitian intervention further; it represents the logical extension of the Roosevelt corollary; it emphasizes the possible implications of that corollary; it makes clear that financial penetration by European states might be regarded by the United States as implying political peril, and might thus fall within the broad scope of the principles of 1823.

In its policy in Haiti the Wilson administration had gone further in the policing of an American state than any administration which preceded it — further, that is, in the extent of power which it exercised, and the degree to which it interfered in the domestic affairs of the state brought under control. But there are signs that still more sweeping applications of the principle of American leadership and control in the Western Hemisphere were at least under consideration. With their innate prejudice against big business interests, especially foreign interests, Wilson and Bryan looked with a cold and critical eye upon the activities of European concessionaires in Mexico; they were annoyed at, and may have brought pressure to bear against, the efforts of the Cowdray interests to secure concessions in Colombia, concessions which were extremely broad in their terms; they watched with apprehension similar activities in Costa Rica and Ecuador. And in June of 1914, Mr. Lansing, Counselor for the Department of State, addressed himself to the problem of whether something ought not to be done about such matters.

Has the time arrived [he wrote], as a result of modern economic conditions in Central and South America, when the Monroe Doctrine, if it is to continue effective, should be restated so as to include European acquisition of political control through the agency of financial supremacy over an American republic? . . . The European power, whose subjects supply the capital to install and operate the principal industries of a small American republic and furnish the funds upon which its government is dependent may, if it so wishes, dominate the political action of the American goverment. . . . Should a new doctrine be formulated declaring that the United States is opposed to the extension of European control over American territory and institutions through financial as well as other means? [78]

Mr. Lansing's suggestion, if carried to its farthest extent, would have gone far indeed. Opposition to European loans would have been a considerable extension of previous policies; opposition to European concessions would have been still more extreme. Here, indeed, was what might almost be called the ultimate extension of the principles of 1823. Here, in the language of altruism, and in the name of self-defense, was marked out for American capitalism, one might fairly say, the whole vast areas of the New World.

We can only speculate as to why these proposals of Mr. Lansing never received the adhesion of Woodrow Wilson and William Jennings Bryan. Perhaps they went further than the President and the Secretary, even with their prejudices against European concessionaires, were ready to go; perhaps the failure of the Cowdray interests to secure the coveted rights in Colombia, and Ecuador and Costa Rica, operated to diminish the seriousness of the problem; perhaps the coming of the Great War gave the administration other things to think about. Whatever may be the reason, the Lansing memorandum never received official approval; but it reappears in a somewhat attenuated form in the latter part of 1915.

Mr. Lansing was now Secretary of State. On November 24 he addressed to the President a memorandum on the "Present Nature and Extent of the Monroe Doctrine." The principles which he had enunciated seventeen months before were now somewhat whittled down. In his memorandum of June 1914, Mr. Lansing had talked of Central and South America. In his memorandum of November 1915, he talked of the republics of the Caribbean. Clearly and definitely, he limited his own principles to a specific, or fairly specific, geographical area; he described a situation which he deemed dangerous to the United States. In some of these states, he declared,

a revolutionary chief finds little difficulty in financing his venture among foreign speculators in exchange for concessions and other privileges and the chance of large profits if the revolution is successful. As a result the people of these countries are the victims of constant strife between rival leaders, and their condition is little improved by the governments, which exist only a short time and which are used to enrich their rulers and those who have financed them. . . . Since the construction of the Panama Canal it is essential . . . that the neighboring nations should not come under the political domination of any European power either directly or by force or by cession or indirectly through the agency of financial control by its subjects. While force and cession are not impossible means if the government of a republic is corrupt or weak, the greater danger lies in the subtlety of financial control. To meet this danger the surest if not the only means is the establishment of a stable and honest government. . . . In order to accomplish this the first thing to do is to remove the prize of revolution, namely the control of the public revenues. If this can be done there will be few revolutions about the Caribbean. In the second place the government must not be dependent on foreign financiers for its continuance in power. In the third place, it must possess a reliable and efficient military force to suppress insurrection against the established authority.

The choice, the Secretary asserted, lay between continual anarchy fomented by foreign intrigue, and American assistance.

It would seem, therefore, that in the case of the republics about the Caribbean Sea the United States should expand the application of the Monroe Doctrine, and declare as a definite Caribbean policy that, while it does not seek domination over the territory of any of these republics, it is necessary for the national safety of the United States, and particularly in view of its interests on the Isthmus of Panama, that it aid the people of those republics in establishing and maintaining honest and responsible governments to such extent as may be necessary in each particular case, and that it will not tolerate control over or interference with the political or financial affairs of these republics by any European power or its nationals, or permit the occupation, even temporarily, by a European power, of any territory of such republics.⁷⁹

To these observations of the Secretary the President replied the very next day. The memorandum, he took for granted, was "only for the guidance and clarification of our own thought, and for informal discussion with our Latin-American friends from time to time" — it was not to serve as the basis of any immediate public declaration; but the argument, he thought, was "unanswerable." ⁸⁰ Thus did Woodrow Wilson, prophet of democracy and friend of self-determination, commit himself to the principles of the Roosevelt corollary, and to a doctrine of intervention in the affairs of independent states. When the United States entered the World War in 1917, American marines had been installed on the soil of three of the New World republics; in one of these the native government had been completely suppressed; in another it was subservient to a high degree to the wishes of the authorities in Washington; in a third it existed by virtue of American arms. By a development as interesting as it appeared continuous, even inexorable, the Roosevelt corollary had led directly to the coercion of the very states it was intended to protect. The Monroe Doctrine, aimed to prevent the intervention of European powers, had become a justification for the intervention of the United States.

Was the Roosevelt corollary an unwise and unwarrantable policy? Perhaps so. We need attempt no dogmatic judgment on the matter. But certain observations ought to be made. It may be stated with definiteness, for example, that in tracing the habit of revolution in the countries of the Caribbean to the machinations of unscrupulous European financiers, Mr. Lansing exaggerated, seeking, as we all do, a simple and diabolic explanation of infinitely complicated facts. A more candid and a broader judgment would call attention to the social conditions of these countries, to their traditions of personal rule, to the absence, in many of them, of a middle class of sufficient proportions, to many other factors. It might even be suggested that not on all occasions, or in every one of these states, had

American business interest been without sin in the fomenting of domestic disorder. It could be added, also, that not everywhere in the Caribbean area had good order needed to wait on American intervention. Time does wonderful things in politics, as in other matters. The turbulent Venezuela of Cipriano Castro, for example, became the tightly governed Venezuela of Gómez, sitting secure in the seat of power for a long quarter of a century; in Colombia, despite a turbulent period in the fifties, much progress has been made in political stability since the days of Theodore Roosevelt; in Mexico the convulsions of the post-Díaz era finally resulted in the emergence of a regime which, whatever the rigorous nature of some of its policies with regard to foreign capital, has not been during the last twenty years in a state of chronic revolution, or distinguished by an "impotence which results in a general loosening of the ties of civilized society." Such considerations tell their own story; they prove, beyond the peradventure of a doubt, that the civilizing influence of the United States can hardly be regarded as an *inevitable* condition of progress in Latin America. Yet we must not fall into the error of unqualifiedly condemning the Roosevelt-Knox-Wilson policy. That the occupation of Nicaragua, of Haiti, of Santo Domingo, resulted in some gains is undoubted. In all of these states communications were improved. In all of them the public health was promoted. In all of them something was done for education. In all of them, it can be argued, the masses of the population were better off under American control than they were under a native dictator, subject to less exploitation, more secure in the protection of their lives and properties, if they had properties. Furthermore, while American occupation cannot be said to have rooted out the revolutionary habit, it does appear to have made revolution less likely. In all the states native constabularies were established, which contributed to comparative stability. In Nicaragua and the Dominican Republic, indeed, the chiefs of these constabularies became President, and substituted a dictatorial but relatively efficient rule for the cycle of revolution. In Haiti, the state soon slipped back into its own ways of turbulence and misgovernment, but some small measure of progress may perhaps have been temporarily attained. It is, therefore, possible to maintain that benefits in the field of material progress, and in the preservation of the public order, have flowed from the American program.

Yet there can be no denying that since 1915 the tide has run against the policy of the Roosevelt corollary. There can be no denying that it earned us immense ill will. There can be no denying that it never received the really unequivocal and hearty support of American public opinion. A survey of the last quarter of a century will make this fact clear. But that is a matter for another chapter.

The period from 1905 to 1916 is that in which we witness the most sweeping extension of the Monroe Doctrine. From it was deduced not only the right of an international police power, but also, though more tentatively, a prohibition on European loans to the distracted states of the Caribbean. These new interpretations came from the executive. But in order to complete the picture a third interpretation or quasi interpretation must be added, a prohibition on the acquisition by foreign governments or corporations of harbors or other sites which might threaten the communications or the safety of the United States. This is related to the well-known episode of Magdalena Bay.

The facts in this matter may be briefly stated. A group of American capitalists owned a considerable strip of territory on the shores of this important harbor in Lower California. In the early months of 1911, they began to discuss a deal with a group of Japanese who desired to acquire the lands in question. Before long rumors began to spread along the Pacific Coast, rumors of nefarious projects on the part of the Foreign Office at Tokio. In July a representative of the American syndicate discussed the matter at some length with the Acting Secretary of State, Mr. Adee. He was told that if the Japanese government was concerned in the matter, the application of the Monroe Doctrine would necessarily be involved. Continuing to press for action, he wrote to Mr. Knox on the ninth of August, asking for the early expression of the opinion of the Department with regard to the whole problem. He received an equivocal reply. The Secretary, apparently aware of the embarrassment involved in prohibiting a purely business transaction, refused to answer categorically; he did, however, declare "that such a transfer would be quite certain to be interpreted in some quarters in a manner to cause a great outcry." With this, for the time being, our enterprising man of business had to be content. Very naturally, he merely modified his plans; instead of an outright sale, there was now contemplated an arrangement by which the Japanese entrepreneurs were to have a 35 per cent interest, with an option of a further 15 per cent, in the properties under discussion, while the American owners were to retain control of the board of directors and continue to direct the affairs of the land company. This plan Mr. Knox received in a manner even more noncommittal. Still a third attempt to elicit information and obtain some positive expression of opinion from the Washington sphinx was made without success.[81]

Such was the situation in the winter of 1912. It was brought to the public attention by Senator Lodge of Massachusetts, than whom no one could have had a more suspicious mind, or a more constant purpose to see perils both where they existed and where they did not. On February 29 Lodge, in the Senate, alluded to the "indirect" efforts to secure control of Magdalena Bay;[82] on April 2, he introduced a resolution calling on the State Department for information. Without waiting for any action from Washington, the Japanese government immediately took action. Mr. Hanihara, the Counselor of Legation, called at the State Department; he declared that the Japanese Foreign Office had been approached by some Japanese who desired encouragement in the project of acquiring land on Magdalena Bay; he asserted that it had discouraged the idea, and added that there was no water frontage to the tract marked for lease.[83] This was on April 5. On April 6, in response to a telegraphic inquiry from the *New York Times*, Marquis Saionji categorically denied that the Japanese government had any interest in the question of a coaling station in Mexico; and this disavowal was

followed by still another by Viscount Chinda, who made "an un-
reserved and categorical denial of the rumored purchase of land
at Magdalena Bay by the Imperial Japanese Government, or by a
Japanese company, characterizing the report as entirely sensa-
tional and utterly without any foundation whatever, the Japanese
Government having never directly or indirectly attempted or contemplated the acquisition of any land at Magdalena Bay for any
purpose." [84]

With this reassurance, reported to the Senate on April 27, the
question seemed for a time to recede into the background. Not im-
probably the Japanese capitalists who had been negotiating with
the American syndicate hoped to buy the lands on the bay as a
speculation and turn them over later to the government; certainly
the negotiations lapsed with the spring of 1912, and with the public
ventilation of the matter. But Senator Lodge was not satisfied. In
July he introduced into the Senate a resolution declaring that "when
any harbor or other place in the American continents is so situated
that the occupation thereof for naval or military purposes might
threaten the communications or the safety of the United States,
the Government of the United States could not see without grave
concern the possession of such harbor or other place by any corporation or association which has such a relation to another government, not American, as to give that Government practical power
of control for national purposes." [85]

This resolution, it will be observed, contained no reference to
the Monroe Doctrine. Nor would Mr. Lodge, when asked what was
the relationship of the new principle to the Doctrine, admit that
the two were united. His proposition rested, he declared, on "a
generally accepted principle of the law of nations, older than" the
tenets of 1823. It was based, as were those tenets, on "the principle
that every nation has a right to protect its own safety." [86] It should
be accepted had these tenets never been promulgated. We must, of
course, take the Senator at his word, and accept his assertion that
he was putting forward a new declaration of policy, unconnected
with the name of Monroe.

On the other hand, the Lodge resolution, as the press comment shows, did not remain dissociated from Monroeism in the debates in Congress or in the public mind, and probably owed at least some of the support which it secured to the same kind of sentiment which gave strength to the principles of 1823. It passed the Senate by a vote of 51 to 4; [87] it had already secured the unanimous approval of the Senate Committee on Foreign Affairs.

Juridically, the Senator from Massachusetts went far indeed in propounding his new theory. He was opposing a veto on the transfer of private property from private individuals to private individuals. He admitted that in the case of Magdalena Bay no government had been concerned. No doubt the theory of national safety will bear this, and almost any other extension; but it is nonetheless true that the resolution marks a new and remarkable application of the general principle of excluding non-American influences from this hemisphere. No doubt the Senate, in voting as it did, correctly expressed American opinion; and on at least four occasions since 1912 the Department of State has invoked the Lodge resolution not in dealing with foreign governments, but in interposing objections to the transfer to foreign interests of lands held by Americans in Mexico.[88] We must conclude, therefore, that though the Lodge formula was, at the time it was enunciated, somewhat distasteful to the administration, its principles have been incorporated into the foreign policy of the United States.

The action of August 3, 1912, was no doubt indicative of the temper of the times. It was indicative of American national sentiment in the second decade of the twentieth century. It was illustrative of the fashion in which the claims of the United States to the wide determination of questions involving American continents were developing and expanding. In all this there was little thought of the reactions of others, little consideration for the susceptibilities of the nations of Latin America. The years from 1905 to 1916 represent the culmination of those aspects of the Doctrine which European critics connect with what they call American "imperialism." Whether such days will come again the historian does not assume to say; he can, however, indeed he must, point out that the mood which they expressed was not lasting. What came after, what new forces entered the field, what new ideas began to flourish, we shall soon see.

VIII

The Doctrine and the League Monroeism and World Peace

I am proposing, as it were, that the nations should with one accord adopt the doctrine of President Monroe as the doctrine of the world: that no nation should seek to extend its polity over any other nation or people, but that every people should be left free to determine its own polity, its own way of development, unhindered, unthreatened, unafraid, the little along with the great and powerful.

I am proposing that all nations henceforth avoid entangling alliances which would draw them into competitions of power; catch them in a net of intrigue and selfish rivalry, and disturb their own affairs with influences intruded from without. There is no entangling alliance in a concert of power. When all unite to act in the same sense and with the same purpose all act in the common interest and are free to live their own lives under a common protection.

—WOODROW WILSON *in the speech of January 22, 1917*

The United States will not submit to arbitration or to inquiry by the assembly or by the council of the League of Nations, provided for in said treaty of peace, any questions which in the judgment of the United States depend upon or relate to its long-established policy, commonly known as the Monroe doctrine; said doctrine is to be interpreted by the United States alone, and is hereby declared to be wholly outside the jurisdiction of said League of Nations and entirely

unaffected by any provision contained in the said treaty of
peace with Germany.

— The Lodge reservation to the Treaty of Versailles

IN THE years of the Great War, and in the decade which followed it, there took form a great new experiment in international
affairs, the League of Nations. Through this instrumentality, con-
structed in 1919, a serious effort was made to organize international
life on some basis other than that of primitive force, to substitute
discussion, negotiation, and compromise for the brutal assertion of
national self-interest through war. We must not exaggerate the
degree to which this effort was carried. The Treaty of Versailles
reflected much of the spirit of intense nationalism. The foreign policy of the great powers remained egoistic in essentials. In our own
country American tariff laws, restriction of immigration, insistence on naval equality and on the repayment of the war debts,
all made it clear that American foreign policy was guided by no
remote idealism or extraordinary consideration for the well-being
of a world society as compared with the well-being of our own
people. But the temper in which diplomacy was conducted in this
period seemed at the time to carry great hopes in its train. It was
the temper of conciliation, of adjustment, and it was based on the
interest of all nations in avoiding war and settling their differences
by peaceful means. It sought to keep force in the background and
diplomatic processes in the foreground in the relations of the great
states of the world. It did not seem, at that time, either romantic
or naïve; it seemed eminently practical. Today the League of Nations system is in collapse; nor is it easy to believe that it will be
soon reconstituted. But the great experiment, if no longer a facile
hope, is none the less a significant memory; and in its working out,
and perhaps in its failure, the Monroe Doctrine played a part. We
shall have to consider how the American attitude toward the
League idea was influenced by the principles of 1823.

First of all, what lay at the heart of the League idea? Three
simple and easily stated principles. One, that all League members

should agree to respect the territorial integrity and political independence of each. Two, that they should agree to submit all disputes arising between them either to arbitration or to conciliation — that is, to either an arbitral or a judicial tribunal, or to a board of adjustment. Three, that they should agree to exercise economic and (conceivably) military pressure in unison against any state which violated the solemn promises just outlined. This is the essence of the matter. These various agreements did not go as far as to ban any and every type of war. On the contrary, war was still permitted, in most instances, if the processes of conciliation did not result in agreement, and after these processes had failed. Putting the matter in another way, there was a generalized obligation under the terms of the Covenant to attempt to settle every controversy with another nation by peaceful means; there was no such generalized obligation to abstain from the use of force if these measures of peaceful adjustment failed. There was also a generalized obligation to apply economic pressure against a lawbreaking nation; there was a less precise — indeed an extremely vague — obligation to resort to military or naval measures against the violator of the public peace.

Were engagements of such a kind contrary to the principles of 1823? Would American adhesion to the League have been a violation of the Monroe Doctrine?

In attempting to answer any such question the first thing to do, obviously, is to go back to Monroe's message itself. What did Monroe actually say with regard to Europe? He declared that "of events in that quarter of the globe, with which we have so much intercourse and from which we derive our origin, we have always been anxious and interested spectators." He went on to state that "in the wars of European powers *relating to themselves* we have never taken any part, nor does it comport with our policy to do. It is only when our rights are invaded or seriously menaced that we resent injuries or make preparations for our defense." In a later paragraph, he expressed himself as follows: "Our policy with regard to Europe, which was adopted at an early stage of the wars which have so long agitated that quarter of the globe, nevertheless remains the same, which is, not to interfere in the internal concerns of any of its powers; to consider the government *de facto* as the legitimate government for us; to cultivate friendly relations with it, and to preserve those relations by a frank, firm and manly policy, meeting in all instances, the just claims of every power, submitting to injuries from none."

These statements may, of course, be construed strictly or loosely, either literally or with regard to the general attitude which they reveal. If we are to construe them literally, we shall, I believe, be loath to draw the conclusion that the League idea and the Monroe Doctrine were incompatible. Monroe declared we should not interfere in the *"internal concerns"* of European states; the Covenant of the League suggested no such interference. He declared that the United States should not intervene in the wars of European powers "relating to themselves"; is it reasonable to assume that participation in a world-wide economic boycott or even military or naval action against a treaty-breaking state would be a violation of this maxim? Monroe, of course, had not the remotest conception that such a thing would ever be proposed; how, then, can his language be assumed to express a prohibition against it?

If it be averred that it is the spirit and not the letter of Monroe's message that must be heeded, there is still a case for the reconciliation of the principles of 1823 and the Covenant of the League of Nations. As we have already indicated in a previous chapter, it is by no means an inevitable deduction from the message that the United States should follow a policy of complete disinterestedness in Europe, or indeed in Asia. In the case of the Orient, the American government had not assumed, and was not assuming in 1917 or 1918, that, because it possessed special or paramount interests in the Western Hemisphere, it was, on that account, excluded from all participation in international politics in the Far East; such a proposition, as we have seen, had been brought forward in attenuated form in the debates of 1898 and 1899; but it had been repudiated in practice. In Europe, too, the sphere of American diplomacy had widened. The Hague Conferences were an illustration of this fact; the participation of the United States in the conference of Algeciras, called to compose a dispute between France and Germany, was no less so. And in 1917 had come the war itself. Was it logical to suggest that the United States could make war in Europe, but that it could not have anything to do with the consolidation of peace? Was not the United States free, in any quarter of the globe, to pursue its national interests as it perceived them; might not one of these interests, a major one, be an interest in maintaining the peace of the world?

This was one side of the matter; but the question, it must be admitted, could be argued from another angle. Behind the declaration of 1823, it could reasonably be contended, rested the principle of the two spheres, the separation of the interests of the New World from those of the Old. Monroe had drawn a line between republican America and monarchical Europe; between the virtuous and the vicious; between one order and another. The United States, it is true, had been swept into a European war in 1917, but it entered the struggle for reasons of its own; and with the defeat of Germany, it could be asserted, its proper policy was to withdraw from any further partnerships with powers of whom it had been only an "associate," in the President's own words, and never an ally. Europe was depraved and exhausted, America was virtuous and full of vigorous life; this had been the theme of many an American pronouncement before 1917 and 1918 — was it not a sound basis of action? Was not the doctrine of the two spheres, which lay behind the Monroe Doctrine, still valid in 1919?

Such are the two sides of the question of American adhesion to the League, looking at the matter as one of theory and relating it quite specifically to the language of Monroe. But what of the matter from the standpoint of practice and precedents? How in actual fact had the American government and the American Senate regarded the problem of American participation in the work of international peace?

We have already seen that as early as 1899, at the First Conference at The Hague, an evil example had been set for others to follow in dealing with this important problem. The United States had made a reservation to the Convention for the Pacific Settlement of International Disputes. It had done the same thing again with regard to the revised convention in 1907. And in 1912 still a third episode of the same general type had occurred. President Taft, conspicuous in his devotion to international good will, had negotiated so-called arbitration treaties with France and Great Britain. These treaties called for the submission to arbitration, not by any means of all disputes, but of all "questions justiciable in their nature," and it provided that a commission of inquiry with three representatives of each nation might decide by a vote of 5 to 1 or 6 to 0 whether a given question were justiciable.[1] This proposal would hardly have seemed, to the cool observer, to imperil the principles of 1823. How could the Monroe Doctrine be described as a "justiciable" matter? What was the chance that two out of three American members of a commission of inquiry would so decide? Yet the majority of the Senate Committee on Foreign Relations professed great concern on this point.[2] As early as August of 1911, just after the treaties had been signed, Elihu Root, eminent lawyer, ex-Secretary of State, and sometimes wavering friend of international peace, suggested a reservation covering the "traditional policy" of the United States. Theodore Roosevelt, more belligerent by nature, was even surer that some such protective qualification was needed.[3] Henry Cabot Lodge, always unbendingly nationalist, was much alarmed.[4] And to complete the picture, the Democratic members of the Senate, almost in a body, united to cast doubts upon the wisdom of the Taft proposal. With a partisanship which invites no admiration they proceeded to emasculate the arbitration agreements. Assisted by seven Republicans, they attached to the resolution of ratification a provision that there should not be submitted to arbitration "any question which affects the admission of aliens to the educational institutions of the several States, of the territorial integrity of the several States or of the United States, or concerning the alleged indebtedness or monied obligation of any State of the United States, or any question which depends upon or involves the maintenance of the traditional attitude of the United States, concerning American questions, commonly described as the Monroe Doctrine, or other purely governmental policy." [5] Disgusted at this exhibition of inconsequence, as he may justly have considered it, President Taft refused to ask the assent of Great Britain and France to the amended agreements. The Senate had made its view clear; and the principles of 1823 had been used to defeat an attempt at understanding between great and friendly nations. Might not the national egotism and the unhappy partisanship of which this Senate vote was an expression be taken as an evil augury for any such experiment as the League of Nations?

Indeed it might, as the event was to prove. But the friends of international peace, in 1918 or 1919, could point to one enheartening fact on the other side of the ledger. They could point to the action of the Senate on the so-called Bryan conciliation treaties. This series of pacts called for the submission of disputes "of every nature whatsoever" either to arbitration or to a commission of inquiry. In the event of the latter type of action, the signatory states were bound to abstain from war until the investigatory commission had rendered its report; they were, however, not bound to accept such a report when published, but could then resume their liberty of action. [6] It was Mr. Bryan's firm conviction that compacts of this kind would, in practice, effectively preserve peace. He negotiated a large number of them, and in August of 1914 no less than eighteen were sent to the Senate, and ratified as they stood by the overwhelming vote of 49 to 0. In view of the subsequent record of the Senate the absence of reservations to the Bryan treaties is both mysterious and miraculous. No adequate explanation of this phenomenon has yet been forthcoming. It may have been due somewhat to the Senate's preoccupation with the war which had just broken out in Europe; somewhat to the heat of a Washington summer; somewhat to the absence of Senator Lodge, who considered the agreements "fatuous" [7] and would have resisted them had he been present. But whatever the explanation, the friends of international understanding may at the time well have drawn heart from it; for here, after all, embodied in international compacts to which the United States was a party, was one of the fundamental principles of the future League of Nations.

It is not necessary in this brief volume to trace the interesting history of the development of the League idea in the United States. Beginning under the sponsorship of such eminent private individuals as William Howard Taft and Abbott Lawrence Lowell, it received the cautious adhesion of President Wilson at the end of May, 1916, and was mentioned in the Democratic Party platform of the same year, in the customarily ambiguous terms of such an instrument. It figured only occasionally, and not particularly concretely, in Wilson's campaign speeches for re-election. But in December discussion became more frequent, and on the twenty-second of January, 1917, in his famous peace-without-victory address, Mr. Wilson committed himself quite definitely to the conceptions later to be embodied in the Covenant. Making it clear that the adhesion of the United States to any such conceptions could be given only if the peace itself were based on sound foundations, on equality of rights, on self-determination, on the freedom of the seas, on limitation of armaments, the President held out the expectation that "the people and Government of the United States will join the other civilized nations of the world in guaranteeing the permanence of peace upon such terms as I have named. I am proposing, as it were," he went on, "that the nations should with one accord adopt the doctrine of President Monroe as the doctrine of the world: that no nation should seek to extend its polity over any other nation or people, but that every people should be left free to determine its own polity, its own way of development, unhindered, unthreatened, unafraid, the little along with the great and powerful." With this pronouncement may be said to have begun the epic struggle which culminated in the defeat of the Covenant, and in the personal humiliation of the President himself.

Why was it that Woodrow Wilson thus related the conception

of the League to the principles of 1823? In all probability because already there seemed to be gathering an opposition to his cherished policy which centered around the Monroe Doctrine. In the last days of 1916 press discussion for the first time raised the question as to whether, under the projected League, European powers would have the right to intervene in the New World to compel two American powers to observe peace. The idea appears to have caused some disquietude at the White House; for a few days the President seems to have hesitated as to the whole conception of a League to *enforce* peace, and to have thought of a League to *insure* peace, acting by moral suasion rather than physical coercion. On the sixth of January, Senator Borah, so long to contend in the forefront of the battle against the Covenant, expressed quite unequivocally his opinion that the League idea was incompatible with the traditional policy of the United States, and developed his theme in some detail.[8] This challenge the President in his speech of January 22 sought to meet by the assertion that an association of nations for the preservation of peace would be nothing less than the affirmation of the principles of 1823. Those principles protected the states of Latin America against conquest, against the subversion of their government; would not a universal pledge such as was contemplated not only universalize, but consolidate the Monroe Doctrine? Would it not give to the New World states a fuller protection against aggression than they had ever possessed? Would it not bring to their support in case of need the whole civilized world? Would it not provide a treaty sanction for the action of the United States itself in protecting them against aggression? Such, at any rate, was the argument brought forward; it may seem sophistical to some, and cogent to others; but it was, as we shall see, to be frequently repeated in the great debates of 1919.

The language of Woodrow Wilson, however, carried no conviction to the tenacious mind of Senator Borah of Idaho; on the twenty-sixth of January, as if in answer to the peace-without-victory address, the Senator introduced a resolution which reaffirmed the validity of the maxims of the Farewell Address, and of the Monroe Doctrine.[9] And more tardily, but more completely, Senator Lodge of Massachusetts, in a speech full of partisan venom, sought to demolish the President's thesis.

How [he asked] are we to reaffirm the first portion of the Monroe Doctrine [that is, the noncolonization principle] so as to give it a world-wide application? . . . If all the European powers accepted that doctrine and agreed with us that they would attempt no colonization here we should have the recognition of the doctrine by European powers, but the doctrine would apply to the same territory as before. How are we to make it a world doctrine in any other way? How are we to turn into a world doctrine President Monroe's second statement that he should regard it as an unfriendly act if any European power interfered with the independence of any American government? Is the transformation to be effected by having Europe and Asia and Africa adopt a doctrine that there shall be no colonies established by any power on any of those great continents and that if, for example, any European power should establish a new colony somewhere in Africa we should regard it as an unfriendly act. . . . The Monroe Doctrine defined our position and nobody else's position, and if we are to extend that doctrine to the other nations the only sanction it would carry would be that we should regard European colonization in all continents as an unfriendly act. Or does the President's proposition mean that the Monroe Doctrine is to be extended to all the world under the law laid down by John Fiske in regard to myths — that when we find a story of something which has happened everywhere we may be quite sure that it never happened anywhere — so that if we have a Monroe Doctrine everywhere we may be perfectly certain that it will not exist anywhere? If we are to abandon the Monroe Doctrine, this is one way of doing it. The Monroe Doctrine [added the Senator] is strictly local in its application; it applies only to the American Hemisphere and is based on the theory that there are two spheres in the world which are entirely separate in their political interests.[10]

Thus was the issue joined with regard to the Monroe Doctrine in relation to a League of Peace; the supporters of such a league claimed that the fundamental tenets of the American dogma would be internationalized by the cause they advocated; the opponents of the new spirit rested their case on that separation of the New World from the Old that was closely connected with the principles of 1823. Just as in religion men have often derived remarkably divergent conclusions from identical articles of faith, so too in politics there can be drawn just such deductions as one wishes to draw from the established and cherished maxims of the past. The struggle over the League illustrates this familiar fact.

The speech of January 22, 1917, and the replies to it, were only the opening guns in a battle which was inevitably delayed. Within a fortnight of the President's pronouncement the American government had severed its relations with Germany; and events moved relentlessly on to the declaration of war of April 6, and to the full participation of the United States in the struggle that was going on in Europe. In entering that struggle Woodrow Wilson again made it clear that one of its principal objectives must be the reorganization of the world for peace; the speech of the Fourteen Points in January of 1918 reiterated this objective; and in the heat of the great effort made by the American people to put down the German power in Europe, and in the lofty mood of the occasion, the purposes of the administration were rarely challenged. In the debates that preceded the great decision of 1917 there were occasionally those who trembled for the principles of 1823. Mr. McLemore of Texas, author in 1916 of a famous resolution which would have warned Americans off the merchant ships of the Allies, declared that he could not vote "to abrogate the Monroe Doctrine." [11] Representative Knutson of Minnesota, and his colleague, Lundeen, later a Senator from that state, thought that American entry into the struggle endangered the great American dogma,[12] Two or three other Congressmen took the same general position, tying the Doctrine, as it has so often been tied, to the conception of the two spheres and the separation of the New World from the Old. But in the Senate not a single voice was raised in lamentation at the ruin of Monroeism, and for many months after the declaration of war the nation devoted itself to the conflict alone, with little or no attention to the wider implications of the struggle. It was only with the coming of the Armistice, with the appeal of the President for a Democratic Congress, with the announcement that he intended to go to Europe to fight for the kind of peace in which he believed, that once more the spirit of opposition awakened, and once more the question began to be raised as to whether the idea of a League of Peace was compatible with the principles of 1823.

When the Congress assembled in December of 1918 the debate opened almost immediately, to continue intermittently through the early months of 1919, while Woodrow Wilson and his colleagues were wrestling with the problem of drafting the Covenant. The most prominent opponents of the President in these early months were undoubtedly Senator Borah, whose deep and sincere convictions were well known, and Senator Lodge. But other Senators took part in the discussion, and those hostile to the new policies and deeply disturbed about the Monroe Doctrine were not all on the Republican side. It could have been no great surprise to anybody to find James A. Reed of Missouri, constitutionally "agin' the government," among the critics of the administration; Senator Hardwick of Georgia was known to be on bad terms with the White House; but when such faithful Democrats as McKellar of Tennessee [13] and Myers of Montana [14] expressed the strong conviction that in any League of Nations the principles of the Monroe Doctrine must be preserved and protected it was clear that the opposition was not wholly captious or entirely partisan, but that it reflected something sincerely thought — or felt — by Senators and, no doubt, by their constituents as well. Though there is much that is unlovely and even mean in the League debate, we must not make the mistake of supposing that it was no more than a vicious partisan onslaught upon the President of the United States.

The opponents of the League, in their discussion of the principles of 1823, rested their case in part, as Senator Lodge had done in his speech of February 1, 1917, upon the principle of the two spheres, upon the separation of the New World from the Old. The Monroe Doctrine, said Senator Borah, was a purely American principle. It had been proclaimed, as President Wilson had himself declared, on the authority of the United States alone. Before the declaration of Monroe, the world was one. "Monroe determined to separate it and divide it, and that was the very object" of his message.[15] "It was the division of two systems; it was the political partition of two continents." In the same way Senator Lodge asserted that the very "essence" of Monroe's principles "is that American questions shall be settled by Americans alone; that the American continents shall be separated from Europe, and from the interference of Europe in purely American questions." [16] But this, of course, was only one of the arguments brought forward. In the familiar fashion of those resisting innovation, the foes of the League brought forward all sorts of hypothetical cases to show that the traditional policies of the United States might be endangered. Under the League system how could we be sure we could prevent the cession of the Danish West Indies or the Galápagos to Germany or some other hostile power? How could we take such action as we had taken in 1916 when Pershing entered Mexico in pursuit of Villa? How could we deal with such an incident as that of Magdalena Bay? Might not the decision of an international body in any of these instances be adverse to the interests and policy of the United States? These were the least of the perils which Senatorial eyes discerned in the developing Covenant. To Senator Borah,[17] to Senator Reed,[18] to Senator Poindexter,[19] to Senator Medill McCormick,[20] there was worse than this — there was nothing less than a British plot to secure the abandonment of the principles of 1823. In the League the United States would be outnumbered; Great Britain through the Dominions would have six votes to our one. The immortal dogma of Monroe, in such circumstances, could come to none but an inglorious end. The country must be protected against such a peril.

To arguments such as these the defenders of the President retorted with such effectiveness as they could summon to their task. Again and again they pointed out that the League was designed to protect the territorial integrity and the political independence of the nations concerned, and was in this sense an extension and reaffirmation of the Monroe Doctrine; [21] the principles of 1823 would be protected not by one nation, but by all, under the terms of the League constitution; [22] the Latin-American states would have a voice in determining these questions, and would, no doubt, act with the United States. As to the danger of submitting questions involving the Doctrine to arbitration or conciliation, had not the Bryan treaties already abandoned the position that certain matters could not be submitted to international investigation? In what respect did the League principles on this point differ from these treaties, which had received the unanimous support of the Senate in the summer of 1914? Unless the United States intended to assert the Doctrine in some offensive sense, unless it intended to claim some kind of hegemony over other American states, a hegemony to which it had no right, what was there to be feared from the development of an international association of nations?

All this, and much more, the reader will doubtless assess according to his prejudices and aspirations. The historian must be content to record the arguments, and one thing more. From a fairly early period in the winter of 1919 it was more and more apparent that if some heed were not paid to the strong feeling reflected in the debates with regard to the Doctrine, American adhesion to any international instrument setting up a League would be seriously endangered. It was not the foes of the League alone who expressed concern with regard to the matter; it was no question of satisfying merely the militant Borah or the vindictive Lodge; McCumber, firm friend of the League, expressed the conviction that some kind of concession should be made to the objections so frequently stated; there was disquietude, as we have seen, among the President's supporters. As early as March 4, 1919, Gilbert Hitchcock, the Democratic leader in the Senate, wrote to the President at Paris that a reservation on the subject of the Doctrine was highly desirable.[23] Outside the Senate William Jennings Bryan, still a leading figure in his party, declared on February 21, after expressing his strong sympathy with the League, that the principles of 1823 should be preserved.[24] "Our nation is not asking," said he somewhat ineptly, "to be permitted to take part in the settlement of European disputes, and . . . it ought not to be asked to give up its paramount influence in the Western hemisphere as a condition precedent to its entry into the League." William Howard Taft, than whom none more cordially supported the work being done at Paris, telegraphed to the President on March 18, urging a reservation as to the Doctrine in the body of the treaty, and prophesying that such a reservation would "probably" carry the treaty through to ratification.[25] There were subtler political thinkers than Bryan; there were shrewder judges of opinion than Taft; but the judgments of these two men were, at the time, no more than typical. There cannot be the faintest question that public sentiment had been aroused on the point in question, and that some kind of concession to Monroeism was an indispensable pre-condition to the drafting of a League Covenant which American opinion would accept.

But one may go further than this. It is interesting to discover these evidences of respect for the Doctrine amongst those not actively engaged in the negotiations at Paris; but it is more than interesting — it is impressive — to discover in the very heart of the American delegation itself the expression of the same point of view. Mr. Lansing, the Secretary of State, had grave doubts as to the relation of Covenant and Doctrine. Conservative by temperament, sensitive by nature, a conscientious rather than an imposing personality, he had watched with some trepidation the evolution of the ideas of his chief. As early as May, 1916, he had expressed his concern lest the project of a League become "a serious menace" to the Doctrine.[26] In particular, he disliked the idea of a positive guarantee of the territory and the political independence of the states of the world, which might "permit European Powers to participate, if they could not act independently, in the forcible settlement of quarrels in the Western Hemisphere whenever there was an actual invasion of territory or violation of sovereignty, while conversely the United States would be morally, if not legally, bound to take part in coercive measures in composing European differences under similar conditions." [27] But Mr. Lansing, in January 1919, no longer possessed the confidence of his chief, and his views were not likely to have great influence. Much more important was the position taken by David Hunter Miller, the legal adviser of the American delegation, a close friend of Colonel House and destined to play a central role in the drafting of the Covenant. In a memorandum drawn up as early as January 18, 1919, Miller launched a slashing attack upon the proposed article of the Covenant which guaranteed the political independence and territorial integrity of the contracting states.

Such an agreement [he declared] would destroy the Monroe Doctrine. Under such an agreement, Germany, as well as the United States and even despite the United States, would have been bound to support Venezuela against Great Britain in 1895. Under such an agreement Great Britain, France and Japan might be bound to intervene in Chile or in Peru according to their views of the Tacna-Arica dispute even in addition to intervention by the United States. . . . What the United States has done, is doing and will do for Europe is enough, without making an unasked sacrifice of her interests and those of Latin America, by giving up a policy which has prevented the countries south of the Rio Grande from being, like Africa, pawns in the diplomacy of Europe. . . . That the future attitude of the United States and its policy and that of Latin America should not be left to inference, but be beyond doubt or question, the constitution of the League of Nations should contain an express recognition of the Monroe Doctrine.[28]

Thus, from a quarter of large influence, and wholly disinterested, and at the Peace Conference itself, there came the same demand that popular and partisan feeling had expressed in the discussions at home.

In the early period of the Peace Conference, however, the question of the Doctrine did not figure importantly. In the early discussions of the special commission appointed to draft the League Covenant, over which President Wilson presided and which produced its first draft in the eleven days between the third and the

thirteenth of February, it played no part at all. The President took
ship for America; on the twenty-sixth he held his famous dinner
with the Senators at the White House, giving no indication that he
was prepared for any concession on the issue of Monroeism; on the
fourth he returned to Paris, and still there was no word of amending
the Covenant to satisfy American prejudices with regard to the
principles of 1823. As late, indeed, as the eighteenth of March, Mr.
Wilson was still reluctant to admit the Doctrine into the Covenant;
the Senate, he declared, would not wish it to be defined; would not
the acceptance of it necessitate the approval of an Asiatic doctrine
for the Japanese? [29]

But the pressure was, after all, very great; and it came from
sources which the President was bound to respect. On the nineteenth Lord Robert Cecil, the British delegate on the League Commission, and T. W. Gregory, Attorney General of the United States,
both handed to Miller suggestions for an article that would incorporate the Doctrine into the Covenant.[30] From that time forward
the question was frequently discussed; and it would be only tedious
to analyze in detail the various suggestions that were brought forward to deal with the important question of Monroeism. The draft
which finally met with general approval, and which was to be incorporated into the Covenant, was of British and not American
origin, and first appeared on March 25, when Sir William Wiseman
came to Miller's office and showed it to him.[31] It read as follows:
"Nothing in this Covenant shall be deemed to impair the validity
of any international engagement or understanding for securing the
peace of the world such as treaties of arbitration or the Monroe
Doctrine."

In one sense it is readily understandable why this rather extraordinary collocation of terms was to prove acceptable to the Americans at Paris. Of all things the most dangerous would have been an
attempt to *define* the Monroe Doctrine. A principle of action so
varied in its application would have been extremely difficult to
describe precisely. Any effort to do so would almost inevitably have
failed. Is it not easy to imagine the ingenious zeal of Senators of the

United States in thinking up corollaries that had been omitted? Is it not easy to imagine the cumbrous phraseology, the interminable clauses, that would have been necessary to satisfy every susceptibility? Should a definition include the idea of the Lodge resolution of 1912? Should it include the Roosevelt corollary? Should it include the Cleveland maxims? It would have been highly embarrassing to answer all such questions; it was much simpler to mention the Doctrine without defining it. President Wilson himself, as we have seen, had stated that the Senate did not want it defined; he had gone even further, and insisted in one of the most important of his speeches that it could *be* defined by the United States alone.[32] From this angle of vision the Wiseman draft seemed admirable indeed.

And yet it is not cynical to assume that the British, in formulating the article of the Covenant in question, were not thinking exclusively of the welfare of the United States. The phrase "any engagement or understanding for assuring the peace of the world" was a generously large one. It could be made to cover much besides the principles of 1823. It could be useful to British as well as to American interests, and useful to the interests of some of Britain's friends, such as the Japanese. It was a highly ingenious and innocent formula, of which much might be made, where convenience suggested.

For some time after the presentation of the Wiseman formula, however, discussion of the Monroe Doctrine receded into the background. That canny gentleman, David Lloyd George, who spoke the language of idealism, of self-interest, and even of bitterness with equal fluency, apparently hoped to make some kind of bargain with the Americans by which acceptance of the principles of 1823 would be set off against the suspension of the vast American naval program which had been initiated in the years immediately preceding Versailles; the issue was definitely raised early in April; and on the tenth of April Colonel Edward House, acting for the President, flatly refused to link together two questions entirely unrelated, or to traffic with the British Prime Minister on the question of Monroeism.[33] In this same interview Colonel House declared that at the meeting of the League Commission that evening an amendment on the Doctrine would be presented; that it would be presented whether the British liked it or not.[34] The strong tone that was here taken was a measure of the importance which had come to be attached by the American delegation to the recognition of the principles of 1823; but Lord Robert, who "seemed very much upset" on this occasion,[35] may have been tranquillized when the evening came, for the amendment submitted was one based on the Wiseman draft, and serving the purposes of Great Britain no less than those of the United States.

The debate in the League Commission on this spring evening of April 10 is one of the most interesting discussions in the long and interesting history of the Peace Conference. The Covenant of the League was being read article by article by the full Commission. When Article 10 was reached, President Wilson proposed the following amendment: "Nothing in this Covenant shall be deemed to affect the validity of international engagements such as Treaties of Arbitration, or regional understandings like the Monroe Doctrine for securing the maintenance of peace." At once discussion broke forth, and lasted till after midnight. Perhaps the most significant opposition to the Wilson proposal came from the French. It is plain to see why; indeed the reason was frankly stated by M. Larnaude, one of the French representatives. He wished, say the minutes of the meeting, "to have an obligation imposed on America to take part in European affairs." [36] In other words, relating the Doctrine to the idea of the two spheres, he feared that the President's proposal might lead to the virtual withdrawal of the United States from the League obligations so far as they related to the Old World. "He had no doubt that the United States would come to the help of Europe if Europe were threatened by absolutism. [An interesting prophecy, indeed!] Future wars might not, however, be wars of liberation. They might be economic in origin. The question was, therefore, whether the United States would come to the help of France should she be engaged in a struggle with a country which happened to be quite as liberal as herself." It would be best, in his judgment, to omit the Wilson proposal altogether. If it were to be included at all, it should be accompanied by a definition of the Monroe Doctrine.

In their opposition to the Wilson amendment, however, the French stood virtually alone. The subtle mind of Wellington Koo, the Chinese delegate, detected in the phraseology of the proposal a danger to the interests of China as against Japan, a veiled admission of Japanese hegemony in the Orient; and with this in view Koo suggested a change in verbiage, but he paid eloquent tribute to the principles of 1823.[37] Lord Robert Cecil rallied to the support of the President. He was opposed to any attempt at definition of the Doctrine, since such action "might extend or limit its application." He pointed out to M. Larnaude that "if he would consult history he would find that the Monroe Doctrine had never in a single instance been applied to American policy with regard to American participation in Europe, but always with regard to European participation in American affairs." With regard to the language, he suavely explained that "there were other understandings such as those concerning the tribes of Arabia" which should be included in the new provision. In every respect he placed himself behind the American proposal.[38] So, too, did the Italians, destined, before many days were gone, to feel the full weight of the Wilsonian opposition to their territorial ambitions, and anxious no doubt to court the President's favor on the matter in hand.[39] M. Orlando reminded the French delegates that the United States, after all, had participated in the war just over, "and if they did so under the principles of the Monroe Doctrine, then the more so would they come in in similar circumstances if they were members of the League." "He could not understand M. Larnaude's doubts," he added sententiously.[40] As for the President himself, he bore himself well and vigorously in this great debate. He reiterated that the Covenant universalized the principles of 1823, in its guarantee of the independence and integrity of the member states. "His colleagues in America had asked him whether the Covenant would destroy the Monroe Doctrine. He had replied that the Covenant was nothing but a confirmation and extension of the Doctrine. He had then been asked whether, if this were so, there would be any objection to making a specific statement to that effect in the text. It was by way of concession to this reasonable request that he was asking the Commission to state definitely what was already implied." In Wilson's mind, there was, in the acceptance of this amendment, no assumption that the United States would withdraw from due participation in European affairs. "If the United States signed this document they would be solemnly obliged to render aid in European affairs, when the territorial integrity of any European state was threatened by external aggression. Did M. Larnaude," he added somewhat touchily, "doubt that the United States would live up to its obligations if it became a signatory to the Covenant?" These observations of the President came fairly early in the discussion; toward midnight he participated once again, in what David Hunter Miller describes as "perhaps the most impressive speech I ever heard." For quite a while he had been silent, listening to the objections of the French. "He became very much stirred, and a sign of his agitation was that his lower lip began to quiver." Finally, he rose to sum up his position, "in words which literally seemed to cast a spell over those present." "Was the Commission going to scruple on words at a time when the United States was ready to sign a Covenant which made her forever part of the movement for liberty? Was this the way in which America's earlier service to liberty was to be rewarded?" A last objection came from the tenacious M. Larnaude. The President fell upon him. "Why were these objections raised? Was it conceivable that he wanted the United States alone of the signatories of the Covenant to say that she would not repudiate her obligations? Did she [France] wish to stop her from signing the Covenant?" With this last challenge the opposition appears to have collapsed. The amendment, though placed in a different position in the Covenant, as Article 21, was unanimously adopted; and in the wee small hours of the morning the Commission adjourned.

In the light of future events, in view of the later collapse of the League, it would be a sterile and futile matter to examine in any measure of detail the question as to whether the adoption of Article 21, and its incorporation in the Treaty of Versailles, constituted a recognition by European states of the legal validity of the Monroe Doctrine. It can hardly be maintained that the article was drawn with complete precision; the differences of opinion as to its meaning, the clamors for a definition of its terms, attest as much.[41] The French and English texts, it was to turn out, though both of them official, were inconsistent with one another. One declared the Doctrine was not "to be considered as incompatible with any one of the provisions of the present pact." The other declared the Doctrine to be "not affected by the engagements of the Covenant." One subordinated the Doctrine to the Covenant; the other the Covenant to the Doctrine. In view of all this imprecision it is very difficult indeed to discover with exactness just what had occurred. And in the years following not much light was to be thrown upon the problem. Attempts to clarify the ambiguities of Article 21 were, one and all, distinguished failures.

In view of all this vagueness it is not strange that the victory which Woodrow Wilson won at Paris was a Pyrrhic victory, so far as the contest with the Senate of the United States was concerned. By no means did it pave the way for easy ratification of the peace treaty. Of course, the President's friends hailed the adoption of Article 21 as a great triumph. David Hunter Miller maintained that "the mention of the Doctrine in an international agreement signed by all the states of the world without any dissent and with approval is *almost* a recognition of the Doctrine." [42] The President's supporters in the Senate, less cautious than his legal adviser, proclaimed that beyond all question the principles of 1823 had been preserved, protected, and explicitly acknowledged at Paris.[43] The President himself, after his return to America in July, insisted upon the same thesis in speech after speech, and in the famous conference which he held in August with the members of the Foreign

Relations Committee of the Senate.[44] But the opponents of the Covenant were implacable. They insisted that the language of Article 21 was not only vague, but incomprehensible. They insisted that the Monroe Doctrine was not "a regional understanding" but the unilateral policy of the United States.[45] In particular they called attention to an interpretation of the Covenant which had been elaborated by Lord Robert Cecil and widely circulated in Great Britain. "In its essence," Cecil had written, the Monroe Doctrine "is consistent with the spirit of the Covenant; and indeed the principles of the league, as expressed in Article 10, represent the extension to the whole world of the principles of the doctrine; while should any dispute as to the meaning of the latter ever arise between the American and European powers, the league is there to settle it." [46] What means this sinister and candid language? asked Senator Johnson, and Senator Knox, and Senator Lodge. Does it not signify that the authority of the League might be exercised to define the Monroe Doctrine? And is not this interpretation virtually the official British one, since Cecil helped to draw the Covenant? How, in the face of such facts as these, can anyone maintain that Article 21 sufficiently safeguards the interests of the United States? How can the Senate do otherwise than take steps of its own to protect the ark of the diplomatic covenant from violation?

Senator Lodge was still more ingenious. He raked up, along with the statement of Cecil, a commentary of Stéphen Lauzanne, whom he described as "solicitor of the treaties and a chief spokesman for M. Clemenceau," the French Prime Minister. In an exuberant passage this prominent journalist had predicted that in due time the League would "control, whether it will or not, the destinies of America. And when the American States shall be obliged to take a hand in every war or menace of war in Europe (art. 11), they will necessarily fall afoul of the fundamental principle laid down by Monroe. . . . If the league takes in the world, then Europe must mix in the affairs of America; if only Europe is included, then America will violate her own doctrine by intermixing in the affairs of Europe." [47] The language of M. Lauzanne showed an imperfect knowledge of the Covenant; and it incorrectly identified the Monroe Doctrine with the doctrine of the two spheres. Yet it sounded ominous, just the same; and indeed the opponents of the President derived, very naturally, strong support for their position from the natural American repugnance to entanglement with the nations of Europe.

It is not necessary for us to sit in judgment on the Senatorial interpreters, the necessarily partisan interpreters, of Article 21. But it may perhaps be said that many of the friends, as well as all of the enemies, of the League were critical of the phraseology. Lord Robert Cecil himself declared that it was "vague in essence"; [48] many Democratic Senators came to the same conclusion; [49] so, too, did ex-President Taft.[50] No authoritative interpretation of the disputed clauses could be brought forward; and taking all the circumstances into account it is not entirely surprising that the clamor for a reservation on the Monroe Doctrine did not die down with the President's victory at Paris. As a matter of fact it swelled into a chorus; it was clear that the Senate, traditionally independent in its view of treaties, and also traditionally partisan, would not rest content with the recognition of the principles of 1823 — if recognition it could be called — which had been incorporated into the Covenant.

It is no part of our purpose to discuss in detail the long debates which took place on the League and the treaty when Woodrow Wilson brought them back to the United States in July 1919. The President assumed, from the outset, a clear and in many respects a logical position; he would not object to interpretative reservations to the treaty, which would not be a part of the instrument of ratification; but he would not accept reservations or amendments which might require the renegotiation of the compact itself. Whatever is to be said for or against such a position, it was certainly not at all novel — Presidents have taken it again and again; and after the numberless painful compromises in the negotiations at Paris it is not strange that Wilson did not wish to go through further long and possibly perilous diplomatic exchanges.

On the other hand, it is not entirely fair to regard the debates of 1919 as nothing more than a miserable partisan controversy. It is true that a malevolent party spirit appears in the maneuvers and speeches of Henry Cabot Lodge and many of his followers; it is true that on the Democratic side there were blind adherents of the President; but it is also true that much of the opposition to the treaty was sincere, and the sentiment for reservations was not the mere expression of a desire to discredit and humiliate the administration. The test in these matters is to be found in the voting; it is of the highest significance that, while the Republicans held their lines practically intact, the Democratic forces weakened when the balloting began. On the question of a reservation with regard to the Monroe Doctrine, for example, it was not possible for the Democrats simply to take their stand on Article 21; they brought forward a reservation of their own; they could not, in the face of public sentiment, apparently, ignore the necessity of some further safeguard for the principles of 1823. Indeed, on this particular issue they went almost as far as did Lodge and his followers, and the difference between the Lodge reservation and the substitute offered by Senator Hitchcock, the Democratic leader, is rather one of suavity of language than divergence of outlook. Thus the Lodge draft declared that the Doctrine was "to be interpreted by the United States alone, and is hereby declared to be wholly outside the jurisdiction of said league of nations and entirely unaffected by any provision contained in the said treaty of peace with Germany"; the Hitchcock draft spoke of "the national policy of the United States, known as the Monroe Doctrine, as announced and interpreted by the United States"; both drafts withdrew the Doctrine from any decision, report, or inquiry by the council or assembly; the Lodge draft added a word as to arbitration.[51] It was clear that in some form the Senate desired to pass on the question of the principles of 1823 in relation to the Covenant; the desire to do so was widespread on both sides of the Chamber. Moreover, as the debate proceeded, the drift was in the direction of a stronger, rather than a weaker pronouncement. Only two Democrats, it is true, voted for the Lodge reservation, and both of these were enemies of the administration; but not a single Republican deserted,[52] on a choice between the Lodge and Hitchcock proposals. And once the Hitchcock reservation had been defeated, no less than nine Democrats gave their approval to the proposition of the Massachusetts Senator.[53] No other of the numerous reservations received a larger number of votes from the Democratic side, and only one commanded as many. Figures such as these are eloquent of the direction of public sentiment; they are eloquent of the place which the Doctrine held in public opinion. For in the long run one may say that our American representative bodies do truly represent; and while men's motives are mixed, and often obscured even from themselves, it seems wholly likely that the Democratic Senators who deserted the administration and cast their votes with the solid phalanx of the Republicans were expressing no mere whim of their own, but a generally held prejudice with regard to the principles of 1823.

As is well known, the voting on the treaty and the Covenant in November of 1919 had an altogether melancholy result, from the standpoint of believers in the League. The Senate adopted no less than fifteen reservations; it made ratification of the treaty as a whole dependent upon the acceptance of these reservations by three out of four of the great powers — Great Britain, France, Italy, and Japan. In this form, of course, the President would not accept it; stricken with paralysis after his Western tour in September, insulated by an all-too-loving wife from those who might have offered him the counsel of compromise, bitterly disappointed and outraged at the spirit which had been displayed in the Senate debates, reluctant, as almost any chief executive would have been, to renegotiate the language of the Covenant and of the treaty, Wilson cast his influence in favor of unconditional ratification; a resolution to this effect introduced in the Senate was defeated by 38 to 53. On this resolution seven Democrats deserted; and if, once again, one believes that Senators are apt to be fairly representative of their constituents, one must conclude that the drift of opinion was opposed to the unqualified acceptance of the great document which had been drawn up in Paris a few months before.

Yet sentiment for some kind of affirmative action on the treaty continued strong; when Congress reassembled a bipartisan conference was called, which set to work to go over the reservations with a view to making them more acceptable to the friends of the Covenant. On the subject of the Monroe Doctrine, however, no agreement could be arrived at. The phrase to which Senator Lodge and his supporters clung was that "the Monroe Doctrine should be interpreted by the United States alone"; this statement, the Senator from Massachusetts declared, carried out "the unbroken history of the United States." "We are claiming here," he declared on the floor of the Senate, "nothing more than we have always claimed; but if, after that claim has been put into a reservation adopted by the Senate, it is stricken out, it would be equivalent to saying to all the world that we are not prepared to interpret the doctrine alone." Such a course appeared to him unthinkable. So, too, it appeared to his colleagues when the test came. Senator Hitchcock's milder reservation, when the Senate voted, commanded only 34 of the 47 Democratic votes; and the Lodge reservation itself was reaffirmed with 17 Democrats in support.[54] Among these were such administration stalwarts as Senator Pittman of Nevada, a future chairman of the Committee on Foreign Relations, and Senator Owen of Oklahoma, author of the Federal Reserve Act of 1913. Unable to break down the Republican position, their own ranks crumbling, the friends of unconditional ratification were again routed; and once again, this time without much hope of renewal, the treaty failed. The President, as early as January, had urged that the issue be taken to the people in the Presidential election of that year; he was as set against compromise as ever; and so a momentous issue of foreign policy was submitted to the passions, the vagaries, and the insincerities of a political campaign.

Into the details of that campaign it is, of course, not necessary to enter. There was the usual amount of equivocation and blurring of the issues, perhaps more than the usual amount; in particular, it was difficult to ascertain the precise position of the Republican candidate, Senator Harding. The campaign approached its end with many sincere, if possibly naïve, leaders of opinion urging the election of Harding on the ground that this was the best way to get the United States into the League; and this fact alone is a sufficient illustration of the confusion which prevailed. But the Republican candidate, though devious in many of his utterances, and mellow toward all shades of opinion (mellowness was Harding's distinguishing fault), did not omit to declare himself unequivocally on the subject of the Monroe Doctrine. That doctrine, he declared in a speech of September 11, "is not a treaty of arbitration or a regional understanding. It is the plain, square, fearless declaration of the United States, which is a warning against European nations asserting undue influence or applying improper pressure upon the helpless republics of the western hemisphere." [55] This statement contained, it must be admitted, more than a trace of condescension toward our Southern neighbors; the statesmen of Argentina or Brazil, had they read the candidate's words, would not altogether have relished the description of their thriving nations as "helpless"; but it must be said to the credit of Mr. Harding that he had assimilated one fact of importance: he asserted the now so often emphasized principle that the Monroe Doctrine was a unilateral doctrine of the United States; he made clear what had been made increasingly clear in the League debates, that the doctrine was to be interpreted by the United States alone. With a political instinct that was acute if not unerring on this as on most other matters, — for example, in his famous promise of a "return to normalcy," — he said precisely what the American people in 1920 most wanted to hear. In November the voters rendered judgment; and by an overwhelming majority Warren Harding was sent to the White House to replace Woodrow Wilson, exemplifying in his triumph the change in the national mood since the heroic days of 1917 and 1918. His inaugural still hinted at the possibility of "engaging under the existing treaty," as the new President put it; but it was not long before this idea was abandoned, in view of the strength of the irreconcilable elements in the Republican Party; and so the United States remained aloof from the hopeful institution of international peace which Woodrow Wilson had had so much to do with founding. The League fight was over.

What conclusions are to be drawn from the events that we have narrated from the standpoint of the Monroe Doctrine? The assertion has sometimes been made that the defeat of the League Covenant was directly due to the loyalty of the American people to the principles of 1823. Such an assertion, however, appears to be very extreme. It is likely that, if the President had been willing to accept the Lodge reservations, the treaty could have been ratified; it is also likely that *had* it been ratified the European signatories would have accepted the modifications which had been made; and while the historian must proceed with the greatest caution in dealing with hypotheses, it seems not improbable that Woodrow Wilson, most unhappily, tipped over his own work in those bitter days of the fall of 1919 and the winter of 1920. No such statement ought to be made dogmatically; one's sympathy for the broken man in the White House, animated by purposes so lofty, makes one reluctant to come to any such conclusion, but a candid judgment on the facts requires that this view of the matter be stated. Surely the experiment of ratification with reservations ought to have been tried; it is rash indeed to assert that it would certainly have failed — and even rasher, then, to declare that the League was defeated because of American attachment to Monroeism.

But if the Monroe Doctrine idea cannot be said to have defeated the Covenant, it is nonetheless true that the debate on the League reveals that there was in the minds of many of its opponents an incompatibility between the principles of 1823 and American adhesion to a League of Nations. This feeling was strongest in those who associated Monroeism with the idea of the two spheres. It was a feeling, after all, which had been more than once expressed before. It was a feeling which rested on long-held prejudices as to the wicked nations of the Old World. It was a feeling, in reality, that antedated Monroe, antedated even the Farewell Address, went back to John Adams at Paris and Thomas Paine in Philadelphia. The reader or the writer of this volume may prefer to construe the message of 1823 entirely differently. But it is impossible to deny that in the course of the League debates of 1919 and 1920 it was used, and used effectively, to discredit or to limit the idea of American participation in an international association for the maintenance of peace.

Something more must be said with regard to the Doctrine and the policy of Woodrow Wilson. The Covenant was conceived in the spirit of internationalism. The Doctrine was a manifestation of the spirit of nationalism. The words of its ardent defenders in the Senate, the insistence on the fact that it was to be interpreted by the United States alone, the appeal to the protection of purely national interests in its name in the course of the debates, all illustrate the same thing — all demonstrate that national egotism is a powerful, indeed a dominating principle in the life of all great states and all great peoples. To many persons, it is true, the League formula was an enticing one; and the theory which lay behind it, of an association of free nations which by collective action should make the world "safe for democracy" and free from the assaults of autocratic power, is a theory which many, in our own day, will wish it had been possible to translate into fact, and which the very optimistic may hope to see vindicated in the future. But, in truth, it required of men and of nations a long, and a relatively disinterested view of affairs; and men being proverbially shortsighted, being in the nature of things most concerned with the present living moment and not with the evolving future, being deeply attached to the formulas of the past and the interests which lie near them, being, for good or bad, deeply infused with national feeling and limited by national selfishness, it was perhaps inherent in the nature of the thing that the great and not irrational ideal which lay behind the Covenant should become diffused and distorted in the moil of partisanship, patriotism, and persistent egotism. So it was elsewhere as well as in America; and he is romantic indeed who conceives today that the ratification of the Treaty of Versailles in the United States would have ushered in a millennial period in the history of mankind.

In the years which followed the great debate over the League, indeed, the spirit which lay behind the Covenant often proved itself insufficiently strong to accomplish important ends. It existed, and at times it brought about real successes, notably in the Washington Conference of 1921–1922, which resulted in the reduction of naval armaments; notably again in the decisive fashion in which it expressed itself at a moment of maximum tension with Mexico in 1927; notably, once more, in the tripartite agreement of 1930 on naval building which set for a few brief years limitations on all types of ships, for the United States, Great Britain, and Japan. But it could not alter the determination of the American people to insist on the payment of the war debts; it could not prevent them from closing the doors of their house to the foreigner in the Immigration Acts of 1921 and 1924; and it was never able to bring about the adhesion of the United States to the World Court of Justice which was set up at Geneva.

This latter problem concerns the Monroe Doctrine, and must therefore be given more than a word of mention. The general facts with regard to it are not difficult to summarize. The judicial settlement of international disputes had been, one might almost say pre-eminently, an American ideal. A commission of jurists under League auspices had outlined a scheme for a World Court which was submitted to the first Assembly in 1920; and after this scheme had been, with some modifications, approved by that body, a protocol embodying the plan was drawn up, and signed by forty-six nations. At the second Assembly judges were elected, according to the new project, and the Court convened at The Hague in January of 1922. An eminent American, Mr. Root, had been one of the most useful members of the commission of jurists; an American judge took his seat upon the Court, elected by a procedure which did not involve the assent of the government of the United States. From these activities that government in 1920, 1921, and 1922 held officially aloof; but in the winter of 1923 the Harding administration, which was gradually modifying its attitude of extreme reserve with regard to even the most harmless of League activities, came forward with a positive proposal for American adhesion to the protocol creating the Court; and thus was precipitated a debate which lasted for more than a decade, and which furnishes an unhappy example of the resistance that may be offered to the most innocent proposal in the field of international action. The Court was, for the most part, a court of voluntary jurisdiction; no nation could be haled before it against its will; yet there arose in the United States on the part of the foes of the League a violent opposition to any connection with an institution which owed its origins to the initiative of Geneva, and the advocacy of four Presidents and the support of a considerable body of opinion were insufficient to break this down.

In submitting the World Court protocol to the Senate in 1923 President Harding had thoughtfully taken account of the Senate's penchant for reservations, and had suggested several. He had not, however, suggested a reservation on the principles of 1823. This almost inevitable gesture was left to Senator Henry Cabot Lodge, who was not unequal to the occasion. Like most of the opponents of the Court proposal, Senator Lodge fixed his attention on the function of the Court which permitted it to give an advisory opinion on any question referred to it by the Council or the Assembly. This function existed for League members under Article 14 of the Covenant; it would have been altered in no fashion whatever by American adhesion to the protocol; and it was, in any case, binding morally only, and not legally. But the enemies of the Court made great play of the possible perils inherent in advisory opinions; and Lodge, in offering an alternative to the proposal before the Senate, made it clear that an international Court of Justice should have no power to give such opinions "in any question which depends on or affects the maintenance of the traditional policy of the United States, concerning American questions." [56] The same position was assumed by Senator Pepper of Pennsylvania and, it will not be surprising to learn, by Senators Borah of Idaho and Reed of Missouri.

It is an evidence of the potency of the Doctrine as a weapon of opposition that though the friends of the administration pointed out more than once the emptiness of the argument that the principles of 1823 were endangered, they were compelled, in the upshot, to admit into the final resolution of ratification a saving clause with regard to those principles. Senators hate to be recorded in opposition to Monroeism. They hated to be so recorded in the struggle over the Court. And so, in due or undue course (perhaps the latter, since the proposal did not come to a vote till 1926) we find Senator Swanson of Virginia, none other than the proponent of the resolution of ratification, on January 23 introducing of his own volition a modification of the original proposal. This modification expressly declared "that adherence to the said protocol and statute hereby approved shall not be so construed as to require the United States to depart from its traditional policy of not intruding upon, interfering with, or entangling itself in the political questions of policy or internal administration of any foreign state, nor shall adherence to the said protocol and statute be construed to imply a relinquishment by the United States of its traditional attitude towards purely American questions." [57]

It was with these saving clauses, amongst a variety of others, that the Senate voted favorably on the World Court proposal on January 27, 1926, approving it by a vote of 76 to 17. At the same time it had added a reservation stipulating that the Court should render no advisory opinion "in any dispute or question in which the United States has or claims an interest" without the consent of the American government. This reservation, also, undoubtedly owed its existence, in part at least, to the fears engendered by the opposition as to the position of the Court with regard to the Monroe Doctrine. Though the debate was less ardent, the issue of the Doctrine drawn less sharply, than in 1919 and 1920, it still remains true in the one case as in the other that the principles of 1823 played their part in the defeat of a new, and extremely modest proposal looking to the advancement of pacific methods of solution for international controversies. The moral effect of this was shown in the form of the treaties of arbitration which the Department of State drew up in 1928, as a contribution to the spirit of international co-operation; these treaties specifically excepted from arbitral consideration questions involving the traditional policy of the United States with regard to American questions, "commonly known as the Monroe Doctrine." There was to be no ambiguity on this score.

The year 1928 is also the year of that extraordinary document known as the Kellogg Pact, or the treaty for the renunciation of war. Taking advantage of a proposal which came from the French government for a bilateral treaty renouncing war, Secretary Kellogg undertook the ambitious project of binding all the nations of the world together in one great international agreement for the preservation of peace. His efforts were, in the main, successful, and on August 27, 1928, was signed an instrument of three articles, an instrument which seemed simplicity itself. This was afterwards accepted by virtually all the nations of the world, Brazil and Argentina excepted. It pledged the signatory power to renounce war "as an instrument of national policy"; it stipulated that "the settlement of all disputes or conflicts of whatever nature or of whatever origin" should "never be sought except by pacific means." [58] But in the working out of this remarkable accord the Monroe Doctrine showed its head once more. In the early phase of the discussion, for example, it appeared prominently in a draft or project of a treaty drawn up by Professors Shotwell and Chamberlain of Columbia University. No two men could have been more disinterested friends of international peace than these; and it is interesting and significant that they found it necessary, in drawing up an agreement for the renunciation of war, to reserve, not only the right of legitimate self-defense, but also "action by the United States of America in pursuance of its traditional policy with reference to the American continents." [59] Secretary Kellogg, despite the precedent of the arbitration treaties, did not, however, fall in with this idea. He hoped to make his projected agreement the very simple document which it did in fact become, free of all unnecessary verbiage and all qualifying language. He aimed to allay distrust of his proposal by making it clear in public addresses, notably that of April 28, 1928, before the American Society of International Law, that the renunciation of war still left intact the right of self-defense; and by assurances of this kind he sought to satisfy the more nervous supporters of the principles of 1823. In a measure he was successful; during the course of the negotiation one hears little of objections to the Kellogg Pact. Up to this time, indeed, practically the only official allusion to the Monroe Doctrine was in the British note of May 19. In that communication, in the main an acceptance of the Kellogg proposal, Sir Austen Chamberlain, the British Foreign Secretary, pointed out somewhat obscurely that there were "certain regions of the world the welfare and integrity of which constitute a special and vital interest for our peace and safety." Declaring that the British government could not surrender its freedom of action with regard to such regions, Mr. Chamberlain went on to say, "The Government of the United States has comparable interests any disregard of which by a foreign power they have declared they would regard as an unfriendly act. His Majesty's Government believe, therefore, that in defining their position they are expressing the intention and meaning of the United States Government." [60]

To these interesting observations Mr. Kellogg made no reply. In the note of June 23, 1928, in which the pact proposal took mature form, he spoke once again of self-defense, but not at all of the principles of 1823. But when the treaty was presented to the Senate, doubts naturally began to present themselves. In vain did its friends argue that those magical words "self-defense" covered the situation amply, and made reservations of any kind unnecessary. To this the critics responded with the argument from history. There always had been reservations to agreements of this kind, they insisted. There had been reservations to The Hague Conventions, to the Taft treaties, to the Covenant of the League of Nations, to the World Court protocol. In the light of all these precedents, why not have a reservation to the treaty for the renunciation of war?

The malcontents came from both sides of the Chamber; there were Republicans as well as Democrats, friends of peace as well as cynics like James A. Reed, who contemptuously described the treaty as "an international kiss." Something had to be done to satisfy them; and fortunately for Mr. Kellogg's *amour-propre*, and indeed for the eventual acceptance of the pact itself, the parliamentary situation was far less bitter and strained than it had been nine years before. In the mellow days preceding the Great Depression, the fires of partisan controversy with regard to schemes of peace seemed to have burned themselves out. The foes of the League were now the friends of the Kellogg Pact; the voice of Senator Borah, raised so often, and so sincerely, in opposition to the Covenant, was now lifted not so much to defend as ardently to advocate the proposed treaty; and except for the irrepressible Reed, most of the other irreconcilables of 1919 and 1920 were silent. Accordingly a way was found to deal with the question of the Monroe Doctrine. The report of the Committee on Foreign Relations, originally presented on December 19, was modified so that it contained a gloss upon the treaty, a *gloss*, be it noted, not a reservation; and this gloss contained the following significant words: "The committee reports the above treaty with the understanding that the right of self-defense is in no way curtailed or impaired. . . . The United States regards the Monroe Doctrine as a part of its national security and defense. Under the right of self-defense allowed by the treaty must necessarily be included the right to maintain the Monroe Doctrine which is a part of our system of national defense." There followed relevant quotations from Monroe, from Cleveland, from Root, from the international lawyer, Theodore Woolsey; and in the last of these it was indicated, no doubt with a view to soothing Latin-American susceptibilities, that the Doctrine "called no new rights into being; therefore, whenever it over-steps the principle of self-defense, reasonably interpreted, the right disappears, and the policy is questionable." In such fashion the principles of 1823 were in a measure defined and reiterated; and in such fashion the Kellogg Pact was preserved from alteration. It passed the Senate by a vote of 85 to 1; we have no way of knowing to what extent the Senate committee's gloss contributed to this brilliant victory; but the fact that that gloss was deemed necessary is one more evidence of the vitality of Monroeism.

It was not possible, however, with regard to other agreements, to repeat the relatively moderate procedure adopted in 1928. Twice thereafter the World Court protocol was to be reported to the Senate; in 1932 the resolution of ratification again contained a saving paragraph, reproducing the reservation to The Hague Convention, designed to protect and preserve the Doctrine. This reservation had the endorsement of every member of the Committee on Foreign Relations, including such friends of international peace as Thomas J. Walsh of Montana and Robinson of Arkansas. In 1935, when, after long delays, the matter was once more taken up in the Senate, Arthur H. Vandenberg of Michigan offered a similar amendment, and it was adopted by a unanimous vote, without a roll call.[61] And even with this safeguarding clause, the protocol failed.

In these numerous maneuvers of the Senate, extending over the years, it is possible if one will, no doubt, to see nothing more than the perversity of individual politicians, or a corporate sense of self-importance which gratified itself in altering, if not in emasculating, the proposals of the Executive. It would be foolish to deny that some such motives may have played, and probably did play, a part in the events that we have been examining. But this explanation can hardly be a complete one. We may fairly assume that there was something more than personal or corporate egotism behind the various reservations on the Monroe Doctrine. It is likely that they expressed a point of view not rarely held by members of the American electorate. It is likely that the temper of American nationalism was reflected in the Senate. The American people cherished the dream of international peace; but they cherished also the principles of 1823. Because they cherished those principles it was easy for Senators to append such reservations as we have been analyzing to agreements widening the area of peaceful settlement, and to reiterate their loyalty to the great American dogma.

IX

The Doctrine and the Good Neighbor
Pan-Americanism and Monroeism

Article I. The High Contracting Parties declare inadmissible the intervention of any one of them, directly or indirectly, and for whatever reason, in the internal or external affairs of any other of the Parties.

* * * * *

Article II. It is agreed that every question concerning the interpretation of the present Additional Protocol, which it has not been possible to settle through diplomatic channels, shall be submitted to the procedure of conciliation provided for in the agreements in force, or to arbitration, or to judicial settlement.

— *The Special Protocol Relative to Nonintervention,*
December 23, 1936

IN THE YEARS from the defeat of the Covenant to the rise of militarist and nationalist Germany, the American continents were in no danger of any kind from the ambitions of any European power. The exhaustion of war would, in and of itself, have explained this important fact; but it ought also to be observed that the whole policy of Great Britain had now been brought into conformity with the principles of 1823, and that postwar France showed no signs of any New World ambitions, having fully enough to do in maintaining its position in Continental Europe. Whether or not the Monroe Doctrine had been explicitly recognized by the language of Article 21 of the Covenant, it was certainly in no wise challenged by the victors of the World War; and optimists might easily have justified to themselves the conclusion that after the defeat of the Reich the New World would enjoy a long period of exemption from the threats or the intrigues of the Old. Such a view was to be proven false in due course; but the tranquillity of the international scene in the twenties, and the absence of any direct challenge to the liberties of the American republics in the thirties, at any rate until the very end of the decade, means that the story of the Doctrine in this period is more concerned with Latin America than with Europe, and centers around the relationship of Monroeism to the movement known as Pan-Americanism.

This movement possessed a very feeble vitality during most of the nineteenth century; it has grown into a phenomenon of increasing significance in the twentieth; and although it would be easy to point out the difficulties that lie in the way of its continued progress, and the divergences of temper and interest between the partners to this understanding, the fact remains that substantial progress has been made in creating a sense of common interest between the various and varied governments of the Western Hemisphere. The spirit of Pan-Americanism in part resembles, and in part differs from, the spirit of 1823. Both assume that there is something distinctive about the way of life and the ideals of the countries on this side of the Atlantic; both rest, in other words, in some measure at any rate, upon the doctrine of the two spheres. But in one important respect the two conceptions are not so much in harmony as in opposition, one to the other. For the Pan-American spirit is the spirit of equality and friendly understanding; the spirit of Monroeism, as we have seen, had by 1915 been deeply charged with an assumption of a right of control, of superior power, of hegemony, over the other states of the New World. In proportion as the Pan-American spirit grows, the assumption of overlordship on the part of the United States naturally tends to disappear, and in proportion as the nations of the Americas tend to co-operate with one another, the purely unilateral character of the principles of 1823 tends to be superseded by a broader view of Monroeism. This evolution is one that we shall have to trace in the pages that lie ahead.

We must not, of course, imagine that Pan-Americanism is a movement unconnected with the material interests of the United States. It had its origins in a broadening interest in the commercial and financial possibilities opening up in Latin America. James G. Blaine, its first conspicuous champion, tied together in his own thought the idea of commercial reciprocity and that of the peaceful settlement of inter-American political controversies. Much of the earlier work of the Pan-American Conferences had to do with questions of an economic, rather than of a political character.

Nor is it to be thought that it was easy to win the friendship or secure the hearty collaboration of the states to the south of us. In their cultural relationships (and in some striking instances in their trade relationships) these states were oriented rather toward Europe than toward the United States. Distrust of the Colossus of the North was often keen. We have seen, for example, how in 1895 in Mexico, in Chile, and in Argentina, the disinterested enthusiasm of Cleveland and Olney for the cause of Venezuela was received with distrust rather than enthusiasm. In Cuba, the publicist Céspedes, whose country had most to hope for from the United States, and who wrote the first Latin-American book on the Monroe Doctrine, was unable to divest himself of suspicion and dread of the North Americans.[1] In the period of the Spanish-American War, the Argentine statesman, Roque Saenz Peña, later to be president of the republic, delivered an eloquent address championing the cause of Spain; [2] in the same year the famous Chilean scholar, Alberto del Solar, gave a lecture on the Monroe Doctrine and Latin America in Buenos Aires, which minced no words as to American imperialism.[3] When this lecture was published, it contained an introduction by Calixto Ayuela, soon to achieve fame in Argentina as literary man and critic. Just a few years later there appeared in Brazil a still more savage attack by Eduardo Prado, entitled *The American Illusion,* an attack so bitter, indeed, that the book was suppressed by the Brazilian government. When the second Pan-American Conference met in Mexico City in 1902, after an interval of thirteen years, and only after some urging on the part of the United States, the spirit of the delegates, while naturally polite, was one of attachment to Europe rather than eager friendship for the United States. To the pessimist, it might well have appeared at this time as if the future of Pan-Americanism were anything but brilliant.

Moreover, in the years between 1902 and 1915 the tide of suspicion of the United States continued to rise. In the literary sphere it becomes increasingly conspicuous. It is evident in the earlier work of the Nicaraguan, Darío; in the writings of the Uruguayan, José Rodó; in the *Latin America* of the Peruvian, García Calderón; and in a still more virulent degree in the Madrid lectures of the Venezuelan Blanco-Fombona, the extraordinarily able and widely read volume of Manuel Ugarte, *The Future of Latin America,* and the works of the Mexican Carlos Pereyra. These authors one and all distrusted the Colossus of the North; one and all expressed doubts as to Pan-Americanism, and emphasized rather what may be described as Pan-Hispanism; and while we might easily exaggerate their influence, it is significant that in the literary sphere relatively few voices were raised against them.[4]

Nor is it to be thought that all was well on the political side in the years we have just mentioned. At Rio de Janeiro in 1906 the suave and friendly diplomacy of Elihu Root had done something to pour oil upon the waters; the last years of the Roosevelt administration were relatively untroubled; but at the fourth Pan-American Conference at Buenos Aires in 1910, a significant episode shows the distrust with which the United States, and its favorite policy of the Monroe Doctrine, were regarded.

Of the larger countries of Latin America, that one most consistently friendly to the United States has been Brazil. The Brazilian Minister to the United States, Senhor Nabuco, had drafted in advance of the Buenos Aires meeting a declaration on the subject of the principles of 1823, which lauded those principles as "a perma-

nent factor of external peace for the American continents" and terminated by addressing to the "great sister of the North . . . the
expression of all her [that is, Latin America's] gratitude for that
noble and disinterested initiative, of such benefit to the western
world." This declaration committed to nothing; one might have
thought that it would be readily accepted, as a pleasant bit of diplomatic flattery, if you will; but it ran afoul of all kinds of objections.
The Chilean delegation had as one of its members Señor Alejandro
Alvarez, who was, perhaps, among Latin-American publicists, the
least grudging in his recognition of the value of the Monroe Doctrine; but the Chileans were not ready to accept the resolution we
have just mentioned. The representatives of some of the other
states were still less enthusiastic; they feared that "in approving
it," says Señor Alvarez, "they would sanction the acts of hegemony
accomplished by the United States, by whom more than one country considered itself as offended in its sovereign dignity." It became clear, therefore, that the introduction of any such resolution
might precipitate an acrimonious debate; the American delegation,
when consulted, indicated that it would prefer inaction to an inharmonious discussion; the whole project had to be dropped. That
so harmless a formula should have awakened antagonism is eloquent proof, however, of the spirit of some of the Latin-American
delegations toward the United States.[5]

Another illustration of a similar temper is to be found in the so-
called Triana plan. Santiago Perez Triana was the Colombian Minister at London. In the spring of 1912 he brought forward a proposal for a multilateral convention of the American states, by which
conquest should be proscribed, and by which the signatories should
agree not to resort to it. The plan got nowhere; but it clearly revealed distrust of the American government, and of the new interpretations which were being placed upon the Monroe Doctrine.
By the time the Taft administration left office, it is undeniable that
the relations of the American government with the states of the
New World were distinctly not harmonious or trustful; in foreign
as in domestic policies Mr. Taft, by some unhappy stroke of for-

tune, or personal idiosyncrasy, found accumulated upon his head all the discontents that had been slowly forming in the administration of his predecessor. It is only fair to say that the President had been by no means uniformly inept or inconsiderate in his relations with Latin-American states; he had shown the greatest patience and self-restraint in dealing with the troubled conditions in Mexico; he had undertaken negotiations with Colombia to smooth over the untoward events of 1903 in Panama; but nonetheless he failed to secure the good will of the nations to the south; and in press and diplomatic correspondence alike one discovers plenty of evidence of the sensitive state of Latin-American feeling toward the United States.

Let us add one more example of the kind of thing that was becoming increasingly common. In 1913, Theodore Roosevelt, ex-President of the United States, undertook his famous exploration and travels in South America. And on at least two occasions, amongst the many on which he was feted and entertained, the speakers of the day went out of their way to say a word about the Monroe Doctrine. In Chile Marcial Martínez, a writer and diplomat of great distinction, was frank indeed. "My opinion," he declared, "is that the Monroe Doctrine lived, that is to say, it has ceased to exist. It is an obsolete document, and to consider it as in force is a striking anachronism. The social, economic, political, and even ethnological conditions of 1823 have absolutely disappeared; and it would be impossible, without being guilty of gross error, to apply at the present time a system which has really become obsolete as a matter of fact." At Buenos Aires the well-known publicist, Estanislao Zeballos, was less crushing, though no less candid. He was able to sympathize with the American attitude in Panama, "the crown of thorns" and the "masterpiece" of his guest's administration. He was able to recognize the wisdom of the principles of 1823 in relation to "smaller countries, some of them inorganic, in constant conflicts with Europe," in the neighborhood of the Caribbean. But Monroe's "attitude" (Zeballos refused to give his sanction to the word "doctrine") degenerated as one went southward. "The Argentine Republic will not be protected by Monroe's attitude because she has completed her evolution in civilization, and is now a respected country and knows how to merit the respect of the world! . . . We do not fear aggressions against our territory, either from Europe or from America, and there is not the slightest danger of our sovereign integrity being threatened by any nation whatsoever. Monroe's attitude is not, then, applicable to our country."

For a not inconsiderable period, while the tide of criticism in some of the states of Latin America rose higher and higher, the American people were, for the most part no doubt, agreeably oblivious of the impression which their cherished Doctrine produced in the breasts of their Southern neighbors; and it is only fair to say that the first striking attempt at enlightenment came in an article by Hiram Bingham, in the *Atlantic Monthly* for June 1913. Boldly, perhaps too boldly, in view of American opinion and of his own subsequent utterances, Professor Bingham proclaimed the great dogma of 1823 to be "an obsolete shibboleth." Vigorously he denounced the Roosevelt gloss on Monroe as implying the assumption of the heaviest responsibility "for the good behavior of all of the American nations." Illuminatingly he discussed the attitude of the three most powerful states of South America, Argentina, Brazil, and Chile, and declared that these states regarded the Doctrine as "long since outgrown, and as being at present merely a display of insolence and conceit on our part." He pointed out that the mere discussion of a project to clean up the Ecuadorian port of Guayaquil with the aid of American sanitary engineers and American capital had produced a real flurry of antagonism in Ecuador, and in some of the newspapers of neighboring Peru. He quoted the British Ambassador to the United States, the learned and highly respected James Bryce, in support of his conclusions. "Since there are no longer rain clouds coming up from the east," said many Latin Americans, according to Bryce, "why should a friend, however well-intentioned, insist on holding an umbrella over us? We are quite able to do that for ourselves if necessary."

The views expressed in his article in the *Atlantic Monthly* Professor Bingham, in this same year of 1913, expanded into a little book, and reiterated in the *Yale Review* the year following. He told of Saenz Peña, now President of Argentina, for whom the Monroe Doctrine was a "gutta-percha doctrine"; he quoted Policarpo Bonilla, President of Honduras, as declaring that the American dogma "instead of being considered as a guarantee of independence by the Latin-American countries had been regarded as a menace to their very existence"; he quoted Dr. Rafael Reyes, an ex-President of Colombia, as declaring that the nations of Latin America "resent the spirit of domination and tutelage which implies that they need the protection of the United States against foreign aggression"; he cited the language of the *Mercurio,* one of the most influential of Chilean journals; in short he massed new authorities, numerous and respectable, in support of the thesis which he had put forward. And he ended with a plea for co-operative action by the United States with the republics of the South, in place of the assumption of superiority.

But Professor Bingham's book and articles were only one sign of the change that was taking place, if not in the offices of the State Department or in the minds of the specialists who worked there, at least in academic opinion, and indeed in the wider circles of American journalism. The article in the *Atlantic Monthly* was followed in December by one in the *North American Review* by George H. Blakeslee, distinguished student of international politics, and teacher of history at Clark University. Professor Blakeslee was more tender of the susceptibilities of his compatriots than his Yale colleague; he did not talk of "obsolete shibboleths"; but he arrived at the same conclusion, that the Monroe Doctrine ought to be transformed from a mere unilateral declaration of policy into a joint policy of the American states. Striking confirmation for his conclusions Professor Blakeslee found in an inquiry which he set on foot in the winter of 1914. "The Monroe Doctrine," a British essayist had written, "is like God or religion to a small child — something fearful, something to inspire awe, something, if necessary, to fight for." Was this statement true? What did the specialists, the teachers of international law and American diplomacy, have to say about the matter? It turned out that they had a good deal. Out of 124 interrogated, only 13 thought that the existing status of the Doctrine was satisfactory; 104 out of 124 thought the United States should share with the ABC states the responsibility of enforcing it; 107 out of 127 thought that its principles should be restated for the benefit of Latin America; 94 out of 126 thought the American people needed a little enlightenment as to its meaning as well. But these men were a small unworldly group, it might be urged, perversely or happily or high-mindedly engaged, as you will, in attempting to make the world of affairs a little better than it had been. It was interesting and important to find that in the field of journalism, closer to the opinion of the mass, the same view was held. Out of 36 papers 30 favored some form of international cooperation with regard to the Doctrine; 30 out of 37 believed that it should be redefined. The *New York Sun* thought the principles of 1823 had become "as elastic as India rubber and as comprehensive as all outdoors"; the *Nation* thought those principles "had been modified to death"; again and again the gentlemen of the press called for a new spirit in applying the dogmas of Monroeism.

There were signs that this new spirit was on the way in some of the acts of the Wilson administration. The declaration of President Wilson at Mobile on October 27, 1913, that the United States would "never seek one additional foot of territory by conquest" undoubtedly produced a favorable impression (though it is only fair to say that it had been anticipated by a similar speech of Philander C. Knox more than a year before). The acceptance of the good offices of the ABC powers after the taking of Vera Cruz in April of 1914 was an earnest of good intentions, as was the evacuation of that seaport six months later. Even more important and far-reaching, though destined to remain abortive, was the administration's plan for a Pan-American pact by which the territorial integrity and the republican form of government of the nations of the New World would be severally and jointly guaranteed. In this proposal, indeed, one discerns, long before the deliberations at Paris, even before the President's acceptance of the program of the League to Enforce Peace, something very like the attempted international-ization of the fundamental tenets of Monroeism.

This idea was born, so it would appear, in the fertile and far-ranging mind of Colonel House. It was proposed to Wilson by House as early as December 16, 1914.[6] Given a free hand by the President the enterprising Colonel proceeded to sound the am-bassadors of the ABC powers in Washington. From Naon, of the Argentine, and Da Gama of Brazil, he received a warm reception, which was echoed by the governments which they represented. At Buenos Aires, indeed, the project was received with especial sym-pathy as "tending to transform the one-sided character of the Mon-roe Doctrine into a common policy of all the American countries." [7] But from the Chilean government the reception was inevitably less enthusiastic. For Chile had a boundary dispute with Peru with re-gard to the territory of Tacna and Arica, and a discussion of guaran-tees of territorial integrity was almost certain to bring this un-pleasant question into the forefront of public discussion. From the first, therefore, the atmosphere at the Chilean capital was one of reserve; indeed, it was Chilean aloofness which in the end led to the collapse of the whole proposal. It is not necessary for us to fol-low the negotiations on the Pan-American pact in their intimate details. The administration was really quite tenacious of this project once it got under way. There was talk, for example, of going ahead with Brazil and the Argentine, and permitting the lukewarm gov-ernment at Santiago to come in later. There were efforts to find such a solution of the problem of Tacna-Arica as would permit Chile to go ahead. The whole matter was discussed, with intervals of qui-escence, down to the days of American participation in the World War.[8] No one can doubt the sincerity or interest of Wilson and House in the idea. But as time went on the attitude of the Chileans communicated itself to the Argentines and Brazilians. Enthusiasm evaporated. The invasion of Mexican territory by the troops of General Pershing, in pursuit of Villa, in the summer of 1916, created an atmosphere in which progress was difficult. And then came

American entry into the European war, first blanketing the project of the pact and then merging it in the larger idea of a League of Nations. Yet despite the unfavorable course of events it is a fact of major importance that the Wilson administration should have brought forward a plan which looked to the translation of the fundamentals of the Doctrine into a general agreement of the American nations. Here was at least the beginning of an alteration in the temper of American relations with the republics of Latin America.

In the period of America's participation in the World War there were some evidences of that solidarity of the American nations which the Wilson administration had, in some measure, glimpsed. Thirteen American states either severed relations with Germany or actually entered the war. But the number is less impressive than it at first appears. For many of the republics in question, Cuba, Haiti, Santo Domingo, the states of Central America (excluding Salvador), were in close political or economic relationships with the United States. And the list of neutrals is impressive — Argentina, Mexico, and Chile, three of the four most important of the Latin-American nations, and Colombia and Venezuela, two of the most significant of the countries of the Caribbean.

In the attitude of some Latin-American states toward the Covenant, moreover, the spirit of distrust of the United States was amply illustrated. An interesting example of this is to be found in the attitude of Salvador. In January of 1920, that little state was considering adherence to the Covenant. Before taking such action it addressed itself directly to Washington for an interpretation of the Monroe Doctrine. Calling attention to the different "applications" of the principles of 1823, deploring the "anarchy of opinions" which existed, expressing the hope that the Doctrine would be converted into a "principle of universal public law," the Minister of Salvador requested of Secretary Lansing an "authentic opinion" as to how "the Government of the White House interprets it in the present and will consider it in the future." At first this curiosity on the part of Salvador bid fair to go completely unsatisfied. Secretary

Lansing on February 10 declared that no new interpretation of the great American dogma was considered necessary. But soon afterward Lansing resigned, and Polk, acting as his successor, sent a reply on February 26 which called attention to the speech of President Wilson before the Pan-American Scientific Congress at Washington in January of 1916. "I have the honor to inform you," he wrote, "that the opinion of this government with regard to the Monroe Doctrine was expressed" in the speech in question. This was not entirely illuminating. For the President, in this well-known address, had declared that "the Monroe Doctrine was proclaimed by the United States on her own authority," and that "it has always been maintained, and always will be maintained, on her own responsibility," and that "it did not disclose the use which the United States intended to make of her power on this side of the Atlantic." He went on, it is true, to say that doubts and suspicions on this last point must be removed. He spoke of guarantees of political independence and territorial integrity and of the settlement of disputes by peaceful means; he spoke of precautions against assistance to revolutionary movements; but however reassuring such references might be, they could hardly be regarded as completely covering the question, or as delimiting in precise terms the highly flexible principles of 1823. The Salvadorean government professed itself satisfied; it adhered to the League Covenant; but the question of the meaning of the Doctrine had not been settled, and was destined within a very few years to arise again.[9]

It was not only Salvador which made known its uneasiness in striking fashion in connection with the inclusion in the Covenant of the reference to the principles of 1823. The Mexico of Venustiano Carranza was undeniably far from friendly to the United States. The oil question had poisoned relations between the two countries. The chase after Villa in 1916 had been violently resented. The existence of German propaganda on a considerable scale was tolerated during 1917 and 1918. Mexican neutrality, while perhaps technically correct, was in spirit distinctly hostile to the American government. The president himself was a man of intractable and contentious spirit, standing all too often on punctilio, playing the game of politics with unceasing appeals to Mexican nationalism and prejudice. And in the spring of 1919, in accordance with the general attitude already assumed, the Mexican Foreign Office sounded off on Article 21 of the Covenant, declaring "publicly and . . . officially . . . that Mexico had not recognized and would not recognize the Monroe Doctrine . . . since it attacks the sovereignty and independence of Mexico and would place the nations of America under a forced tutelage." [10] This statement apparently had no effect whatsoever upon the drafters of the League instrument; indeed, Mexico was one of the few nations not invited to join the League itself. Accordingly, in his message of September 1, President Carranza pronounced himself in terms more bilious than ever, declaring that Mexico had not done, and would not do, anything "to enter into that international society, because the bases upon which it was formed do not establish, either as to its functions or as to its organization, a perfect equality for all nations and races. . . ." [11] No doubt the President was an unusually prickly person; his successor, General Obregón, was to take a very different attitude toward the League; but the Mexican position of 1919, whatever else might be said of it, was one more evidence that something less than complete harmony reigned in the American family.

In a sense, moreover, the world organization that was set up at Geneva by the Treaty of Versailles seemed to substitute a larger ideal for that of Pan-Americanism. Of the thirteen states which had either severed relations with Germany or declared war, eleven became members of the League by adhering to the treaty. Most of the other Latin-American States shortly joined. Though the degree of enthusiasm which they manifested was greatly to vary, though in course of time withdrawals became unhappily numerous, for a little space, at any rate, it appeared as if in the new machinery set up across the water the republics of the South might find a useful counterpoise to the influence of the United States. And from time to time it is clear that they sought to use it in just this fashion. The evidence lies in the appeals of three Latin-American states to

League authority in the early days of its existence, and in the atmosphere of hostility to the United States which at least one American observer noted at the first Assembly in Geneva.

The three appeals which we have mentioned each ran a different course. Peru, which had a long-standing boundary controversy with Chile, with regard to the districts of Tacna and Arica, took action as early as November 1, 1920. Invoking Article 19, which declared that the League Assembly might "advise the reconsideration . . . of treaties which have become inapplicable," it brought its long-cherished grievance before the League by a letter to the Secretary General. But to many of those at Geneva it seemed highly imprudent to challenge American susceptibilities by interference in an American dispute at the very outset of the League's career. After much urging, as it would appear, Peru withdrew its request.[12]

The Bolivians, however, were not so complacent. Like Peru, they had a grievance against Chile, and like Peru they asked to have the question put on the agenda for the first Assembly under Article 19. They insisted that the matter be at least considered, finally conceding only that it be carried over to the meeting of 1921. And there the guns of oratorical debate were unlimbered. The Chileans protested vigorously against action. They challenged the applicability of Article 19, and, what is more interesting to the student of the Monroe Doctrine, they invoked, in their documentary presentation of the case, though not in the oral debates, the authority of Article 21, and produced three distinguished international lawyers who were ready to testify that under that article the Assembly was incompetent to deal with the dispute in question.[13] The problem was referred to a committee of jurists, which, prudently refraining from any interpretation of the Monroe Doctrine clause, construed Article 19 in such fashion as to put Bolivia to rout.[14] How far concern for American susceptibilities played a part in this decision it is impossible to say.

The third case of an appeal to the League was from the Republic of Panama. In 1914 Chief Justice White of the United States had awarded to Costa Rica the so-called Coto district, in dispute be-

tween Costa Rica and Panama, but the award had never been carried out. In 1921, its patience exhausted, the Costa Rican government seized the territory by force of arms. On March 2, Panama
appealed to the League. It made a second protest on March 5. But
in this case American diplomacy was on the alert. As early as the
first of the two dates just mentioned, Washington had proffered its
good offices. The offer was repeated by Secretary Hughes on the
very day of his taking office, along with a reminder that the parties
had agreed to seek American mediation in case of disputes arising
between them. On the eighth, Costa Rica informed the Secretary
General that she had accepted American interposition. As to Panama, the American government insisted that she carry out her
obligations under the decision of 1914. The Panamanians made one
more appeal to the League on March 8, but received only a suave
reply expressing satisfaction that "an honorable settlement of the
dispute, in accordance with the spirit of the Covenant, is in sight." [15]

These three episodes, in one sense, lie on the periphery rather
than at the heart of our subject. Strictly construed, the Monroe
Doctrine did not operate to prevent the use of European good offices in controversies between American states, and *a fortiori* of
League good offices. The United States had never objected on the
ground of principle to any such offers in the past. The Spanish
government, for example, had served as the arbiter of a dispute
between Venezuela and Colombia in the early 1880's, and though
Secretary Frelinghuysen, when sounded, had declared that the decision of American questions pertains to America itself, he had also
stated that no opposition would be offered to such arbitration. In
the case of a dispute between Colombia and Costa Rica, Spain
again served as arbiter, without protest from Washington. In 1880
the Emperor of Austria had arbitrated a dispute between Nicaragua
and Great Britain. In at least two cases, that of the San Juan de
Fuca water boundary and that of American claims against Mexico,
a difference to which the government of the United States was a
party was submitted to a European arbitrator. On the ground of
the precedents, therefore, there was no reason to look askance at

League efforts to preserve peace. But on the other hand League interposition in American controversies, once begun, might conceivably be carried beyond the point of mere deliberation or mediation. From this point of view, the prompt action of the State Department in the controversy of Panama and Costa Rica is understandable. However, it is clear that at Geneva there existed a very real desire to avoid a controversy with the United States. As a counterpoise to American influence, the League proved from the beginning a feeble instrument. And the fact was underlined by the submission, in 1922, of the Tacna-Arica dispute to the arbitration of the government at Washington.

Yet the distrust which Latin-American states felt toward the Colossus of the North was by no means dispelled in the days of Mr. Hughes's incumbency as Secretary of State. Progress was being made; the treaty of 1921 with Colombia, liquidating the long-standing dispute over the Panama revolution of 1903, was a step forward, and so too were the preparations which were being made for the withdrawal of American marines from the soil of the Dominican Republic and Nicaragua. But at the fifth Pan-American Conference at Santiago, in the spring of 1923, there was by no means a cordial attitude toward the United States. With a view to diminishing somewhat American influence, a successful attempt was made to modify the structure of the Pan-American Union. Many of the states present displayed a positive discontent with American policy. Nor did the attitude of the American delegation toward the Uruguayan proposal for an American League of Nations increase the sum total of understanding.

The idea of such a league had been brought forward three years before by the then President of Uruguay, Dr. Baltásar Brum. At the time he spoke, the Senate had, for the second time, rejected the Treaty of Versailles. Assuming that this action was final, Dr. Brum proposed an American League of Nations, which he desired to base upon the Monroe Doctrine. He admitted that the Doctrine had been abused, and that it was in a sense "vexatious for the nations of America, because it constitutes something like a protectorate over them." [16] But he pointed out that it protected the nations of America from foreign conquest, no less in 1923 than in 1823, and he urged that the Doctrine be universalized, each nation making "a similar declaration to Monroe's, binding themselves to intervene in favor of any of them, including the United States, in case they should be engaged at war with an over-seas country in defense of their rights." [17] "Such a declaration," he declared, "would create a situation of great dignity, placing them [that is, the nations of Latin America] on a footing of perfect moral equality with the United States." [18]

The constitution of the League, he went on, with an allusion to Article 21, "in recognizing and expressly accepting the Monroe Doctrine, seems to be desirous of limiting its sphere of action as far as American affairs are concerned." Why not build on this foundation? Why not constitute an American Association of Nations, which should include the United States, the most powerful nation of the continent, and one which had repudiated the institution of Geneva?

Dr. Brum's proposals had no important immediate repercussions. There was some little discussion of regional groupings within the general framework of Geneva in the Assembly of 1920, and again in 1921. But no action of any kind was taken, and nowhere was the Uruguayan project hailed with much enthusiasm. In preparation for the conference of 1923, however, Uruguay again brought it forward, and it figured on the agenda of the conference itself, and was discussed at length in the session of April 30.[19] It gave rise to at least one attack upon the principles of 1823. The delegate from Colombia rehearsed some of the familiar arguments of the foes of the American dogma. He recalled the major role of Great Britain in forestalling the designs of the Continental powers a century before. He pointed out, not always with historical accuracy, how often the Doctrine had been honored in the breach. "The United States," he declared, "did not take advantage of the message when in 1833 Great Britain occupied the Falkland Islands; nor in 1834 when Great Britain blockaded the port of San Juan de Nicaragua; nor even at the time of the Anglo-American intervention in La Plata

in 1835; in this same year the republic of Guatemala could not succeed in persuading General Jackson to oppose the founding of
British establishments in Belize, although it recalled the Doctrine
to his attention; nor in 1838 when a squadron bombarded the
fortress of San Juan de Ulloa; nor afterwards when Le Blanc blockaded the port of the Río de la Plata; nor when it vacillated before
the threatened usurpation of England on the Colombian coast of
Mosquitia; nor when Spain reconquered Santo Domingo; nor when
Napoleon III founded in Mexico the Empire of Maximilian of Austria." What faith, then, could be placed in "this sinuous document,
contradictory because it proclaims the same principle that it
condemns, and whose doctrine has never been adopted by the Congress of the United States, notwithstanding the numerous efforts
that have been made to get it so adopted in the century of its existence?" "It was necessary," he declared in a thinly veiled attack
on American policies of intervention, to "organize the means of
defense," not only in relation to Europe, but in "every case of menace, as President Wilson expressed it with admirable propriety." [20]

In the face of this attack on the Uruguayan proposal, and on the
United States, what was the position of the American delegation?
It gave no encouragement to any continentalization of the Doctrine in its reply. On the contrary, speaking briefly yet positively,
Henry P. Fletcher, head of the delegation, declared that the principles of 1823 did not enter into the discussion "because the tasks of
the Committee did not permit," but that it could be stated that the
United States considered those principles as "original and essentially national." And he went on to declare that he must "recall to
the Committee that Article 21 of the League of Nations had no
obligatory force for this, or any other American Assembly; and that
the disjointed allusions of Article 21 with regard to the Monroe
Doctrine are highly inexact." [21] The declaration of Mr. Fletcher
appears to have had a somewhat chilling effect upon the deliberations of the committee. The Uruguayan proposal was in any case
slated for postponement, that favorite device of diplomatic assem-
blies, but the fact that the debate terminated shortly after the

American pronouncement was made may have a significance of its own. At any rate, that pronouncement certainly cannot be said to have contributed positively to the harmony of the conference, or to have removed the widespread suspicions which were felt in Latin America with regard to the imperialistic connotations of the principles of 1823.

The Secretary of State of the United States in 1923, however, was Charles Evans Hughes, not unlikely to be recorded as one of the most competent who have held that important office. Hughes was well aware of the problem of winning Latin-American good will; he took, as we have already said, significant steps in that direction in the cases of Santo Domingo and Nicaragua; and he was perhaps led by the events at Santiago and by the fact that 1923 was the centennial year of the Monroe Doctrine to take further measures toward allaying the hostility sometimes felt toward it in the capitals of the South. In the course of the next few months he made two important speeches on the Doctrine, one in Minneapolis on August 30 and one in Philadelphia exactly four months later. These discourses remain among the most enlightening and perspicuous that have ever been delivered in connection with the great American dogma.

It is not necessary for us here to analyze these commentaries in every detail. In both the Secretary iterated and reiterated one fundamental point — namely, that the Monroe Doctrine did not "attempt to establish a protectorate over Latin-American States." "I utterly disclaim, as unwarranted," he declared at Minneapolis, "the observations which occasionally have been made implying a claim on our part to superintend the affairs of our sister republics, to assert an overlordship, to consider the spread of our authority beyond our own domain as the aim of our policy, and to make our power the test of right in this hemisphere. I oppose all such misconceived and unsound assertions and intimations. They do not express our national purpose; they belie our sincere friendship; they are false to the fundamental principles of our institutions and of our foreign policy which has sought to reflect with rare exceptions, the ideals of liberty; they menace us by stimulating a distrust which has no real foundation. They find no sanction whatever in the Monroe doctrine." [22] In the Philadelphia address the same idea is reiterated. "We have not sought," said the Secretary, "to establish a protectorate or overlordship of our own with regard to these republics. Such a pretension not only is not found in the Monroe Doctrine but would be in opposition to our fundamental affirmative policy." [23]

But while thus striking a conciliatory note with regard to the imperialist connotations of the Monroe Doctrine, the Secretary took his stand firmly on traditional ground with regard to the strictly national character of its principles. "As the policy embodied in the Monroe doctrine is distinctively the policy of the United States, the government of the United States reserves to itself its definition, interpretation, and application. . . . This implies neither suspicion nor estrangement. It simply means that the United States is asserting a separate national right of self-defense, and that in the exercise of this right it must have an unhampered discretion. . . . The United States has never bound itself to any particular course of conduct in case of action by other powers contrary to the principles announced." [24]

Secretary Hughes did not by any means renounce the so-called right of intervention, so offensive to much Latin-American opinion. But he divorced it from the Doctrine itself in clear-cut language and he sought to localize it. "The Monroe doctrine as a particular declaration in no way exhausts American right or policy; the United States has rights and obligations which that doctrine does not define. And in the unsettled condition of certain countries in the region of the Caribbean it has been necessary to assert these rights and obligations as well as the limited principles of the Monroe doctrine." [25] This was the language of the speech at Minneapolis. It was reiterated at Philadelphia. "Disturbances in the Caribbean region," the Secretary there declared, "are . . . of special interest to us not for the purpose of seeking control over others but of being assured that our own safety is free from menace. . . . It is the policy of this government to make available its friendly assistance to promote stability in those of our sister republics which are specially afflicted with disturbed conditions involving their own peace and that of their neighbors." [26]

These declarations have a very large significance. They propounded what might be described as a Caribbean doctrine in supplement to and distinguished from the earlier Doctrine. They tended, therefore, to give the assurance that the interference of the United States would be limited to a relatively narrow geographical area. They were aimed at conveying reassurance as to the manner in which that interference would be undertaken, and as to the objectives which would be sought. In a sense, they can be said to narrow the application of the Roosevelt corollary in the field of theory, just as the negotiations for withdrawal of the marines from Nicaragua and Santo Domingo represent a retreat in the field of practice. Not, of course, that such assurances as Hughes gave had never been given before; even in the days of the Rough Rider himself there had been talk of soothing nature with regard to the great states of South America as the co-guarantors of the Doctrine; the idea of special interest in the Caribbean was not original with Mr. Hughes. But the points we have been discussing were presented with striking clarity and force; they were, so to speak, made essential to the elaboration of American foreign policy; and they represented, therefore, a genuine clarification of the principles of 1823.

There were other points on which Mr. Hughes was equally specific. As early as 1902, in the Venezuela question, Mr. Roosevelt had used the phrase "non-American" instead of "European" power in speaking of the Monroe Doctrine; the debates of 1912 had made it clear that the interference of Japan would be no less resented than that of any other nation; the Secretary of State in his speeches of 1923 underlined this fundamental fact. Moreover, he defined the Doctrine positively. The original declaration, he pointed out, opposed the colonization of the American continents by European powers, and the extension of their political system to this hemisphere, or any interposition for the purpose of oppressing or controlling the destiny of the new American republics. The only modification of these principles, he declared, lay in the no-transfer concept and in the extension of the warning to *all* foreign states, wherever situated.[27] Our policies in the East and in Europe, as they had actually evolved, contained, in his judgment, not the slightest inconsistency with the language of Monroe.

These declarations of the Secretary are, like the ones previously noted, of high importance. They are the closest approach that we have to a positive and therefore a limiting definition of the principles of 1823. They contained, in this sense, a definite reassurance. And for those confused persons who have imagined that the Monroe Doctrine meant that we must abdicate all diplomatic interest or influence in Europe or the Orient, they could not fail to be illuminating. Whoever belongs to this school of thought should read with careful attention, and in full, the observations of Mr. Hughes with regard to our policy in those two sections of the globe.

The Secretary also had a word to say to those who declared the Doctrine to be an "obsolete shibboleth." And his words seem particularly interesting today. "The fact that intervention of non-American powers in this hemisphere is not threatened at this moment cannot be deemed to be controlling," he declared. "The future holds infinite possibilities, and the doctrine remains as an essential policy to be applied whenever any exigency may arise requiring its application. To withdraw it, or to weaken it, would aid no just interest, support no worthy cause, but would simply invite trouble by removing an established safeguard of the peace of the American continents." [28] These words have the ring of wisdom in them many years after they were written.

All in all, indeed, there is no more remarkable exposition of the principles of 1823 than that by Secretary Hughes. It represents a distinct contribution to the literature of the Doctrine and to its understanding. But it did not, of course, allay all suspicions of American intentions; and what the scholars of Latin America thought of the matter may be seen from the deliberations of a committee of the American Institute of International Law at Ha-

vana in the winter of 1925. There the sentiment against outside interference on the part of one state in the affairs of another was
strong indeed; the committee drew up a project, one article of
which denied the right of intervention in the most unequivocal
terms. That in its thought this right was connected with the Doctrine is plain from the language of Dr. James Brown Scott, who
went so far as to declare that the project "Americanized Monroe's
declaration," made it "co-extensive with the continent, and associated all the American republics in its application." [29]

Unhappily for the policy of conciliation, it was not long before
the United States was drawn into a new intervention. The American marines had withdrawn from Nicaragua early in August, 1925.
In October, by a *coup d'état*, Emiliano Chamorro, long a conspicuous figure in Nicaraguan politics, forced President Solórzano to
appoint him commander of the army; in January 1926 he seized the
supreme power; in May revolution broke out; and in the months
that followed Nicaraguan politics became confusion worse confounded. The United States, by a policy of nonrecognition, finally
forced Chamorro out of office. By a procedure whose regularity
was open to question, Adolfo Díaz, an old friend, was elected to
the presidency and recognized by Washington; but the vice-president under Solórzano, Sacasa, protested the election, and took the
field against Díaz at the end of the year. Now Sacasa had been a
refugee in Mexico; the State Department, rightly or wrongly, believed him hostile to the United States; it gazed upon his aspirations
to the presidency with a cold and fishy eye. The credulous Mr. Kellogg, now Secretary of State, and his still more credulous assistant,
Mr. Olds, managed somehow to connect Sacasa's activities with
Bolshevist propaganda emanating from Mexico City; before long
(by the end of 1926, to be specific) American marines were once
more in Nicaragua, to protect American interests, and to do so in a
manner which seemed to cynics to offer every assistance to the
government of Adolfo Díaz. These cynics could hardly fail to be
re-enforced in their opinions when, by the middle of January,
American troops appeared at the capital, Managua, amidst the de-

lirious joy of the partisans of the president in office.[30] Once again the United States was faced with the hostile reaction of Latin America. The press of the republics of the South resounded with denunciations; a commission of jurists appointed by the Pan-American Conference in 1923, and meeting at Rio, adopted by acclamation a declaration declaring intervention illegal; the conciliatory gestures of the Hughes period were for the moment forgotten. As the time came for the sixth Pan-American Conference at Havana, it was clear that it would be the occasion for a slashing attack upon the policy of the United States.

In the strict sense, it ought here to be said, the intervention of 1926–1927 in Nicaragua had precious little to do with the Monroe Doctrine. There was no threat from any European power, real or alleged. It is true that the British and Italian representatives notified our minister at Managua that unsettled conditions menaced the lives and property of their nationals; this was obviously a gentle hint that intervention would be welcome; but it does not prove that either the British or the Italian government intended to act itself. In justifying the acts of the American government President Coolidge, in his message to Congress of January 10, 1927, made no reference whatever to the principles of 1823, nor did he in the speech of April 10, in which he again alluded to the Nicaraguan intervention and related it to the interest of the United States in the countries this side of the Panama Canal. The State Department chose to rest its case upon the danger of Bolshevism; Secretary Kellogg was silent as to the magical name of Monroe. Only in Congress was there any disposition to invoke the great American dogma, and this almost exclusively on the part of the Republican supporters of the administration. Senator Hiram Bingham, curiously enough, forswore his views of earlier days, and, more royalist than the king, invoked the Doctrine in unequivocal terms. He was followed by such men as Irving Lenroot and Hiram Johnson. But it was significant that Senator Borah, by now a dominating figure on the Republican side, took a very different view, declaring that he did "not see in the entire situation any facts or circum·

stances which would justify an appeal to the Monroe doctrine."
"The Monroe doctrine," he went on, "was the outgrowth of a controversy between hemispheres. It has nothing whatever to do and
furnishes us no guide with reference to dealing with different factions or different conditions internal in any Central American country. . . . Those who believe in the Monroe doctrine, and think it
of vital importance to the people of this country, are doing it a
great disservice by undertaking to invoke it in aid of any kind of
interference in those countries, either Central or South American." [31] As for the Democrats, they naturally seized their partisan
opportunity. In both House and Senate there were numerous
denunciations of the policy of the administration, numerous de-
nials of the applicability of the principles of 1823. And Representative Moore of Virginia, afterwards to be a prominent officer
of the State Department, introduced in the House of Representatives a resolution specifically declaring that there was nothing in
the famous declaration of Monroe which authorized intervention
in the affairs of independent states.[32]

Still more interesting were the proceedings of the Commission
of Jurists which assembled at Rio de Janeiro in April of 1927, with
a mandate from the governing board of the Pan-American Union
to draw up a code of international law. This body had scarcely assembled when a telegram arrived from the Minister of Nicaragua
to Mexico, asking the Congress to make an express declaration
condemning the policy of the United States. Very naturally this
request was not complied with; American influence would have
been feeble indeed if it could not have prevented this. But the
question of intervention was hotly debated by the jurists, and very
extreme proposals with regard to the problem were brought forward by Haiti and Santo Domingo, both of which had some practical experience with the matter at issue, and by Argentina, in this
as in some other instances not unwilling to take the lead in opposition to the United States. Nor was it possible to evade the question. On the contrary, the conference adopted a formula which
declared that "no state could interfere in the internal affairs of

another." [33] This was not, to be sure, by any means unequivocal; what were "internal affairs"? Might not many an intervention be justified as involving "external affairs"? Such was one way of looking at the matter, at least. But the general trend of Latin-American opinion was by no means doubtful; and the conference at Rio paved the way for a more heated and a more significant debate at Havana, when the sixth Pan-American Conference convened in that city the next year.

In one sense, the remarkable discussion at Havana lies on the periphery of our subject. When the legal theory of intervention came to be debated there, it was discussed as an abstract question rather than one involving the interpretation of the principles of 1823. Long before 1928 American statesmen had learned that it was prudent to soft-pedal references to Monroe in international Pan-American Conferences. As for Latin Americans, it is difficult to see what effect the mention of the Doctrine by them could have had except to arouse an emotional opposition on the part of many citizens of the United States, and even of their diplomatic representatives. It is not strange that both sides avoided such irritating references. The American delegation was headed not by Secretary Kellogg, but by Charles Evans Hughes. It contended vigorously against the formula which had been adopted at Rio; in language almost invariably urbane — not quite invariably so — the former Secretary of State defended the existence of a certain right of "interposition" as falling well within the principles of international law. A formula less rigid than that of Rio brought forward by Senor Maúrtua, of the Peruvian delegation, he ardently supported. There were some who rallied to the American position, or at any rate supported the Maúrtua substitute — notably the Cubans, who, under the regime of Machado, had good reason to court American favor. But the trend of the debates was by no means favorable to the United States. Thirteen of the twenty-one states at the conference made strong declarations in support of the Rio declaration. Eight states, led by Argentina, took an even stronger position. So intense was the feeling that the secret discussions of the subcommittee were inevitably supplemented by debate at a plenary session, and, temporarily stilled in the morning, the controversy continued in the afternoon. There could, after all this, be not the slightest doubt of the trend of sentiment. Action on the nonintervention resolution was indeed postponed. But the American delegation left Havana with a clear understanding of the depth and breadth of the opposition to those policies of the United States which had all too often been connected with the name of Monroe.[34]

The year 1928, indeed, was remarkable for more than one renewed attack upon the principles of 1823. Toward the end of February the Argentine delegate at Geneva, speaking before the Commission on Arbitration and Security, served notice that in the opinion of his government the Doctrine was no more than a unilateral declaration, and not a regional agreement in any sense of the word.[35] Only a fortnight later, Señor Uriburu, the Argentine envoy to Brussels, declared that the Monroe dogma meant only "America for the United States." [36] In August came a still more interesting evidence of feeling, in the application of Costa Rica for enlightenment with regard to the language of the Covenant. Costa Rica had joined the League, but had in 1924 signified its intention to withdraw. Four years later an attempt was made to persuade the authorities at San José to reconsider their decision. On July 18, 1929, the Costa Rican government responded with a request addressed to the President of the Council of the League, M. Hjalmar Procopé, that the Council express itself as to the interpretation to be placed upon Article 21. The question was a thorny one, but on September 1 an answer was forthcoming. "In regard to the scope of the engagements to which the article relates," read the brilliantly executed reply, "it is clear that it cannot have the effect of giving them a sanction or validity which they did not previously possess. It confines itself to referring to these engagements, such as they may exist, without attempting to define them; an attempt at definition being, in fact, liable to have the effect of restricting or enlarging their sphere of application. Such a task was not one for the authors of the Covenant; it only concerns the states having accepted *inter se* engagements of this kind." Thus, in diplomatic language, the Council avoided any political commitment; indeed, it went further: it recognized that the terms of the Doctrine were not to be fixed by the League, but by the states "having accepted *inter se*" some interpretation of their own. At the same time it was stated that Article 21 "gives the states parties to international engagements the guarantee that the validity of such of these engagements as secure the maintenance of peace would not be affected by accession to the Covenant of the League." This discreet phraseology seemed to say that the Monroe Doctrine is unaffected *so far as it looks toward the preservation of international tranquillity;* but the point was not embroidered. "The Covenant of the League forms a whole; the articles of which it is composed confer upon all the Members of the League equal obligations and equal rights," reads another sentence, intended no doubt to reassure the states of Latin America as to the effect of the Doctrine upon their relations with the United States. But these ingenious phrases are in no way amplified; and taking the matter as a whole it cannot be said that the note of September 1 made precise and definite what was indefinite before.[37]

It was possible for the Council of the League thus dexterously to avoid the pitfalls which beset it in connection with the Monroe Doctrine. But for the United States the year 1928 was crucial. At Havana no ground had been yielded, no pledges of any kind made. But the reorientation of American policy had become more and more a necessity; and in that reorientation something had to be done about the Monroe Doctrine. Speaking at Princeton in May, Charles Evans Hughes denounced the use of the Doctrine as a "cover for extravagant utterances and pretensions"; in November a supervised election in Nicaragua was followed by the withdrawal of a portion of the American forces there; in December President-elect Hoover embarked upon a good-will tour of Latin America; in January of 1929, in its gloss upon the Kellogg Pact, the Senate struck a blow at the Roosevelt corollary.

In this period, too, there was prepared at the State Department, though not yet given to the world, a remarkable memorandum on the Monroe Doctrine. This memorandum was the work of Mr. J. Reuben Clark, Undersecretary of State, and a man of considerable experience in diplomatic affairs. It was requested (and it is a mere act of justice to record the fact) by Secretary Kellogg; and it was transmitted under date of December 17, 1928. It may well have influenced the Senate discussions on the Kellogg Pact early in 1929; and it may, in particular, have had something to do with Senator Borah's interpretation of the principles of 1823.

It is not necessary here to analyze the Clark memorandum in detail; but it is of fundamental importance to understand it in its broad lines. Mr. Clark, like many a commentator before him, based the Monroe Doctrine fundamentally on the principle of self-preservation; it was intended, to revert to the message itself, to prevent those acts which were "dangerous to our peace and safety." It was, of course, less broad than the principle from which it sprang; it had to do with only one aspect of that principle, the peril of European attack upon states in the New World; and it did not regulate and it did not affect, therefore, wide areas of American policy. "In particular," says Mr. Clark, it "does not apply to purely inter-American relations. Nor does the declaration purport to lay down any principles that are to govern the inter-relationship of the states of this Western Hemisphere as among themselves. The Doctrine states a case of United States vs. Europe, not of United States vs. Latin America." [38] So viewed, certain acts are obviously forbidden by the terms and application of the language of 1823. The occupation of territory by European powers, either temporary or permanent, is one of them.

And then, in words which constitute the most striking part of his paper, Mr. Clark goes on to discuss the Roosevelt corollary. "The so-called Roosevelt corollary," he writes, "was to the effect, as generally understood, that in case of financial or other difficulties in weak Latin-American countries, the United States should attempt an adjustment thereof lest European governments should intervene, and intervening should occupy territory — an act which would be contrary to the Monroe Doctrine. . . . It is not believed that this corollary is justified by the terms of the Monroe Doctrine, however much it may be justified by the application of the doctrine of self-preservation." Thus, in a manner more specific than that of Mr. Hughes in 1923, the Clark memorandum sought to divorce Monroeism from the idea of intervention and, in its own words, "relieve the Doctrine of many of the criticisms which have been aimed against it." [39]

The Clark memorandum, as originally framed, was not a public document; and for some time after it was drawn it remained hidden in the State Department; but the Hoover administration, which came into office in 1929, and Henry L. Stimson at the State Department in particular, were intent upon improving our relations with Latin America, and hastened to put into practice that policy of the "good neighbor" which was to be continued and brilliantly executed by their successors. After some delay, the State Department made the Clark memorandum its own, and in identic notes to the governments of Latin America indicated that it would be guided by the principles therein laid down. In this sense, by June of 1930, the Roosevelt corollary had been definitely and specifically repudiated; and since that time there has been no scholarly foundation for the proposition that the Monroe Doctrine as officially interpreted either makes necessary or even tolerates interventions in the affairs of the other states of the New World. The United States had not renounced the right of intervention, but it gave notice that it no longer intended to rest this right upon the principles of 1823.

It must not be imagined, however, that the Clark memorandum automatically terminated the distrust that was felt in Latin America with regard to the American dogma. In Argentina, perhaps particularly bitter in 1930 on account of the Hawley-Smoot tariff, the press was irreconcilable. *La Prensa,* an important paper, declared the Doctrine to be "nonexistent." "The United States," it added, "has merely sought by capricious interpretation of certain chance phrases in the President's message of 1823 to give a juridical aspect to a thesis which is nothing but an insulting outrage against the American republics." [40] *La Razón,* more moderately, declared that the Doctrine was "no longer needed." [41] So, too, did *La Nación.*[42] These utterances were, sometime later, to have their counterpart in official action. In September of 1932, when the Argentine chamber voted that Argentina should rejoin the League of Nations, it declared "that the Argentine republic regards the Monroe Doctrine, mentioned in Article 21, as a unilateral political declaration which in its time performed a notable service to the cause of American emancipation, but holds that it does not constitute a regional agreement." [43]

In Mexico, too, the spirit of suspicion of the United States was by no means wholly exorcised, despite the success of the Morrow mission of 1928. "For Mexico the Monroe Doctrine does not exist," declared one of the justices of the Mexican Supreme Court. In his judgment, indeed, it was "an infantile theory, to cloak a tutelage on the part of the United States over Latin America." [44] This statement was made in July 1930. In 1931 Mexico, arriving about as others were leaving, entered the League of Nations. The Foreign Minister of the republic on this occasion stated in his covering letter to Geneva that "Mexico has never admitted the regional understanding mentioned in Article 21 of the League Covenant." [45] This declaration, received in silence at Geneva, was hailed as "a complete triumph of our Chancellery" by the rector of the National University of Mexico, who did not hesitate to express his belief that the Doctrine ought to be eliminated altogether.[46] Something of the same view had already been expressed by an important Chilean newspaper, *El Mercurio,* some time before.[47]

It is not to be thought, of course, that comments such as these expressed a viewpoint universally held throughout the countries of the South. To state this would doubtless be an exaggeration. But in truth there was still much apprehension, apprehension which made itself clearly felt when the states of the New World assembled at Montevideo in the seventh Pan-American Conference in the last days of 1933. Once more there was brought forward the nonintervention formula that had caused so much heat at Havana, amended so as to prohibit interference in the "internal or external concerns" of the states concerned. In the debate on this resolution there were relatively few references to the Monroe Doctrine, but those that were made were anything but friendly. From Haiti, from Cuba, and from Peru came derogatory allusions to the principles of 1823.[48] And from all the republics together came pleas addressed to the United States to give its adhesion to the concept of nonintervention. This, while boggling a bit, and complaining that the terms of the formula needed closer definition, Mr. Hull, the American Secretary of State, consented to do; the nonintervention resolution was embodied in a convention, and on June 14, 1934, this convention, *mirabile dictu,* was ratified unanimously by the Senate of the United States.[49]

Thus, so far as the words of a treaty are effective, the United States put behind it not only the Roosevelt corollary, but the pretension to interfere by force of arms in the affairs of the states of the New World; and what it promised in the verbiage of an international agreement it carried out in practice. As far back as November of 1932 the last marine had left the soil of Nicaragua; in May of 1934 the Roosevelt administration negotiated with Cuba a treaty for the abrogation of the Platt amendment, and this treaty was promptly ratified by the Senate; in August, after an occupation of nineteen years, the troops of the United States left the Haitians to their own devices, and their own notions of self-government. In a period when finance capitalism was as widely discredited in this country as it was in 1934, these gestures of abnegation were no doubt easier than they would have been a quarter of a century before; for the policies of intervention had been identified in the minds of many simple and some sophisticated persons with the interests of the bankers; but no one can deny that they were effectively carried through, and at the close of 1934, for the first time in a period of more than two decades, not a single American soldier thwarted the will or the policy of the ruler of any Latin-American state.

Moreover, the doctrine of nonintervention was to undergo still further elaboration with the consent of the United States before the end of President Roosevelt's first term. At Buenos Aires in 1936 was signed a new protocol which reiterated and strengthened the declaration of 1933. This protocol declared "inadmissible" the intervention of any American state in the affairs of another, "directly or indirectly, and for whatever reason." It went further. It stipulated that "the violation of the provisions of this Article shall give rise to mutual consultations, with the object of exchanging views and seeking methods of peaceful adjustment." Finally, it provided that "every question concerning the interpretation of the present Additional Protocol, which it has not been possible to settle through diplomatic channels," should be submitted either to conciliation, or to arbitration, or to judicial settlement.[50] This protocol was ratified by the Senate of the United States without a roll call (and without a dissenting vote on the floor) on June 29, 1937.[51] It received the unanimous approval of the Foreign Relations Committee, and the especial commendation of Senator Borah. Thus, not only was the Roosevelt corollary stricken out of the Monroe Doctrine, but the right of intervention itself was renounced, and the term "intervention" itself was to be interpreted through an international tribunal, or through an international agency of conciliation. It is not too much to say, perhaps, that there had been a complete reversal of the policies of the period 1905 to 1915. A new epoch was opening with regard to the principles of 1823.

X

The Doctrine Broadened

That any attempt on the part of a non-American State against the integrity or inviolability of the territory, the sovereignty or the political independence of an American State shall be considered as an act of aggression against the States which sign this declaration.

In case acts of aggression are committed or should there be reason to believe that an act of aggression is being prepared by a non-American nation against the integrity or inviolability of the territory, the sovereignty or the political independence of an American nation, the nations signatory to the present declaration will consult among themselves in order to agree upon the measure it may be advisable to take.

All the signatory nations, or two or more of them, according to circumstances, shall proceed to negotiate the necessary complementary agreements so as to organize cooperation for defense and the assistance that they shall lend each other in the event of aggressions such as referred to in this declaration.

— *The Declaration of Reciprocal Assistance and Cooperation for the Defense of the Nations of the Americas*

THE CONFERENCES of Montevideo and Buenos Aires mark an end, as we have seen, to that interpretation of the Monroe Doctrine which justified and gave sanction to the intervention of the United States in the affairs of the states of the New World. It was perhaps easier for the American government to submit to this curtailment of its freedom of action because in the early thirties the possibility of interference by any European power was extremely small. In other words, it was no longer necessary to defend American intervention as a preventative of action by a European power. Nor has American policy ever again revived the notion of the Roosevelt corollary.

But the sense of immunity from danger which perhaps had something to do with American abandonment of the policy of interference was not long to last. In Germany Adolf Hitler had come to power in 1933, and with the consolidation of his power a new menace arose from across the seas. At first the threat was hardly understood and reaction against it was therefore slow; but the occupation of the Rhineland in 1936 was a warning of what lay ahead, a warning which in some degree was heeded; the signs of the times became more ominous with 1937, positively threatening with the occupation of Austria and the Czechoslovak crisis of 1938, clearly pointing to war with the Franco-British guarantee to Poland in 1939, until at last the decisive moment came and the German legions entered Poland on the fateful first of September, 1939. Each step in Europe led to new steps taken in America; and by a remarkably wise and successful statesmanship, the countries of the New World were brought closer and closer together in the face of German violence and ambition.

In the development of this *rapprochement* we must consider the Pan-American political conferences that followed upon that of Montevideo: the Buenos Aires conference of 1936; the Lima conference, the eighth in the regular Pan-American series, in 1938; and the Havana conference in the summer of 1940.

The conference at Buenos Aires was called at the suggestion of President Roosevelt to deal with the general problem of the maintenance of peace. It met at the Argentine capital in December of 1936. Since this is not a treatise on Pan-Americanism, we need not study the many ways in which the Pan-American idea was there implemented, but we must call attention to those conventions which looked toward the acceptance of the principles of the Monroe Doctrine by the states of Latin America.

One of these, the most important, is the Convention for the Maintenance, Preservation and Re-establishment of Peace. In the form in which this convention was originally prepared by the government of Brazil, one suspects not wholly without the knowledge of the United States, it specifically alluded to the message of 1823, and referred to the possibility of attack by a non-American power. This language was regarded with some distaste by Dr. Saavedra Lamas, the Argentine Foreign Minister, who indeed complained that it would imply "a kind of Monroeism." [1] To meet the susceptibilities of this sensitive nature, the phrase was modified, but the convention was, by this fact, hardly altered in its tenor, and as it was finally adopted it provided that "in the event that the peace of the American Republics is menaced" the signatory powers should "consult together for the purpose of finding and adopting methods of peaceful co-operation." A second article provided also for consultation "in the event of an international war outside America." This, of course, went beyond the purport of the Monroe Doctrine. [2]

In addition to the convention just mentioned, there was signed at Buenos Aires what was described as a "declaration of principles of inter-American solidarity and co-operation." This declaration laid down the principle that "every act susceptible of disturbing the peace of the Americas affects each and every one of them, and justifies the procedure for consultation provided for in the Convention for the Maintenance, Preservation and Re-establishment of Peace," and like the convention itself it was ratified by an almost unanimous vote by the Senate of the United States. [3]

The documents we have just mentioned were only a first step along the road of international agreement with regard to the principles of 1823. They prescribed no specific course of action; they did not, in fact, even set up machinery for the protection of interests common to the Americas; they asserted an academic principle of common deliberation. It was for the eighth Pan-American Congress at Lima to implement the decisions of the conference of Buenos Aires, and to take another and a longer step toward the solidarity of the American states. This Congress met in December of 1938.

The climate of opinion at Lima was by no means that of two years before. In Europe the year had been signalized by the annexation of Austria in March, and by the crisis over the Sudetenland in August and September. War had, it is true, been avoided, but only by a narrow margin. And while the Munich conference prevented an actual clash of arms, it was clear that the tension was rising, and that "appeasement," hailed with enthusiasm by many at the time, was unlikely to survive new acts of aggression on the part of the Chancellor of the Reich. Only the optimists or the ill-informed faced the future with a confident hope of the preservation of peace.

But the aggressive temper of the National Socialist regime was not illustrated in Europe alone. The states of Latin America had, by this time, much reason to fear its activities on this side of the Atlantic. In Brazil, for example, there had now appeared the so-called "green shirts" or Integralistas, organized on a national basis, with representation in each of the twenty-two states of the republic, and obviously German in inspiration. In the spring of 1938 a revolt fomented by this new group was discovered and put down, only to blaze up again in May and again to be repressed. The Brazilian government refused to receive any longer Herr Ritter, the German Ambassador, who was thought by some to have been implicated in the events just described. Popular feeling was rising against Germany; and in the field of trade as in that of politics the drift of Brazilian policy was more and more toward the United States. In Chile, the elections of 1937 had for the first time brought three Nazi deputies, drawn from the German populations of South Chile, into the Chambers; in 1938 President Alessandri, in his address to the Congress, had denounced the "introduction of political conflicts or the diffusion of creeds or ideologies which agitate other peoples"; in September the Nazi agitators had a part in an outbreak of violence; as in Brazil the tide of popular feeling began to rise, and the victory of the parties of the Left in the presidential elections was a further indication of the direction of opinion. In Uruguay the government became alarmed at the activities of the local German schools, and at the propaganda which, it was demonstrated, was being carried on in them. In Argentina also there were some signs of rising sentiment against the Reich.

We must not exaggerate the significance of such events as we have just described. They did not revolutionize the diplomatic situation; and they had little to do with the interests or the attitude of many of the twenty states that constituted the Latin-American galaxy. But undoubtedly they were not without influence; and combined with the good-neighbor policy they did something to provide for the United States at Lima an atmosphere more friendly and even cordial than at any previous Pan-American Conference.

Not, of course, that there was no rift whatever in the lute. The Argentine government had never displayed any very passionate enthusiasm for a movement toward American solidarity in which the United States played so important a role. Its economic interests oriented it toward Europe rather than toward the Colossus of the North; the restrictions placed on the importation of Argentine beef into this country were widely resented, in view of the importance of the cattle-raising industry to the Argentine. The large European populations of the republic, especially the large Italian population, affected its outlook on foreign affairs. In such circumstances it was not strange, perhaps, that the Argentine Foreign Minister played no very gracious role at Lima. He arrived in a battleship for a state visit just at the time of the conference; he stayed only a few days; and during the most critical of the sessions he was making a leisurely tour of the Chilean lake districts, in chilling disregard of the necessities of the occasion. But Argentina was isolated at Lima; there was a very strong body of anti-Nazi sentiment; and not only the smaller states of the Caribbean area, but Cuba, Mexico, Venezuela, and Colombia were all in favor of a far-reaching program of continental guarantees. In its search for unanimity, the United States, which perhaps favored such a program in principle, adopted a middle ground; and it is possible that had it not done so, several other states, such as Paraguay and Bolivia, often within the Argentine orbit, would have followed the government of Buenos Aires into opposition.

As it was, new and important steps were taken. The most significant of these was the Declaration of Lima, signed on December 24, 1938, which was nothing less than a reaffirmation of the ideals that might be thought to unite the world of the Americas. The declaration began by declaring, perhaps somewhat extravagantly, that the "peoples of America have achieved spiritual unity through the similarity of their republican institutions, their unshakable will for peace, their profound sentiment of humanity and tolerance, and through their absolute adherence to the principles of international law, of the equal sovereignty of states and of individual liberty without religious or racial prejudices." It went on to declare that "they reaffirm their continental solidarity and their purpose to collaborate in the maintenance of the principles upon which the said solidarity is based," and that "they reaffirm their decisions to maintain them and to defend them against all foreign intervention or activity that may threaten them. . . . In case the peace, security or territorial integrity of any American Republic is thus threatened by acts of any nature that may impair them, they proclaim their common concern and their determination to make effective their solidarity." This they were to do by the process of consultation, and, unlike the convention of Buenos Aires, the Lima Declaration provided a machinery for this purpose. It was stipulated by its terms that the Ministers of Foreign Affairs of the American republics, "when deemed desirable and at the initiative of any one of them," would "meet in their several capitals by rotation, and without protocolary character. . . . Each government may, under special circumstances, or for special reasons, designate a representative as a substitute for its Minister for Foreign Affairs." [4]

There are, no doubt, cynics who would scoff at the resounding phrases of the Declaration of Lima. "Spiritual unity" is a fairly comprehensive matter; and one may doubt that it has been completely attained in any phase of international relations. The ideals which were so glowingly set forth in the first sentences of the declaration have, in one state or another, sometimes been honored in the breach rather than in the observance. The declaration, while making much of common action, declared that "the governments of the American Republics will act independently in their individual capacity, recognizing fully their juridical equality as sovereign states." And it did not bind to anything more than consultation. But it is often wise statesmanship to affirm as a fact what is really an ideal aspired to; and it is also wise statesmanship to let the spirit of co-operation grow rather than try to force it into full bloom. Looked at from this angle, Lima was another milestone in the hopeful evolution of Pan-Americanism; and it marked a step, also, toward common international action in the defense of the principles of 1823.

Within a year of Lima came the outbreak of the European war; the new machinery began to function; the representatives of the Latin-American states met at Panama to concert common measures with regard to the defense of their neutrality; but such measures did not fall within the scope of the Monroe Doctrine. It is otherwise, however, with the meeting at Havana in July of 1940. This meeting has a very direct relationship to the great American dogma since it concerned the possibility of the transfer of territory from one European power to another in the New World.

The conquest of Holland by the legions of National Socialism, and still more the conquest of France, were obviously calculated to arouse American opinion from the kind of torpor into which it had settled back during the spring of 1940. Could Germany, enthroned in the Netherlands, claim for herself the Dutch West Indies? Could Germany, installed in France, demand the cession of the French islands of the Caribbean, or of French Guiana? These questions were bound to arise in June and July of 1940, and on them public opinion expressed itself with the greatest definiteness. The Monroe Doctrine was on the lips of many of our public men; by an almost unanimous vote, a thing unprecedented, both Houses of Congress went on record in support of the no-transfer principle.[5] Contemporaneously with the passage of this Congressional declaration, a similar pronouncement came from the Secretary of State, and a diplomatic note of June 18 put the government of the Reich on warning against any attempt to thrust its power into the New World.

There followed an exchange of compliments between Secretary Hull and Foreign Minister von Ribbentrop that is worth recording. In combating the American view the German objected that this position would deny to certain European states the right to possess territories in the American region. Such an interpretation, he declared, would obviously be untenable. Furthermore, he went on, "the non-intervention in the affairs of the American continent by European nations which is demanded by the Monroe Doctrine can in principle be legally valid only on condition that the American nations for their part do not interfere in the affairs of the European continent."[6]

The argument advanced by von Ribbentrop was not put forward for the first time. We have already seen that it was by no means convincing. But the answer to it was never better stated than by Secretary Hull in a note of July 5 to the German government. "It" [the Monroe Doctrine], declared the Secretary, "contains within it not the slightest vestige of any implication, much less assumption, of hegemony on the part of the United States. It never has resembled, and it does not today resemble, policies which appear to be arising in other geographical areas of the world, which are alleged to be similar to the Monroe Doctrine but which, instead of resting on the sole policies of self-defense and of respect for existing sovereignties, as does the Monroe Doctrine, would in reality seem to be only the pretext for the carrying out of conquest by the sword, of military occupation, and of complete economic and political domination by certain powers of other free independent peoples." "The United States," Hull continued, "pursues a policy of non-participation and non-involvement in the purely political affairs of Europe. It will, however, continue to co-operate with all other nations, whenever the policies of such nations make it possible, and whenever it believes that such efforts are practicable and in its own best interests, for the purpose of promoting economic, commercial and social rehabilitation, and of advancing the cause of international law and order." [7]

Having thus put von Ribbentrop to rout, the administration went on to implement its unilateral action with action on a broader basis. As early as the fall of 1939 it had been suggested at the conference of Panama that the nations of the New World should consult if the territorial equilibrium of the Western hemisphere was threatened. The threat was now obvious, and toward the end of July the representatives of the Americas met in Havana and drew up a remarkable document which provided for the international control of territories which might be in danger of falling into the rapacious maw of the conquerors of Continental Europe. The Havana declaration declared that "the American republics would consider any transfer or attempt to transfer sovereignty, jurisdiction, possession or any interest or control in any of these regions to another non-American state as contrary to American sentiments, principles and rights of American states to maintain their security and political independence." In case of extreme emergency, it authorized any American state to take action in a "manner required for its defense or the defense of the continent." It provided that if it became necessary to occupy the territories menaced by German power, these territories should be under an "Inter-American Commission of Territorial Administration." This commission might depute the actual administration to one or more states, but it was to have the last word as to control. And it would, presumably, see to it that the elaborate rules for the protection, the benefit, and the progress of the people of the occupied territory were observed in practice. Furthermore, when the emergency of the war was over, the territories which had been occupied were under the convention to return to their former situation, or to be constituted as autonomous states, "provided it is not detrimental to the safety of the American republics." [8] Thus, in an elaborate instrument, the United States adopted not a unilateral but a co-operative policy toward the problem of the French and Dutch colonies in the New World. Thus another step had been taken toward the internationalization of the principles of 1823.

But the conference of Havana went further. It adopted a declaration which, for the first time since the League fight of 1919, brought the principle of collective security into the field of practical politics so far as the states of America were concerned. In a protocol termed a Declaration of Reciprocal Assistance and Co-operation for the Defense of the States of America it declared that "any attempt on the part of a non-American state against the integrity or inviolability of the territory, the sovereignty, or the political independence of an American state shall be considered as an act of aggression against the states which sign this declaration," and added: "In case acts of aggression are committed or should there be reason to believe that an act of aggression is being prepared by a non-American nation against the integrity or inviolability of the territory, the sovereignty or the political independence of an American nation, the states signatory to the present declaration will consult among themselves in order to agree upon the measures it may be advisable to take." [9] The pledge made in this paragraph was to be honored when the day of Pearl Harbor came in December, 1941.

Before considering the further steps towards the solidarity of the New World which were taken with the advent of war, it will be convenient to turn back and examine briefly what amounts to an extension of the dictum of Monroe to areas other than those of Latin America. Perhaps the most significant of these was the virtual inclusion of the Dominion of Canada within the ample folds of the principles of 1823.

In general, the question of the relationship of Canada to the American dogma was hardly broached in the nineteenth or the early twentieth century. A contributor to the *Revue des Deux Mondes* in 1879 discussed the subject in the vaguest and most general terms, identifying the Doctrine with American imperialism, as so many Europeans have done, and treating at some length the prospects of annexation to the United States.[10] But he was not able to cite any case in which the famous message had ever been applied to the regions of the North, unless it were that of Polk on the Oregon controversy. The plain truth of the matter was, of course, that throughout the nineteenth and early twentieth century, so great was the power of imperial Britain, so unquestioned her naval supremacy, that it could have occurred only to the boldest and most speculative mind that, so far as Canada was concerned, it would be challenged. Even in the years of the World War this was for the most part the case. Indeed, the question might have slumbered entirely had it not been for the gratuitous statement of Dr. Bernhard Dernburg, a German propagandist in the United States. Dr. Dernburg asserted that it was "a breach of the Monroe Doctrine for an American self-governing dominion to go to war, thereby exposing the American Continent to a counter-attack from Europe and risking to disarrange the present equilibrium." He added graciously that America need not be disturbed. "I at least would most emphatically say that no matter what happens the American Doctrine will not be violated by Germany, either in North or South America. When she is victorious there will be enough property of her antagonists over the four parts of the globe to keep Germany from the necessity of looking any farther, and causing trouble where she seeks friendship and sympathy." [11] These reassuring observations apparently caused very little public discussion. Indeed, the only reference to Canada and the Monroe Doctrine in the early years of the war appears to have come from William Howard Taft, who asserted on November 28, 1914, that if the Dominion were attacked the United States would be drawn into the struggle.[12] No one ventured to deny the reasoning of our German friend — though in truth it would have been easy to point out that nothing in the message of 1823 forbade an American state to go to war with a European state, and that every independent nation is free to consult its own interests as to so vital a matter as engaging in hostilities.

The question of invasion of the New World remained a happily academic one in the years from 1914 to 1918; and although there were those who feared it, there were none who could at any moment regard it as imminent. The war ended with Britain still enthroned; and the decade of the twenties seemed to suggest, not only that no peril existed as to Canada, but also that a new international order might conceivably be in process of development. These were the happy days when Mr. Kellogg and Senator Borah appeared to believe that war could be exorcised by a magical formula; when a glamorous illusion made men forget that, until the last great nation has disarmed, force is, and will be, the ultimate arbiter between nations; when a new world war appeared not only improbable, but almost inconceivable. And then came the decade of the thirties, the discrediting of the League in the Far East, the rise of Hitler, the successful violence of Italy in Abyssinia, the inexorable advance of National Socialism. In America men still refused to believe the implications of what was happening in Europe; Senator Gerald Nye as late as August, 1939, declared that not in months had there been less danger of war in Europe;[13] Senator Borah could still, with monumental self-assurance, tell Secretary Hull that he had better sources of information than the State Department, and that these led him to disbelieve in the imminence of hostilities; the significance and the scope of the great unfolding drama were hidden from many who considered themselves specialists in international affairs. Considering all this, it is all the more remarkable that in the midst of the Czechoslovak crisis of 1938 President Roosevelt, speaking in Kingston, Ontario, could declare categorically that "the United States would not stand idly by" if Canada were attacked. The statement had a kind of abstract flavor at the time; but it was to prove of great historical significance. In his press conference next day the President related it to the Monroe Doctrine, citing the terms of the message, and affecting to believe that Monroe's own words covered the case in point; and although it was fantastic to assert that the fifth President of the United States even dreamed of protecting Canada against aggression, it was true that the noncolonization clause of the famous declaration had no strings tied to it in any fashion, and had been provoked by a controversy, not over Latin America, but over the Northwest. At any rate, the President's statement appears to have aroused almost no dissent; and it was destined, when the war came, to be supplemented by action. In August of 1940 Mr. Roosevelt announced the formation of a joint counsel of defense for Canada and the United States; again public opinion sustained him; such a prominent Republican as Senator Vandenberg, no militant advocate of strong measures, endorsed the President's stand; and hardly anyone commented on the curious anomaly of an agreement for defense with a nation that was already at war. The implications of this new step were still hidden in the future, yet one thing was certain: Canada had now in striking fashion been brought within the purview of the principles of 1823.

The summer of 1940 also saw another bold move which may be regarded as an extension of the Monroe Doctrine. By the declaration of August 18, 1938, the United States had made it clear that it would defend the Dominion of Canada. By the destroyer-bases deal, formally announced on September 3, 1940, the American government not only underlined its previous resolution, but went further. It was normal and natural, speaking purely in historical terms, that the United States should seek to strengthen its position in the Caribbean; the leaseholds of Antigua, Santa Lucia and Trinidad, perhaps also of the Bahamas, might conceivably have been thought of as falling within the limits of a traditional sphere of interest; but when Newfoundland and Bermuda were added to the list, the significance of such action was obvious, and the intention of the Roosevelt administration to defend the outposts as well as the mainland of the North American continent became as clear as words, coupled with action, could make it.[14] And here again the note of popular approval was unmistakable. It was inevitable that in the midst of a Presidential campaign some criticism should be addressed to the manner in which the agreement was made, to the use of the form of an executive agreement in a matter of such momentous importance; but this makes it even more impressive that so stanch an exponent of isolationist policy as Senator Wheeler of Montana applauded the President's action.

A still more striking application of the fundamental conception of the Monroe Doctrine in relation to the North American continent came to fruition in the early spring of 1941. This was the extension of the Monroe Doctrine to Greenland. As long ago as 1916, Rear Admiral Robert E. Peary, in an article recommending the purchase of this island, had written as follows: "Geographically Greenland belongs to North America and the Western hemisphere, over which we have formally declared a sphere of influence by our Monroe Doctrine. Its possession by us will be in line with the Monroe Doctrine, and will eliminate one more possible source of future complications for us from European possession of territory in the Western hemisphere." [15] The Admiral's words created very little repercussion; no urgent problem of hemispheric defense presented itself to the American imagination at that time. That Peary was right in his assertion there can be very little doubt. Indeed, one of the highest of authorities in such matters, Vilhjalmur Stefansson, asserted in an article in *Foreign Affairs* (January 1941): "All geographers concede that Greenland is in the Western Hemisphere." [16] But the need of protective measures of any kind did not become clear until after the conquest of Denmark by Hitler. In March of 1941 came the passage of the lend-lease bill, pointing the lesson of Greenland's importance, and in April the administration took action. By an agreement with the Danish Minister in Washington (an agreement which cost him a rebuke and disavowal by the intimidated government at Copenhagen), the United States took the island under its protection and was accorded the right to adopt such measures as might be necessary to ensure that the territory was not used by Germany. In announcing and clarifying this decision, both the State Department and the President specifically and definitely declared that such action was taken under the Monroe Doctrine.[17] And once again they were sustained by the overwhelming body of American public opinion.

The case of Greenland clearly fell within the limits of the Monroe Doctrine. Was Iceland also to be included? The question had been raised by Stefansson in his book, *Iceland, the First American Republic*, published about 1940. In his ingenious article in *Foreign Affairs*, mentioned above, the famous Arctic explorer developed the theory that the proper dividing line between America and Europe, or, more properly, between the hemispheres, was what he called the line of the "widest channel," or a line equidistant from the American continents on the one hand, and the African and European continents on the other.[18] This principle brought Iceland within the Western Hemisphere, and it could be buttressed by a State Department report of 1868. In July, the administration determined upon the occupation of this new outpost. Yet its tone with regard to the Monroe Doctrine in this case was less certain than in the previous instances. Questioned in regard to the occupation, President Roosevelt made no appeal this time to the principles of 1823. Not the Doctrine but the necessities of national defense furnished the basis and justification for his action. And numerous dissents from the thesis that Iceland is a part of the Western Hemisphere indicate that he was wise in avoiding a debate on this geographical issue. Other and more solid grounds could be adduced for a measure intended to ensure the practical success of the policy of aid to Britain, solemnly adopted four months earlier.

In the meantime the clouds of war loomed always darker. Before the day of decision came, the American government had taken other steps towards the implementation of the Monroe Doctrine. It is not necessary to describe each of these in detail, but it is worth noting that Uruguay, far removed from the area which traditionally had preoccupied Americans in previous applications of the famous dogma, accepted the assistance of the United States

in the construction of a great air and naval base on the River
Plate, and that an agreement was actually concluded in November,
1941, by which it was made clear that, if the Uruguayan government so requested, that base might be utilized by the forces of the
great nation far away to the north.

And so we come to the dramatic day in 1941 when the bombs
fell on Pearl Harbor, and when the American continents were
challenged as never before.

Before tracing the developments of the war period it may be
useful to point out that American public opinion, lukewarm in
the early stages of Hitler's rise to power, had come to view with
more and more anxiety the position in the New World. In 1937,
for example, when the question was posed in the magazine *Fortune:* Would you be in favor of the United States defending by
force any Latin-American country from foreign attack? only 28
per cent of the persons interrogated responded in the affirmative
and 61.4 per cent in the negative.[19] The rest said they did not
know.

But by the summer of 1940 an overwhelming body of sentiment
was ready to fight for the defense of the Caribbean area, and by
February of 1941 86 per cent of those interrogated were ready
to fight even for Argentina and Brazil if these countries were actually attacked.[20] Though the proportion oscillated somewhat in
the course of the year, it seems clear that the great body of the
American people were entirely ready to accept the concept of
hemispheric solidarity and, if necessary, to enter the world struggle in defense of the liberties of the New World. The administration paid some heed to this feeling in the way in which it put the
case for lend-lease and for the extension of the naval patrols into
the Atlantic by representing these measures — at any rate, at
times — as steps which were necessary for the protection of the
hemisphere.

Furthermore, the principle of defense against aggression was
accepted by most of the states of Latin America, though with
varying degrees of enthusiasm. When the United States was swept

into the world struggle, a conference of New World states was promptly summoned to meet at Rio. And here, despite the obstructive attitude of the Argentineans, and the cautious attitude of the military leaders of Brazil, a declaration was adopted recommending the breaking of relations with Germany, Italy and Japan "in conformity with the position and circumstances obtaining in each country." This resolution was in general followed, and many of the Latin-American republics, indeed all but six, went further and in due course actually declared war, among them Mexico and Brazil. The Chileans delayed a rupture for a time, and the Argentine government acted only under heavy pressure when the conflict was well advanced, but the display of solidarity was impressive as compared with the somewhat similar situation that existed in 1917. The principles of the Monroe Doctrine, insofar as they implied the necessity for resisting aggressive action against the New World, were given a very substantial adhesion by most of the republics of the American continent.

It is not necessary here to trace the many measures that were taken in the field of common action during the period of the war, measures of economic assistance, measures against subversion and espionage, and the creation of an Inter-American Defense Board composed of representatives of all the twenty-one republics. It will be sufficient to say that, generally speaking, intimate collaboration among the American states existed during the war and that the only gross deviation from the principles of Monroeism came from the Argentine republic, which became a focus for Nazi intrigue and propaganda. But, as the war drew near its close, this collaboration was threatened, and threatened by circumstances which have a profound significance in connection with the Doctrine and its place in contemporary affairs. The essential issue was this: Was the idea of the defense of the Americas, asserted at Havana and carried into practice in the succeeding years, to give way to a more general principle? Was inter-American collaboration to be submerged in a world-wide international organization for the preservation of peace? There were those at Washington who answered these questions in the affirmative. In the preparations for the drafting of the United Nations charter and in the conversations which took place at Dumbarton Oaks between the representatives of the great powers, the Latin-American states, much to their chagrin, were virtually ignored. And powerful elements in the State Department seem to have looked down their noses at the idea of inter-American defense, and to have treated the whole concept as one that was outmoded in the world of 1944 and 1945.

But a countercurrent set in. Under pressure from the republics of the South, the American government consented to the calling of a conference at Mexico City, a conference generally alluded to as the conference of Chapultepec. Here the principles of inter-American action were again asserted; the declarations of previous conferences were reasserted; once more an act of aggression against any American state was declared to be an aggression against all; once more the obligation to consult in case of danger was underlined; and a whole variety of measures was listed by which the individual states, "within the scope of their constitutional powers" and as might "be found necessary," would take action against the aggressor state.[21]

The principle of hemispheric defense laid down at Chapultepec was rediscussed and reinforced at the famous Charter conference at San Francisco. It was well enough to talk of the idea of universality that was embodied in the Charter; it was well enough to stress the significance of the new world organization that was coming into being; but the Latin-American states were quite aware of the fact that this new organization operated on principles somewhat restricted; for the Charter was so drafted as to give to the permanent members of the Security Council a veto on the deliberations of that body, and thus to diminish its effectiveness as an instrument of peace. It was suspected that trouble lay ahead; and these suspicions, directed, of course, against Russia, were felt in great degree by the Latin Americans and were sharpened and accentuated by the rather contemptuous attitude of Mr. Molotov towards the smaller Latin-American sovereignties. As the

Charter finally emerged from the discussions at San Francisco, substantial concessions, indeed fundamental concessions, were made to the hemispheric point of view. Most important, Article 52 stipulated that nothing in the Charter itself would "preclude the existence of regional arrangements for dealing with such matters relating to the maintenance of international peace and security, if these arrangements were consistent with the purpose and principles of the United Nations." [22] Thus, unless and until the Security Council has acted, the machinery of inter-American collaboration could readily be brought into play. And let it again be observed that it could be operated without a veto.

There was more to follow, however, with regard to intercontinental defense. The decisions taken at Chapultepec had not been embodied in a treaty and, so far as the United States was concerned, had been taken under the wartime powers of the President. But it was clearly understood that a treaty was to follow and, although the bad state of our relations with the Argentineans led to a delay, a new conference met at Rio de Janeiro in the late summer of 1947. This conference drew up a treaty of inter-American assistance, framed in far-reaching terms. In the first place, the scope of common action was so defined as to include Greenland, Canada, and much of the polar regions within the operation of a collective guarantee. The treaty defined aggression in explicit terms as an unprovoked armed attack against the territory, the people, or the land, sea and air forces of another state, or as an invasion of the territory of another state; it listed measures of sanction, including the possible use of armed force, and it even went so far as to provide that common action against a lawbreaking state might be taken by a two-thirds vote, and that the decision so taken should be binding on all states, with the sole exception that no state should be required to use armed force without its own consent. [23]

The events which we described have certainly marked an important evolution in the history of the Monroe Doctrine. Insofar as formal treaty agreements could guarantee security, the states of the New World (all of which have ratified the treaty of Rio) were bound to act together against aggression, and against aggression not only in Latin America but in the Western Hemisphere broadly defined. Moreover, the obligation so to act (we repeat) might be brought about through a two-thirds vote of the Council of the Organization of American States, and the United States might be bound by such a vote even if it were in the minority. Further still, if the precedent of the conference of Havana were to be followed in the future, the transfer of territory in the New World from one Old World state to another would be a matter of concern to the cis-atlantic republics, all the more certainly since there was to arise in Latin America an increasing agitation for the termination of all colonial situations on this side of the ocean. All in all, therefore, it is fair to say that immense steps had been taken towards the generalized acceptance of the principles of 1823, and that the dream of an American league of states, put forward by Baltásar Brum in 1919, had attained at least a measure of substance.

But it is quite another matter to proclaim, as certain publicists have proclaimed, that the Doctrine had been internationalized, and to speak as if it had been discarded in favor of some wider formula. Here, too, no doubt, a change from the situation thirty or forty years ago is clear. The United States, by the conventions of Montevideo and Buenos Aires, has forsworn the right of physical intervention to protect its interests under the Doctrine, and it would be a serious matter to violate this pledge. But the American government has not forsworn all independent action. It could still, without the violation of any existing engagement, and with the limitation just mentioned, be its own judge of a situation which violated its essential interests. The Charter of the United Nations itself reserves to each individual nation the right of self-defense if the Security Council fails to act in case of aggression. This right is inherent in national sovereignty; and as long as it exists, in a sense, the Monroe Doctrine will exist also. This is not to say that wise policy and a decent respect for the opinions of mankind will not dictate on the part of any American government a prudent restraint in the taking of independent action. But such action is not barred by the understandings which we have been outlining.

We must go a bit further in discussing this important question. The Doctrine has not, strictly speaking, been internationalized. But a great deal has been learned since 1905 or 1919 by those most intimately concerned with the conduct of American foreign policy. And one thing that has definitely been learned is that admirable as are the principles of 1823, the words "Monroe Doctrine" convey a definite impression of hegemony, of supercilious arrogance, of interference to the minds of our Latin-American neighbors. They still suggest the Roosevelt corollary; they still suggest the nationalism of the debates on the League; they still suggest a protective attitude offensive to the pride of the growing states of the South. And because they suggest these things, it is well not to talk too much of Monroe.

Strange to say, this fact seems to have been assimilated. In general, it cannot be said that silence is an American virtue in foreign affairs, or that restraint in proclaiming its own high purposes is characteristic either of the American people or of its government. But there is no denying that in this particular matter there was for a time a distinct change of tone. It is a fact, striking beyond measure, for example, that in the debates on the Charter of the United Nations, debates that extended over more than a fortnight in the Senate, the Doctrine was hardly mentioned. Compare this situation with the tremendous outpouring of Senatorial eloquence in 1919 and 1920 and with the impassioned nationalism of which the discussions of that time were the expression. In 1945 only two Senators, Langer of North Dakota and Bushfield of South Dakota, had even a critical word to say on the subject.

There are various explanations, to be sure, of this fact. The delegation at San Francisco was a bipartisan delegation, containing among others one of the ablest and most influential men in the Senate, Vandenberg of Michigan, an ardent supporter of the idea of international organization and an extraordinarily subtle and skilled parliamentarian. The existence of the veto in the Charter must have done something to soothe Senatorial susceptibilities, for here was a guarantee, as it must have seemed, that no action could be taken contrary to the principles of 1823. To add another point, the psychology of the summer of 1945 was distinctly favorable to the movement for the organization of peace. No postwar reaction, no return to normalcy had yet occurred, and there were vivid and suggestive memories of the failure of twenty-six years before. But even taking all these facts into account, it still remains remarkable that so little attention was paid to Monroe.

The same thing applies to the convention of Rio. In discussing an instrument so intimately related to the great American dogma, one would have expected spates of oratory on the past policy of the United States. Nothing of the sort occurred.

There is also a third international engagement which should be mentioned here which might have led Senators of the United States to descant on the principles of the past. In 1949 the American government took one of the most significant steps in our diplomatic history when it promoted and signed the North Atlantic treaty and brought this country, for the first time since February 6, 1778, into an actual alliance with European powers. There was, it is true, nothing in this that definitely ran counter to the Monroe Doctrine. The necessity for protecting the American hemisphere, we have already pointed out, does not mean, and ought not to mean, that the United States has no security interests elsewhere. But we may be very sure, nonetheless, that in an earlier period of American history such an engagement would have brought many Senators to their feet with comments on our "traditional policy," and with references to 1823. The fact that the subject of Monroeism was hardly mentioned is therefore of substantial interest.

We may go even further. The fact is undeniable that since 1947, or even since 1945, there was a decline in the public interest in the Monroe Doctrine, indeed, the late forties and early fifties might have thought that the Monroe Doctrine had ceased to command attention. In the periodicals, in the published books, even in the pages of the *Congressional Record*, it was barely mentioned.

Yet it would have been dangerous to say, as Senator Pittman had said in the thirties, that the Doctrine had been outmoded. When, in 1953, there seemed some danger that a Communist or proto-Communist regime would establish itself in Guatemala, cries for the recognition of the Monroe Doctrine again were heard. Senator Johnson of Texas, an influential figure in the Upper House, introduced a resolution calling for its defense, and John Foster Dulles, the Secretary of State, described the course of events as a direct challenge to the principles of 1823. Fortunately the danger soon passed, the government of President Arbenz was deserted by the army and overthrown, very possibly with some assistance to the rebels from the United States.

But worse was to come. In Cuba a revolution brought Fidel Castro to power. His government soon moved in the direction of Communism. Relations with the United States were broken off. More and more insolent and reckless, the Cuban dictator not only threw himself into the arms of the Soviet Union, but actually began to build on his soil, with the assistance of Russia, missile bases which might well endanger the security of the United States. New demands arose for the enforcement of the Monroe Doctrine. The government of the United States established a partial blockade of Cuba, and made it clear that it would take whatever action was necessary to put an end to the new menace.

Yet an important new fact appeared. In his speech to the nation of October 22, 1962, President Kennedy said not a word of the message of 1823. Instead he rested his action on the pact of Rio de Janeiro and, to the vast satisfaction of most Americans, the nations of the New World rallied to the side of the United States.

The point is one that deserves to be emphasized. For it marks realization of the fact that the words "Monroe Doctrine" still retain for our Latin American friends connotations of imperialism and of offensive interference in their affairs. It is wiser and more tactful to place our defensive action in the New World on the basis of Pan-Americanism rather than on the formulas of a hundred and forty years ago.

The result, of course, is the same. The United States today, as in earlier times, will brook no European invasion of this continent, no indirect control of any Latin American state by another and alien power. In the deepest sense, the Monroe Doctrine remains today, fused with the common determination of the states of the hemisphere to regulate their own affairs and to develop in their own way the institutions which they wish for themselves.

XI

~~~~~

Retrospect and Prospect
Monroeism in Its Broad Lines—The Future

~~~~~~

WERE history nothing more nor less than narrative, it would be possible to end the story of the Monroe Doctrine with the concluding sentences of the last chapter. But generalization and interpretation are an indispensable part of every historical subject; a problem studied in detail must be seen also in large perspective; nor can the historian refrain from the hope that the experience of the past may be useful in the elucidation of the problems of the present, and suggestive — though certainly not prophetic — with regard to the future. What is to be said, then, with regard to the larger aspects of the Doctrine? What principles, what broad conceptions, what vistas, should a study of the Doctrine make more clear?

The famous message of December 2, 1823, the product of the combined genius of Adams and Monroe, rested upon a broad philosophical conception that has not been without influence upon the history of the United States. This country of ours in its social structure and its political ideals was, in the days of its youth, the herald of a new order. Americans of the early period of our history felt that there was building on this side of the Atlantic a fresh and confident society on a new model, one which in its optimism, its freedom from trammeling convention and outworn custom, held out a great hope to the world at large, and stood sharply opposed to the monarchies and feudalisms of the Old World. The revolutions that took place in Latin America in the first and second decades of the nineteenth century only sharpened this feeling and widened it; and while there might be some skeptics, like John Quincy Adams, who were by no means convinced that the history of the new republics of the South would run parallel to that of the North, no doubt the more acceptable view was that of men like Henry Clay, and indeed of Monroe himself, who saw in the turn of events in Latin America new signs of the triumph of the New World ideals. At the same time, experience seemed to have demonstrated to the Americans the inexpediency of close connection with the nations of Europe. The French alliance had, indeed, been helpful in the gaining of independence; but it had been irksome in the making of peace, and more than irksome in 1793 when a great international war broke out in Europe. Though American statesmen for some time flirted with the idea of a closer political connection with one or another European state in some special situation, such, for example, as that created by the informal war with France in 1798, or by the cession of Louisiana to France in 1800, the voice of experience more and more affirmed the wisdom of an independent course, of a separation, in the political sphere, of the New World from the Old. This idea had become dominant by the decade of the twenties; and it was firmly held by John Quincy Adams, whose strong will and bold and hardy intelligence had so much to do with the declaration of 1823. In the deliberations which led to that famous declaration it is worth noting — indeed worth underlining — that the chance of common action with Great Britain against the Continental powers in their assumed hostility to the new republics was put aside. Jefferson and Madison, venerable and respected counselors of the President, advised collaboration with the Court of St. James's; Monroe himself was not flatly averse to the idea; but the cabinet discussions and in particular the opinion of Adams led to its rejection, and the government of the United States spoke out boldly and independently with regard to the colonial question, not, it is true without the knowledge that in a pinch it might be supported by the mistress of the seas, but asking no pledge of support, and giving no pledge of its own. The circumstances of its enunciation have inevitably connected the Monroe Doctrine in the minds of Americans with the conception of the two spheres, the separation of the New World from the Old.

This conception had an obvious measure of validity in 1823. The distinction between the social and political ideals of the United States and those of Europe was a real one. And often in their constitutions and theories the new states of Latin America, in putting aside the idea of monarchy, seemed to associate themselves with the new spirit. While the broadest generalizations are always the most dangerous, there was truth in the idea of a clash of political ideals between the countries of the West and those of old Europe. As the nineteenth century wore on, the generalization became for a time less relevant. Democracy, the fruit of our pioneer soil, and our boundless individual opportunity, became the creed not only of America, but of some of the leading European peoples. On the contrary, it seemed hardly to flourish, except in theory, in the countries to the south. Not Argentina or Brazil, but Great Britain, despite its social cleavages and its landholding class, became outside the United States the best model of the democratic ideal. The France of the Third Republic was nearer to the American conception of popular government than Venezuela or Colombia.

The doctrine of the two spheres, indeed, was already becoming outmoded by the end of the nineteenth century. It was to be dealt a deadly blow by the events of the twentieth. Reluctantly, but at long last vigorously, the United States became involved in a European struggle, and Woodrow Wilson crossed the seas at the end of the conflict to participate in the decision of many questions that were predominantly European. There was, it is true, reaction against the larger American role with the end of the war. But before two decades had gone by, the rise of German National Socialism raised a new peril. Once more the United States responded, and the legions of Hitler were crushed on the beaches of Normandy and on the banks of the Meuse and of the Rhine. Again the impulse for withdrawal asserted itself, but this time the reaction was brief indeed. The aggressiveness and the far-reaching ambitions of Russian Communist imperialism led the American government to form closer ties with the states of Western Europe, and by 1949 the United States had entered an alliance with these states, the first formal alliance in its history since February 6, 1778. No well-informed person today would be likely to try to draw a sharp line between the New World and the Old; the doctrine of the two spheres no longer has any validity. In a recent book of much penetration and sound scholarship, Professor Arthur Whitaker of the University of Pennsylvania has contributed some interesting observations to this shift of opinion. The same theme is underlined in the late Professor Spykman's *America's Strategy in World Politics* and in Eugene Staley's article on "The Myth of the Continents," which appeared in *Foreign Affairs* as early as 1941.

But the doctrine of the two spheres is one thing; the Monroe Doctrine is another. The latter owed its origins to the former, in some degree; but it must be emphasized that it possesses an original force of its own, and that, as our story has shown, it never was intended to bar the way to the larger defense of American interests, or to American diplomatic or physical action in other parts of the globe.

The sentences of Monroe's message which relate to Europe are cautiously and conservatively phrased. They speak of abstinence from intermeddling in the "internal affairs" of European powers, and of abstinence from the wars of European countries "relating to themselves." There is nothing in these phrases that suggests the fixing of an absolute and an irrevocable standard with regard to diplomatic co-operation with European powers. Monroe himself, as the history of the period shows, approached the problems of foreign affairs in no narrow and doctrinaire spirit. He was decidedly ready to consider the possibility of common action with Great Britain in a matter in which the interests of his own country and of the British were identical. Even Adams, less than a year after the famous declaration, was not averse to consultation with the Court of St. James's in the interests of Spanish America, and was ready, if the peril was great enough, to go further. We cannot, therefore, say of the statesmen of 1823 that they were isolationists in the extreme sense of the term. Their problems were so very different from those of our own time that it is perhaps not very useful to cite their position in defense of either isolation or intervention in Europe.

The Scriptures can always be quoted to any purpose. It would be futile to deny that the opponents of American diplomatic action in the Old World or in Asia have sometimes appealed to the message of Monroe. It was so in the debates over the acquisition of Hawaii and the Philippines. It was so in connection with The Hague Conventions. It was so, in some few instances, in connection with our entry into the First World War. It was so in connection with the contest over the League. But it was so hardly at all in 1940 and 1941. The notion that our foreign policy must be circumscribed by a formula of over one hundred years ago, and that formula misinterpreted, had very little to do with the debates that preceded our entry into the Second World War. It was on other grounds that the foes of Roosevelt's policy attacked the administration.

In reality, of course, Monroe probably never intended to proclaim a doctrine at all. John Quincy Adams, in formulating the so-called noncolonization clause, may have had it in mind to generalize for a long future. At any rate, he talked of "principle." But Monroe was dealing with a specific situation, and an assumedly immediate, if illusory, peril. He reiterated the warning of 1823 in 1824, it is true. But there seems no reason to believe that he thought of himself as laying down maxims of conduct for the long future; and the history of the Monroe Doctrine is the history of an interesting evolution, alike in the field of ideas and of public opinion.

The message of 1823 was undoubtedly popular in the United

States; it produced a very considerable contemporaneous impression. But it is worth noting that in the years following its enunciation there was manifested, on the part of both the legislative and the executive branch of the government, a very distinct reluctance to translate its general phrases into more concrete terms, and especially into any binding engagement toward the states of Latin America. This reluctance is comprehensible, and wholly consonant with the general traditions of our foreign policy; nothing is more characteristic of American diplomacy than its general aversion to far-reaching contractual commitments. Yet it argues something less than an unqualified enthusiasm for the cause of the new republics; and it cannot be said that the declaration of Monroe was followed by very intimate political relationships with the nations of the New World. There was no great zeal for American representation at the Congress of Panama; indeed, it was possible to make the matter one of partisan controversy, even possible to question the wisdom of the message of so short a time before; and after 1826 there is a considerable period in which one hears almost nothing of the 1823 pronouncement. Occasional appeals to its wisdom there might be, but little that can be taken as evidence that it had been assimilated by the wide reaches of American public opinion.

It is necessary to give to President James K. Polk the credit of reviving the Monroe message and placing it in the forefront of great diplomatic controversies. This does not mean that the idea of such revival was necessarily original with him; on the contrary, the references to the message become more frequent in 1842 and 1843 than they had been in previous years; the issues of Texas and Oregon provided important concrete interests which might be defended in terms of Continental doctrine; Polk did not pluck out of the air the idea of restating the declaration. Nonetheless, there is a vast difference between the vagrant utterances of members of Congress and the utterance of a President of the United States; and there cannot be the slightest question that the message of December 2, 1845, was a vital step in the evolution of the Monroe Doctrine. It seems strange that a Chief

Executive as prosaic as Polk, one with so hard and narrow a mind, should be responsible for an important step in the development of an idea; there are those who have sought to give the credit for the message to Buchanan, a subtler intelligence, if a less forceful personality; but Polk, it will be remembered, had expressed himself in substantially the terms of the message as early as April 1844, and it seems just therefore that he should be conceded the authorship of the declaration of 1845, and be recorded as an outstanding figure in the history of the great principle of action we have been examining.

One thing, however, Polk could not do. He could not, in days of narrow partisanship, and with his far from imposing personality, command general popularity for his new enunciation of policy. Monroe's declaration became a matter of partisan debate, and while Democrats threw up their caps and huzza'd for the principles of 1823, Whigs maintained a supercilious indifference to what they were sometimes ready to brand as mere demagogy. As happens in such cases, the opposition found an intellectual basis for its point of view, and this was clearly expounded, if not by a Whig, nonetheless by an opponent of the President, the disgruntled Democrat, Calhoun. The thesis put forward was a simple and appealing one: why tie the foreign policy of the United States to an abstraction; why enunciate a general theory; why not permit a wise opportunism to guide our foreign policy? There was much to be said for this proposition, and the Whigs, when they came into office, and when they were confronted with the delicate question of trans-isthmian communication and the clash of British and American interests in Central America, founded their policy, not on any appeal to dogma, but on a treaty which recognized the wisdom of, but did not mention, the principles of 1823. Throughout the early fifties, perhaps a little later, there existed a strong current of feeling against the crystallization of Monroe's message into a fixed maxim of foreign policy; and this feeling was frequently reflected in the debates in Congress.

In a democracy simple and broad generalizations, appealing

to deep-seated sentiments and prejudices, are bound to exercise a considerable weight in politics; it is easier to generalize than to analyze; and it must be conceded in addition that the formulas of 1823 and 1845 expressed not only American feeling but to a very substantial degree American national interests. Attachment to the Doctrine grew; the word "doctrine" itself began to appear; and when the Republicans entered office in 1861, Seward, the very man who in 1855 had expressed his doubts as to the wisdom of Monroeism, speedily made appeal to the name of Monroe with the Spanish reoccupation of Santo Domingo. If he did this, it was not because much was to be hoped from the Doctrine so far as the intimidation of Spain was concerned; it was because he realized, incomparable politician that he was, the strong appeal to national feeling that could be made on the basis of the principles of 1823. Nor could there be any doubt of the accuracy of his judgment; for in the period of the Civil War, when the French invasion of Mexico put to the test in most striking form the loyalty of the American people to the testaments according to Monroe, the outpouring of feeling was extraordinary, expressing itself in innumerable speeches and articles, and in the famous Davis resolution of the House of Representatives.

When the war came to an end, and the hands of the American government were freer, the tide of opinion rose even higher; men like General Grant and General Schuyler were ardent for intervention in Mexico; the President himself shared to a considerable degree their bellicosity; and while Seward never mentioned the Monroe Doctrine by name in his correspondence with the French government, he appealed constantly to its spirit in that skillful series of diplomatic notes by which he helped to persuade the French to abandon the unhappy Maximilian, the puppet Emperor, to the untender mercies of the forces of Benito Juárez. From this great episode the principles of 1823 emerged, clearly not a party, but a national, dogma; and for well-nigh half a century after 1865 the great bulk of American public opinion united behind the maxims of Monroe. Sober men like John A. Kasson began to speak of these maxims in terms not untouched with a kind of mystical nationalism; Congressmen found them useful in rallying American sentiment behind the movement for an American-controlled canal; Grover Cleveland discovered, quite remarkably, that they made necessary the submission to arbitration of a dispute between Great Britain and Venezuela; Andrew D. White, properly coached by Alfred Thayer Mahan, concluded that they could not be subjected to even the most delicate international inquiry; and a succession of Presidents and Secretaries of State enunciated a theory, suggested by Polk but continuously reiterated from the days of Grant, that the interests of the United States demanded that no territory in the New World be transferred from one European power to another, or from an American power to a European. Each one of these interpretations of the Doctrine found widespread, indeed almost unanimous, support in American public opinion; none were successfully refuted or put down; and the growing power of the American people, and their widening interests, were reflected in the evolution of the principles of 1823, and in their well-nigh universal popularity. Before turning to trace the further evolution of the Doctrine in the twentieth century, it may be well to inquire as to its practical efficacy in the period already traversed. Did the Doctrine prevent the conquest of the states of Latin America by Europe?

The answer to this question must, in my judgment, be a negative, perhaps a qualified negative, but still a negative. There can be no doubt at all, for example, that Monroe's message of 1823 was directed against an illusory danger. There never was any fixed purpose to reconquer the Spanish colonies. The matter never even became a subject of important diplomatic discussion. Let us get any other idea out of our minds once and for all. In the period from 1823 to the Civil War, the Doctrine had influence, but by no means dominating influence. It did not prevent the British seizure of the Falklands; it did not prevent the expansion of British jurisdiction in Belize; and in the controversy between Great Britain and the United States over Central America in the fifties, it was cited ineffectively in the diplomatic discussions. The most effective diplomatic weapon in the American armory was the Clayton-Bulwer Treaty, not the Monroe message; it was only at home that the Doctrine played a part in the arousing of public opinion. In the case of Maximilian, the role assigned to the principles of 1823 was more important; the spirit of these principles, if not their letter, was constantly present in the dispatches of Seward; and the knowledge of American feeling as to the Doctrine was a factor in the final withdrawal of the French from Mexico. But it was not the only factor, and, to repeat a judgment already made, it seems not improbable that the Emperor Louis Napoleon would, for other reasons, and in any case, have abandoned his Mexican protégé.

In the period from 1865 to the First World War, the influence of the Doctrine was real, but is easily subjected to exaggeration. It was wise, for example, to enunciate the no-transfer principle; and it is probable that the German naval lords would have been able to get the consent of the Foreign Office for their frequently expressed desires for bases in the Caribbean and South America had it not been clear that any project of this kind would meet with strenuous opposition from the United States. But we must put out of our minds the idea that the first Reich meditated ambitious schemes of control, and specifically that it meditated such schemes with regard to Venezuela in 1902–1903; here again is legend rather than fact. No project of conquest with regard to any Latin-American state can be discovered in this era; the colonizing energies and acquisitive instincts of the great powers were satisfied in Africa and Asia. Great Britain, easily the dominant power of the time, came more and more to defer to American prejudice; never very much excited about the Guiana boundary, the British government bowed before American opinion and consented to arbitration; and the arbitral award kept the British away from the mouth of the Orinoco, and gave to Venezuela considerable territories in the basin of the Cuyuni. Once again, on the question of the canal, the Foreign Office bent before

American pressure; and the Hay-Pauncefote Treaty of 1901 conceded that the United States should control the highway across the isthmus. In the discussions on this question, the Monroe Doctrine had played a part, not a very effective one in the diplomatic debates, as Mr. Frelinghuysen discovered, but a more effective one in the integration of American opinion. At any rate, in one important matter, European influence was excluded from this hemisphere.

And in connection with these and other episodes, an important fact stands out. During the nineteenth and early twentieth centuries, the United States was, in physical power, far inferior to Great Britain. Its navy was puny in 1823; puny in the 1850's when there came the clash on Central America; puny, by comparison, in 1895, when the Guiana boundary question agitated American opinion. One weakness there was in the British position, the long-exposed flank of Canada, and this would have been important in time of war. But was it fear of consequences that led Great Britain to defer to the United States? Or was it rather other factors — the immense British economic stake in the prosperity of this country, the variety and extent of British commitments in other quarters of the globe, the opportunities for expansion in Asia and Africa, already alluded to? May it not also have been due in part to the substantial economic and political progress made by many of the states of the New World? In part to the technical difficulties involved in large-scale military and naval operations against the republics of the South? We cannot answer such questions since they involve delicate problems of motive; but this much we can and ought to say. There is not the faintest evidence of any genuinely aggressive purpose on the part of the British in America in the long period from 1852 to the outbreak of the Great War in 1914. Needless to say, there has been none since.

It is not possible to speak of France or Germany in quite the same terms. France obviously took advantage of the Civil War to pursue an ambitious policy in Mexico, inimical to the interests of the United States. The German Foreign Office pursued a correct, and even a cautious, policy in the main in the years prior to the First World War; but in no country was opposition to the Monroe Doctrine more violently expressed; and in none were the naval authorities so definitely hostile. It may be that a German victory in the First World War, accompanied by the collapse of the British fleet, would have exposed the New World to serious danger; but the danger was averted by the triumph of the Allies. For the first century of their history, at least, it may well be doubted whether the principles of 1823 were a decisive factor in protecting the liberties of the American states.

But let us turn back to sketch the further evolution of the Doctrine in the twentieth century. One interpretation of it gained currency and fell into decline in the period between 1904 and 1933. I refer, of course, to the Roosevelt corollary. It is easy to see how that corollary arose. Undoubtedly the American people were becoming more sensitive to European interpositions in the New World at the close of the nineteenth and the beginning of the twentieth century. The Roosevelt administration, in its first year of office, did not foresee that the blockade of Venezuela, the chastisement of the unlovely Castro, would awaken resentment in the United States; despite the later imaginings of the President on the subject it is clear that the intense reaction to German activity took those in authority by surprise. But the reaction *was* intense, beyond a doubt; and it was a plausible thesis that if we were not going to permit European coercion of American states, we might be called upon to take measures to forestall such coercion. This notion was encouraged by more than one European publicist and statesman, particularly by those of Great Britain; and it derived an added impetus from the temper of the times. The America of the first decade of the twentieth century had been touched with dreams of colonial expansion, of what its enemies bluntly described as "imperialism"; the control of other less competent and more simple peoples seemed attractive to many members of that generation; and it had a positive lure for Theodore Roosevelt himself. We had taken upon ourselves the elevation of the

Filipinos; we had set out to do good to the prolific inhabitants of Puerto Rico; withdrawing from Cuba, we left in the Platt amendment a legal basis for further paternal guidance of the affairs of this newborn republic. What more natural, therefore, than that the Americans who regarded the steps just outlined with complacency and pride should find it easy to propose a new exercise of the reforming spirit, and that they should bring to its support the great tradition of the Monroe Doctrine?

The lines just penned are written in no spirit of censure or mockery. No candid man can view the events of the turn of the century or study the influence of the United States over the peoples which, in one way or another, came under its control without perceiving much that was good in the process. The amelioration of the lot of those under tutelage always played a part in American colonialism; and the direction of the national effort was always toward a greater measure of self-government and freedom for the peoples under control. There is no denying this elementary fact. Moreover, it can be argued with some cogency that real gains flowed from American interventions; in countries such as Haiti, Santo Domingo, and Nicaragua the cause of political stability was undeniably promoted by the coercive action of the United States. In each of these cases the existence of a constabulary, the product of the American regime, has made revolution less likely, though it has not made for genuinely popular government. It is true that the perspective is by no means a very long one — American marines withdrew from Nicaragua only in 1932, from the Dominican Republic in 1924; but the comparative peace of these countries since that time is nonetheless suggestive. Nor is it possible to deny that public improvements, if not on a grandiose, at least on a substantial, scale, followed in the wake of American occupations.

Yet the American people never responded with enthusiasm to the idea of a general tutelage over the Latin-American republics. The Dominican policy of Theodore Roosevelt met with much opposition from the Democrats; it was an administration and not a national policy. Under Secretary Knox, whose touch was anything but light, it seemed to many to be connected with ambitious schemes of finance, and the words "dollar diplomacy" took on a hint of invidiousness; under Woodrow Wilson it seemed patently and flagrantly inconsistent with the lofty professions of the President himself, and with the self-restraint and patience which the United States showed in dealing with the problem of Mexico. It was the object of attack by Warren Harding in the campaign of 1920; the fact that the Wilsonian interventions were in the Roosevelt-Knox tradition did not prevent partisan onslaught upon them; and in 1927 when the Coolidge administration imprudently intervened in Nicaragua, the Democrats, now the outs again, advanced gaily to the charge. It has always been politically possible, if not profitable, to criticize these various manifestations of American "imperialism," as they have invariably been called by their critics.

Moreover, the drift of opinion since the twenties was in the noninterventionist direction. Interventions had been connected in the popular mind with the machinations of wicked financiers; and the years of the depression and the default of so many of the loans of the twenties produced a kind of reaction against the export of capital which found its reflection in the trends of foreign policy. It was obvious, also, that intermeddling in the affairs of Latin-American states was viewed with a general resentment by our neighbors to the south; and although it could not mathematically be demonstrated that a policy of abstinence from interference would have direct results in increased trade, there existed a widespread feeling that good political relations were the best foundations for economic collaboration. Nor could it be stated that American intervention was a *necessary* condition of progress among our neighbors. It had done good, in some ways; but states like Venezuela and Colombia went forward without the blessing of American marine rule; and Nicaragua after two periods of American policing was no further advanced than Guatemala, which had escaped attention of this kind. Considerations such as these have weight; and it is a fact of very large importance that the surrender by the administration of Franklin D. Roosevelt of the right of intervention, first at Montevideo, and in still more explicit terms at Buenos Aires in 1936, met with the virtually unanimous approval of the members of the United States Senate. Indeed, there was nothing partisan about the retreat from the Theodore Roosevelt corollary. Senator Borah lent his powerful influence to the movement at the time of the ratification of the Kellogg Pact; the Clark memorandum was drawn up in the closing days of the Coolidge administration; the Hoover administration published it to the world. Republicans and Democrats alike subscribed to the policy of the good neighbor and to the divorcement of the Monroe Doctrine from the policy of intervention.

But if the American people and their government had by 1933 repudiated the Roosevelt corollary, they remained true to the fundamental principles of the Doctrine. For a few years, years when the war clouds were only gathering and did not as yet hang heavy over the world, the principles of 1823 seemed to have fallen into innocuous desuetude, and in 1937 Senator Pittman, then chairman of the Committee on Foreign Relations in the Senate of the United States, could pronounce them to be outmoded. But there came an abrupt change before long; in 1938 Cordell Hull reiterated the fundamentals of Monroeism at the conference of Lima, and his words were echoed by Alfred M. Landon, the titular head of the Republican Party at that time. The President's association of Canada with the Doctrine in the same year was, so far as I know, nowhere challenged. By 1940 matters had gone further. At the conference of Havana the no-transfer principle was solemnly confirmed in a gathering of all the states of the New World and the solidarity of the republics of the West asserted with the enunciation of the famous declaration that an aggression against any one of them should be considered an aggression against all. The Congress went on record by an overwhelming vote in favor of the first of these two declarations. And in this same year of 1940, the Danish colony of Greenland was brought within the scope of the pronouncement of Monroe. In these various measures was the clearest indication of the loyalty of the American people to the principles of 1823.

It is not to be contended, though, that at all times in their history the American people would have fought for the maintenance of Monroeism. The cautious language of Adams in his reply to Salazar in 1824 makes it at least doubtful whether the Monroe administration itself would have been willing to translate the bold words of the 1823 message into warlike action. The Polk administration compromised on the question of Oregon. The notion that Theodore Roosevelt's administration forced the Germans to give up overambitious designs against Venezuela in 1902–1903 is now no more than discredited legend. This country might conceivably have come to war on the question of Mexico in 1865–1867 had it not been for the wise restraint and mingled caution and firmness of a great Secretary of State. Had the British government in 1895 persisted in its first refusal to submit the Guiana boundary to arbitration, the Cleveland administration undoubtedly would have had to go forward along the lines laid down in the message of December 17, 1895, and this might have led to armed action. But the Mexican matter and the Venezuela crisis of 1895 were, in fact, liquidated without war. In the twentieth century there was for a long time no direct challenge to the Doctrine. But the American people more than once showed their devotion to the principles of 1823, and when the peril appeared greatest, the popular support of the dogma was strongest. There is no doubt of the set of American public opinion in 1940 and 1941.

The Second World War marked an important step in the development of Monroeism. No doubt, as has already been said, there are many Americans who would still insist on the unilateral character of the President's declaration. No doubt it is an incontrovertible fact (and one that ought not to be dodged) that the defense of the republics of the free world depends, so far as actual physical attack is concerned, on the power and resolution of the United States of America. Nonetheless, something important has happened since 1940 and 1941. The change of emphasis is unmistakable. The fact has been assimilated, apparently, that the phrase "the Monroe Doctrine" conveys to the Latin-American mind some not too subtle suggestion of hegemony, that it awakens recollections, not all of them to the advantage of the United States, and that it is wiser and better to talk and to act as if a common interest were involved, so far as the rest of America is concerned, rather than as if this nation were the lord of the two continents. This by no means implies that the principles of 1823 are outmoded; were the republics of the New World to stand in physical danger from the Old, the American people would doubtless rally, as they have rallied in the past, to the dogma of Monroe. They would, nevertheless, wisely assume that action, if possible, should be a matter of common consultation and agreement rather than of the United States alone.

But the danger of actual invasion, in the world of 1955, may well be regarded as remote; the strategic factors at this time suggest that, if a third world war *should* come, the principal fields of action will be in the Northern rather than in the Southern Hemisphere — in Europe, in Asia, perhaps over the Pole, rather than in Latin America. The really serious question today is the question of how to deal with the possible penetration of totalitarian ideals into the states of the New World. In raising the question it is to be emphasized that there is no evidence that in 1823 Monroe intended to insist that the political organization of the American republics should be precisely like our own. Let us examine his position on this matter.

The message of 1823 stated: "The political system of the allied powers is essentially different . . . from that of America. This difference proceeds from that which exists in their respective Governments . . . We owe it, therefore, to candor and to the amicable relations existing between the United States and those powers to declare that we should consider any attempt on their part to extend their system to any portion of this hemisphere as dangerous to our peace and safety." Just exactly what did these phrases mean? Do they imply opposition to monarchy? Or do they merely connote hostility to the system of the Holy Alliance, and to the dogma of intervention for the preservation of legitimacy? In behalf of the latter viewpoint, it is worthwhile to point out that the United States, in 1822, had recognized the Mexican Empire of Itúrbide, and that shortly after the Presidential declaration it extended recognition to Brazil. These facts suggest that opposition to the monarchical system was not unqualified in the minds of Adams and Monroe. Monarchical forms were no doubt regarded as inferior to republican ones, but they were apparently particularly odious only when they implied a connection between a New World and an Old World state. In other circumstances they might perhaps be tolerated, but in these particular instances they could not be regarded as otherwise than dangerous to the peace and safety of the United States.

Now this distinction is one worth bearing in mind today. The United States has not taken the position, in its intercourse with Latin-American governments, that to command our favor or friendship they should operate a democratic system of government similar to our own. Americans dislike revolutions, except revolutions remote in time, like their own; but, generally speaking, the United States has not denied recognition to regimes that came to power through violence, and it has not inquired as to whether the rulers of the republics to the south were observing the forms of their own constitutions. It has dealt with such ruthless dictators as Cabrera in Guatemala and Gómez in Venezuela; it was welcomed to the Congress of Lima in 1938 by General Benavides, whose own regime was something less than democratic in the American sense; it did not frown upon — on the contrary it approved — the so-called corporative state which General Getulio Vargas set up in Brazil. Were it to ask of its Southern neighbors that they be governed precisely as it is governed, it would find co-operation with them difficult, if not impossible.

On the other hand, as recent events have clearly demonstrated, the United States will not permit the establishment of a Communist-satellite state in the New World, or, to put the matter more cautiously, will not permit any state to associate itself so closely with Russia as to jeopardize the security of the Americas. The fact has become crystal-clear in this year 1962.

Is the Cuban situation likely to be repeated? One cannot say. But the Cuban imbroglio has probably diminished rather than increased the danger. The follies of Castro may, perhaps, be repeated. But his own difficulties do not suggest that his experiment will be tried again soon, and the unanimous adhesion of the Latin American states to the view of the United States certainly provides hope for the future.

Where, then, do these reflections lead us? In one sense the Monroe Doctrine, or at least verbal reference to the Monroe Doctrine, is likely to be less frequent than in the past, especially on the diplomatic level. But the essential idea behind it is even more valid than it was in 1823. Then the danger was illusory, nor, as we have shown, was it ever really very great in the nineteenth or even in the early twentieth century. Today the Russian menace has been dramatized by the folly of the Kremlin; the threat has been recognized; and in principle, if not by direct allusion, the governments of the New World are likely to be governed by the principles enunciated by James Monroe.

The Original Monroe Doctrine

CONTAINED IN THE PRESIDENT'S MESSAGE OF
DECEMBER 2, 1823

❖   ❖   ❖   ❖   ❖   ❖

At the proposal of the Russian Imperial Government, made through the minister of the Emperor residing here, a full power and instructions have been transmitted to the minister of the United States at St. Petersburg to arrange by amicable negotiation the respective rights and interests of the two nations on the northwest coast of this continent. A similar proposal had been made by His Imperial Majesty to the Government of Great Britain, which has likewise been acceded to. The Government of the United States has been desirous by this friendly proceeding of manifesting the great value which they have invariably attached to the friendship of the Emperor and their solicitude to cultivate the best understanding with his Government. In the discussions to which this interest has given rise and in the arrangements by which they may terminate the occasion has been judged proper for asserting, as a principle in which the rights and interests of the United States are involved, that the American continents, by the free and independent condition which they have assumed and maintain, are henceforth not to be considered as subjects for future colonization by any European powers.

❖   ❖   ❖   ❖   ❖   ❖

It was stated at the commencement of the last session that a great effort was then making in Spain and Portugal to improve the condition of the people of those countries, and that it appeared to be conducted with extraordinary moderation. It need scarcely be remarked that the result has been so far very different from what was then anticipated. Of events in that quarter of the globe, with which we have so much intercourse and from which we derive our origin, we have always been anxious and interested spectators. The citizens of the United States cherish sentiments the most friendly in favor of the liberty and happiness of their fellow-men on that side of the Atlantic. In the wars of the European powers in matters relating to themselves we have never taken any part, nor does it comport with our policy so to do. It is only when our rights are invaded or seriously menaced that we resent injuries or make preparation for our defense. With the movements in this hemisphere we are of necessity more immediately connected, and by causes which must be obvious to all enlightened and impartial observers. The political system of the allied powers is essentially different in this respect from that of America. This difference proceeds from that which exists in their respective Governments; and to the defense of our own, which has been achieved by the loss of so much blood and treasure, and matured by the wisdom of their most enlightened citizens, and under which we have enjoyed unexampled felicity, this whole nation is devoted. We owe it, therefore, to candor and to the amicable relations existing between the United States and those powers to declare that we should consider any attempt on their part to extend their system to any portion of this hemisphere as dangerous to our peace and safety. With the existing colonies or dependencies of any European power we have not interfered and shall not interfere. But with the Governments who have declared their independence and maintained it, and whose independence we have, on great consideration and on just principles, acknowledged, we could not view any interposition for the purpose of oppressing them, or controlling in any other manner their destiny, by any European power in any other light than as the manifestation of an unfriendly disposition toward the United States. In the war between those new Governments and Spain we declared our neutrality at the time of their recognition, and to this we have adhered, and shall continue to adhere, provided no change shall occur which, in the judgment of the competent authorities of this Government, shall make a corresponding change on the part of the United States indispensable to their security.

The late events in Spain and Portugal shew that Europe is still unsettled. Of this important fact no stronger proof can be adduced than that the allied powers should have thought it proper, on any principle satisfactory to themselves, to have interposed by force in the internal concerns of Spain. To what extent such interposition may be carried, on the same principle, is a question in which all independent powers whose governments differ from theirs are interested, even those most remote, and surely none more so than the United States. Our policy in regard to Europe, which was adopted at an early stage of the wars which have so long agitated that quarter of the globe, nevertheless remains the same, which is, not to interfere in the internal concerns of any of its powers; to consider the government *de facto* as the legitimate government for us; to cultivate friendly relations with it, and to preserve those relations by a frank, firm, and manly policy, meeting in all instances the just claims of every power, submitting to injuries from none. But in regard to those continents circumstances are eminently and conspicuously different. It is impossible that the allied powers should extend their political system to any portion of either continent without endangering our peace and happiness; nor can anyone believe that our southern brethren, if left to themselves, would adopt it of their own accord. It is equally impossible, therefore, that we should behold such interposition in any form with indifference. If we look to the comparative strength and resources of Spain and those new Governments, and their distance from each other, it must be obvious that she can never subdue them. It is still the true policy of the United States to leave the parties to themselves, in the hope that other powers will pursue the same course.

NOTES AND BIBLIOGRAPHY

Notes

NOTES FOR CHAPTER I

1. *Thomas Paine, The Great Works of.* New York, 1877. P. 24.

2. *John Adams, Works of.* Edited by Charles Francis Adams. Boston, 1856. 10 vols. I, 200–01.

3. *Ibid.,* II, 488–89.

4. *Benjamin Franklin, Writings of.* Collected and edited by A. H. Smyth. New York, 1905–07. 10 vols. VII, 20.

5. Malloy, William M. *Treaties, Conventions, International Acts, Protocols, and Agreements between the United States of America and other Powers, 1776–1909.* Washington, 1910. 2 vols. I, 481.

6. *J. Adams,* III, 316.

7. *Journals of the Continental Congress.* Washington, 1904–34. 31 vols. XXIV, 394.

8. *The American Secretaries of State and their Diplomacy.* Edited by S. F. Bemis. New York, 1927–29. 10 vols. I, 242–43.

9. *James Monroe, Writings of.* Edited by S. M. Hamilton. New York, 1898–1903. 7 vols. I, 134.

10. Guttridge, G. H. *David Hartley. An Advocate of Conciliation.* Berkeley, 1926. Pp. 318–19.

11. *American Historical Review,* VIII (1902–03), 728.

12. *Alexander Hamilton, Works of.* Edited by H. C. Lodge. New York, 1904. 12 vols. IX, 327.

13. *Richard Henry Lee, Letters of.* Edited by J. C. Ballagh. New York, 1911–14. 2 vols. II, 280.

14. *Samuel Adams, Writings of.* Edited by H. A. Cushing. New York, 1904–08. 4 vols. IV, 281.

15. Rowland, K. M. *Life of George Mason, 1725–92.* New York, 1892. 2 vols. II, 47.

16. *J. Adams,* VIII, 37.

17. *Thomas Jefferson, Works of.* Edited by P. L. Ford. New York, 1904–05. 12 vols. IV, 469.

18. *Records of the Federal Convention.* Edited by Max Farrand. New Haven, 1911. 3 vols. I, 492.

19. *James Madison, Writings of.* Edited by Gaillard Hunt. New York, 1900–10. 9 vols. IV, 290 and 405.

20. *George Washington, Life and Writings of.* Edited by Jared Sparks. New York, 1847–48. 12 vols. X, 108.

21. *Jefferson, Works*, I, 207.

22. *Washington, Life and Writings of*, X, 331.

23. *Jefferson, Works*, IV, 6.

24. *Thomas Jefferson, The Writings of*. Monticello Edition. Washington, 1903–04. 20 vols. VI, 333.

25. *Jefferson, Works*, VI, 145.

26. *Madison, Writings*, VI, 128.

27. *Monroe, Writings*, I, 257.

28. *Hamilton, Writings*, IV, 396–408.

29. *Jefferson, Works*, VI, 223.

30. *Annals of Congress, 1789–1824*. Washington, 1834–56. 42 vols. IV, 17–18 and 138–39.

31. Richardson, James D. *Messages of the Presidents, 1789–1897*. Washington, 1896. 10 vols. I, 222.

32. *Ibid.*, p. 223.

33. *Ibid.*, p. 311.

34. *Jefferson, Works*, VIII, 145.

35. For a convenient summary, see J. S. Robertson, *Hispanic-American Relations with the United States*. New York, 1923. Pp. 14–25.

36. *Annals of Congress*, XXIII, 428.

37. For a fuller explanation of Jefferson's view, see T. R. Schellenberg, *Jeffersonian Origins of the Monroe Doctrine. Hispanic American Historical Review*, XIV (1934), 1–32.

38. *Jefferson, Works*, IX, 431.

39. *John Quincy Adams, Writings of*. Edited by W. C. Ford. New York, 1913–17. 7 vols. VII, 50–51.

NOTES FOR CHAPTER II

1. *John Quincy Adams, Memoirs of*. Edited by C. F. Adams. Philadelphia, 1874–77. 12 vols. IV, 438 f.

2. *Ibid.*, V, 252 f.

3. *Ibid.*, VI, 104.

4. *Alaskan Boundary Tribunal Proceedings*, Senate Documents, 58th Congress, 2nd Session. Washington, 1904. 7 vols. II, 25.

5. *Adams, Memoirs*, VI, 163.

6. *Alaskan Boundary Proceedings*, II, 52–56.

7. *Ibid.*, 71 f.

8. For the text of this convention, see *Treaties and Conventions Concluded between the United States of America and other Powers since July 4, 1776*. Washington, 1889. Pp. 931 ff.

9. London. Public Record Office, F.O., France. Vol. 305, no. 8. Jan. 12, 1824.

10. Rush, Richard. *Memoranda of a Residence at the Court of London*. Philadelphia, 1845. P. 629.

11. Reddaway, W. F. *The Monroe Doctrine,* 2d. ed. New York, 1905. Pp. 101 f.

12. Richardson, *Messages of the Presidents.* II, 193 f.

13. Monroe Manuscripts, Library of Congress, quoted in W. A. McCorkle, *The Personal Genesis of the Monroe Doctrine.* New York and London, 1923. P. 64.

14. London. P.R.O., F.O., France. Vol. 284, no. 29. March 31, 1823.

15. London. P.R.O., F.O., 352, vol. 8. Stratford Canning Papers. Stratford Canning to George Canning.

16. *Adams, Memoirs,* VI, 152.

17. *Ibid.*

18. Rush, *Court of London,* pp. 412 ff. The text of Canning's note is to be found in T. B. Edgington, *The Monroe Doctrine.* Boston, 1905. Pp. 7 ff.

19. Rush, *Court of London.* Pp. 418 ff.

20. *Albert Gallatin, Writings of.* Edited by Henry Adams. Philadelphia, 1879. 3 vols. II, 271.

21. *Ibid.*

22. *Ibid.,* p. 272.

23. Monroe Manuscripts, Library of Congress.

24. Ford, W. C. "John Quincy Adams and the Monroe Doctrine," I, in *American Historical Review* (July 1902). VII, 685 f.

25. *Op. cit.,* II, in *American Historical Review* (Oct. 1902). VIII, 30 ff.

26. *Adams, Memoirs,* VI, 190.

27. *Ibid.,* p. 185. In the quotation the pronoun "him" has been substituted for Adams's "the President" to avoid repetition of the latter phrase in the same sentence.

28. *Ibid.,* p. 186.

29. *Ibid.,* p. 177.

30. *Ibid.,* p. 207.

31. *Ibid.*

32. *Ibid.,* p. 186.

33. *Ibid.,* pp. 190 and 196.

34. *Ibid.,* p. 179.

35. *Ibid.,* p. 194.

36. *Ibid.,* p. 195.

37. *Ibid.,* pp. 197 f.

38. *Ibid.,* p. 199.

39. *Ibid.,* p. 202.

40. *Ibid.,* p. 205.

41. *Ibid.,* pp. 207 f.

42. *Pennsylvania Magazine of History,* VI (1882), 358.

43. This letter is quoted in full in W. C. Ford's article, *A.H.R.* (July 1902), VII, 685 f. See also *Monroe, Writings,* VI, 323 ff.

44. For Jefferson's letter, see *Writings of Thomas Jefferson* (Memorial ed.). Washington, 1903. 20 vols. XV, 479–80.

45. *Monroe, Writings,* VI, 394.

46. See original and revised text of his instructions to Rush in W. C. Ford's article, "John Quincy Adams and the Monroe Doctrine," II. *A.H.R.* (Oct. 1902), VIII, 33–38.

47. *Ibid.*, p. 47.

48. *Ibid.*, p. 38.

49. *Adams, Memoirs,* VI, 194.

50. *Ibid.*, p. 201.

51. *Ibid.*, p. 203.

52. *Ibid.*, p. 209.

53. This note is published in full in W. C. Ford's "John Quincy Adams and the Monroe Doctrine," II, in *A.H.R.* (Oct. 1902), VII, 43 f.

54. Jean, Comte de Villèle, *Mémoires et correspondance.* Paris, 1889–90. 5 vols. IV, 201.

55. *Ibid.*, p.188.

56. Paris. Ministère des Affaires Etrangères. Correspondance Politique. Espagne. Vol. 722, fol. 56. June 9, 1823.

57. *British and Foreign State Papers,* XI. 1823–24, 49–54. Reprinted in *Monroe's Writings,* VI, 416–19.

58. Paris. Aff. Etr., Corr. Pol., Angleterre. Vol. 617, fol. 145. Oct. 5, 1823. "Nous avons rappellé le seul vaisseau de guerre, le *Jean Bart,* que nous eussions dans les Antilles."

59. Washington, State Department. Dispatches, France. Vol. 22, no. 16. Nov. 29, 1823. "The French government is putting out of commission several of their ships of war, and have already discharged and are discharging numbers of their seamen."

60. Paris. Aff. Etr., Corr. Pol., Espagne. Vol. 724, fol. 147. Oct. 30, 1823.

61. Paris. Aff. Etr., Méms. et Docs., Amérique. Vol. 39 and Paris. Archives Nationales, Minist. de la Marine, BB⁴ 405 bis. These instructions are published almost in full in C. A. Villaneuva, *La Santa Alianza.* Paris, 1912. Pp. 44–50.

62. Paris. Aff. Etr., Corr. Pol., Espagne. Vol. 724. Dec. 6, 1823.

63. St. Petersburg. F.O., Expédiés, no. 8829. Nov. 25, 1823.

64. St. Petersburg. F.O., Expédiés, no. 9044. Jan. 9, 1824.

65. St. Petersburg. F.O., Reçus, no. 21,221 (Encl.).

66. Berlin. Staats-Archiv, Russland. Rep. I, 82. Dec. 19, 1823.

67. St. Petersburg. F.O., Reçus, no. 21,224 (Encl.). Dec. 25, 1823.

68. London. P.R.O., F.O., France. Vol. 296, desp. 568. Nov. 4, 1823.

69. St. Petersburg. F. O., Reçus, no. 21,224 (Encl.). Dec. 25, 1823.

70. Washington. State Department. Special Agents' Series, McRae Papers. Nov. 3, 1824.

71. *Monroe, Writings,* VI, 435.

72. St. Petersburg. F.O., Reçus, no. 21,224. Jan. 19, 1824.

73. London. P.R.O., F.O., France. Vol. 305, no. 8. Jan 12, 1824.

74. St. Petersburg. F.O., Expédiés, no. 9241. Mar. 5, 1824. The original text read, in place of "that it merits only the most profound contempt," "that it would hardly be possible to mention it to the Government of the United States without

haughtily reproving language so strange. However, such action not being for the moment within the pretensions of His Majesty, he invites you to preserve," etc., as above.

75. Paris. Aff. Etr., Corr. Pol., Etats-Unis. Vol. 80. Dec. 11, 1823.

76. Seville. Archivo Géneral de Indias. Estado, América en Géneral. Legajo 5. Jan. 2, 1824.

77. St. Petersburg. F.O., Reçus, no. 21,341. Feb. 2, 1824.

78. See my work, *The Monroe Doctrine, 1823–26*. Cambridge, 1927. Pp. 228–35.

79. Antea, p. 41.

80. Stapleton, A. G. *George Canning and his Times*. London, 1859. P. 395.

81. London. P.R.O., F.O., Buenos Aires and Mexico, Confidential. Dec. 30, 1823, and Feb. 6, 1824, respectively.

82. Festing, Gabrielle. *John Hookham Frère and his Friends*. London, 1899. Pp. 267 f.

83. See my work, *op. cit.*, pp. 238 f.

84. London. P.R.O., F.O., Spain. Vol. 284, no. 14 (secret). April 2, 1824.

85. London. P.R.O., F.O., America. Vol. 185, no. 1. Jan. 5, 1824.

86. St. Petersburg. F.O., Reçus, no. 21,298. Jan. 30, 1824.

NOTES FOR CHAPTER III

1. *Annals of Congress*. 18th Congress, 1st Session. Washington, 1856. I, col. 1104.

2. *Ibid.*, col. 1188.

3. Washington. State Department. Notes from Ministers. Colombia. Vol. I.

4. *Ibid.* Notes to Ministers. Colombia. Vol. I.

5. Washington. State Department. Notes from Foreign Legations. Brazil. Vol. I. Jan. 28, 1825.

6. *Ibid.* Notes to Foreign Legations. Vol. III.

7. American State Papers. *Foreign Relations*, V, pp. 909 f.

8. *Ibid.*, p. 834.

9. *Ibid.*, p. 835.

10. Register of Debates. 19th Congress, 1st Session. II, col. 2369.

11. For these two episodes, see my work, *The Monroe Doctrine, 1826–67*. Baltimore, 1933. Pp. 40–48 and 48–57.

12. For the Falkland Islands question, see *ibid.*, pp. 6–9.

13. Washington. State Department. Special Agents. Galindo.

14. See my work, *The Monroe Doctrine, 1826–67*, pp. 39–40.

15. *Ibid.*, p. 66.

16. Richardson. *Messages of the Presidents*. IV, 197.

17. *Histoire Parlementaire de France*. Recueil Complet des Discours Prononcés dans les Chambres de 1819 à 1848 par M. Guizot. Paris, 1864. 5 vols. IV, 562–64.

18. *Congressional Globe*, 27th Congress, 3rd Session, p. 154.

19. *Ibid.*, App., p. 91.

20. 28th Congress, 1st Session. Reports of Committees. Vol. 1, Report of March 12, 1844, p. 18.

21. Washington. State Department. Consular Dispatches. Mexico. July 10, 1845.

22. On this subject, see E. D. Adams, *British Interests and Activities in Texas, 1838–46*. Baltimore, 1910. Addendum, pp. 234–64, and also *A.H.R.*, XIV, 744–64.

23. *The Diary of James K. Polk*. Edited by M. M. Quaife. Chicago, 1910. 4 vols. I, 71.

24. *Niles's Register*, LXVIII, June 7, 1845.

25. Washington. State Department. Dispatches. Argentine Republic. Aug. 2, 1845.

26. Library of Congress. *Polk Papers*. Published in *Washington Globe*, May 6, 1844.

27. Richardson. *Messages of the Presidents*. IV, 398.

28. This note is published in *A.H.R.*, VIII, 43–44.

29. American State Papers. *Foreign Relations*, V, 856.

30. Richardson. *Messages of the Presidents*. IV, 399.

31. *New York Tribune*, Dec. 3, 1845.

32. *Congressional Globe*, 29th Congress, 1st Session, p. 197.

33. *Ibid.*

34. *London Morning Chronicle*, Dec. 30, 1845.

35. *London Times*, Dec. 27, 1845.

36. Washington. State Department. Dispatches. France. Jan. 1, 1846.

37. Guizot. *Histoire Parlementaire. Op. cit.*, V, 30.

38. Thiers, L. A. *Discours sur les rélations de la France avec les Etats-Unis d'Amérique*, prononcé dans la séance de la Chambre des députés du 20 janvier 1846. Paris, 1846. P. 16.

39. *La Quotidienne*, Dec. 26, 1845. *Le National*, Dec. 25, 1845. *Le Siècle*, Dec. 26, 1845.

40. *James Buchanan, Works of*. Edited by J. B. Moore. Philadelphia, 1908–11. 12 vols. VI, 445.

41. *Ibid.*

42. *Ibid.*, VIII, 81.

43. For this episode, see my work, *The Monroe Doctrine, 1826–1867*, pp. 150–54.

44. Washington. State Department. Ecuador, Notes to. Vol. I, no. 3.

45. *Ibid.* Consular Letters. Lima. Dec. 9, 1846.

46. *Ibid.* Instructions to Ministers. Ecuador. Vol. I, no. 3.

47. Consular Letters. Lima. Feb. 1, 1847.

48. *Ibid.* Dispatches. Peru. Jan. 12, 1848.

49. *Ibid.* Dispatches. Colombia. Sept. 12, 1846.

50. Barranda, Joaquín. *Recordaciones Históricas*. Mexico. 1913. 2 vols. II, 23.

51. British and Foreign State Papers, 1860–61. LI, 1202–04.

52. Richardson. *Messages of the Presidents*. IV, 582.

53. *John C. Calhoun, The Works of*. Edited by Richard C. Crallé. New York, 1851–56. 6 vols. IV, 464.

54. *Ibid.*, App., p. 611.

55. *Ibid.*, p. 624.

56. *Ibid.*, pp. 738 and 773.

57. *Ibid.*, p. 640.

58. *Ibid.*, p. 615.

59. *Ibid.*

60. *Hispanic American Historical Review*, XVI, 358–59.

61. London. P.R.O., F.O., Guatemala. Vol. 57. April 2, 1849, and April 14, 1849.

62. *Ibid.* America. Vol. 497. June 28, 1849. Encl.

63. *Ibid.* Guatemala. Vol. 60. Oct. 25, 1849.

64. British Parliamentary Papers. 1856. LX, 5.

65. *American Historical Review*, V, 101.

66. 32nd Congress, 2nd Session. Senate Reports. Doc. 407, p. 17.

67. Richardson, *Messages of the Presidents*. V, 200.

68. *Congressional Globe*. 32nd Congress, 2nd Session. App., p. 126.

69. 34th Congress, 1st Session. House Exec. Doc. no. 1, p. 63.

70. *Ibid.*, p. 83.

71. *Ibid.*, p. 109.

72. Hansard, *Parliamentary Debates*, 3rd Series. CXLII, cols. 1511 and 1513. June 16, 1856.

73. *Congressional Globe*. 34th Congress, 1st Session. P. 110.

74. LXXXII, 478–512.

75. Paris. Min. des Affaires Etrangères, Corr. Pol. St. Domingue. Vol. II.

76. Pelletier de Saint Rémy. *Etude et Solution Nouvelle de la Question Haïtienne.* Paris, 1846.

77. *Revue des Deux Mondes.* X (1851–2nd vol. for that year), 193–224 and 459–501.

78. For Cazneau's defense, see London, P.R.O., F.O., Santo Domingo. Vol. 19. Nov. 23, 1854. Encl.

79. For these episodes, see my work, *The Monroe Doctrine, 1826–67*, pp. 245–50.

80. *Documentos Relativos á la Cuestión de Santo Domingo.* Sometidos al Congreso de los Diputados. Ministerio del Estado. Madrid, 1865. P. 4.

81. Torrente, M. *Política Ultramarina.* Madrid, 1854.

82. See my work, *The Monroe Doctrine, 1826–67.* Pp. 250–51.

NOTES FOR CHAPTER IV

1. London. P.R.O., F.O., Mexico. Vol. 60, no. 30. March 25, 1830.

2. de Mofras, Eugène Duflot. *Exploration du territoire de l'Orégon, des Californies, et de la Mer Vermeille, exécutée pendant les années 1840, –41, –42.* Paris, 1844. 2 vols. I, 36.

3. *Carta al E. S. Presidente de la República,* par Don J. M. Gutiérrez de Estrada, antiguo Ministro de Relaciones interiores y exteriores. Mexico, 1840.

4. For this episode, see Antonio Pirala, *Historia Contemporánea de la España.*

Anales desde 1843 hasta la Conclusión de la Actual Guerra Civil. Madrid, 1875–79. 6 vols. Especially I, 432–33.

5. London. P.R.O., Mexico. Vol. 196, no. 57. April 29, 1846.

6. London. P.R.O., F.O., Spain. Vol. 711.

7. Paris. Min. des Aff. Etr., Corr. Pol., Mexique. Vol. 41. April 30, 1853.

8. *Ibid.*, Oct. 10, 1853.

9. Encl. in *ibid.*, vol. 43, May 15, 1855.

10. Washington. State Department. Dispatches. Mexico. April 4, 1857.

11. Richardson. *Messages of the Presidents.* V, 512.

12. Paris. Min. des Aff. Etr., Corr. Pol, Mexique. Vol. 45. Dec. 26, 1858.

13. *Ibid.*, April 18, 1859.

14. *Ibid.*, Dec. 19, 1859.

15. *Ibid.*, Sept. 27, 1858.

16. *La Cuestión de Méjico.* Si la monarquía constitucional es conveniente y posible en Aquel País bajo el punto de vista de los Intereses Mexicanos y de la Política Española. P. 25.

17. Quoted in Corti, E. G., *Maximilian and Charlotte of Mexico.* New York, 1928. 2 vols. I, 362.

18. *Ibid.*

19. Documents Diplomatiques, 1863.

20. Library of Congress. Transcripts. Haus-Archiv. Maximilian.

21. Washington. State Department. Dispatches. Austria. Feb. 12, 1862.

22. Quoted in Corti, *op. cit.*, I, 378.

23. *Ibid.*, p. 280.

24. Mercier de La Combe. *Le Mexique et les Etats-Unis.* Paris, 1863. P. 121.

25. *Moniteur,* Jan. 31, 1863.

26. *Ibid.*, Jan. 26, 1864.

27. *Ibid.*, Dec. 18, 1863.

28. *Ibid.*, Jan. 28, 1864.

29. Randon, J. L. *Mémoires du Maréchal.* Paris, 1875–77. 2 vols. II, 74.

30. Quoted in Niox, G. *Expédition du Mexique.* Paris, 1874. Pp. 315 et seq.

31. Library of Congress Transcripts. Haus-Archiv. Wyke-Herzfeld. Nov. 27, 1863.

32. *Ibid.*

33. 37th Congress, 2nd Session. H. Exec. Doc. no. 100, p. 15.

34. *Ibid.*, p. 201. Dispatch of Nov. 1. See also pp. 193–94. Dispatch of Sept. 28.

35. *Ibid.*, p. 212. Dispatch of Sept. 27.

36. 37th Congress, 3rd Session. H. Exec. Doc. no. 54, p. 552. Dispatch of March 26, 1862.

37. 37th Congress, 2nd Session. H. Exec. Doc. no. 100, p. 49.

38. *Ibid.*, pp. 17–18.

39. *Ibid.*, p. 189.

40. *Ibid.*, p. 188.

41. *Correspondencia de la Legación Mexicana durante la Intervención Extranjera.* Edited by Matías Romero. Mexico City, 1870–92. 10 vols. I, 604 and 618.

42. 37th Congress, 3rd Session. H. Exec. Doc. no. 54, pp. 529–30.

43. 37th Congress, 2nd Session. H. Exec. Doc. no. 100, pp. 216–17.

44. 37th Congress, 3rd Session. H. Exec. Doc. no. 54, p. 75.

45. *Congressional Globe.* 38th Congress, 1st Session. P. 1408.

46. Papers Relating to Foreign Affairs, Accompanying the Annual Message of the President, more commonly known as *Diplomatic Correspondence.* 1863. P. 726.

47. *Ibid.,* 1865–66. Part III, p. 357.

48. *Century Magazine,* XVI, 839–46.

49. Wallace, Lew. *An Autobiography.* New York, 1906. 2 vols. II, 812 ff.

50. Romero, *Correspondencia.* V, 296–98.

51. Welles, G. *Diary of Gideon Welles.* New York, 1909. 3 vols. II, 317.

52. For this episode, see Wriston, H. M. *Executive Agents in American Foreign Relations.* Baltimore, 1929. Pp. 780–89.

53. Romero, *Correspondencia.* V, 466.

54. *Ibid.*

55. *Ibid.,* p. 477.

56. *Ibid.,* p. 504.

57. Paris. Min. des Aff. Etr., Corr. Pol., Etats-Unis. Vol. 135. Sept. 5, 1865.

58. *Ibid.,* pp. 662 and 477.

59. Bigelow, John. *Retrospections of an Active Life.* New York, 1909. 5 vols. II, 46.

60. *Ibid.,* III, 152–54.

61. Welles, G. *Diary.* II, 333.

62. Richardson. *Messages of the Presidents.* VI, 368.

63. *Diplomatic Correspondence.* 1865, pt. 3, p. 757.

64. Paris. Min. des Aff. Etr., Corr. Pol. Vol. 132. Aug. 1, 1864.

65. *Ibid.,* vol. 133, Jan. 24, 1865.

66. García, Genaro, and Pereyra, Carlos. *Documentos inéditos e muy raros para la historia de Mexico. Correspondencia secreta de los principales Intervencionistas Mexicanos.* Mexico, 1903. 36 vols. XXIV, 246.

67. 39th Congress, 1st Session. H. Exec. Doc. no. 73. Pt. I, p. 266.

68. Bigelow, III, 123.

69. Paris, Min. des Aff. Etr., Corr. Pol., Etats-Unis. Vol. 135. Aug. 17, 1865.

70. Bigelow, III, 175 ff.

71. *Ibid.,* pp. 193–94, and Paris. Min. des Aff. Etr., Corr. Pol., Etats-Unis. Vol. 135. Oct. 18, 1865.

72. Bigelow, III, 190.

73. Paris. Min. des Aff. Etr., Corr. Pol., Mexique. Vol. 64. Aug. 15, 1865.

74. Gaulot, P. *La Verité sur l'Expédition du Mexique.* Paris, 1889–90. 3 vols. II, 169.

75. *Ibid.,* p. 172.

406 *Notes*

76. *Diplomatic Correspondence.* 1865, pt. 3. Pp. 421 ff.

77. Bigelow, III, 235.

78. Gaulot, II, 201.

79. 39th Congress, 1st Session. H. Exec. Doc. no. 73. Pp. 347–48.

80. Bigelow, III, 288–92.

81. *Ibid.*

82. *Ibid.*, pp. 298–300.

83. *Moniteur,* March 10, 1865.

84. *Ibid.*, April 11, 1865.

85. Bigelow, III, 49 and 267.

86. *Ibid.*, p. 497.

87. *Ibid.*

88. The figures are in G. L. Niox, *Expédition du Mexique 1861–67.* Paris, 1874. P. 763. From this there might perhaps be subtracted Mexican reimbursements to France amounting to 64,000,000 francs.

89. Paris. Min. des Aff. Etr., Corr. Pol., Mexique. Vol. 63, *passim,* but especially Aug. 15, 1865.

90. Washington. State Department. Dispatches. France. Feb. 9, 1865.

91. Madrid. Ministerio del Estado. Negociación 171. Legajo 2. Dec. 8, 1860.

92. For further details, see my work, *The Monroe Doctrine, 1826–67,* pp. 282–83.

93. London. P.R.O., Spain. Vol. 1005. April 22, 1861.

94. Washington. State Department. Notes to Spain.

95. *Ibid.* Dispatches. Spain. Vol. 43.

96. *Ibid.*

97. *Ibid.*

98. Ministerio del Estado. Legación 171. Legajo 4 (22). July 8, 1861.

99. *Ibid.* (23), Anejo.

100. *Documentos Relativos à la Cuestión de Santo Domingo,* remitidos al Congreso de los Diputados por el Ministerio de la Guerra. Madrid, 1865. P. 37.

101. *Ibid.*, p. 109.

102. El General Gándara. *Anexión y Guerra de Santo Domingo.* Madrid, 1884. 2 vols. II, 112.

103. *Ibid.*, p. 473.

104. *Diplomatic Correspondence.* 1864, pt. 4, p. 21.

105. *Ibid.*, p. 24.

106. *Ibid.*, p. 30.

107. Colsón, P. de Novo y. *Historia de la Guerra de España en el Pacífico.* Madrid, 1882. Pp. 203–06.

108. *Diplomatic Correspondence,* 1864, pt. 4, p. 100.

NOTES FOR CHAPTER V

1. Stolberg-Wernigerode, Otto Graf zu. *Germany and the United States during the Era of Bismarck.* Reading, Pa., 1937. App. P. 298.

2. Vagts, Alfred. *Deutschland und die Vereinigten Staaten in der Weltpolitik.* New York, 1935. 2 vols. II, 1682.

3. *Ibid.*

4. Stolberg-Wernigerode, Otto Graf zu. *Op. cit.*

5. Washington. State Department. Dispatches. Haiti. Vol. 18. Dec. 24, 1884.

6. Washington. State Department. Dispatches. France. Vol. 96. April 2, 1885.

7. For an account thereof, see my work, *The Monroe Doctrine, 1826–67,* pp. 539–44.

8. *Diplomatic Correspondence.* 1866. II, 413.

9. Mackenna, Vicuña. *Diez Meses de Misión à los Estados Unidos.* Santiago, 1867. 2 vols. I, 412 ff.

10. This note is published in full in W. C. Ford's "John Quincy Adams and the Monroe Doctrine," *A.H.R.,* VIII, 43–44.

11. *Congressional Globe.* 32nd Congress, 2nd Session. P. 199.

12. Richardson. *Messages of the Presidents.* VI, 3886.

13. Sumner, Charles. *Works.* Boston, 1870–1883. 15 vols. XI, 221–22.

14. *Congressional Globe.* 40th Congress, 1st Session. P. 392.

15. Washington. State Department. Instructions. Denmark. Vol. 14. May 16, 1867.

16. Richardson, *Messages of the Presidents.* VI, 3986.

17. *Ibid.,* V, 4016.

18. *Ibid.*

19. Washington. State Department. Consular Letters. West Indies. Vol. 10. Cited in C. C. Tansill, *The Purchase of the Danish West Indies.* Baltimore, 1932. P. 159.

20. Tansill, *op. cit.,* p. 154.

21. *Ibid.,* p. 167.

22. Washington. State Department. Instructions. France. Vol. 21. Feb. 28, 1885.

23. Washington. State Department. Instructions. Great Britain. Vol. 6. Feb. 24, 1887.

24. Washington. State Department. Haiti. Vol. 3. Jan. 1, 1891. The Haitian government rejected this condition as an "outrage on the National sovereignty." (*Ibid.* Dispatches. Haiti. Vol. 25. April 23, 1891, Encl.)

25. Moore, J. B. *A Digest of International Law.* Washington, 1906. 8 vols. VI, 428.

26. For this episode, see R. H. Luthin, "St. Bartholomew: Sweden's Colonial and Diplomatic Adventure in the Caribbean," in *Hispanic American Historical Review,* XIV, 322–23.

27. See my book, *The Monroe Doctrine, 1826–67,* pp. 156–62.

28. See my book, *The Monroe Doctrine, 1867–1907,* pp. 66–69.

29. *Congressional Record.* 46th Congress, 2nd Session. Vol. 10, pt. 1. Pp. 13–14.

30. *The Nation,* XXX (1880), 90–91.

31. *Ibid.*

32. *North American Review,* CXXX (1880), 499–511; *ibid.,* Dec. 1881.

33. Richardson, *Messages of the Presidents.* VI, 4537–38.

34. *North American Review*, CXXXIII, 241.

35. Washington. State Department. Colombia, Notes from. Vol. 7. Dec. 1, 1880.

36. *Foreign Relations*, 1881, pp. 537–40.

37. *Ibid.*, p. 549.

38. *Ibid.*, p. 531.

39. *Popular Science Monthly*, XVI, 842–49.

40. 46th Congress, 3rd Session. House Reports. Vol. 1, no. 224, pt. 1, pp. 1–3.

41. *The Nation*, XXXIV, 9–11.

42. *Edinburgh Review*, CLV, 222.

43. *Preussische Jahrbücher*, XLIX, 589–654, especially 643–44.

44. *Zeitschrift für die gesammte Staatswissenschaft*, XXXVIII, 331–43.

45. *Foreign Relations*, 1880, p. 385.

46. Moore, *op. cit.*, VI, 531.

47. *Ibid.*

48. *Ibid.*

49. *Ibid.*, p. 532.

50. *Foreign Relations*, 1881, p. 1217.

51. Washington. State Department. Dispatches. Haiti. Vol. 3. Jan. 13, 1869.

52. *Ibid.*, vol. 4, Oct. 9, 1871.

53. *Ibid.*, vol. 11, June 21, 1872.

54. *Foreign Relations*, 1878, pp. 418–27.

55. Washington. State Department. Dispatches. Haiti. Vol. 14. Oct. 3, 1883; also *Foreign Relations*, 1883, pp. 594–96.

56. Washington. State Department. Dispatches. Haiti. Vol. 15, April 7, 1885.

57. *Ibid.*, vol. 21, *passim*.

58. 50th Congress, 1st Session. S. Exec. Doc. no. 226. Vol. 11, pp. 3–4.

59. *Ibid.*, pp. 12–13, Dec. 21, 1880.

60. Washington. State Department. Venezuela, Notes from. Vol. 4.

61. 50th Congress, 1st Session. S. Exec. Doc. no. 226. Vol. 11, p. 50. March 31, 1895.

62. *Ibid.*, pp. 70, 96, 194.

63. *Ibid.*, p. 14, Jan. 31, 1881.

64. Washington. State Department. Instructions. Venezuela. Vol. 3. July 25, 1884.

65. 50th Congress, 1st Session. S. Exec. Doc. no. 226. Vol. 11, p. 68.

66. *Congressional Globe.* 50th Congress, 1st Session. Vol. 19, pt. 2, p. 1419.

67. 50th Congress, 1st Session. S. Exec. Doc. no. 226. Vol. 11, p. 205.

68. *Ibid.*, pp. 70 and 96.

69. Washington. State Department. Instructions. Venezuela. Vol. 4. Oct. 28, 1892.

70. *Congressional Record.* 53rd Congress, 3rd Session. Vol. 1, p. 837.

71. *Ibid.*, vol. 2, p. 1834.

72. *Ibid.*, p. 1833.

73. *Ibid.*, vol. 3, p. 2113.

74. *Ibid.*, p. 2642.

75. *New York Tribune*, March 23. Also see the *Atlanta Constitution, New York Recorder, Chicago Tribune,* and *New York Telegram.*

76. Nevins, Allan. *Grover Cleveland. A Study in Courage.* New York, 1932. P. 631.

77. *North American Review*, CLX, 651–58.

78. *Ibid.*, p. 652.

79. James, Henry. *Richard Olney and His Public Service.* Boston, 1923. P. 110.

80. *Foreign Relations*, 1895, pp. 545–62.

81. *Ibid.*

82. *Ibid.*

83. *Ibid.*

84. *Ibid.*

85. *Ibid.*

86. This note has been frequently published. Perhaps the most convenient reference is *Foreign Relations*, 1895, I, 563–76.

87. *Ibid.*

88. *Ibid.*

89. Library of Congress. Cleveland Papers.

90. *Ibid.*

91. The message is in Richardson, *Messages of the Presidents*. VII, 6087 ff.

92. London *Times*, Dec. 18, 1895.

93. *Congressional Record*. 54th Congress, 1st Session. Pp. 234–35.

94. Senator Allen of Nebraska spoke of the "unanimous agreement" of the members on the Monroe Doctrine, *Congressional Record*, 54th Congress, 1st Session, p. 244. Senator Voorhees declared that "we all have a very firm faith in what is known as the Monroe Doctrine" (*ibid.*, p. 243), and Senator Lodge declared, "We will sustain the Monroe Doctrine with all the strength of the republic" (*ibid.*, p. 243), while Senator Teller spoke of it as "the American doctrine" (*ibid.*, p. 246).

95. *New York World*, Dec. 19, 1895.

96. *The London Telegraph*, Dec. 18, 1895.

97. London *Times*, Dec. 17, 1895.

98. *New York World*, Dec. 22, 1895.

99. Elliott, A. D. *The Life of Lord Goschen.* London, 1911. 2 vols. II, 204.

100. Gardiner, A. G. *The Life of Sir William Harcourt.* London, 1923. 2 vols. II, 396 ff.

101. *Ibid.*

102. Gardiner, *op. cit.*, II, 397.

103. *New York World*, Dec. 25, 1895.

104. *Ibid.*

105. *Ibid.*, Dec. 25. This interesting episode is treated in Sir Sidney Lee, *King Edward VII.* New York, 1925. 2 vols. I, 715–16.

106. Reid, W. *Memoirs and Correspondence of Lord Playfair.* New York and London, 1899. Pp. 416–26.

107. James, *op. cit.*, p. 228.

108. *Ibid.*, p. 229.

109. *Public Opinion,* XIX, 840.

110. See the *Christian Advocate,* vol. 70, p. 834, Dec. 26, 1895; the *Christian Register,* vol. 74, p. 847, Dec. 26, 1895; the *Congregationalist,* vol. 80, p. 1024, Dec. 26, 1895. Each of these papers declared the Monroe Doctrine to be inapplicable to a boundary dispute. For utterances from many clerics and others, see the *Congregationalist,* vol. 70, p. 1028, Dec. 26, 1895.

111. Canterbury. P.R.O., F.O., 115. Vol. 996. Dec. 24, 1895.

112. James, *op. cit.,* p. 229.

113. *Revue générale de droit international public.* III, 151.

114. *Ibid.,* p. 152.

115. *Ibid.,* p. 251.

116. Quoted in London *Times,* Dec. 20, 1895. See also *Literary Digest,* XII, 244.

117. Quoted in *London Standard,* Dec. 20, 1895.

118. *Die Grosse Politik,* IX, 423.

119. Vagts, *op. cit.,* II, 1704.

120. Quoted in *London Standard,* Dec. 20, 1895.

121. *American Magazine of Civics,* VIII, 576 and 578.

122. *Schmollers Jahrbuch,* 1896, pp. 1362, 1364, 1381. Von Halle was not the only German navalist who found a convenient specter in the message of Cleveland. Compare the following from the Münchener *Allgemeine Zeitung,* by a member of the Bavarian Center Party. "Who, then, gives the Yankees the right to say, America belongs to us? On what principle of natural or divine law can they rest their case? Or can they appeal only to the law of force in defense of their monstrous pretension? They are obviously imagining this and Europe believes it is Germany's next duty to thrust aside the Monroe Doctrine, either in good spirit, or by force. This is, in our judgment, the principal reason which makes unconditionally desirable the existence of a strong sea force for Germany." Quoted in Vagts, *op. cit.,* II, 1706.

123. Quoted in *London Standard,* Dec. 20, 1895.

124. *Literary Digest,* XII, 324.

125. Washington. State Department. Dispatches. Austria. Dec. 21, 1895. Goluchowski was violently anti-American. In 1897 he declared that the peoples of Europe must fight shoulder to shoulder and arm against the coming struggle with America which threatens the economic existence of Europe. *Literary Digest,* XV, 964.

126. Washington. State Department. Dispatches. Italy. Vol. 29, Jan. 22, 1896.

127. *Literary Digest,* XII, 324.

128. For this and the following descriptions of Venezuelan sentiment, see the interesting article by Professor W. S. Robertson in the *Hispanic American Historical Review,* III, 1–16, entitled "Hispanic–American Appreciations of the Monroe Doctrine."

129. *Ibid.,* p. 3.

130. *Ibid.,* pp. 3–4.

131. *Ibid.,* pp. 12–13.

132. For the Senate resolution, see *Foreign Relations*, 1895, pp. 75–76. For the House resolution, see Washington. State Department. Dispatches. Brazil. Vol. 59. Encl. in Dec. 23, 1895.

133. Washington. State Department. Dispatches. Peru. Vol. 55. Dec. 23, 1895.

134. See the dispatch of Mr. Baker in Washington, State Department. Dispatches, Nicaragua, vol. 60, Dec. 24, 1895, in which it is declared that "the President of Nicaragua and the people here without regard to party, most heartily endorse the sentiments of President Cleveland." See also Robertson, *op. cit.*, pp. 10–11.

135. Washington. State Department. Dispatches. Argentina. Vol. 32. Encl. in Dec. 26, 1895.

136. *Archivo histórico diplomático mexicano.* Mexico City, 1926. XIX.

137. *Ibid.*

NOTES FOR CHAPTER VI

1. *Congressional Record.* 55th Congress, 2nd Session. P. 3774.

2. *Ibid.*

3. *Ibid.*, p. 3782.

4. De Beaumarchais, Maurice D. *La doctrine de Monroe; l'évolution de la politique des Etats-Unis au XIXme siècle.* Paris, 1898. Pp. 192–93.

5. Kraus, Herbert. *Die Monroe Doktrin, in ihren Beziehungen zur amerikanischen Diplomatie und zum Völkerrecht.* Berlin, 1913. P. 338.

6. *Congressional Record.* 55th Congress, 2nd Session. P. 6634.

7. *Ibid.*, pp. 6522–23.

8. *Ibid.*, 3rd Session, p. 501.

9. *Ibid.*, p. 1298.

10. *Literary Digest*, XVI, 573.

11. *Ibid.*

12. *Congressional Record.* 55th Congress, 2nd Session. Pp. 6362–63.

13. *Literary Digest*, XVI, 113–14.

14. *Das Echo*, Dec. 8, 1898.

15. Pétin, Hector. *Les Etats-Unis et la doctrine de Monroe.* Paris, 1900. P. 423.

16. Barton, W. E. *The Life of Clara Barton.* Boston, 1922. 2 vols. II, 146.

17. *Ibid.*, p. 150.

18. See my work, *The Monroe Doctrine, 1867–1907*, p. 129.

19. White, Andrew D. *Autobiography.* New York, 1905. 2 vols. II, 255.

20. *Ibid.*, pp. 338–39.

21. *Ibid.*, p. 340.

22. *Ibid.*, p. 341.

23. *Review of Reviews*, XX, 563.

24. *Ibid.*

25. *American Journal of International Law*, III, 318.

26. *Revue générale de droit international public*, XIV, 279.

27. Vagts, II, 1705.

28. Von Schierbrand, Wolf. *Germany. The Welding of a World Power.* New York, 1902. P. 352.

29. Vagts, II, 1418.

30. *Ibid.*

31. *New York Times,* May 1900.

32. *Congressional Record.* 56th Congress, 1st Session. Pp. 5402–03.

33. Tansill, *op. cit.,* p. 423.

34. Vagts, II, pp. 1492–94.

35. *Ibid.*

36. *Ibid.,* p. 1730.

37. *Ibid.*

38. *Ibid.,* p. 1495.

39. Harrison, A. *The Pan-Germanic Doctrine.* London, 1904. P. 233.

40. *Ibid.,* p. 249.

41. *Ibid.,* p. 240.

42. *Ibid.,* p. 234.

43. *Ibid.,* p. 241.

44. Vagts, II, 1476.

45. *Die Grosse Politik,* XV, 109–10.

46. Vagts, II, 1457.

47. *Ibid.,* p. 1428.

48. *Ibid.,* p. 1427.

49. *Ibid.,* p. 1505.

50. Tansill, *op. cit.,* pp. 436 and 451–53.

51. *Vagts,* II, 1472.

52. *Ibid.*

53. *Ibid.,* p. 1537.

54. *Ibid.*

55. *Ibid.,* p. 1731.

56. *Ibid.*

57. *Ibid.,* p. 1738.

58. *Ibid.*

59. *Ibid.,* p. 1747.

60. Thayer, W. R. *Theodore Roosevelt, an intimate biography.* Boston, 1919. Pp. 411 ff.

61. 57th Congress, 1st Session. H. Exec. Doc. no. 1. Vol. 1, pp. 192–94.

62. Vagts, II, 1537.

63. Berlin. Auswärtiges Amt. Nov. 20, 1902. Also Canterbury. P.R.O., F.O. Vol. 446. Nov. –, 1902.

64. *Foreign Relations,* 1902, p. 791.

65. Berlin. Auswärtiges Amt. Dec. 14, 1902.

66. Dennett, Tyler. *John Hay; from Poetry to Politics.* New York, 1933. Pp. 392–93.

67. *New York World,* April 3, 1903.

68. Widener Library. Muensterberg Papers. Jan. 23, 1903.
69. *British Documents*, II, 164.
70. Canterbury. P.R.O., F.O. Vol. 479.
71. *Ibid.*, vol. 481.
72. *Ibid.*, vol. 482.
73. Berlin. Auswärtiges Amt. Jan. 25, 1903.
74. Harrison, *op. cit.*, p. 347.
75. *Gegenwart*, LXIII, 17–19.
76. *New York Tribune*, Jan. 5, 1903.
77. *Ibid.*
78. *Literary Digest*, XXVI, 92.
79. *New York Tribune*, March 4, 1903.
80. *Ibid.*
81. *Ibid.*
82. *Review of Reviews*, XXVII, 131–38.
83. *New York Herald*, Jan. 31, 1903.
84. *Verhandlungen des Reichstags*, IX, 7967.
85. *Ibid.*, X, 8719–22.
86. Vagts, *op. cit.*, II, 1753.
87. *Ibid.*, p. 1754.
88. *Ibid.*, p. 1755.
89. *Ibid.*, p. 1602.
90. *British and Foreign State Papers*, XCV, 1081–82.
91. *Ibid.*, p. 1082.
92. Hansard, *op. cit.*, CXVI, 1263.
93. London *Times*, Feb. 14, 1903.
94. Hansard, *op. cit.*, CXVIII, 1065–66.
95. *Ibid.*, pp. 1082–83.
96. *Ibid.*, p. 60.
97. *Ibid.*, p. 119.
98. *British Documents*, II, 164.
99. See my work, *The Monroe Doctrine, 1867–1907*, p. 394.
100. *Ibid.*
101. Library of Congress. White Papers. Dec. 31, 1902.

NOTES FOR CHAPTER VII

1. *Congressional Record*. 56th Congress, 2nd Session. P. 3145.
2. *Ibid.*, p. 3146.
3. *Ibid.*, p. 3147.
4. CCXXV, 86.
5. Hansard, 4th Series, CXVIII, 83.
6. *Ibid.*, p. 26.
7. Dec. 15, 1902.

8. Dec. 12, 1902.
9. Dec. 17, 1902.
10. Dec. 19, 1902.
11. Dec. 20, 1902.
12. Dec. 16, 1902.
13. Canterbury. P.R.O., F.O., 5. Vol. 2522, March 26, 1903.
14. Berlin. Auswärtiges Amt. Dec. 29, 1902.
15. Vagts, *op. cit.*, II, 1625.
16. Berlin. Auswärtiges Amt. March 3, 1903.
17. State Department. Dispatches. Santo Domingo. Vol. 8.
18. *Ibid.*, Sept. 16, 1903, Encl.
19. *Ibid.*, vol. 9, Oct. 29, 1903.
20. *Ibid.* Notes from Santo Domingo. Vol. 5. March 28, 1904.
21. *Literary Digest*, XXVIII, 318.
22. State Department. Dispatches. Santo Domingo. Vol. 10. Feb. 26, 1904. Encl.
23. See the article by J. Fred Rippy, "The Initiation of the Customs Receivership in the Dominican Republic," in *Hispanic American Historical Review*, XXVII, 419–44.
24. Cited in H. Pringle, *Theodore Roosevelt*. New York, 1931. P. 294.
25. *Foreign Relations*, 1904, pp. 274–79.
26. Richardson. *Messages of the Presidents*. 2nd Supplement. P. 857.
27. 59th Congress, 1st Session. H. Exec. Doc. no. 1. P. 298.
28. *Ibid.*, pp. 342–43.
29. Bishop, J. B. *Theodore Roosevelt and His Time*. New York, 1902. 2 vols. I, 434.
30. *Current Literature*, XXXVIII, 108.
31. *Political Science Quarterly*, XLIX, 201.
32. Jessup, Philip C. *Elihu Root*. New York, 1938. 2 vols. I, 496.
33. *Ibid.*
34. *Ibid.*
35. *Literary Digest*, XXX, 104.
36. XII, 204.
37. *Ibid.*, XIII, 263.
38. *Literary Digest*, XXX, 250.
39. Vagts, *op. cit.*, II, 1783.
40. *Ibid.*, p. 1803.
41. *Ibid.*, pp. 1758 ff.
42. Gwynn, Stephen. *The Letters and Friendships of Sir Cecil Spring-Rice*. London, 1929. 2 vols. II, 10.
43. Washington. State Department. Dispatches. Argentina. Vol. 44. Dec. 12, 1904. Encls.
44. *Ibid.*, Notes from. Argentina. Vol. 5. June 8, 1906.
45. *New York Times*, Aug. 12, 1905.
46. Richardson. *Messages of the Presidents*. 2nd Supplement. P. 1179.

47. *Latin America and the United States.* Addresses by Elihu Root. Collected and edited by Robert Bacon and James Brown Scott. Cambridge, 1917. P. 10.

48. *Foreign Relations,* 1903, p. 3.

49. *Hearings.* Senate Foreign Relations Committee. 1927. P. 62.

50. *Foreign Relations,* 1911, pp. 549–50.

51. *Ibid.,* p. 562.

52. *Foreign Relations,* 1909, pp. 455–57.

53. *Ibid.,* 1910, pp. 743–57.

54. *Ibid.,* 1912, p. 1073.

55. *Ibid.,* p. 1092.

56. *Ibid.,* 1911, p. 670.

57. *Ibid.,* 1912, p. 508.

58. *Ibid.,* 1913, pp. 557–72.

59. Library of Congress. Bryan Papers. June 12, 1914.

60. *Foreign Relations,* 1914, p. 248.

61. Washington. State Department. File 874:00, no. 497. Feb. 5, 1909.

62. *Ibid.* Memorandum of April 28, 1909.

63. See my work, *The Monroe Doctrine, 1867–1907,* pp. 255–63.

64. Vagts, *op. cit.,* II, 1794–95.

65. *Ibid.,* p. 1800.

66. *Ibid.,* p. 1803.

67. Washington. State Department. File 874:00, no. 585. April 17, 1909.

68. *Inquiry into the Occupation of Haiti and Santo Domingo.* Hearings before a Select Committee on Haiti and Santo Domingo. Washington, 1921. 2 vols. I, 105.

69. 67th Congress, 2nd Session. Senate Report no. 794. Pp. 32–35.

70. Washington. State Department. File 838:51, no. 330. March 12, 1914.

71. *Ibid.,* no. 343, July 30, 1914.

72. *Ibid.,* no. 385, Feb. 20, 1915.

73. *Ibid.,* no. 354.

74. *Ibid.,* Sept. 16, 1914.

75. *Papers Relating to the Foreign Affairs of the United States. The Lansing Papers.* Washington, 1940. 2 vols. II, 466.

76. *Ibid.*

77. *Foreign Relations,* 1915, p. 433.

78. *Lansing Papers, op. cit.,* II, 460–465.

79. *Ibid.,* pp. 468–70.

80. *Ibid.,* p. 470.

81. For these negotiations, see 62nd Congress, 2nd Session, Sen. Exec. Doc. no. 694, pp. 3–6.

82. *Literary Digest,* April 20, 1912.

83. Washington. State Department. File 894:20:212. Memorandum of April 5, 1912.

84. 62nd Congress, 2nd Session. Sen. Exec. Doc. no. 640. P. 3.

85. *Congressional Record.* 62nd Congress, 2nd Session. P. 9923.

86. *Ibid.*, p. 10045.

87. *Ibid.*, p. 10046.

88. For these episodes, see the article by T. A. Bailey, "The Lodge Corollary to the Monroe Doctrine," in *Political Science Quarterly*, XLVIII (1933), 235–36.

NOTES FOR CHAPTER VIII

1. *Congressional Record.* 62nd Congress, 2nd Session. Vol. 48, pt. 1, p. 963.

2. *Ibid.*, pt. 1, p. 644.

3. Jessup, Philip C., *op. cit.*, II, 272–75.

4. *Congressional Record.* 62nd Congress, 2nd Session. Vol. 48, pt. 3, p. 2603.

5. *Ibid.*, p. 2953.

6. The text of these treaties is in 62nd Congress, 1st Session, S. Exec. Docs. 91 and 92.

7. Holt, W. Stull. *Treaties Defeated in the Senate.* Baltimore, 1933. P. 245.

8. *Congressional Record.* 64th Congress, 2nd Session. Vol. 54, pt. 1, pp. 892–96.

9. *Ibid.*, pt. 2, p. 1950.

10. *Ibid.*, pt. 3, p. 2367.

11. *Ibid.*, 65th Congress, 1st Session. Vol. 55, pt. 8. App., p. 29.

12. *Ibid.*, pt. 8, p. 363.

13. *Ibid.*, 65th Congress, 2nd Session. Vol. 57, pt. 2, p. 920.

14. *Ibid.*, p. 1319.

15. *Ibid.*, pt. 4, p. 3911.

16. *Ibid.*

17. *Ibid.*, p. 3914.

18. *Ibid.*, vol. 59, p. 3513.

19. *Ibid.*, pt. 4, p. 3739.

20. *Ibid.*, p. 3746.

21. *Ibid.*, vol. 58, pt. 3, p. 3137 (Smith of Arizona); pt. 5, p. 4262 (Nugent of Idaho); pt. 6, p. 5450 (Overman of North Carolina); pt. 6, p. 6199 (Wolcott of Delaware).

22. *Ibid.*, vol. 57, pt. 4, p. 4131.

23. Miller, David H. *The Drafting of the Covenant.* New York, 1928. 2 vols. I, 276–77.

24. *Congressional Record*, vol. 57, pt. 5, p. 4845.

25. Miller, *op. cit.*, I, 277.

26. Lansing, Robert. *The Peace Negotiations. A Personal Narrative.* New York, 1921. Pp. 38–40.

27. *Ibid.*, p. 168.

28. Miller, *op. cit.*, II, 71.

29. *Ibid.*, I, 295.

30. *Ibid.*, p. 297.

31. *Ibid.*, p. 336.

32. *The New Democracy, The President's Speeches, Addresses and Other Papers,*

1913–17, by Woodrow Wilson. Edited by R. S. Baker and W. E. Dodd. New York, 1926. 2 vols. I, 443.

33. Miller, *op. cit.*, I, 425.

34. *Ibid.*

35. *Ibid.*

36. *Ibid.*, II, 373.

37. *Ibid.*, p. 369.

38. *Ibid.*, p. 372.

39. *Ibid.*

40. *Ibid.*

41. For the best discussion of this subject see the article by John H. Spencer, "The Monroe Doctrine and the League Covenant," in the *American Journal of International Law*. XXX, 400–13.

42. Miller, David Hunter. *Diary of the Peace Conference.* Privately published, 1928. 21 vols. VIII, 311. Doc. 781.

43. *Congressional Record.* 66th Congress, 2nd Session. Vol. 58, pt. 2, p. 1273 (McCumber of North Dakota); pt. 2, p. 2057 (Gerry of Rhode Island); pt. 3, p. 2537 (Swanson of Virginia); and many others.

44. *Ibid.*, pt. 4, p. 4014.

45. *Ibid.*, pt. 1, pp. 505–06 (Johnson of California); pt. 3, p. 3142 (Borah of Idaho); pt. 4, p. 3781 (Lodge of Massachusetts); and many others.

46. *Ibid.*, p. 3781.

47. *Ibid.*

48. *Ibid.*, p. 3746.

49. *Ibid.*, pt. 3, p. 2930 (Pomerene of Ohio); pt. 6, p. 6335 (King of Utah); pt. 8, p. 7955 (Gore of Oklahoma).

50. *American Academy of Political and Social Science*, XCVI, 42.

51. *Congressional Record.* 66th Congress, 2nd Session. Vol. 58, pt. 9, pp. 8560 and 8563.

52. *Ibid.*, p. 8560.

53. *Ibid.*, p. 8563.

54. *Congressional Record.* 66th Congress, 2nd Session. Pt. 4, p. 3748.

55. *New York Times*, Dec. 25, 1938, 7:1.

56. 68th Congress, 1st Session. Sen. Exec. Doc. no. 107.

57. *Congressional Record.* 69th Congress, 1st Session. Pt. 3, p. 2656.

58. For the history of the treaty, see James T. Shotwell, *War as an Instrument of National Policy.* New York, 1929.

59. *Ibid.*, p. 272.

60. *Ibid.*, pp. 293–94.

61. *Congressional Record.* 74th Congress, 1st Session. Vol. 79, pt. 1, p. 893.

NOTES FOR CHAPTER IX

1. See the article by J. Fred Rippy, "Literary Yankeephobia in Hispanic America," in *Journal of International Relations*, XII, 352.

418 *Notes*

2. *Ibid.*

3. *Ibid.*

4. *Ibid.*, pp. 353–71 and 524–27.

5. For this episode, see *Revue générale de droit international public*, XVIII, pp. 37–44.

6. *Intimate Papers of Colonel House*. Arranged as a Narrative by Charles Seymour. Boston and New York, 1926–28. 4 vols. I, 209.

7. *Ibid.*, p. 215.

8. *Lansing Papers, op. cit.*, II, 471–500.

9. For this episode and the text of the correspondence, see *Revista mejicana del derecho internacional.* June 1921, pp. 277 ff.

10. *New York Times*, April 25, 1919, 8:2.

11. *Ibid.*, Sept. 2, 1919, 1:3.

12. For this episode, see Warren H. Kelchner, *Latin–American Relations with the League of Nations.* Philadelphia, 1930. Pp. 103–04.

13. Barcía Trelles, C. *La Doctrina de Monroe y la Cooperación Internacional.* Madrid, 1931. P. 638.

14. Kelchner, *op. cit.*, pp. 80–81.

15. *Ibid.*, pp. 120–22.

16. Brum, Baltásar. *American Solidarity.* Conference by the president of the Republic of Uruguay, Dr. Baltásar Brum, at the University of Montevideo, on the 21st of April, 1920. Montevideo, 1920. P. 12.

17. *Ibid.*, p. 13.

18. *Ibid.*

19. *Quinta Conferencia Internacional Americana. Actas de las Sesiones de las Comisiones.* Santiago, 1923. Pp. 184–205.

20. *Ibid.*, p. 191.

21. *Ibid.*, p. 199.

22. Hughes, Charles E. *The Pathway of Peace.* New York, 1925. P. 126.

23. *Ibid.*, p. 157.

24. *Ibid.*, pp. 122 and 123.

25. *Ibid.*, p. 128.

26. *Ibid.*, p. 162.

27. *Ibid.*, pp. 146–47.

28. *Ibid.*, pp. 153–54.

29. Barcía Trelles, *op. cit.*, p. 691.

30. For an excellent discussion of this episode, see Isaac J. Cox, "Nicaragua and the United States," in *World Peace Foundation Pamphlets*, X, 783–97.

31. *Congressional Record.* 69th Congress, 2nd Session. Vol. 68, pt. 2, pp. 1555–56.

32. *Ibid.*, p. 2136.

33. For this episode, see Barcía Trelles, *op. cit.*, pp. 693–99.

34. For an excellent discussion, see *Foreign Policy Association Reports*, IV, 50–85.

35. *New York Times*, Feb. 29, 1928, 4:2.

36. *New York Times*, March 13, 1928, 5:3.

Notes

37. League of Nations. Official Journal. 9^{II}, p. 1608.
38. State Department. *Memorandum on the Monroe Doctrine*. Prepared by J. Reuben Clark. Washington, 1930. P. XIX.
39. *Ibid.*, pp. XXIII–XXIV.
40. *New York Times*, April 28, 1930, 6:2.
41. *Ibid.*, June 29, 1930, 21:3.
42. *Ibid.*, May 4, II, 1:7.
43. *Ibid.*, Sept. 29, 1932, 1:6.
44. *Ibid.*, July 26, 1930, 16:2.
45. *Ibid.*, Sept. 10, 1931, 1:4.
46. *Ibid.*, Sept. 13, 1931, II, 1:3.
47. *Ibid.*, Aug. 15, 1930, 6:60.
48. Seventh International Conference of American States. First, Second, and Eighth Committees. Minutes and Antecedents. Montevideo, 1933. Pp. 106, 111, 145.
49. *Congressional Record*. 73rd Congress, 2nd Session. P. 11589.
50. *Ibid.*, 75th Congress, 1st Session, p. 6494.
51. *Ibid.*, p. 6496.

NOTES FOR CHAPTER X

1. *American Journal of International Law*, XXXI, 203.
2. Inter-American Conference for the Maintenance of Peace. *Proceedings*. Buenos Aires, 1937. P. 682.
3. *Congressional Record*. 75th Congress, 1st Session, Pp. 6493–508.
4. *New York Times*, Dec. 25, 1938, 7:1.
5. *New York Times*, June 6, 1940, 12:1.
6. State Department. *Bulletin*, July 6, 1940.
7. *Ibid.*
8. *New York Times*, July 29, 1940, 6:2.
9. State Department Conference Series, 1940–42. P. 71.
10. Varigny, A. *Le Canada et la Doctrine de Monroe.*
11. Hart, A. B. *The Monroe Doctrine*. Boston, 1916. Pp. 280–81.
12. *New York Times*, Nov. 28, 1914, 12:8.
13. *New York Times*, Aug. 19, 1938, 1:3.
14. The agreement is printed in *New York Times*, Sept. 4, 1940, 1:3–8.
15. *Foreign Affairs*, XXIIII, 120.
16. *Foreign Affairs*, XIX, 344.
17. State Department. *Bulletin*, April 12, 1941.
18. *Foreign Affairs*, XIX, 345.
19. *Fortune*, April 1937. P. 202.
20. *Public Opinion Quarterly*, V, 333.
21. *New York Times*, March 9, 1945, 12:2.
22. *Britannica Book of the Year*, 1946. P. 754.
23. *New York Times*, Aug. 31, 1947, 26:2.

Bibliographical Note

AFTER much reflection, I have decided not to append a formal bibliography to this work. That indispensable monument of scholarship, *Guide to the Diplomatic History of the United States*, by Samuel F. Bemis and Grace Gardener Griffin (Washington, 1935), has made it seem rather futile to attempt here an exhaustive list of sources and of secondary materials. In addition, Mr. H. H. B. Meyer's *List of References on the Monroe Doctrine* (Washington, 1919) and Professor Phillips Bradley's *Bibliography of the Monroe Doctrine, 1919–1929* (London, 1929) point the way to the greater part of the materials. In such circumstances, it has seemed sufficient to add to the notes for each chapter a list of the most useful works referred to. It is needless to say that these represent only a fraction of the works consulted.

Much of this study is based on unpublished documents. It rests upon an examination of masses of the diplomatic correspondence of the United States from 1823 to 1919. In Great Britain, through the courtesy of the officials of the Public Record Office and the Foreign Office, I have seen desired materials from 1823 to 1905. At Berlin, I was granted an opportunity to examine the diplomatic exchanges in connection with the Venezuela episode of 1902–1903. In Paris, I was able to pursue my researches at the Quai d'Orsay down to the year 1871. I have had transcripts made of materials in Madrid, and have used the great collection of manuscripts in the Library of Congress, notably the transcript of the Haus-Archiv of Maximilian.

There are certain fundamental sources that might be cited once for all in this brief note. Such, for example, are the *Congressional Record* (Washington, 1874–) under its various names, *Annals of Congress*, 1789–1824 (Washington, 1834–1856, 42 vols.) and *Con-*

gressional Globe, 1833–1873 (Washington, 1834–1873, 46 vols.), and Hansard's *Debates* (London, 1812–1908), for the discussions in the American and British legislative bodies. Such is Richardson's *Messages of the Presidents* (Washington, 1789–1897, 10 vols.). Such are the great series generally known as *Foreign Relations,* beginning in 1861 (*Papers Relating to Foreign Relations of the United States, with the annual message of the President to Congress.* Washington, 1862–), and its predecessor, *American State Papers, Class I. Foreign Relations* (Washington, 1832–1859, 6 vols.) for the period 1789–1828, and the British analogue, *British and Foreign State Papers*, 1812–1929 (London, 1841–). Of perennial value for the period which they cover are the *Literary Digest* (New York, March 1, 1890–February 12, 1938) and the *New York Times Index* (New York, 1913–).

There are many general works on the Monroe Doctrine, of which the most useful to the investigator are that of Herbert Kraus, *Die Monroe-Doktrin, in ihren Beziehungen zur amerikanischen Diplomatie und zum Völkerrecht* (Berlin, 1913), and that of Alejandro Alvarez, *The Monroe Doctrine; Its Importance in the International Life of the States of the New World* (New York, 1924). Barcía Trelles's study of the Doctrine in relation to international cooperation, *La Doctrina de Monroe y La Cooperación Internacional* (Madrid, 1931), is a work of the first order, indispensable in its field. Every student of American foreign relations in the period between 1890 and 1905 must admire — and use — the monumental work of Alfred Vagts, *Deutschland und die Vereinigten Staaten in der Weltpolitik*, 1890–1906 (New York, 1935, 2 vols.). These books so far stand out above all others that I call attention to them here, rather than in the bibliography by chapters.

Bibliography by Chapters

CHAPTER I

Source Material

Obviously, the main source for this introductory chapter must be the views of the fathers, found in the works listed below:

John Adams, Works of. Edited by Charles Francis Adams. Boston, 1856. 10 vols.

John Quincy Adams, Writings of. Edited by W. C. Ford. New York, 1913–17. 7 vols.

Samuel Adams, Writings of. Edited by H. A. Cushing. New York, 1904–08. 4 vols.

Benjamin Franklin, Writings of. Collected and edited by A. H. Smyth. New York, 1905–07. 10 vols.

Alexander Hamilton, Works of. Edited by H. C. Lodge. New York, 1904. 12 vols.

Thomas Jefferson, Works of. Edited by P. L. Ford. New York, 1904–05. 12 vols.

Thomas Jefferson, The Writings of. Monticello Edition. Washington, 1903–04. 20 vols.

Richard Henry Lee, Letters of. Edited by J. C. Ballagh. New York, 1911–14. 2 vols.

James Madison, Writings of. Edited by Gaillard Hunt. New York, 1900–10. 9 vols.

James Monroe, Writings of. Edited by S. M. Hamilton. New York, 1898–1903. 7 vols.

Thomas Paine, The Great Works of. New York, 1877.

and in:

Journals of the Continental Congress. Washington, 1904–34. 31 vols.

Records of the Federal Convention. Edited by Max Farrand. New Haven, 1911. 3 vols.

Secondary Material

American Historical Review, VIII (1902–03), 709–733. "Correspondence of the Comte de Moustier with the Comte de Montmorin, 1787–1789."

Deals with Jay's effort to liberate the United States from the treaty of 1778.

Guttridge, G. H. *David Hartley. An Advocate of Conciliation.* Berkeley, 1926.

Of mild value in connection with our subject.

Schellenberg, T. R. "Jeffersonian Origins of the Monroe Doctrine." *Hispanic American Historical Review,* XIV (1934), 1–32.

A valuable article.

Rippy, J. F., and Debo, A. *Historical Background of the American Policy of Isolation.* Northampton, 1924.

A path-breaking article.

CHAPTER II

Source Material

John Quincy Adams, Memoirs of. Edited by C. F. Adams. Philadelphia, 1874–77. 12 vols.

Indispensable, fascinating, and the *sole* source of importance on the cabinet debates of the fall of 1823.

Alaskan Boundary Tribunal Proceedings, Senate Documents, 58th Congress, 2nd Session. Washington, 1904. 7 vols.

Contains the most important correspondence on the Northwest question.

Festing, Gabrielle. *John Hookham Frère and his Friends.* London, 1899.

Contains an occasional letter of interest.

Ford, W. C. "John Quincy Adams and the Monroe Doctrine," I and II, in *American Historical Review,* VII (July 1902), 676–696, VIII (Oct. 1902), 28–52.

Contains some documentary material not to be found in published form elsewhere, and is in addition a pioneer study on the origins of the Doctrine.

Albert Gallatin, Writings of. Edited by Henry Adams. Philadelphia, 1879. 3 vols.

Contains an occasional letter of significance.

Thomas Jefferson, Writings of. Memorial edition. Washington, 1903. 20 vols.

With an occasional letter of significance.

James Monroe, Writings of. Edited by S. M. Hamilton. New York, 1898–1903. 7 vols.

With an occasional letter of significance and supplementary documentary materials of much value.

Rush, Richard. *Memoranda of a Residence at the Court of London.* Philadelphia, 1845.

Most interesting on the Rush-Canning negotiations and with some material on the Northwest controversy.

Stapleton, A. G. *George Canning and his Times.* London, 1859.

An account of the Spanish colonial question from the British angle by Canning's secretary.

Secondary Material

Perkins, Dexter. *The Monroe Doctrine, 1823–26.* Cambridge, 1927.

A much more intensive treatment of the subject discussed in this chapter, with a comprehensive bibliography.

CHAPTER III

Source Material

Adams, E. D. *British Diplomatic Correspondence Concerning the Republic of Texas.* Texas State Historical Association. Austin, 1918.
Contains interesting material.

d'Alaux, Gaston. "La République Dominicaine et l'Empereur Soulouque," *Revue des Deux Mondes,* X (1851, 2nd vol. for that year), 193–224, 459–50ᵀ.

James Buchanan, Works of. Edited by J. B. Moore. Philadelphia, 1908–11. 12 vols.
Invaluable.

John C. Calhoun, Works of. Edited by Richard C. Crallé. New York, 1851–56. 6 vols.

Contains the great speech in which Calhoun set up the opportunist theory of the Doctrine.

Documentos Relativos á la Cuestión de Santo Domingo. Sometidos al Congreso de los Diputados. Ministerio del Estado. Madrid, 1865.
The most important Spanish correspondence.

Guizot, M. *Histoire Parlementaire de France.* Recueil Complet des

Discours Prononcés dans les Chambres de 1819 à 1848. Paris, 1864. 5 vols.

Pelletier de Saint Rémy. *Etude et Solution Nouvelle de la Question Haïtienne*. Paris, 1846.

Illustration of the French attitude toward the Caribbean.

James K. Polk, The Diary of. Edited by M. M. Quaife. Chicago, 1910. 4 vols.

An important source.

Thiers, L. A. *Discours sur les rélations de la France avec les Etats-Unis d'Amérique*, prononcé dans la séance de la Chambre des députés du 20 janvier 1846. Paris, 1846.

View of the opposition to Guizot.

34th Congress, 1st Session. House Exec. Doc. no. 1.

Secondary Material

Adams, E. D. *British Interests and Activities in Texas, 1838–46*. Baltimore, 1910.

Useful not only on the question of Texas, but on that of California.

Barranda, Joaquín. *Recordaciones Históricas*. Mexico, 1913. 2 vols.

The Yucatán problem treated in detail.

Cady, J. F. *Foreign Intervention in the Río de la Plata 1838–50*. Philadelphia, 1929.

A good study with an excellent bibliography.

Destruge, C. *La Expedición Flores — Proyecto de monarquia Americaná, 1846–7*. Guayaquil, 1906.

Perkins, Dexter. *The Monroe Doctrine, 1826–67*. Baltimore, 1933.

A more intensive treatment of the matters dealt with in this chapter, with bibliography.

Rivas, Raimundo. *Colombia y los Estados-Unidos, 1810–1850*. Bogotá, 1915.

Based on the archives of Colombia.

Van Alstyne, R. W. "The Central American Policy of Lord Palmerston, 1846–48," in *Hispanic American Historical Review*, XVI, 339–59.

Welles, Sumner. *Naboth's Vineyard, The Dominican Republic 1844–1924*. New York, 1928.

Most thorough treatment of the history of the Dominican Republic and its relations with the United States to be found in English, and it is written from the sources, containing excellent commentary and much material not to be found elsewhere.

Williams, M. W. "Secessionist Diplomacy of Yucatán," in *Hispanic American Historical Review*, X, 132–43.

——— *Anglo-American Isthmian Diplomacy 1815–1915*. Washington, 1916.

An excellent study with bibliography.

CHAPTER IV

Source Material

Bigelow, John. *Retrospections of an Active Life*. New York, 1909. 5 vols.

The memoirs of our minister in Paris — of great value.

Carta al. E. S. Presidente de la República, par Don J. M. Gutiérrez de Estrada, antiguo Ministro de Relaciones interiores y exteriores. Mexico, 1840.

Interesting pamphlet on Mexican monarchy.

Correspondencia de la Legación Mexicana durante la Intervención Extranjera. Edited by Matías Romero. Mexico City, 1870–92. 10 vols.

The result of indefatigable industry. Contains much information not only on the diplomatic exchanges but on the state of American public opinion.

Corti, E. G. *Maximilian and Charlotte of Mexico*. New York, 1928. 2 vols.

Publishes important source materials not easily found elsewhere.

La Cuestión de Mexico. (Si la monarquía constitucional es conveniente y posible en Aquel País bajo el punto de vista de los Intereses Mexicanos y de la Política Española.)

Interesting pamphlet on Mexican monarchy.

Documents Diplomatiques. Paris, 1861–67. For the year 1863.

An indispensable collection of diplomatic documents.

García, Genaro, and Pereyra, Carlos. *Documentos inéditos y muy raros para la historia de Mexico. Correspondencia secreta de los principales Intervencionistas Mexicanos*. Mexico, 1903. 36 vols.

A great and valuable collection for the Mexican and the French side of things.

Gaulot, P. *La Verité sur l'Expedition du Mexique.* Paris, 1889–90. 3 vols.
Contains a few important letters.
Randon, J. L. *Mémoires du Maréchal.* Paris, 1875–77. 2 vols.
Important for occasional letters.
Welles, G. *Diary of Gideon Welles.* New York, 1909. 3 vols.
Always salty and occasionally useful.
37th Congress, 2nd Session. H. Exec. Doc. no. 100.
37th Congress, 3rd Session. H. Exec. Doc. no. 54, *and*
39th Congress, 1st Session. H. Exec. Doc. no. 73, pt. 1.
Of the first importance. Much of the crucial correspondence.

Secondary Material

Callahan, J. M. *Evolution of Seward's Mexican Policy.* West Va. Studies
   in Am. Hist. Morgantown, 1908.
A systematic account.
Corti, Egon C. *Maximilian and Charlotte of Mexico.* New York, 1928.
   2 vols.
A chef-d'oeuvre, though written largely from one archive.
Duniway, C. A. "Reasons for the Withdrawal of the French from Mex-
   ico." *Annual Report of the American Historical Association for
   1902.* I, 313–28.
A perspicacious analysis.
García, José Gabriel. *Compendio de la Historia de Santo Domingo.*
   Santo Domingo, 1896.
A useful general work.
Lally, F. E. *French Opposition to the Mexican Policy of the Second Em-
   pire.* In Johns Hopkins University Studies in Historical and Po-
   litical Science. Series XLIX, No. 3. Baltimore, 1931.
Interesting as it shows the French reaction to the Mexican interven-
tion.
Perkins, Dexter. *The Monroe Doctrine, 1826–67.* Baltimore, 1933.
Intensive treatment on the subject.
Rippy, J. F. *United States and Mexico.* New York, 1926.
A useful summary.
Welles, Sumner. *Naboth's Vineyard, The Dominican Republic, 1844–
   1924.* New York, 1928.
The only treatment of Dominican history in English. Invaluable.

Wriston, H. M. *Executive Agents in American Foreign Relations.* Baltimore and London, 1929.

Some interesting pages on the Schofield mission.

CHAPTER V

Source Material

Archivo histórico diplomático mexicano. Mexico City, 1923–30. 32 vols. Vol. XIX.

Important for the conference of 1896 at Mexico City.

50th Congress, 1st Session. S. Exec. Doc. no. 226. Vol 11.

An important collection of documents, especially for the background of the crisis of 1895.

Elliott, A. D. *The Life of Lord Goschen.* London, 1911. 2 vols.

A few interesting letters.

Gardiner, A. G. *The Life of Sir William Harcourt.* London, 1923. 2 vols.

Gives the view of the leader of the Liberal opposition in the clash of 1895.

Mackenna, Vicuña. *Diez Meses de Misión a los Estados Unidos.* Santiago, 1867. 2 vols.

Memoirs of the Chilean agent in the United States at the time of the Chilean-Spanish war.

Moore, J. B. *A Digest of International Law.* Washington, 1906. 8 vols, especially Vol. VI, pp. 368–604.

One of the significant selections of source materials on the Doctrine.

Reid, W. *Memoirs and Correspondence of Lord Playfair.* New York and London, 1899.

Important for the Playfair memorandum.

Sumner, Charles. *Works.* Boston, 1870–83. 15 vols.

Contains no references to the Doctrine, but stresses here and there the idea of a "continental policy."

The following periodical articles are of value for the canal question:

Edinburgh Review. CLV, 207–24. "The Panama Canal."

Kasson, John A. "The Monroe Declaration," in the *North American Review.* CXXXIII, 241–54.

Koerner, Gustave. "The True Monroe Doctrine," in the *Nation.* XXXIV, 9–11.

Nation. XXX, 90–91. "The United States Government and the Panama Canal."

North American Review. CXXX, 499–511. "The Monroe Doctrine and the Isthmian Canal."

Popular Science Monthly. XVI, 842–49. "Some Features of the Interoceanic Canal."

Rümelin, Carl. "Die Monroe-Doctrin," in *Zeitschrift für die gesammte Staatswissenschaft.* XXXVIII, 331–43.

Schleiden, Rudolph. "Die rechtliche und politische Seite der Panama-canal-frage," in *Preussische Jahrbücher.* XLIX, 589–654.

These two periodical articles are valuable for the Venezuela question:

Lodge, H. C. "England, Venezuela, and the Monroe Doctrine," in *North American Review.* CLX, 651–58.

Moore, John B. "The Monroe Doctrine," in *Political Science Quarterly.* XI, 1–29.

Secondary Material

Cleveland, Grover. *Venezuelan Boundary Dispute.* New York, 1901.

James, Henry. *Richard Olney and his Public Service.* Boston and New York, 1923.
Of first importance.

Jervey, T. D. "William Lindsay Scruggs, a Forgotten Diplomat," in *South Atlantic Quarterly.* XXVII (1928), 292–309.

Nevins, Allan. *Grover Cleveland; a Study in Courage.* New York, 1933.
A brief but stimulating treatment by a distinguished scholar.

Perkins, Dexter. *The Monroe Doctrine, 1826–67* and *The Monroe Doctrine, 1867–1907.* Baltimore, 1933 and 1937 respectively.

Rippy, J. F. "Some Contemporary Mexican Reactions to Cleveland's Venezuelan Message," in *Political Science Quarterly.* XXXIX (1924), 280–92.

Stolberg-Wernigerode, Otto Graf zu. *Germany and the United States during the Era of Bismarck.* Reading, Pa., 1937.
A brilliant study of the period.

Tansill, C. C. *The Purchase of the Danish West Indies.* Baltimore, 1932.
A standard account of the matter. Invaluable.

CHAPTER VI

Source Material

British Documents on the Origins of the War, 1898–1914. Edited by G. P. Gooch and Harold Temperley. London, 1926–33. 10 vols.

Die grosse Politik der Europäischen Kabinette, 1871–1914. Berlin, 1922–27. 40 vols.

Standard German collection of prewar documents.

Verhandlungen des Reichstags. Berlin, 1871–1938.

The debates in the Reichstag.

Von Schierbrand, Wolf. *Germany. The Welding of a World Power.* New York, 1902.

Contains a report of a famous interview with Bismarck.

White, Andrew D. *Autobiography.* New York, 1905. 2 vols.

Chiefly interesting in connection with the Monroe Doctrine and the first Hague Conference.

Magazine articles on the Hague Conference:

> Alvarez, Alejandro. "Latin-America and International Law," in *American Journal of International Law.* III, 269–353.

> Drago, Luis M. "Les Emprunts d'Etat et leurs rapports avec la politique internationale," in *Revue générale de droit international public.* XIV, 251–87.

> Holls, F. W. "The Results of the Peace Conference in Their Relation to the Monroe Doctrine," in *Review of Reviews.* XX, 560–67.

Review of Reviews. XXVII, 131–38. "The Venezuela Affair."

A contemporary article on the Venezuela question.

Secondary Material

de Beaumarchais, Maurice D. *La doctrine de Monroe; l'évolution de la politique des Etats-Unis au XIXme siècle.* Paris, 1898.

A French study of mediocre value.

Dennett, Tyler. *John Hay; from Poetry to Politics.* New York, 1933.

Important for a memorandum of Hay's on the Venezuela question.

Harrison, A. *The Pan-Germanic Doctrine.* London, 1904.

An excellent study.

Bibliography

Hill, H. C. *Roosevelt and the Caribbean*. Chicago, 1927.

An analysis of Roosevelt's Caribbean policy.

Perkins, Dexter. *The Monroe Doctrine, 1867–1907*. Baltimore, 1937.

Pétin, Hector. *Les Etats-Unis et la doctrine de Monroe*. Paris, 1900.

Tansill, Charles C. *The Purchase of the Danish West Indies*. Baltimore, 1932.

Thayer, W. R. *Theodore Roosevelt, an intimate biography*. Boston, 1919.

Important for Theodore Roosevelt's account of the Venezuela episode.

CHAPTER VII

Source Material

Inquiry into the Occupation of Haiti and Santo Domingo. Hearings before a Select Committee on Haiti and Santo Domingo. Washington, 1921.

Important for American policy, especially in Haiti.

The Lansing Papers (Papers Relating to the Foreign Affairs of the United States). Washington, 1940. 2 vols.

Of first importance in connection with an extended interpretation of the Monroe Doctrine.

Rippy, J. F. "The British Bondholders and the Roosevelt Corollary of the Monroe Doctrine," in *Political Science Quarterly*. XLIX, 195–206.

Senate Foreign Relations Committee. *Hearings*. 1927.

Throws important light upon American policy in Nicaragua.

59th Congress, 1st Session. H. Exec. Doc. no. 1.

Important in connection with the Dominican affair.

62nd Congress, 2nd Session. Sen. Exec. Doc. no. 694.

Important for the Magdalena Bay episode.

67th Congress, 2nd Session. Senate Report no. 794.

Important for German attitude toward Haiti.

Secondary Material

Bishop, J. B. *Theodore Roosevelt and His Time*. New York, 1902. 2 vols.

By an ardent admirer of the President, reflecting his viewpoint.

Jessup, Philip C. *Elihu Root*. New York, 1938. 2 vols.

Gives some interesting sidelights on our Latin-American policy.

Perkins, Dexter. *The Monroe Doctrine, 1867–1907*. Baltimore, 1937.
  Deals with the evolution of the Roosevelt corollary.
Pringle, H. *Theodore Roosevelt*. New York, 1931.
  A masterpiece of biography.
Rippy, J. F. "The Initiation of the Customs Receivership in the Domini-
  can Republic," in *Hispanic American Historical Review*. XXVII,
  419–44.
  A very valuable article.

CHAPTER VIII

Source Material

Lansing, Robert. *The Peace Negotiations. A Personal Narrative*. New
  York, 1921.
  Gives the conservative view of Wilson's Secretary of State.
Miller, David H. *The Drafting of the Covenant*. New York, 1928. 2 vols.
——— *Diary of the Peace Conference*. Privately published, 1928. 21 vols.
  Invaluable documentary material.
Wilson, Woodrow. *The New Democracy, The President's Speeches,
  Addresses, and other Papers, 1913–17*. Edited by R. S. Baker and
  W. E. Dodd. New York, 1926. 2 vols.
  A standard collection.

Secondary Material

Holt, W. Stull. *Treaties Defeated in the Senate*. Baltimore, 1933.
  Serviceable for both 1912 and 1919.
Jessup, Philip C. *Elihu Root*. New York, 1938. 2 vols.
  Useful on the treaties of 1912, as well as on the League.
Shotwell, James T. *War as an Instrument of National Policy*. New York,
  1929.
  Standard for the Kellogg Pact.
Spencer, John H. "The Monroe Doctrine and the League Covenant,"
  in the *American Journal of International Law*. XXX, 400–13.
  Excellent.

CHAPTER IX

Source Material

Brum, Baltásar. *American Solidarity*. Conference by the President of the Republic of Uruguay, Dr. Baltásar Brum, at the University of Montevideo, on April 21, 1920. Montevideo, 1920.

A proposal for an American League of Nations by the President of Uruguay.

State Department. *Memorandum on the Monroe Doctrine*. Prepared by J. Reuben Clark. Washington, 1930.

Fundamental, as expressing the views of the State Department.

Hughes, Charles E. *The Pathway of Peace*. New York, 1925.

Contains Mr. Hughes's two fundamental speeches on the Doctrine.

Inter-American Conference for the Maintenance of Peace. *Proceedings*. Buenos Aires, 1937.

Lansing Papers. Washington, 1940. 2 vols.

Useful for the negotiations on the Pan-American pact.

League of Nations. Official Journal. 9^{II}.

Contains the reply to Costa Rica's request for a definition of Article 21.

Quinta Conferencia Internacional Americana. Actas de las Sesiones de las Comisiones. Santiago. 1923.

The minutes of the conference.

Revista mejicana del derecho internacional. June 1921.

Gives the exchange of notes between Salvador and the United States.

Seventh International Conference of American States. First, Second, and Eighth Committees. Minutes and Antecedents. Montevideo, 1933.

Seymour, Charles. *The Intimate Papers of Colonel House*. Boston and New York, 1926–28. 4 vols.

Useful for the negotiations on the Pan-American pact.

Secondary Material

Cox, Isaac J. "Nicaragua and the United States," in *World Peace Foundation Pamphlets*. X, 783–97.

Excellent on the Nicaraguan intervention.

Fenwick, Charles G. "American Conference for the Maintenance of Peace," in *American Journal of International Law*. XXXI, 201–25.

Suggestion of Canada's entering the Pan-American Union.

Foreign Policy Association Reports. IV, 50–85. "The Sixth Pan-American Conference."

First-rate summary of the Havana Conference.

Hart, A. B. *The Monroe Doctrine*. Boston, 1916.

Interesting on Canada and the Doctrine.

Kelchner, Warren H. *Latin-American Relations with the League of Nations*. Philadelphia, 1930.

A careful treatment.

Rippy, J. F. "Literary Yankeephobia in Hispanic America," in *Journal of International Relations*, XII (1922), 350–71, 524–38.

CHAPTER X

Source Material

Meeting of Foreign Ministers. Second. *Diario de las Sesiones*. Havana. 1940.

Meeting of Foreign Ministers. Third. *Diario das Sessões*. Rio de Janeiro. 1942.

Inter-American Conference on the Means of Consolidating Peace and Security. *Diario de la Conferencia*. Mexico. 1946.

Documents on American Foreign Relations. Vols. III–VIII, 1940–46. Vols. III–VI, Boston. Vols. VII and VIII, Princeton.

Inter-American Conference for the Maintenance of Peace and Security. Rio de Janeiro. 1947. Inter-American Treaty of Reciprocal Assistance. Rio de Janeiro. 1947.

Secondary Material

Bemis, S. F. *The Latin American Policy of the United States*. New York, 1943.

Indispensable for the period covered.

Duggan, Laurence. *The Americas: The Search for Hemisphere Security*. New York, 1949.

A convenient summary of the conferences on inter-American affairs.

Whitaker, Arthur P. *The Western Hemisphere Idea.* Ithaca, 1954.
A provocative view of Pan-Americanism.

Wilcox, F. O. "The Monroe Doctrine and World War Two," in *American Political Science Review.* XXXVI, 433–53.

Perkins, D. "Bringing the Monroe Doctrine Up to Date," in *Foreign Affairs.* XX, 253–65.

INDEX

Index

Clark memorandum on (1928), 342–343, 385; repudiation of Roosevelt corollary, 343, 346, 385; criticized by Latin-American press, 343–344; tendency to become more an international than a national doctrine, 349, 350, 353, 356, 357; no-transfer principle, 354, 385; extension of, to Canada, Caribbean, Newfoundland, 356–359; and the United Nations Charter, 363–366; declining interest in, 367–369; implied conception of two spheres, 371–375; isolationists' appeal to, 375; became a fixed maxim of foreign policy (1865–1900), 377, 378, 379; strong appeal to national feeling (1923–1945), 378–379; practical efficacy of, 379–380; right of intervention by U. S. withdrawn, 384, 385; adverse implications in the words, 387. *See also* Noncolonization dogma

Appeal to: by Colombia (1824), 69, 386; by New Granada (1837), 75, (1846), 89; by Ecuador and Peru (1846), 87-88; by Yucatán (1848), 90; by Nicaragua (1848), 95; by Nicaragua, Honduras, and Salvador (1849), 96; by Mexico (1862 and following), 122, 127; by Venezuela (1876, 1880, 1881, 1884, 1887), 171–172; by Dominican agent (1905), 237; by Argentina (1902–1903), 247

Criticized: by an acute student, 33; by Metternich (1823), 56–57; by Congressmen (1823), 69; by Guizot (1846), 83–84; by Lord Clarendon (1854), 100; by Disraeli (1856), 101; in *North American Review* (1856), 102, (1913), 321–322; in Spanish pamphlets (1861), 116; by Calderón Collantes (1861), 142–143; by Chilean Minister to United States (1865), 155; by Lord Granville (1882), 166; by writers in various periodicals (1882), 166–167; by Lord Salisbury (1895), 177–178, 190; by French and German newspapers (1895), 186–187, (1905), 245; by Bismarck (1896, 1897, 1898), 187, 208; by Mexico City

Congress (1896), 189; by European publicists (1898), 197; by the German Emperor (1898), 199, 211–212; by German newspapers 1898), 199, 221–222; by the Duke of Devonshire, 233; by Latin Americans (1913), 319–320; by Hiram Bingham (1913, 1914), 320–321; by the Mexican government (1919), 326

Discussed in Congress: (1844), 76; (1845), 81–82; (1848), 90–91, 92; (1852–1853), 98–99 (1855), 102; (1898), 196, 198–199; (1901), 231–232; (1905), 242; (1912), 274; (1917), 286; (1918–1919), 287–288, 300–301, 304–305; (1923, 1926), 307–309; (1928), 309–312; (1932, 1935), 312; (1927), 337–338

Ignored: (1823–1841), 67–75; by Whigs when in power, 93; in Spanish book (1852), 103; in Congressional debate on Cuba (1857–1858), 156; by Hayes in message on canal (1880), 163–164; by McKinley in Cuban intervention (1898), 196, 231; in Platt amendment (1901), 231; by French government (1905), 245; by Lodge (1912), 273

Importance recognized: after 1845, 87; by Forsyth (1856), 113; by Seward in case of Dominican Republic (1861), 122, 378; by Seward in case of Mexico (1861), 125, (1865), 132–135, 380; by Spanish government (1860), 138, (1864), 146; by Europe (1865), 147, 148; by Germany (1893), 151; by France (1884), 152; by John A. Kasson (1881), 164; by Great Britain (1896), 183, 184; by German Minister at Rio, 214; by Sternburg (1903), 222; by British statesmen (1902–1903), 224, 225; by British newspapers (1902–1903), 227

Invoked: by Caleb Cushing (1838), 72; by Buchanan (1845), 85–86; by Polk in connection with Yucatán (1848), 90; by U. S. agent in Haiti (1854), 103; by Seward in connection with Spanish reoccupation of Dominican Republic